A great follow-up to Volume I! Volume II is an in-depth guide to the mathematical and geometric concepts indispensable to advanced Maya programmers.

—Larry Gritz, Exluna/NVIDIA

From Volun

David's boo   Maya
developers a   Maya
API by appl   Alias

David Goul   People
who need to   ntend
to do extens   what's
going on un   I, and
is written to   nded!
    rMan

This book   expert
alike. For t   ds-on
tutorial an   hat in
it David sh   hitec-
ture, so tha   ower-
ful program

    hor of
    aphics

Having pro   ming,
I must say   nt for
Maya. Nev   gram-
ming for M   it.
    Studio
    ornia"

If you ever   by-step
instructions,   create
your own ex

    Magic

The Morgan Kaufmann Series in Computer Graphics and Geometric Modeling

COMPLETE MAYA PROGRAMMING

VOLUME II

An In-depth Guide to 3D Fundamentals,
Geometry, and Modeling

David A. D. Gould

AMSTERDAM • BOSTON • HEIDELBERG
LONDON • NEW YORK • OXFORD
PARIS • SAN DIEGO • SAN FRANCISCO
SINGAPORE • SYDNEY • TOKYO

ELSEVIER

Morgan Kaufmann Publishers is an imprint of Elsevier

MORGAN KAUFMANN PUBLISHERS

Senior Editor	Tim Cox
Publishing Services Manager	Simon G. Crump
Senior Project Manager	Angela G. Dooley
Assistant Editor	Richard Camp
Editorial Assistant	Jessica Evans
Cover Design Direction	Cate Rickard Barr
Cover Illustration	Sean Platter, Studio Splatter
Text Design Direction	Julio Esperas
Composition	Integra Software Services Pvt. Ltd., Pondicherry, India
Technical Illustration	Dartmouth Publishing Inc.
Copyeditor	Daril Bentley
Proofreader	Phyllis Coyne et al.
Indexer	Northwind Editorial
Interior Printer	Maple-Vail Manufacturing Group
Cover Printer	Phoenix Color Corp.

Morgan Kaufmann Publishers is an imprint of Elsevier.
500 Sansome Street, Suite 400, San Francisco, CA 94111

This book is printed on acid-free paper.

Library of Congress: Application submitted

ISBN: 0-12-088482-8
ISBN: 978-0-12-088482-8

For information on all Morgan Kaufmann publications,
visit our website at www.mkp.com.

Printed in the United States of America
05 06 07 08 09   5 4 3 2 1

To Agnes, my foundation.

About the Author

With over thirteen years of experience in the computer graphics industry, David Gould has pursued the dual paths of programmer and artist. This rare ability to combine both the technical and artistic has won him many awards and credits. He has played a key role in the development of an eclectic mix of technology, including an award-winning laser rendering system for Pangolin. He developed software for controlling the Kuper motion-control rig, as well as the Monkey stop-motion puppet. He personally developed Illustrate, the market leading toon and technical illustration renderer. This renderer is used by NASA, British Aerospace, Walt Disney Imagineering, and Sony Pictures Entertainment, among others.

David's career has spanned a wide variety of companies and continents. In Paris, he supervised the production of 3D stereoscopic scientific films, including the award winning film *Inside the Cell*. In London he developed a patented facial animation system. Further broadening his experiences, he worked in New York in the post-production industry where he contributed to many high-profile commercials.

While at Walt Disney Feature Animation, Los Angeles, David developed cutting-edge animation and modeling technology that was used in the production of their animated feature films. He diversified further by joining Exluna, Berkeley, the software company founded by former Pixar rendering researchers, including Larry Gritz. While there, he played an active role in the design and development of Entropy, the Renderman-compatible renderer, as well as other products. David continued his rendering development efforts while at NVIDIA, in Santa Clara, California, by aiding in the design of their future 3D graphics chips.

David has since joined the academy awarding winning studio WETA Digital in New Zealand. Having completed work on *The Lord of the Rings* trilogy he is currently working on *King Kong*. His varied roles in production include research and development, shader writing, lighting, and effects.

Contents

Preface

Given the depth and breadth of Maya's programming functionality, it became quickly clear that a single book couldn't possibly cover it all. The first volume focused on giving the reader a solid understanding of how Maya works and on its two programming interfaces: MEL and the C++ application programming interface (API). This book extends on that work, while paying particular attention to the areas of geometry and modeling. Clearly, in order to have a deeper understanding of these areas it is important to first understand the fundamentals of computer graphics, and in particular the mathematical foundations on which they are built. This book, therefore, explains the fundamental building blocks of computer graphics so that a complete understanding of geometry and modeling is possible.

Although the mathematics and principles of computer graphics are explained in other books, I felt it necessary to place these in the context of Maya programming. So, rather than explain the theory alone, sample source code and scripts are provided so that the reader can see how the mathematics and principles can be directly applied and implemented. Many of the examples can be used directly in your own implementations.

Because the first book was focused on teaching the fundamentals of MEL and the C++ API, these two areas were covered separately. This book takes a more problem-solving approach. The utility of a particular mathematical concept is explained together with both the MEL and C++ source code used to implement the concept. The key is to understand the concept; the syntax then follows. By building up a wider understanding of computer graphics concepts, you will have a larger toolbox of solutions from which to draw when tackling your own problems.

This book contains a great deal of knowledge I have accumulated over the years. Much of it is taken from experience, books, courses, and notes. All of this information isn't of much use if you can't readily access it. As such, another important goal of this book is to provide the reader with a pertinent reference resource. By dividing the book by concept, rather than by programming language, it is easy to refer to particular sections as needed. The subject index has been extensively expanded and is more useful for finding when and where a particular function or command can be used.

Although every attempt was made to present each area with an equal emphasis on MEL and the C++ API, it will soon become obvious to the reader that the C++ API is clearly more powerful and versatile when it comes to handling larger and more complex problems. With the ever-increasing need for more detailed and complex models, it becomes even more important that your solution work quickly and efficiently. In addition to the speed gains it makes possible, the C++ API offers a great many convenience classes. For example, because MEL doesn't have direct support for quaternions, you would need to implement them yourself. The C++ API has the **MQuaternion** class, which provides a complete implementation of quaternions. This class can be used directly in your plug-ins. You can also rest assured that the class has been extensively tested so that it is guaranteed to be both robust and stable. Integrating your solutions into Maya in a clean and seamless manner is often only possible through the C++ API. Your users will be more appreciative of a solution that resembles the standard Maya implementation than one that is compromised simply because of MEL's limitations. Admittedly, the learning curve for the C++ language is steeper than that for MEL, but in the long run the additional functionality provided by knowing C++ will pay off. You will have a greater scope for handling more diverse and complex problems, some of which may be difficult, if not impossible, to implement in MEL. Ideally, a solid knowledge of both programming interfaces will give you the maximum freedom of choice.

ACKNOWLEDGEMENTS

The process of writing a book can be likened to a marathon and like any successful athelete the role of the support staff is critical to their success. I would like to make a particular acknowledgement to my editor, Tim Cox, and his very capable assistants Richard Camp and Jessie Evans. They pressed ahead, undaunted, as the book continued to grow ever larger and more complex.

If each page looks as outstanding as it does it is due to the professionalism and hard work of Angela Dooley and her great team of designers and copy editors.

To my reviewers I'd like to thank them for their critical eye and abundant feedback. Their ideas and opinions assisted me greatly in defining the book's core goals and focus. My dream team of reviewers included Scott Firestone, Bryan Ewert, Christophe Hery, Michael Lucas, André Mazzone, Philip Schneider, and Andre Weissflog.

CHAPTER 1

Introduction

This book endeavors to build upon your existing experience in Maya programming. As such, this book assumes that you are already familiar with basic MEL and/or C++ API programming. If you have never written MEL scripts or C++ plug-ins, you are highly encouraged to read the first volume. It covers all of the basics of Maya programming, as well as how Maya works internally. This knowledge will be critical when developing more advanced scripts and plug-ins.

All too often your work in Maya will involve problem solving. Although it is often easy to formulate a solution in general abstract terms, the task of actually implementing the solution can be daunting. If you read the first volume, you have a strong understanding of how Maya works, as well as of the MEL and C++ API programming interfaces. Thus, the actual task of writing a script or plug-in shouldn't be too difficult. The next step will be to apply your knowledge of computer graphics principles and mathematics to implement the solution.

This often proves to be the greatest hurdle. The most common reason for not being able to implement a solution is due to a lack of understanding of computer graphics principles. Without a solid grasp of basic computer graphics concepts, all problem solving will become more difficult. Computer graphics is based on mathematics, and many people are quite reluctant to learn mathematics. A common reason for this is that the mathematics is presented in abstract and theoretical terms with little application to solving real-world problems. This book presents the most important fundamental mathematical concepts without diverging into esoteric mathematical areas that have little practical use. For instance, the *dot product* is covered in detail. This mathematical operation is used extensively in computer graphics for calculating such things as angles, rotations, sidedness, lengths, areas, and the amount of light reflected from a surface. All of this is possible from an operation that involves little more than a few multiplications and additions. Independently of Maya programming, a solid grasp of these computer graphics concepts will hold you in good stead for all of your future work. As your knowledge increases, you will become more adept at combining and using these mathematical building blocks to create more robust and efficient solutions.

The explanation of each mathematical concept is accompanied by ample source code and scripts that demonstrate how to implement the concept. The source code and scripts can be used as a starting point for your own solutions. The entire spectrum of computer graphics concepts through to geometry and modeling is covered.

The most fundamental building blocks of computer graphics are points and vectors. Many problems can be solved using the simple point and vector operations, and thus understanding them will provide a strong foundation for all further chapters. Rotations merit their own chapter in that they can often be the source of much confusion. There are many ways to represent rotations and orientations, and thus it is important to understand their advantages and disadvantages in order to best apply them to your work. Integral to computer graphics is the process of transforming (scaling, shearing, rotating, translating, and projecting) objects. Transformations are most efficiently implemented using matrices, covered in this book in detail. Transformations provide an important level of abstraction for building hierarchies of objects. Being able to retrieve and transform points at any level in a hierarchy are particularly useful skills in many computer graphics applications.

Progressing from the basic building blocks, the next topic covered is geometry. Geometry uses points and vectors to represent more complex shapes such as curves and surfaces. All of Maya's supported geometry types are covered in their own respective chapters. Each chapter covers the tasks of displaying, editing, and creating each geometry type. A detailed explanation of the components that make up each type is also given. The most basic, yet most pervasive, type of geometry — polygonal meshes — is covered first. NURBS curves and surfaces are subsequently explained in detail.

Finally, the increasingly popular geometry type, subdivision surfaces, is covered. Each different type of geometry has its strengths and weaknesses. Some are better suited for games development, whereas others are more appropriate for industrial design. The reader will gain a greater understanding of each geometry type's advantages and disadvantages, so that an informed decision can be made as to which one is best to use. The process of writing geometry importers and exporters is greatly simplified once you have a greater understanding of Maya's various geometry types. Custom modeling tools can also be created that are adapted to a given geometry type. Developing your own tools will provide you with a far greater level of control and functionality than those provided with Maya.

1.1 EXAMPLE FILES

Note that all files used in this book are available at:

www.davidgould.com

Information available at the site includes the following.

- MEL scripts, C++ source code, and makefiles for all examples in the book
- Additional example MEL scripts
- Additional example C++ source code
- Errata for this book
- Continually updated glossary
- Updated list of other relevant web sites and online resources

1.1.1 COMPILING EXAMPLE PLUG-INS

New versions of both Maya and C++ compilers are being constantly released. Rather than provide potentially outdated and obsolete instructions in this book, the complete set of instructions for downloading and compiling the companion files for this book are available at:

www.davidgould.com

Here you will find all C++ source code and makefiles necessary to compile the plug-ins on your own computer. There are also instructions for creating your own plug-in makefiles from scratch.

1.1.2 SOURCING EXAMPLE MEL SCRIPTS

To source any of the example MEL scripts, Maya must be able to locate them. It is possible to include the complete path to the `source` command, but if multiple MEL scripts are being sourced it is easier to set up the `MAYA_SCRIPT_PATH` environment variable correctly. This variable simply needs to be updated, as follows, to include the directory where the example MEL scripts are located.

1. Open the **Script Editor**.

2. Execute the following to initialize the `$exampleScripts` string to the path of the directory containing the example MEL scripts.

```
string $exampleScripts = <example_mel_scripts_directory>;
```

For example:

```
string $exampleScripts = "C:/DavidGould/MEL Scripts";
```

When specifying a path in Windows with backslashes, be sure to use two back-slashes. A single backslash will be interpreted as an escape sequence. The same path with backslashes would therefore be written as follows.

```
string $exampleScripts = "C:\\DavidGould\\MEL Scripts";
```

Maya will automatically convert all directory paths with backslashes to forward slashes.

3. Execute the following:

```
string $newScriptPath=$exampleScripts + ";" +`getenv "MAYA_SCRIPT_PATH"`;
putenv "MAYA_SCRIPT_PATH" $newScriptPath;
```

The first line initializes the `$newScriptPath` variable to the example MEL scripts path and then appends the current setting for the MAYA_SCRIPT_PATH variable. The second line uses the `putenv` command to set the MAYA_SCRIPT_PATH variable to the path.

With the MAYA_SCRIPT_PATH environment variable now updated, sourcing any MEL script can be done the same way. For example, to source the **foobar.mel** script the following code would be executed:

```
source foobar.mel;
```

The previous steps need to be completed for each new Maya session. Thus, if Maya is restarted the previous steps should be performed.

1.2 EXECUTING MEL CODE IN THE SCRIPT EDITOR

There are a lot of snippets of MEL code throughout this book. Many readers will want to type this MEL code into the **Script Editor** and then execute it. This will work fine in most cases. There will often be a problem when you execute different blocks of MEL code that use the same variable name but assume a different type. This problem is demonstrated in Maya as follows.

1. Open the **Script Editor**.

2. Execute the following.

```
$myVar = 1.0
```

The result is displayed.

```
// Result: 1 //
```

This creates the $myVar and assigns it an initial value.

3. To see what would happen if there were another piece of MEL code that used the same variable but as a different type, execute the following.

```
$myVar = "hi"
```

This produces an error.

```
// Warning: Converting string "hi" to a float value of 0. //
// Result: 0 //
```

4. Execute the following.

```
whatIs "$myVar"
```

The variable's data type is printed out.

```
// Result: float variable //
```

The problem is that although you are executing another piece of MEL code the `$myVar` variable still exists. The attempt to assign a string to it failed because the variable is already defined as a float. Once the data type (string, float, int, and so on) is defined for a variable it can't be changed.

The underlying problem is that all variables defined in the **Script Editor** are automatically made global variables, even if you don't explicitly make them. Thus, executing the statement

```
$myVar = 1.0
```

in a script would make it a local variable. This same statement executed in the **Script Editor** is the equivalent of writing

```
global $myVar = 1.0
```

The variable is implicitly made global. Once a variable is global there is no way to delete it. The only way is to restart Maya and thereby remove all global variables and start afresh. Note that this behavior also extends to procedures. Any procedure defined in the **Script Editor** will automatically become global.

What is needed is a way of defining the variable to be local. Unfortunately there is no explicit keyword (an opposite to the `global` keyword) that makes a variable local. This is, however, a way of implicitly making a variable local. By using code blocks, a variable is implicitly made local. At the end of the code block the variable is automatically deleted. This is precisely what is needed to ensure that running several sections of MEL code doesn't define the same global variable. This also prevents a "contamination" of the global name space of variables with variables you intended only for learning and testing.

5. Restart Maya by closing it and then opening it again.

6. Execute the following in the **Script Editor**.

```
{
$myVar = 1.0;
print $myVar;
}
```

The value of $myVar is printed out.

```
1
```

Because the definition of the variable was enclosed in braces, this created a separate code block. All variables defined within the block are automatically local. When the closing brace (}) is reached, all variables defined within the block are deleted. This ensures that the $myVar variable no longer exists after the code is executed and prevents it being added to the list of global variables.

7. Execute the following.

```
{
$myVar = "hi";
print $myVar;
}
```

The value of $myVar is printed out.

```
hi
```

There was no error this time when $myVar was defined because it is local to the block and is deleted when the block is finished.

Thus, the general rule is that if you ever intend on executing MEL code in the **Script Editor** simply enclose it in braces to ensure that it runs as a separate block. There may be times when you want to determine if a given variable is global. The following MEL procedure is designed to return `true` if the supplied variable is global, and `false` otherwise.

```
global proc int isGlobal( string $var )
{
  string $globals[] = `env`;
  for( $glob in $globals )
  {
   if( $glob == $var )
     return true;
  }
  return false;
}
```

This procedure can then be used to test if $myVar is a global variable.

```
isGlobal( "$myVar" )
```

The result is 0 (false). Note that the variable name is enclosed in quotation marks (").
This ensures that the variable name is passed to the procedure and not its value. Also
note that this procedure is a global procedure and thus can be called from anywhere
within Maya (script, **Script Editor**, and so on) once it is defined.

Points

Points and vectors provide the fundamental building blocks upon which geometry is based. Before covering the specifics of Maya's point and vector types it is important to understand the mathematical basis for points and vectors.

2.1 DIMENSIONS

The dimension of a point is the number of coordinates it has. Maya doesn't provide an explicit 2D point or vector, although a 3D point or vector can be used for the same purpose. Maya provides 3D points in MEL and 4D points (homogenous points) in the C++ API.

2.2 CARTESIAN COORDINATES

A 3D Cartesian point is represented as follows.

$$p = (x, y, z)$$

Cartesian coordinates are based on distances from the origin *(0,0,0)*. Each coordinate is a distance measured along an axis, starting at the origin. Because each of the axes is perpendicular to the others, the combination of coordinates defines a precise position in space.

For 3D points, the three coordinates define the distance along the standard X *(1,0,0)*, Y *(0,1,0)*, and Z *(0,0,1)* axes. Figure 2.1 shows a point with Cartesian coordinates (3, 4, 1). This point is located by starting at the origin and moving three

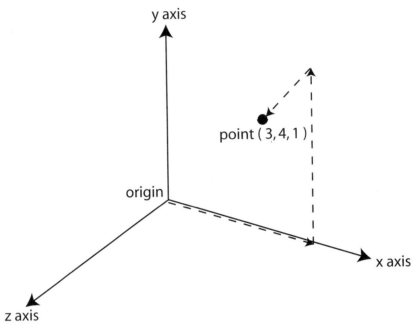

FIGURE 2.1 Cartesian coordinates.

units along the X axis. Next, move four units along the Y axis, followed by one unit along the Z axis. This is the final position of the point.

2.3 HOMOGENEOUS COORDINATES

A point can also be represented in homogeneous coordinates. Such a point has four dimensions and is represented as follows.

p = (x, y, z, w)

The additional coordinate, **w**, can be thought of as providing a scaling of the point. Keeping the **x**, **y**, and **z** components the same and simply varying the **w** component will produce a series of points along a line. The line runs through the origin and the point (**x**, **y**, **z**). Homogeneous coordinates are particularly useful for calculating projections. A projection is where a 3D point is projected onto a 2D point. A good example of this is the perspective projection, wherein a point in the scene is projected onto the image plane. The result is a 2D pixel in the image plane.

The addition of another coordinate is also very useful for applying more generalized transformations to points. This is covered in the transformation section.

2.4 POLAR AND SPHERICAL COORDINATES

A 2D point can be represented using polar coordinates, as follows.

p = (r, θ)

The **r** coordinate is a distance from the origin. The θ (Greek theta symbol) is the angle (in radians) rotated around from the X axis. (See **Section 4.1** for further details on angles and angle units.) The direction of rotation is counterclockwise. Figure 2.2 shows a point at polar coordinates (1.5, 0.78). The angle 0.78 is 45 degrees in radians.

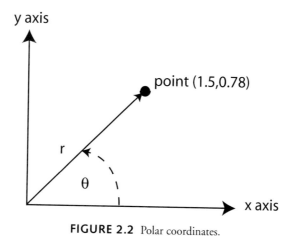

FIGURE 2.2 Polar coordinates.

To represent a 3D point in a similar manner, an additional angle — φ (Greek phi symbol) — is needed.

p = (r, φ, θ)

The point is now located on a sphere with radius **r**. The θ angle specifies the rotation about the *Z* axis from the *X* axis. The φ angle is rotation from the *Z* axis. Both rotations are counterclockwise. Figure 2.3 shows a point with spherical coordinates (1, 0.78, 0.78). Note that the vertical axis is the *Z* axis.

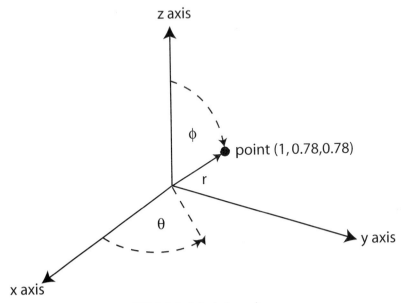

FIGURE 2.3 Spherical coordinates.

The final position is constructed as follows. Move from the origin along the *Z* axis by a distance of r. Rotate the position around the *Y* axis by an angle of ϕ. The point is on the *X-Z* plane. Rotate the point around the *Z* axis by the angle θ. The point is now in its final position.

The θ angle has a range of 0 to π radians (0 to 180 degrees). The ϕ angle has a range of 0 to $\pi/2$ radians (0 to 90 degrees).

2.5 CONVERSIONS

This section defines how to convert points between the various representations.

2.5.1 CARTESIAN TO HOMOGENEOUS

Any point with *n* dimensions can be converted to a point with *n* + 1 dimensions by multiplying each coordinate by a scalar. The *n* + 1*th* coordinate is then set to this scalar. Thus, to convert from a 3D Cartesian point

$$\mathbf{p} = (\mathbf{x}, \mathbf{y}, \mathbf{z})$$

to a 4D homogeneous point

$$p' = (x', y', z', w)$$

the original coordinates are multiplied by a scalar. The simplest scalar is obviously 1.

$$p' = (1 \cdot x, 1 \cdot y, 1 \cdot z, 1)$$
$$= (x', y', z', 1)$$

2.5.2 HOMOGENEOUS TO CARTESIAN

To convert from a homogeneous point back to a Cartesian point, the opposite operation is performed. All coordinates are divided by the last coordinate, w.

$$p = (x' / w, y' / w, z' / w, w / w)$$
$$= (x, y, z, 1)$$
$$= (x, y, z)$$

When implementing this formula it is important to check for w = 0. This will cause a division-by-zero error. If w = 0 the vector can be immediately set to the zero vector.

2.5.3 CARTESIAN TO POLAR

Because a polar coordinate only has two dimensions, the z coordinate is ignored. To convert the Cartesian coordinates

$$p = (x, y, 0)$$

to polar coordinates, the r coordinate is calculated as the distance from the point to the origin. The angle is the arc tangent of the y and x values.

$$p' = (r, \theta)$$
$$= (\sqrt{x^2 + y^2}, \tan^{-1}(y, x))$$

2.5.4 POLAR TO CARTESIAN

The polar coordinate

$$p = (r, \theta)$$

is converted to Cartesian coordinates as follows.

$$\mathbf{p'} = (x, y, z)$$
$$= (r\cos(\theta), r\sin(\theta), 0)$$

2.5.5 CARTESIAN TO SPHERICAL

To convert a Cartesian point

$$\mathbf{p} = (x, y, z)$$

to spherical coordinates, use the following.

$$\mathbf{p'} = (r, \phi, \theta)$$

where

$$r = \sqrt{x^2 + y^2 + z^2}$$
$$\phi = \tan^{-1}(\sqrt{x^2 + y^2}, z)$$
$$\theta = \tan^{-1}(y, x)$$

2.5.6 SPHERICAL TO CARTESIAN

To convert the spherical coordinates

$$\mathbf{p} = (r, \phi, \theta)$$

to Cartesian coordinates, use the following.

$$\mathbf{p'} = (x, y, z)$$

where

$$x = r\sin(\phi)\cos(\theta)$$
$$y = r\sin(\phi)\sin(\theta)$$
$$z = r\cos(\phi)$$

2.6 **MEL**

MEL's use of the term *vector* is more closely related to the computer science definition of a vector: a one-dimensional array of scalars. As such, there are very few restrictions on what operations can be performed on a vector.

A vector's elements can be accessed through its x, y, and z components. Vectors can be added, subtracted, and multiplied by other vectors, resulting in another vector. These operations are simply performed in a component-wise fashion.

Because a vector has just three components, it can only be used to represent Cartesian coordinates. The lack of a fourth component prevents it from being used in homogenous calculations. A point is defined as follows.

```
vector $p;                      // Initialized as (0,0,0)
vector $p = 3;                  // Initialized as (3,3,3)
vector $p = <<4.5, 3.8, 3.2>>;  // Initialized as (4.5, 3.8, 3.2)
```

Although the vector data type is convenient for performing vector operations, many of Maya's MEL commands and procedures don't support vector operations. For instance, a quite common task is getting the position of a transform. The command

```
getAttr transform1.translate;
```

will return an array of three floating-point numbers:

```
// Result: 0 0 0 //
```

From Maya 6.0 onward, it is valid to explicitly assign this array of three scalars to a vector as follows.

```
vector $t = `getAttr transform1.translate`;
```

In earlier versions of Maya, this would have caused an error. In all versions it isn't possible to directly assign a vector to an attribute.

```
vector $t = << 1, 2, 3 >>;
setAttr transform1.translate $t; // Causes an error
```

Instead, the vector must be assigned in a component-wise fashion.

```
setAttr transform1.translate ($t.x) ($t.y) ($t.z); // OK
```

2.7 C++ API

The C++ class for points is the **MPoint** class. The **MPoint** class is a homogeneous point with four coordinates: x, y, z, w. Each coordinate is stored as a double. There also exists a float variation of this class, **MFloatPoint**. The default constructor initializes the coordinates to the following.

```
MPoint pt; // x=y=z=0, w=1
```

The point can be converted from a Cartesian point to a homogeneous point via the homogenize function.

```
MPoint pt;
pt.homogenize(); // pt = (w*x, w*y, w*z, w)
```

This function simply multiplies each component by the w component. Note that if w is 0 then a zero vector (0,0,0,0) will result. To convert the point from a homogeneous point to a Cartesian point the cartesianize function is used.

```
MPoint pt;
pt.cartesianize(); // pt = (x/w, y/w, z/w, 1)
```

This function is the inverse of the homogenize function and thus divides all components by w. There also exists a final conversion function, rationalize, that works similarly to cartesianize, but instead of setting w to 1 at the end it leaves it.

```
MPoint pt;
pt.rationalize(); // pt = (x/w, y/w, z/w, w)
```

It is important to note that Maya doesn't explicitly store which form (Cartesian, homogeneous, rational) the point is in. It is up to the developer to ensure that only those functions that are valid for a given form are used. There is nothing to prevent the rationalize function from being called twice, which will clearly result in an incorrect point. For convenience the predefined class instance, origin, exists.

```
MPoint::origin // point at (0,0,0)
```

These can be used like regular class instances, as in the following example.

```
MPoint p0;
if( p0 == MPoint::origin )
 MGlobal::displayInfo( "point is at the origin" );
```

2.8 LOCATORS

Maya doesn't have a geometry shape for a single point. However, locators can be used for this purpose. Locators are visual guides that are drawn in viewports but are not rendered. To create a locator at a given position, use the following.

```
spaceLocator -p 1 3 6;
```

Because a locator has its own transform node it can be scaled, rotated, and translated like any other geometry. The position of a locator can be retrieved in object and world space as follows.

```
xform -query -objectSpace -translation;
xform -query -worldSpace -translation;
```

CHAPTER 3

Vectors

A vector has both a direction and a *magnitude*. The magnitude of a vector is simply its length. Vectors are often used to define the difference between points, which is the *displacement* from the first point to the second. A series of vectors (combined with an origin) can also define a coordinate frame. This can then be used for defining a custom space in which to define other points and vectors.

In Maya, all vectors are 3D. The three components are named x, y, and z. It is important to understand that while many books show vectors located somewhere in space, vectors don't have a location. A vector is a relative movement, an offset. In terms of position, a vector has no meaning without a point. The vector is added to the point to give a new point. At no time does the vector represent a position.

It is sometimes more intuitive to think of vectors as arrows sticking out of the origin. This helps understand that they are not positions but simply directions. Imagining all vectors being grouped around the origin makes such operations as comparing two vectors, flipping their direction, or rotating them more intuitive.

3.1 MEL

A vector is defined using the `vector` data type. Because MEL doesn't make the distinction between points and vectors, all operations that can be performed on points can be applied to vectors.

3.2 C++ API

The C++ API makes a distinction between points and vectors. Whereas points are represented by the **MPoint** class, vectors are represented by the **MVector** class. The operations that can be performed on them conform to the mathematical rules set out previously. The **MVector** class has three coordinates: x, y, and z. All coordinates use the double data type. There also exists a float variation of this class, **MFloatVector**. The default constructor initializes the instance to the zero vector.

```
MVector vec; // x=y=z=0
```

Even though Maya makes the mathematical distinction between points and vectors, for convenience the **MPoint** and **MVector** classes can be easily converted from each other.

```
MPoint pt;
MVector vec;
pt = vec;
vec = pt;
```

Instances of **MFloatPoint** and **MFloatVector** can be converted to instances of **MPoint** and **MVector**, respectively. Note that when converting an **MPoint** to an **MVector** Maya assumes that the point is already in Cartesian coordinates. If it isn't, simply call the cartesianize function before assignment. For convenience, several predefined instances of **MVector** exist.

```
MVector::zero  // vector (0,0,0)
MVector::xAxis // vector (1,0,0)
MVector::yAxis // vector (0,1,0)
MVector::zAxis // vector (0,0,1)
MVector::xNegAxis // vector (-1,0,0)
MVector::yNegAxis // vector (0,-1,0)
MVector::zNegAxis // vector (0,0,-1)
```

These can be used like regular class instances, as in the following example.

```
MVector v0;
if( v0 == MVector::xAxis )
    MGlobal::displayInfo( "vector is the same as the x axis" );
```

3.3 ADDING

Adding two vectors **a** and **b** produces another vector, **c**, as shown in Figure 3.1. The dotted lines show another way of looking at vector addition. By placing each successive vector at the end of the previous one, the final vector offset is determined.

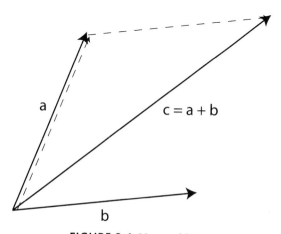

FIGURE 3.1 Vector addition.

To add two vectors, the individual components are added, resulting in a new vector.

$$\begin{aligned} \mathbf{c} &= \mathbf{a} + \mathbf{b} \\ &= (a_x + b_x, a_y + b_y, a_z + b_z) \end{aligned}$$

The algebraic rules for vector addition are:

$\mathbf{a} + \mathbf{b} = \mathbf{b} + \mathbf{a}$	(Commutative property)
$\mathbf{a} + (\mathbf{b} + \mathbf{c}) = (\mathbf{a} + \mathbf{b}) + \mathbf{c}$	(Associative property)
$\mathbf{a} + \mathbf{0} = \mathbf{a}$	(Additive identity)
$\mathbf{a} + (-\mathbf{a}) = \mathbf{0}$	(Additive inverse)

3.4 SUBTRACTING

Subtracting two vectors **a** and **b** results in another vector, **c**, as shown in Figure 3.2.

c = a − b

The dotted lines in the figure show a more intuitive way of looking at vector subtraction. Subtracting can be thought of as addition, but with the second vector's direction flipped.

c = a + (−b)

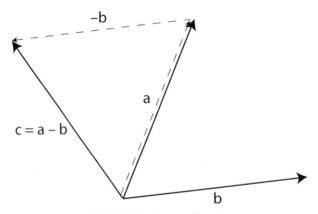

FIGURE 3.2 Vector subtraction.

The algebraic rules for vector subtraction are:

a − b ≠ b − a   (Noncommutative property)
a − (b − c) ≠ (a − b) − c   (Nonassociative property)
a − 0 = a   (Subtractive identity)

3.5 SCALING

A vector's length can changed by scaling it. A vector, **a**, is scaled by multiplying each component by a scalar, *s*.

b = *s***a**

Figure 3.3 shows the result of scaling the vector a by 2 and −1. A scaling of −1 will cause the vector to be flipped. That is, its direction is reversed.

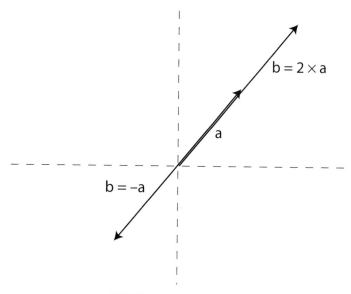

FIGURE 3.3 Vector scaling.

The algebraic rules for vector scaling are:

(st)a $= s(t$a$)$ (Associative property)
$(s + t)$a $= s$a $+ t$a   (Distributive property)
$s($a $+$ b$) = s$a $+ s$b   (Distributive property)
1a $=$ a   (Multiplicative identity)

3.6 LENGTH

Calculating the length of a vector is done using the standard Pythagorean theorem, shown in Figure 3.4. This is a right triangle. That is, a triangle with one angle at 90 degrees.

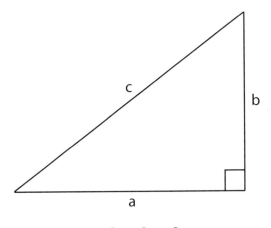

$$c^2 = a^2 + b^2$$

FIGURE 3.4 Pythagorean theorem.

The variable **c** is the hypotenuse, which is the longest side of the triangle. This is also the length of the 2D vector (**a, b**). Given the Pythagorean theorem, the value of **c** is derived as follows.

$$c^2 = a^2 + b^2$$

Taking the square root of both sides results in

$$c = \sqrt{a^2 + b^2}$$

The double vertical bar, ‖, is used to denote the length of the vector.

$$\|c\| = \sqrt{a^2 + b^2}$$

Note that this differs from the single vertical bar, |, which is used to denote the absolute value operation (|c| is the absolute vector). The values **a** and **b** can be replaced by the **x** and **y** coordinates of the vector. For any 2D vector, the length is simply

$$\|c\| = \sqrt{x^2 + y^2}$$

For a 3D vector, the length is

$$\|c\| = \sqrt{x^2 + y^2 + z^2}$$

The same process is applied to vectors of n dimensions. All of the coordinates are squared, then summed. The square root of the result is the length of the n-dimensional vector.

3.6.1 MEL

VECTOR

To calculate the length of a vector, use the mag command.

```
vector $v;
float $length = mag( $v );
```

If you need to calculate the length of a 2D vector, the hypot command can be used.

```
vector $v = <<2.4, 4.6, 0.0>>;
float $length = hypot( $v.x, $v.y );
print $length; // Prints 5.188449
```

FLOAT ARRAY

To calculate the length of a vector as a float array, use the following procedure.

```
proc float len( float $v[] )
{
   return sqrt( $v[0]*$v[0] + $v[1]*$v[1] + $v[2]*$v[2] );
}
```

The following is an example of use of this procedure.

```
float $v[] = {2.4, 4.6, 7.3};
float $length = len( $v );
print $length; // Prints 8.956004
```

3.6.2 C++ API

The length of a vector is returned using the `length` function.

```
MVector v;
double len = v.length();
```

3.7 DISTANCE BETWEEN POINTS

The Euclidean distance between two points is the length of the vector between the two points. Given two points, **p0** and **p1**, the vector and distance between them is

$$\mathbf{v} = \mathbf{p0} - \mathbf{p1}$$
$$\mathbf{distance} = \|\mathbf{v}\|$$

Another useful distance is the Manhattan distance. This is calculated as the sum of the absolute values of the components.

$$\mathbf{distance} = \left|\mathbf{v_x}\right| + \left|\mathbf{v_y}\right| + \left|\mathbf{v_z}\right|$$

3.7.1 MEL

VECTOR

To calculate the distance between two points, use the following.

```
vector $p0 = <<1, 0, 0>>;
vector $p1 = <<2, 0, 0>>;
vector $v = $p0 - $p1;
float $len = mag( $v );
```

FLOAT ARRAY

Calculate the vector between the two points by subtracting them, and then use the `len` procedure (shown in the previous section) to calculate the distance separating them.

3.7.2 C++ API

The distance between two points is calculated using the **MPoint**'s `distanceTo` function.

```
MPoint p0( 1.0, 0.0, 0.0 );
MPoint p1( 2.0, 0.0, 0.0 );
double distance = p0.distanceTo( p1 );
```

3.8 NORMALIZING VECTORS

A vector that has a length of 1 is called a *unit vector*. To turn any vector into a unit vector, it needs to be *normalized*. This is done as follows.

$$\hat{\mathbf{u}} = \frac{\mathbf{u}}{\|\mathbf{u}\|}$$

Each component of the vector is divided by the vector's current length. The vector's length will then be 1. Unit vectors are represented with the "hat" character (^) above them. For a 3D vector the calculation is as follows.

$$\hat{\mathbf{u}} = \left(\frac{\mathbf{u}_x}{\|\mathbf{u}\|}, \frac{\mathbf{u}_y}{\|\mathbf{u}\|}, \frac{\mathbf{u}_z}{\|\mathbf{u}\|} \right)$$

Vectors with a length of 1 are also sometimes referred to as *normal vectors*. This can cause some confusion, in that the term *normal* has another meaning with regard to vectors. However, the action of *normalizing* only ever means to scale a vector so that its length is 1.

3.8.1 MEL

VECTOR

To normalize a vector, use the `unit` command.

```
vector $v = <<2.4, 4.6, 7.3>>;
float $len = mag( $v );
print $len; // Prints 8.9560041
```

```
$v = unit( $v );
$len = mag( $v );
print $len; // Prints 1.0
```

FLOAT ARRAY

If the vector is a float array, the `normalize` command can be used.

```
float $v[] = {2.4, 4.6, 7.3};
float $len = normalize( $v );
print $len;
```

3.8.2 C++ API

To normalize the vector, call the `normalize` function. This will perform an in-place normalization.

```
MVector v;
v.normalize();
```

To get a copy of the vector, but with unit length, use the `normal` function. This makes a copy of the vector, normalizes it, and returns it. The original vector is left untouched.

```
MVector v;
MVector norm = v.normal();
```

3.9 DOT PRODUCT

The dot product is denoted using the middle dot (·) character. Given two vectors, **a** and **b**, the dot product is calculated as follows.

$$\mathbf{a} \cdot \mathbf{b} = a_x b_x + a_y b_y + a_z b_z$$

Note that the result is a single scalar value. The dot product is also referred to as the *inner product*, or more precisely the *Euclidean inner product*.

3.9.1 ANGLE BETWEEN

Figure 3.5 shows two vectors, **a** and **b**, and the angle between them, θ. (Angles and angle units are covered in detail in Section 4.1.)

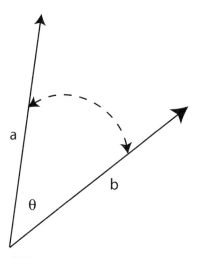

FIGURE 3.5 Angle between vectors.

The calculation of the angle is based on the dot product (·) of two vectors. The dot product can also be calculated as follows.

$$\mathbf{a} \cdot \mathbf{b} = \|\mathbf{a}\| \, \|\mathbf{b}\| \cos(\theta)$$

This equation is derived from the Law of Cosines. With the goal of determining the value of θ, this equation can be rewritten as follows.

$$\frac{\mathbf{a} \cdot \mathbf{b}}{\|\mathbf{a}\| \, \|\mathbf{b}\|} = \cos(\theta)$$

$$\cos^{-1}\!\left(\frac{\mathbf{a} \cdot \mathbf{b}}{\|\mathbf{a}\| \, \|\mathbf{b}\|}\right) = \theta$$

Note that the resulting angle, θ, is in radians. The value ranges from 0 (when the two vectors are exactly colinear) to π radians (180 degrees), when the two vectors are in exactly opposite directions.

MEL

Vector

The `angle` command can be used to calculate the angle between two vectors.

```
vector $v0 = <<1,0,0>>;
vector $v1 = <<0,1,0>>;
rad_to_deg( angle( $v0, $v1 ) );
// Result: 90.000001 //
```

The functionality of the `angle` command can be replicated using other commands. The dot product of two vectors is calculated using the `dot` command. The `acos` command returns the arc-cosine ($\cos^{-1}$) of the given angle.

```
vector $v0 = <<1,0,0>>;
vector $v1 = <<0,1,0>>;
rad_to_deg( acos( dot( $v0, $v1 ) / (mag($v0) * mag($v1)) ) );
// Result: 90.000001 //
```

Float Array

The `dotProduct` command is designed to calculate the dot product of two float arrays.

```
float $v0[] = {1.0, 0.0, 0.0};
float $v1[] = {0.0, 1.0, 0.0};
rad_to_deg( acos( dotProduct( $v0, $v1, true ) ) );
// Result: 90.000001 //
```

C++ API

The `angle` function is used to calculate the angle between two vectors.

```
MVector v0( 1.0, 0.0, 0.0 );
MVector v1( 0.0, 1.0, 0.0 );
double a = v0.angle( v1 ); // Angle in radians
```

The calculation of the angle can be broken down into separate parts. The dot product is calculated using the **MVector**'s multiply operator (*). It has been overloaded to provide the dot product of two vectors.

```
MVector v0( 1.0, 0.0, 0.0 );
MVector v1( 0.0, 1.0, 0.0 );
double a = acos( (v0 * v1) / (v0.length() * v1.length()) );
```

3.9.2 LENGTH SQUARED

Recall that the length of the vector is the square root of the sum of the individual coordinates squared. Given a vector **v** with components x, y, and z, the length is calculated as follows.

$$\|\mathbf{v}\| = \sqrt{x^2 + y^2 + z^2}$$

Working back to the original Pythagorean theorem results in

$$\|\mathbf{v}\|^2 = x^2 + y^2 + z^2$$

The dot product of the vector, **v**, with itself will give the squared length of the vector.

$$\|\mathbf{v}\|^2 = \mathbf{v} \cdot \mathbf{v}$$

Often the length of a vector needs to be compared against some predefined length.

```
if( v.length() < 0.1 )
    . . .
```

The squared length can be used to implement this more efficiently. The sqrt function can be quite long to calculate compared to the multiplications and additions required to calculate the dot product. The sqrt function can be avoided entirely if the length being compared is itself squared ($0.01 = 0.1^2$). The faster comparison is therefore

```
if( v * v < 0.01 )
    . . .
```

3.9.3 PERPENDICULAR PROJECTION

The dot product can be used to project one vector onto another. Figure 3.6 shows the result of projecting vector **a** onto vector **b**.

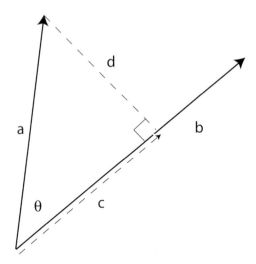

FIGURE 3.6 Perpendicular projection.

To calculate the length of vector **c**, the same trigonometry used to convert from polar coordinates to Cartesian coordinates is used.

$$x = r\cos(\theta)$$

Substituting $\|\mathbf{a}\|$ for **r** and $\|\mathbf{c}\|$ for **x** gives

$$\|\mathbf{c}\| = \|\mathbf{a}\|\cos(\theta)$$

The dot product can be used to calculate the $\cos(\theta)$ part of the equation.

$$\cos(\theta) = \frac{\mathbf{a} \cdot \mathbf{b}}{\|\mathbf{a}\|\,\|\mathbf{b}\|}$$

Substituting this into the initial equation results in

$$\|\mathbf{c}\| = \|\mathbf{a}\|\cos(\theta)$$
$$= \|\mathbf{a}\|\frac{\mathbf{a} \cdot \mathbf{b}}{\|\mathbf{a}\|\,\|\mathbf{b}\|}$$

The $\|\mathbf{a}\|$ in the numerator and denominator cancel each other out, leaving

$$\|\mathbf{c}\| = \frac{\mathbf{a} \cdot \mathbf{b}}{\|\mathbf{b}\|}$$

If the vector **b** is normalized, resulting in the unit vector $\hat{\mathbf{b}}$, the equation is even simpler. The length of vector **c** is simply the dot product of the vectors **a** and $\hat{\mathbf{b}}$.

$$\|\mathbf{c}\| = \frac{\mathbf{a} \cdot \hat{\mathbf{b}}}{1}$$
$$= \mathbf{a} \cdot \hat{\mathbf{b}}$$

The projection vector **c** is then

$$\mathbf{c} = (\mathbf{a} \cdot \hat{\mathbf{b}})\hat{\mathbf{b}}$$

DISTANCE TO LINE

This same method can be used to calculate the perpendicular distance from a point **p** to a line, running through the points **p0** and **p1**. Referring to Figure 3.6, the length of vector **d** is the distance from the vector **a** to its projection on the vector **b**. The vector **a** is calculated as follows.

$$\mathbf{a} = \mathbf{p} - \mathbf{p0}$$

Vector **b** is used to represent the line. It is normalized to ensure that it has a unit length.

$$\mathbf{b} = \mathbf{p1} - \mathbf{p0}$$
$$\hat{\mathbf{b}} = \text{normalize}(\mathbf{p1} - \mathbf{p0})$$

As shown previously, the vector **c** is

$$\mathbf{c} = (\mathbf{a} \cdot \hat{\mathbf{b}})\hat{\mathbf{b}}$$

The vector **d** is

$$\mathbf{d} = \mathbf{a} - \mathbf{c}$$
$$= \mathbf{a} - (\mathbf{a} \cdot \hat{\mathbf{b}})\hat{\mathbf{b}}$$

The length of vector **d** is the perpendicular distance to the line.

$$\|\mathbf{d}\| = \|\mathbf{a} - (\mathbf{a} \cdot \hat{\mathbf{b}})\hat{\mathbf{b}}\|$$

MEL

Vector

The perpendicular distance is calculated as follows.

```
vector $p = <<1,3,4>>;
vector $p0 = <<0,0,0>>;
vector $p1 = <<1,0,0>>;

vector $a = $p - $p0;
vector $b = unit( $p1 - $p0 );
vector $c = dot( $a, $b ) * $b;
vector $d = $a - $c;
float $dist = mag( $d );
// Result: 5 //
```

C++ API

The distance from the point to the line is calculated as follows.

```
MPoint p( 1.0, 3.0, 4.0 );
MPoint p0( 0.0, 0.0, 0.0 );
MPoint p1( 1.0, 0.0, 0.0 );
MVector a = p - p0;
MVector b = p1 - p0;
b.normalize();
MVector c = (a * b) * b;
MVector d = a - c;
double dist = d.length();
MGlobal::displayInfo( MString("distance: ") + dist );
```

The result is

```
// distance: 5
```

3.10 CROSS PRODUCT

The cross product is a very useful operation for calculating the vector perpendicular to two others, the area of a parallelogram or triangle, and the sine of the angle between two vectors. The cross product is also known as the *vector product*.

3.10.1 PERPENDICULAR VECTOR

Figure 3.7 shows two vectors, **a** and **b**, and a third vector **c**, which is perpendicular to the first two vectors. This is written using the perpendicular symbol ⊥.

$$\mathbf{c} = \mathbf{a} \perp \mathbf{b}$$

The vector **c** is guaranteed to be at 90 degrees to the flat plane formed by the **a** and **b** vectors.

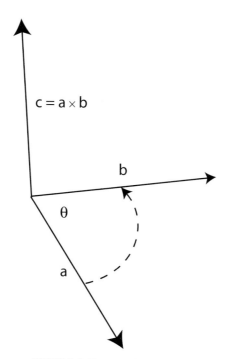

FIGURE 3.7 Perpendicular vector.

The perpendicular vector is calculated using the cross product of two vectors, as follows.

$$\begin{aligned} \mathbf{c} &= \mathbf{a} \times \mathbf{b} \\ &= (a_y b_z - a_z b_y,\, a_z b_x - a_x b_z,\, a_x b_y - a_y b_x) \end{aligned}$$

The direction of the perpendicular vector is defined by the right-hand rule. The dotted line in Figure 3.7 shows the direction to curl the fingers of your right hand. Vector $\mathbf{c}$ points in the direction of the thumb. The cross product is not commutative, and thus the order of the vectors is important.

$$\mathbf{a} \times \mathbf{b} \neq \mathbf{b} \times \mathbf{a}$$

If the order of the vectors is reversed, the perpendicular vector will point in the opposite direction.

$$\mathbf{a} \times \mathbf{b} = -(\mathbf{b} \times \mathbf{a})$$

Note that if the vectors $\mathbf{a}$ and $\mathbf{b}$ are colinear (parallel), the perpendicular vector will be the zero vector. The reason is that two colinear vectors define a line and not a plane. A line has an infinite number of normalized perpendicular vectors. A plane has only two. The right-hand rule defines which of these two possible vectors is produced by the cross product. The perpendicular vector for a 2D vector, $\mathbf{a}$, is calculated as follows.

$$\begin{aligned} \mathbf{a} &= (x, y) \\ \perp\mathbf{a} &= (-y, x) \end{aligned}$$

When using 2D vectors, the *perpendicular dot product*,

$$(\perp\mathbf{a}) \cdot \mathbf{b} = \|\mathbf{a}\| \, \|\mathbf{b}\| \sin(\theta)$$

can be used to calculate θ, which is the signed angle between $\mathbf{a}$ and $\mathbf{b}$. When the smallest rotation from $\mathbf{a}$ to $\mathbf{b}$ is in a clockwise direction, θ will be negative. Likewise, if the smallest rotation is in a counterclockwise direction, θ will be positive. The absolute value of the perpendicular dot product gives the area of the parallelogram with sides $\mathbf{a}$ and $\mathbf{b}$.

$$\text{area} = \left| (\perp\mathbf{a}) \cdot \mathbf{b} \right|$$

The algebraic rules for the cross product are:

$$a \times b = -(b \times a)$$
$$a \times (b + c) = (a \times b) + (a \times c)$$
$$(a + b) \times c = (a \times c) + (b \times c)$$
$$s(a \times b) = (sa) \times b = a \times (sb)$$
$$a \times 0 = 0 \times a = 0$$
$$a \times a = 0$$

MEL

Vector

The cross product is calculated using the `cross` command.

```
vector $a = <<1,0,0>>;
vector $b = <<0,1,0>>;
vector $c = cross( $a, $b );
// Result: <<0, 0, 1>> //
```

FLOAT ARRAY

The `crossProduct` procedure can be used to calculate the cross product for float arrays. The procedure also takes two Boolean values, `$normalizeInputs` and `$normalizeResult`, which control, respectively, whether the input vectors and final vector are normalized.

```
float $a[] = {1.0, 0.0, 0.0};
float $b[] = {0.0, 0.0, 0.0};
float $c[] = crossProduct( $a, $b, false, false );
```

C++ API

The cross product is calculated using the **MVector**'s overloaded ^ operator.

```
MVector a( 1.0, 0.0, 0.0 );
MVector b( 0.0, 1.0, 0.0 );
MVector c = a ^ b;
```

3.10.2 AREA OF TRIANGLE

The length of the perpendicular vector, **c**, resulting from the cross product is the area of the parallelogram formed by the two vectors **a** and **b**.

c = a × b
‖c‖ = area of parallelogram

This is shown in Figure 3.8.

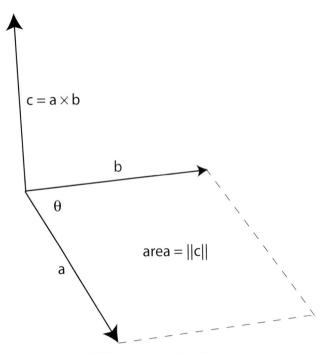

FIGURE 3.8 Area of parallelogram.

The area of the parallelogram is exactly twice the area of the triangle formed by the vectors **a** and **b**. The area of the triangle is, therefore, calculated as follows.

triangle area = ‖a × b‖ / 2

Another interesting property of the cross product is that it can be used to calculate the sine of the angle between the two vectors **a** and **b**.

$$\| a \times b \| = \| a \| \| b \| \sin(\theta)$$

$$\frac{\| a \times b \|}{\| a \| \| b \|} = \sin(\theta)$$

The angle between the two vectors, θ, is then calculated as follows.

$$\sin^{-1}\left(\frac{\| a \times b \|}{\| a \| \| b \|} \right) = \theta$$

A common misconception with the cross product is that if both vectors **a** and **b** have unit length that the perpendicular vector **c** will have unit length. This is only true when the angle θ is $\pi/2$ (90 degrees).

$$\| a \times b \| = \| a \| \| b \| \sin(\theta)$$
$$= 1 \cdot 1 \cdot \sin(\pi/2)$$
$$= 1 \cdot 1 \cdot 1$$
$$= 1$$

Otherwise, the length of the perpendicular vector is scaled by the sine of the angle θ.

MEL

The area of the triangle is calculated as follows.

```
vector $a = <<1,0,0>>;
vector $b = <<0,1,0>>;
float $triArea = 0.5 * mag( cross( $a, $b ) );
// Result: 0.5 //
```

C++ API

The triangle's area is calculated using the following.

```
MVector a( 1.0, 0.0, 0.0 );
MVector b( 0.0, 1.0, 0.0 );
MVector c = a ^ b;
double triArea = 0.5 * c.length();
```

3.11 POINTS VERSUS VECTORS

Because a point and a vector both have three dimensions, it may seem logical to consider them equivalent. They are, in fact, geometrically and mathematically different. Geometrically, a vector has a direction and a length, whereas a point has a position. Mathematically, a point and a vector are represented by homogeneous coordinates as follows.

$$\mathbf{p} = (p_x, p_y, p_z, 1)$$
$$\mathbf{v} = (v_x, v_y, v_z, 0)$$

Note that the only difference is the w coordinate. The point, $\mathbf{p}$, when converted to Cartesian coordinates will result in the following.

$$\mathbf{p'} = (p_x / 1, p_y / 1, p_z / 1)$$
$$= (p_x, p_y, p_z)$$

When the homogeneous point, $\mathbf{v}$, is converted to Cartesian coordinates, the result is infinity due to the division by 0.

$$\mathbf{v'} = (v_x / 0, v_y / 0, v_z / 0, 0)$$
$$= (\infty, \infty, \infty)$$

This is because as the value of w approaches zero the division by w results in a point that is larger and larger. The point is therefore further and further away. When w is set to zero, the point is so far away that it is at infinity. Such a point no longer defines a position but instead a direction from the origin; a vector. Thus, points have a w homogeneous coordinate of 1 and all vectors have a w homogeneous coordinate of 0. What happens when a point is added to another point? Starting with two points

$$p0 = (p0_x, p0_y, p0_z, 1)$$
$$p1 = (p1_x, p1_y, p1_z, 1)$$

they are added component by component, resulting in the following point.

$$
\begin{aligned}
p' &= p0 + p1 \\
&= (p0_x + p1_x, p0_y + p1_y, p0_z + p1_z, 1 + 1) \\
&= (p0_x + p1_x, p0_y + p1_y, p0_z + p1_z, 2)
\end{aligned}
$$

Note that the homogeneous coordinate w is 2. Thus, when the homogeneous point is converted back to Cartesian coordinates by dividing by w, the result isn't what you would expect because it has been divided by 2, halving the result. Because the homogenous coordinate isn't 1, the result isn't a point. It is invalid.

It is valid to add two vectors together. To see why, consider the following example. Two vectors

$$v0 = (v0_x, v0_y, v0_z, 0)$$
$$v1 = (v1_x, v1_y, v1_z, 0)$$

added together result in the vector

$$
\begin{aligned}
v' &= v0 + v1 \\
&= (v0_x + v1_x, v0_y + v1_y, v0_z + v1_z, 0)
\end{aligned}
$$

The resulting vector has a homogenous coordinate of 0, and is thus a valid vector. Therefore, adding a vector to another vector results in a vector. Adding a vector to a point is demonstrated using the following point and vector.

$$p0 = (p0_x, p0_y, p0_z, 1)$$
$$v0 = (v0_x, v0_y, v0_z, 0)$$

When added, the result is

$$
\begin{aligned}
p' &= p0 + v0 \\
&= (p0_x + v0_x, p0_y + v0_y, p0_z + v0_z, 1 + 0) \\
&= (p0_x + v0_x, p0_y + v0_y, p0_z + v0_z, 1)
\end{aligned}
$$

Note that the final homogeneous coordinate is 1. As such, the result of adding a point and a vector is a point, in that all points have a w homogeneous coordinate of 1. It follows logically that subtracting two points results in a vector. Given two points

$$p0 = (p0_x, p0_y, p0_z, 1)$$
$$p1 = (p1_x, p1_y, p1_z, 1)$$

the result is a vector (as follows), in that the w coordinate is 0.

$$\begin{aligned}
p' &= p0 - p1 \\
&= (p0_x - p1_x, p0_y - p1_y, p0_z - p1_z, 1 - 1) \\
&= (p0_x - p1_x, p0_y - p1_y, p0_z - p1_z, 0)
\end{aligned}$$

Maya doesn't make any distinctions between points and vectors in MEL. The vector data type is used to represent both. However, in the C++ API, Maya makes the distinction. There are separate data types for points and vectors. Because Maya mixes interpretations, it is obvious that there is no right or wrong way. The advantage with considering both the same is that only one type is needed and the same operations can be performed. It is the responsibility of the developer to make the semantic distinction between the two. When there are distinct types, as in the C++ API, the advantage is that there is stricter type checking. For instance, it isn't possible to add two points together. This results in more mathematically correct code. The source code is also clearer, in that the developer's intentions are more explicit because distinct data types are used. Without explicit data types, the code should include more comments to help clarify the operations being performed.

CHAPTER 4

Rotations

Rotations are often a source of much confusion, and thus an entire chapter is devoted to them here. Before delving into rotations, however, it is important to understand what an angle is.

4.1 ANGLES

An angle is the rotational distance between two vectors. Angles can be measured in both degrees and radians. Degrees are the most common unit of measurement. There are 360 degrees in a circle. There are 2π radians ($\cong 6.2831$) in a circle. Although degrees are more intuitive, all mathematical functions that take angles use radians. Fortunately, the conversion between degrees and radians, and vice versa, is simply a matter of scaling.

4.1.1 MEL

To convert from degrees to radians, use the `deg_to_rad` command.

```
deg_to_rad( 360 );
// Result: 6.283184 //
```

To convert from radians to degrees, use the `rad_to_deg` command.

```
rad_to_deg( 6.283184 );
// Result: 359.999928 //
```

Note that the result isn't exactly 360. Because conversions from one unit to another may not be exact, it is important to use tolerances to check values. The inexactness of the conversions is often due to limited floating-point precision.

4.1.2 C++ API

The **MAngle** class can be used to convert between angle units. The **MAngle** class accepts angles in degrees, radians, angle-minutes, and angle-seconds. To convert an angle in degrees to radians, use the following.

```
MAngle a( 90.0, MAngle::kDegrees );
double r = a.asRadians();
```

The asDegrees function can be used to convert the given angle to degrees. Although the **MAngle** class is convenient, it does require the instantiation of a class object. The conversion from degrees to radians, and vice versa, can be done using simple inline functions.

```
const double DEG_TO_RAD = M_PI / 180.0;
const double RAD_TO_DEG = 180.0 / M_PI;

inline double degToRad( const double d )
{
    return d * DEG_TO_RAD;
}

inline double radToDeg( const double d )
{
    return d * RAD_TO_DEG;
}
```

4.2 ROTATIONS

A rotation is used to turn a given point or vector about an *axis of rotation* by an amount given as the *angle of rotation*. The center of rotation is the point about which the rotation will occur. This allows an object to be rotated about any arbitrary point. By default, the center of rotation is the origin. The axis, angle, and center of rotation together completely define a rotation. For a 2D vector, **v**, it is rotated in a counter-clockwise direction, resulting in the final vector **v'**, as shown in Figure 4.1.

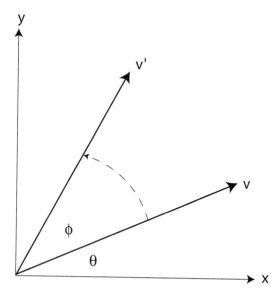

FIGURE 4.1 Rotation in 2D.

The center of rotation is the origin. The angle is given in radians and is typically specified using the Greek symbol theta (θ). In the case of a 2D rotation, the axis of rotation can be thought of as an invisible Z axis that points out of the page, toward the reader. To rotate a vector

v = (x, y)

the vector is first converted into polar coordinates as follows.

v = (r, θ)

See Section 2.5.3 for an explanation of this conversion. Polar coordinates include an implicit angle, θ, and thus it is easy to imagine a rotation as simply adding to or subtracting from this angle. Thus, to rotate the vector by +45 degrees ($\pi/4$ radians), the additional angle is added to the existing angle.

v' = (r, θ + $\pi/4$)

These polar coordinates can then be converted back to Cartesian coordinates. Fortunately, there is a faster way to perform a rotation if the complete series of operations is taken into account. Given the additional angle of rotation ϕ, the final angle is $\theta + \phi$. The conversion of the final angle back to Cartesian coordinates can be defined as

$$x' = r \cos(\theta + \phi)$$
$$y' = r \sin(\theta + \phi)$$

By applying trigonometric identities, this can be expanded to

$$x' = r \cos(\theta) \cos(\phi) - r \sin(\theta) \sin(\phi)$$
$$y' = r \cos(\theta) \sin(\phi) + r \sin(\theta) \cos(\phi)$$

Referring to the equations for converting from polar to Cartesian coordinates, it is known that

$$x = r \cos(\theta)$$
$$y = r \sin(\theta)$$

and thus all instances of these in the equation can be replaced by x and y as follows.

$$x' = x \cos(\phi) - y \sin(\phi)$$
$$y' = x \sin(\phi) + y \cos(\phi)$$

Extending this to three dimensions, the rotation about the Z axis will be exactly the same as the 2D case.

$$x' = x \cos(\phi) - y \sin(\phi)$$
$$y' = x \sin(\phi) + y \cos(\phi)$$
$$z' = z$$

The z coordinate doesn't change because this is the axis of rotation. Rotations around the X axis are performed using

$$x' = x$$
$$y' = y \cos(\phi) - z \sin(\phi)$$
$$z' = y \sin(\phi) + z \cos(\phi)$$

Rotations around the Y axis are performed using

$$x' = z \sin(\phi) + x \cos(\phi)$$
$$y' = y$$
$$z' = z \cos(\phi) - x \sin(\phi)$$

4.3 ORIENTATION REPRESENTATIONS

Now that you have an understanding of what rotations involve, let's examine the various possible orientation representations. An orientation is a way of defining the way an object is angled relative to a given coordinate system.

4.3.1 EULER ANGLES

With Euler angles, an orientation is defined by three angles (*rx*, *ry*, and *rz*) relative to the standard axes *X*, *Y*, and *Z*. The three angles are also referred to as *roll, pitch,* and *yaw.* The order in which the angles are applied is important. If the order is *x-y-z,* the *rx* rotation is applied first, followed by the *ry* rotation, then finally the *rz* rotation. Using the same rotation angles but changing their order to *y-z-x* will most likely result in a different orientation.

GIMBAL LOCK

When an object seems to be only rotating about two axes even though three rotation angles were specified, the object is most likely exhibiting *gimbal lock.* To understand gimbal lock it is important to understand what exactly a gimbal is and its application in real-world navigation systems. A gimbal is a ring with a central rod about which it can rotate. Figure 4.2 shows a gimbal assembly with three gimbals.

Gimbals are used in gyroscopic compasses. These compasses are used for navigation in airplanes, space shuttles, space stations, and just about any craft that needs to precisely know its orientation. A gyroscopic compass consists of three gimbals and an inertial platform at the center. The gyroscopic compass is rigidly attached to the craft. It is the inertial platform that relays the craft's exact orientation based on the separate orientations of the three gimbals. To be accurate it is very important that the inertial platform be able to freely assume any orientation. Unfortunately, if certain gimbals align themselves, one of the rotation axes is lost and the inertial

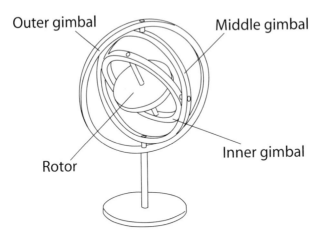

Outer gimbal   Middle gimbal

Inner gimbal

Rotor

FIGURE 4.2 Gimbal assembly.

platform can't orient itself freely. The inertial platform is now in lockstep with the craft it is attached to. Its orientation calculation is therefore no longer valid because its orientation isn't independent of the craft's orientation. Hence the term *gimbal lock*.

Because the gimbal assembly has three gimbals it has three degrees of freedom. Each gimbal can revolve relative to the gimbal it is attached to. However, this creates an inherent dependency among the gimbals. Starting with the inner gimbal, it can rotate freely. It is attached to the middle gimbal, and thus any rotation of the middle gimbal will clearly affect the inner gimbal's final orientation. Likewise, the middle gimbal is attached to the outer gimbal. Any rotation of the outer gimbal will therefore affect the orientation of both the middle and inner gimbals.

It is this ordering of separate, yet dependent, rotations that can cause a gimbal lock. A gimbal lock occurs when the rods (axes of rotations) of the outer and inner gimbals are aligned. A degree of freedom is lost, in that the axis of rotation of the inner gimbal isn't different from the outer gimbal. Their rotations are now along the same axis. The system is reduced to just two degrees of freedom. Figure 4.3 shows the result of gimbal lock.

It is the middle gimbal's orientation that causes the gimbal lock. Because the middle gimbal orients the inner gimbal it is directly responsible for the outer and inner axes aligning.

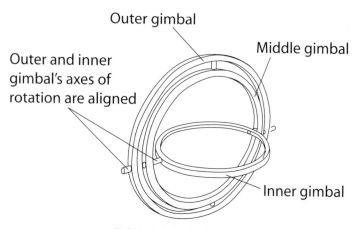

FIGURE 4.3 Gimbal lock.

A gimbal lock can still occur in a gimbal assembly with more than three gimbals. It is easy to imagine an assembly with four or more gimbals. The moment certain gimbals align with each other there will be a loss of one or more degrees of freedom.

Euler angles operate in a very similar way to an assembly with three gimbals. As such, they are also prone to gimbal lock. Given a 3D coordinate system, the inner gimbal can be considered the *X* axis, the middle gimbal the *Y* axis, and the outer gimbal the *Z* axis. When the *X* and *Z* axes align there will be a gimbal lock. In Maya, the order in which the rotations are accumulated can be changed, and thus in more general terms when the first and last axes of rotation are aligned there will be a gimbal lock. The axes don't have to point in the same direction. They can be pointing in opposite directions. They simply have to be colinear.

Figure 4.4 shows two coordinate systems. The one drawn with dashed lines is the world space. This is the Cartesian coordinate system. It is immovable and provides a reference to compare the orientation of the other coordinate system. The one drawn with solid lines is the coordinate system that will undergo a series of rotations. The two systems are drawn offset from each other for clarity. In reality they are precisely aligned with each other.

The coordinate system will undergo a series of three rotations about the main axes: *x* rotation = 23 degrees, *y* rotation = 90 degrees, and *z* rotation = 10 degrees. The rotation order is *x-y-z*. The 23-degree rotation about the *X* axis happens as expected. Figure 4.5 shows the resulting axes.

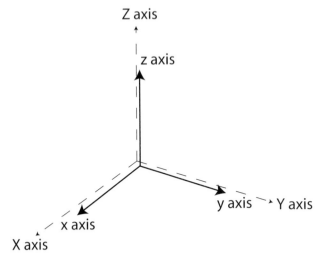

FIGURE 4.4 Initial orientation.

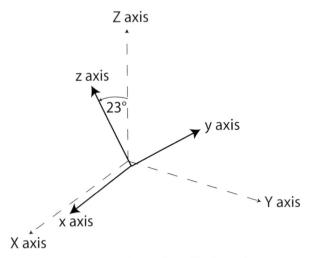

FIGURE 4.5 After 23-degree X-axis rotation.

The rotation of 90 degrees about the Y axis rotates all axes but now the X axis is aligned with the Z axis. Because the X axis is now the same as the Z axis, one degree of freedom is lost. The result is shown in Figure 4.6.

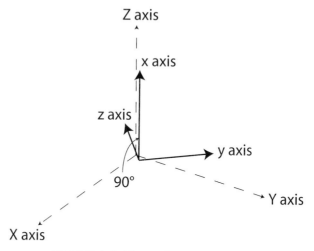

FIGURE 4.6 After 90-degree Y-axis rotation.

The final 10-degree rotation about the *Z* axis now happens as a rotation about the *X* axis, as shown in Figure 4.7. It is as if the *Z* axis no longer exists. The *Z* axis of rotation is the degree of freedom that is lost.

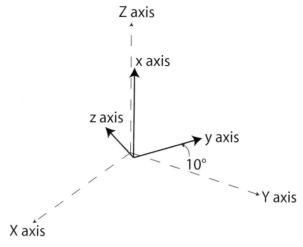

FIGURE 4.7 After 10-degree Z-axis rotation.

Due to the gimbal lock, the rotation about the Z axis is redundant, and thus the series of rotations (23, 90, and 10 degrees) is actually the equivalent, respectively, of 33, 90, and 0 degrees. Therefore, a combined rotation of 33 degrees around the X axis followed by a 90-degree rotation around the Y axis would have produced the same result.

The problem is that the rotations are evaluated in a particular order. The x-y-z ordering of rotations allowed the X axis to align with the Z axis (the 90-degree y-axis rotation), thereby rendering the Z-axis rotation redundant. Because earlier rotations are affected by later rotations, a way of fixing gimbal lock is to change the order of rotations or to add another gimbal. Alternative approaches in Maya are explored in the following.

1. Select **File | New Scene** from the main menu.

2. Select **Create | NURBS Primitives | Cone** from the main menu.

3. Press the **f** key or select **View | Frame Selection** from the viewport's menu.

4. If the origin axis is not displayed, select **Display | Heads Up Display | Origin Axis** from the main menu. These are the world axes.

5. Select **Display | Component Display | Local Rotation Axes**.

   The local axes of the cone are displayed.

6. Open the **Channel Box**.

7. Set to the **Rotate X** field to **23**.

   The cone tilts to the left.

8. Set the **Rotate Y** field to **90**.

   The cone rotates about the vertical axis. Note that the cone's X axis is now aligned with the world's $-Z$ axis.

9. Set the **Rotate Z** field to **10**.

   The cone rotates around the world's Z axis. There is no rotation about the cone's Z axis.

10. Select the **Rotate Z** field label.

11. Right click and drag horizontally in the viewport to interactively update the **Rotate Z** attribute.

Note how the cone's *z* rotation is happening about the *X* axis. To prove that the cone's *Z* axis is now redundant, the *x* rotation can be changed.

12. Select the **Rotate X** field label.

13. Right click and drag horizontally in the viewport to interactively update the **Rotate X** attribute.

    The *x* rotation is equivalent to the *z* rotation. Clearly a gimbal lock has occurred. Will flipping the direction of the *y* rotation fix this?

14. Set the **Rotate Y** field to −90.

15. Select the **Rotate Z** field label.

16. Right click and drag horizontally in the viewport to interactively update the **Rotate Z** attribute.

    The *z* rotation is still the same as the *x* rotation. Flipping has no effect, in that the axes are still aligned. What about changing the rotation order?

17. Open the **Attribute Editor**.

18. Set the **Rotate Order** attribute to **xzy**.

19. Interactively change the **Rotate X** and **Rotate Z** attributes.

    The *x* and *z* rotations no longer produce similar results. The reason for this is that the *x* rotation is applied first, then the *z* rotation, and finally the *y* rotation. When the *z* rotation is applied, none of the axes are aligned and thus no gimbal lock has occurred. A downside of this approach is that when the rotation order changes, the orientation of the object also changes. The object would have to be re-rotated to assume its original orientation. Another approach is to add degrees of freedom by parenting the object under a new transform.

20. Set the **Rotate Order** attribute back to **xyz**.

21. Select **Edit | Group** from the main menu.

    The cone now has a new transform parent node, **group1**.

22. Interactively change the **Rotate X, Rotate Y,** and **Rotate Z** attributes of the **group1** node.

    The cone, through its parent, can now be freely oriented in any direction, even though it is itself in gimbal lock. The parent's three axes of rotation have contributed three additional degrees of freedom. This will not entirely eliminate gimbal lock but it will reduce its possibility of arising. The parent itself, like its children, could become gimbal locked. There will always be certain rotation configurations that will cause a gimbal lock. That being said, the chance of the cone not being able to assume any given orientation is considerably reduced.

As an aside, NASA's later Apollo missions included a gyroscope with four gimbals. This additional "redundant gimbal" reduced the possibility of gimbal locks significantly because it provided more degrees of freedom than were theoretically necessary. It was mounted outside the existing outer gimbal. A three-gimbal gyroscope was used in earlier missions because, ironically enough, such a gyroscope is more reliable, less prone to drift, and weighs less.

The fundamental cause of gimbal locks is that the rotations are evaluated consecutively rather than as a whole. Quaternions provide a means of evaluating the final rotation as a whole. Unfortunately, quaternions come with the cost of additional complexity, due to their mathematical formulation, as well as a reduction in the intuitiveness by which rotations can be specified.

MEL

To get the three local rotation angles for a given object, use the following.

```
xform -query -rotation transform1;
// Result: -12.58062 18.728048 37.908005 //
```

The resulting angles are in the current angular unit. To query the current angular unit, use the following.

```
currentUnit -query -angle;
// Result: deg //
```

To set the rotation angles, use the following.

```
xform -rotation 45deg 0 0;
```

This sets the object's rotation to 45 degrees around the *X* axis. Note the explicit use of the deg unit following the 45 value. It is best to use explicit units because there is no guarantee what the user may have set the current units to. No rotation occurs around the other axes. To add a relative rotation to an object, use the -relative flag, as follows.

```
xform -relative -rotation 15deg 0 0;
```

The object is now rotated a total of 60 degrees (45 + 15 degrees) around the *X* axis. Given two vectors **a** and **b**, to calculate the rotation needed to rotate **a** onto **b** use the following.

```
angleBetween -euler -v1 1 0 0 -v2 0 1 0;
// Result: 0 0 90 //
```

This returns the three Euler angles in the current angular unit. The result indicates that a 90-degree rotation about the *Z* axis is needed to align the *X* axis onto the *Y* axis.

C++ API

The **MEulerRotation** class is used for defining Euler angles. To get an object's rotation in Euler angles, use the getRotation function, as follows.

```
MFnTransform transformFn( dagPath );
MEulerRotation er;
transformFn.getRotation( er );
MGlobal::displayInfo( MString( "rotation: " ) +
                     er.x + ", " + er.y + ", " + er.z +
                " order: " + er.order );
```

This results in

```
// rotation: 0.523599, 0.349066, 0.174533 order: 0
```

All rotation angles are in radians. To set the absolute rotation for an object, use the following.

```
MEulerRotation rot( degToRad( 45.0 ), 0, 0 );
transformFn.setRotation( rot );
```

To add a relative rotation, use the following.

```
MEulerRotation rotOffset( degToRad( 15.0 ), 0, 0 );
transformFn.rotateBy( rotOffset );
```

A vector can be rotated using Euler angles.

```
MEulerRotation r( 0.0, degToRad( 15.0 ), 0.0 );
MVector v( 1.0, 0.0, 0.0 );
MVector vRotated = v.rotateBy( r );
```

There is no equivalent for points. Care must be taken when converting from Euler angles to matrices and back.

```
MEulerRotation r( degToRad( 1523.0), degToRad( -315.0 ), degToRad( 0.5 ));
MGlobal::displayInfo( MString( "rotation: " ) + radToDeg(r.x) + ", " +
radToDeg(r.y) + ", " + radToDeg(r.z) + " order: " + r.order );
```

The Euler angles are exactly the same (though in radians) as the angles passed in.

```
// rotation: 1523, -315, 0.5 order: 0
```

This is converted to a matrix as follows.

```
MMatrix m;
m = r.asMatrix();
```

The matrix can be reconverted to Euler angles by using the static decompose function.

```
r = MEulerRotation::decompose( m, r.order );
MGlobal::displayInfo( MString( "rotation: " ) + radToDeg(r.x) + ", " +
radToDeg(r.y) + ", " + radToDeg(r.z) + " order: " + r.order );
```

The Euler angles don't match the original.

```
// rotation: 83, 45, 0.5 order: 0
```

Although the angles are not the same, the orientation is. Rotating by the first set of Euler angles will result in the same orientation as rotating by the matrix decomposed Euler angles. This makes an important case for distinguishing between rotation and orientation.

It is important to note that there are many different Euler angles that match a given matrix. The Euler angles calculated from a matrix will all be within the range [0°, 360°]. This means that any negative Euler angles or angles over 360 degrees will be converted to their 0- to 360-degree equivalents.

4.3.2 QUATERNIONS

A quaternion is an orientation representation that suffers fewer of the shortcomings of Euler angles. Quaternions don't have problems of gimbal lock because all three rotation axes are evaluated at the same time rather than sequentially. This is inherent to the mathematics behind quaternions. Quaternions can also be concatenated efficiently. They are the best representation when interpolating between angles. Quaternions can be thought of as the combination of an axis and angle of rotation. The formulation of a quaternion is

$$q = w + x * i + y * j + z * k$$

The vectors, **i**, **j**, and **k** are the standard basis vectors, and thus it is possible to write a quaternion using just four components.

$$q = (w, x, y, z)$$

This is the general representation of quaternions. Quaternions have many uses outside computer graphics, where they originated. When using quaternions for representing rotations, an additional constraint is imposed; quaternions must have unit length. Because a quaternion is a 4D vector, normalizing it is done as follows.

$$\|q\| = \sqrt{w^2 + x^2 + y^2 + z^2}$$
$$\hat{q} = \frac{q}{\|q\|}$$

The x, y, and z components can be reduced to a vector, and thus a quaternion is written as the **w** and vector **v** pair

$$\mathbf{q} = (\mathbf{w}, \mathbf{v})$$

The **w** component and **v** vector can be likened to the angle and axis of rotation, respectively. Given an angle θ and axis of rotation **a**, the conversion to quaternions is

$$\mathbf{w} = \cos(\theta/2)$$
$$\mathbf{v} = \sin(\theta/2) * \hat{\mathbf{a}}$$

Note that the angle of rotation is halved: $\theta/2$. Note also that the normalized version of the axis of rotation $\hat{\mathbf{a}}$ is used.

A vector can be used to indicate an orientation. In terms of a quaternion, the vector is the axis of rotation and there is no rotation about this axis. A given vector **a**, when converted to a quaternion, is

$$\mathbf{q} = (0, \hat{\mathbf{a}})$$

There is no rotation angle and the axis of rotation is normalized. It is important to note that the result of negating a quaternion results in the same orientation.

$$\mathbf{q} = -\mathbf{q}$$
$$\mathbf{q} = (-q_w, -q_x, -q_y, -q_z)$$

This may seem counterintuitive, but a closer look at the equation reveals that both the angle q_w and the axis of rotation $(q_x, q_x, -q_z)$ are negated. This flips the axis of rotation and rotates it in exactly the opposite direction. The result is a rotation that represents rotating around in the opposite direction, resulting in the same final orientation.

Two quaternion rotations concatenate via multiplication. Given two quaternions

$$\mathbf{q} = (q_w, q_v)$$
$$\mathbf{r} = (r_w, r_v)$$

the result of multiplying them is

$$\mathbf{q} * \mathbf{r} = (q_w * r_w - q_v \cdot r_v, q_w * r_v + r_w * q_v + q_v \times r_v)$$

It is important to note that quaternion multiplication is not commutative.

q * r ≠ r * q

This is exactly what you would expect, in that the order of rotations is important. A series of rotations applied in a different order will most likely produce a different final orientation.

MEL

MEL doesn't directly support quaternions, but there are commands that provide axis-angle functionality. To find the axis and angle of rotation to rotate one vector onto another, use the following.

```
angleBetween -v1 1 0 0 -v2 0 1 0;
// Result: 0 0 1 90 //
```

The resulting angle is in the current angular unit. This indicates that a 90-degree rotation is needed about the Z axis. To rotate a point given an axis and angle of rotation, use the rot command.

```
vector $p = <<1, 0, 0>>;
vector $rotAxis = <<0, 0, 1>>;
float $rotAngle = deg_to_rad(90);
rot $p $rotAxis $rotAngle;
// Result: <<2.26795e-007, 1, 0>> //
```

Note that the final point should be $(0,1,0)$ but is instead a point very close to that. This gives further emphasis to the importance of using tolerances when comparing points and vectors. Note also that the rot command takes the angle in radians and not degrees.

C++ API

The **MQuaternion** class is provided for creating and manipulating quaternions. To get the rotation of an object as a quaternion, use the following.

```
MFnTransform transformFn( dagPath );
MQuaternion q;
transformFn.getRotation( q );
```

To set the absolute rotation of an object, use the following.

```
MQuaternion r( degToRad( 10.0 ), MVector( 1.0, 0.0, 0.0 ) );
transformFn.setRotation( r );
```

This sets the rotation to 10 degrees around the *X* axis. To add a relative rotation to an existing rotation, use the following.

```
MQuaternion r( degToRad( 20.0 ), MVector( 1.0, 0.0, 0.0 ) );
transformFn.rotateBy( r );
```

Alternatively, quaternion concatenation could be used on the original rotation.

```
transformFn.getRotation( q );
MQuaternion r( degToRad( 20.0 ), MVector( 1.0, 0.0, 0.0 ) );
q * = r;
transformFn.setRotation( q );
```

To calculate the quaternion rotation necessary to rotate one vector onto another, use the following.

```
MVector v0( 1.0, 0.0, 0.0 );
MVector v1( 0.0, 1.0, 0.0 );
MQuaternion r = v0.rotateTo( v1 );
```

A vector can be rotated by a quaternion using the rotateBy function.

```
MQuaternion r( degToRad( 35.0 ), MVector( 1.0, 0.0, 0.0 ) );
MVector v( 0.0, 1.0, 0.0 );
MVector vRotated = v.rotateBy( r );
```

CHAPTER 5

Transformations

Transformations are critical to so many aspects within Maya that they are covered in detail in this chapter, including their theoretical basis. Any operation that moves, scales, rotates, shears, or projects a point involves a transformation. A transformation is simply a mapping of a point from one place to another.

p' = p * transformation

The input point **p** is transformed into another point **p'**. The coordinates of $p = (p_x, p_y, p_z)$ are mapped, respectively, to new coordinates $p' = (p_x', p_y', p_z')$.

If a transformation is applied to a point and the resulting point **p'** is the same as the original **p**, no effective transformation has taken place. Such a transformation is called an *identity transformation*. Applying an identity transformation to a point will not change its coordinates.

p = p * identityTransformation

Typically, you will want to apply a series of transformations to a point, rather than just one. For instance, a movement of two units to the left followed by a scale of ten followed by a rotation of eight degrees would result in the following series of transformations.

p' = p * translateByTwo * scaleByTen * rotateByEight

To transform the original point **p** to its final location **p'**, the series of transformations would need to be stored and then applied in turn. This example has just three transformations, but what if there were a lot more? It is conceivable that a jointed skeleton would have many joints and therefore many transformations. A finger at the end of the joints would need to go through all transformations defined by the rotations of the joints leading down to the finger. This would require a lot of storage for all of the individual transformations that would need to be applied to a point in the finger to give its final position. Fortunately, there is an extremely compact way of storing all such transformations into a single unit, a matrix.

5.1 MATRICES

Matrices are a powerful means of combining a series of transformations into a single transformation. Rather than store the series of transformations, a single transformation matrix can be stored that holds the result of applying all transformations. This single transformation compactly encodes all transformations of which it is composed.

The process of combining transformations is called *concatenation*, which is denoted using the multiplication operator (*). Given the series of transformations mentioned previously, a final transformation matrix can be created that embodies all individual transforms.

transformMatrix = translateByTwo * scaleByTen * rotateByEight

This final transformation matrix can then be applied to the point.

p' = p * transformMatrix

It is clear that using matrices reduces the amount of storage needed, in that all individual transformations can be combined into a single transformation matrix. An added benefit is that because only one transformation matrix needs to be applied the calculation happens much faster. These two benefits have seen matrices become the standard method of recording as well as applying transformations.

A matrix is simply a 2D array of numbers. They can be shown as a table of numbers in which each number occupies a given row and column location. A 3×2 matrix is a table of numbers having three rows and two columns. Mathematically, matrices can have any number of rows or columns, but for the purposes of this discussion transformation matrices will always have four rows and four columns (i.e., each will be a 4×4 matrix). Figure 5.1 shows an example of a 4×4 matrix.

$$\begin{bmatrix} 3 & 0 & 34 & 0 \\ 15 & 10 & 0 & 17 \\ 8 & 0 & 1 & 0 \\ 2 & 0 & 8 & 5 \end{bmatrix}$$

FIGURE 5.1 Example 4 × 4 matrix.

Each element in the matrix is referred to by its row and column index. A particular element is referenced using the following notation.

$$(M)_{i,j}$$

Here, **M** is the matrix, **i** is the row, and **j** is the column. This index is base 0, and thus the elements will have a row and column index between 0 and 3. The first element is at *row* = 0 and *column* = 0. The value of the element at this location is 3.

$$(M)_{0,0} = 3$$

Similarly, the element on the second row (*row* = 1) and last column (*column* = 3) has a value of 17.

$$(M)_{1,3} = 17$$

5.1.1 MATRIX MULTIPLICATION

Concatenation of two matrices into one is done using matrix multiplication. This is where two matrices are multiplied together to produce another one.

$$C = A * B$$

Expanding this out to show the individual matrix elements is shown in Figure 5.2. The row and column index is given per element. For instance, the C matrix's element at *row* = 3, *column* = 1 is referred to as C31.

$$C \quad = \quad A \quad * \quad B$$

$$
\begin{bmatrix} C00 & C01 & C02 & C03 \\ C10 & C11 & C12 & C13 \\ C20 & C21 & C22 & C23 \\ C30 & C31 & C32 & C33 \end{bmatrix}
=
\begin{bmatrix} A00 & A01 & A02 & A03 \\ A10 & A11 & A12 & A13 \\ A20 & A21 & A22 & A23 \\ A30 & A31 & A32 & A33 \end{bmatrix}
*
\begin{bmatrix} B00 & B01 & B02 & B03 \\ B10 & B11 & B12 & B13 \\ B20 & B21 & B22 & B23 \\ B30 & B31 & B32 & B33 \end{bmatrix}
$$

FIGURE 5.2 Matrix multiplication.

The process of multiplying two matrices together may initially seem complex but in fact it is just a continual repetition of the same rule. To calculate the value of element C00, simply multiply the elements in row A0 by the elements in column B0, adding the result as you go.

C00 = A00 * B00 + A01 * B10 + A02 * B20 + A03 * B30

You may notice the pattern that has emerged.

$$C_{i,j} = \sum_{m=0}^{3} A_{i,m} B_{m,j}$$

The operation can be written using a series of *for* loops.

```
int row, column, i;
for( row=0; row < 4; row++ )
{
  for ( column=0; column < 4; column++ )
  {
  C[row][column] = 0;
  for( i=0; i < 4; i++ )
    C[row][column] += A[row][i] * B[i][column];
  }
}
```

The concatenation of a series of transformations is simply the result of applying the matrix multiplication one after another. The result of the first multiplication is multiplied with the second, and so on.

M = A * B * C * D
step 1: M = A * B
step 2: M = (A * B) * C
step 3: M = (((A * B) * C)) * D

Note the order in which the multiplications are performed. Starting with A, the matrix B is then multiplied on the right; then C is multiplied on the right. This ordering is known as *postmultiplication*. Each matrix is successively multiplied on the right. This is how all of Maya's matrix multiplications are performed. In contrast to this, a *premultiplication* of the matrices would look as follows.

M = (D * (C * (B * A)))

Mathematically, premultiplication is just as valid as postmultiplication. However, postmultiplication is clearly more intuitive, in that each additional operation is added to the right. Scanning the sequence from left to right lets you easily see the ordering of the operations.

5.1.2 MATRIX TRANSPOSE

To calculate the *transpose* of a matrix, simply reverse the row and column positions of the matrix's elements. The transpose is represented by $\mathbf{M^T}$.

$(\mathbf{M^T})i,j = (\mathbf{M})j,i$

Thus, given a 3 × 3 matrix **A**, its transpose is

$$
\begin{bmatrix}
A00 & A01 & A02 & A03 \\
A10 & A11 & A12 & A13 \\
A20 & A21 & A22 & A23 \\
A30 & A31 & A32 & A33
\end{bmatrix}^T
=
\begin{bmatrix}
A00 & A10 & A20 & A30 \\
A01 & A11 & A21 & A31 \\
A02 & A12 & A22 & A32 \\
A03 & A13 & A23 & A33
\end{bmatrix}.
$$

Because each element's row and column positions are simply reversed, the matrix doesn't necessarily have to be square. Given the row matrix

$$A = [A00 \quad A01 \quad A02 \quad A03]$$

its transpose is

$$A^T = \begin{bmatrix} A00 \\ A01 \\ A02 \\ A03 \end{bmatrix}$$

Some textbooks will represent points and vectors using row-major order, whereas others will use column-major order. Because there is no one convention for matrix multiplication, some textbooks will use premultiplied matrices and others will use postmultiplied matrices. Premultiplied matrices will have the point or vector represented using column-major order. A point would be represented using the column matrix

$$P = \begin{bmatrix} x \\ y \\ z \\ w \end{bmatrix}$$

Such a point would be transformed using premultiplied matrices.

M = (D * (C * (B * A)))
P' = P * M

A column matrix must be used in order for matrix multiplication to be valid: the number of columns of the first matrix must match the number of rows in the second matrix. This can be represented as $1 \times 4 * 4 \times 4 = 1 \times 4$.

For postmultiplied matrices, a row-major matrix is used. A point would be represented as follows.

$$P = [x \quad y \quad z \quad w]$$

The point representation would be transformed using postmultiplied matrices.

M = (((A * B) * C)) * D
P' = M * P

The resulting point, **P'**, is also a row matrix. This follows from the rules governing matrix multiplication: $4 \times 1 * 4 \times 4 = 4 \times 1$.

Maya uses postmultiplied matrices, which are more intuitive. When consulting a textbook that uses premultiplied matrices, simply apply the transpose to the matrix to get a postmultiplied matrix. The algebraic rules for matrix transposes are:

$$(\mathbf{M^T})^T = \mathbf{M}$$
$$(a\mathbf{M^T}) = a\mathbf{M^T}$$
$$(\mathbf{A} + \mathbf{B})^T = \mathbf{A^T} + \mathbf{B^T}$$

5.1.3 IDENTITY MATRIX

There is a special matrix, called the *identity matrix*, that when multiplied by another matrix doesn't change it.

M = M * identity

This particular matrix is often denoted using a capital **I**.

M = M * I

The identity matrix is shown in Figure 5.3. It contains a single diagonal row of ones, and the rest of the elements are zero. Try multiplying it by another matrix to see that the result is the same as the original matrix.

$$\begin{bmatrix} 1 & 0 & 0 & 0 \\ 0 & 1 & 0 & 0 \\ 0 & 0 & 1 & 0 \\ 0 & 0 & 0 & 1 \end{bmatrix}$$

FIGURE 5.3 Identity matrix.

By default, all matrices in Maya are initialized to the identity matrix.

5.1.4 INVERSE MATRIX

A transformation matrix will transform a point **p** from one location to another, **p'**. What if you had point **p'** and wanted to transform it back to point **p**? What you want is to do the opposite, or inverse, transformation. Fortunately, matrices allow for this type of operation by using the *inverse matrix*. An inverse matrix will apply the exact opposite transformation of the original matrix. It can be thought of as an "undo" method. The inverse of a matrix **M** is denoted M^{-1}. This indicates that it is the original matrix but inverted. If an inverse matrix is the opposite of the original matrix, it follows logically that when the inverse matrix is concatenated to the original matrix, nothing will be transformed.

$$p = p * M * M^{-1}$$

Breaking this down into steps results in the following. The point **p** is transformed by the matrix **M**, resulting in a new point **p'**. The point **p** has thus been transformed.

$$p' = p * M$$

The resulting point **p'** is then transformed by the inverse matrix M^{-1}. Because the inverse matrix is the opposite of the original matrix, it transforms point **p'** back to its original position **p**.

$$p = p' * M^{-1}$$

Applying both transformations **M** and M^{-1} didn't have any effect on point **p**. As mentioned in the previous section, there is just such a matrix that when applied to another matrix has no effect: the identity matrix. It follows then that concatenating **M** with its inverse, M^{-1}, results in the identity matrix.

$$I = M * M^{-1}$$

Thus, the original transformation can be written as follows.

$$p = p * M * M^{-1}$$
$$= p * I$$
$$= p$$

The inverse matrix is an extremely useful tool when performing complex transformations. It allows certain transformations to be erased, while leaving others. Its uses are covered in greater detail in a later chapter. The algebraic rules of matrix inversion are:

$$(M^{-1})^{-1} = M$$
$$M * M^{-1} = I$$
$$M^{-1} * M = I$$
$$M^{-1} * (M^{-1})^{-1} = I$$
$$(M * N)^{-1} = M^{-1}N^{-1}$$

It is important to note that although mathematically the inverse is the opposite transformation, in reality, due to floating-point precision issues, this may not always be the case. Transforming a point by a transformation matrix and then transforming the point by the inverse matrix may not give the exact same original point. The resulting point will often be very close.

5.1.5 MEL

The **matrix** type provides the general functionality of matrices within MEL. Because matrices can have any positive number of rows and columns, for the purposes of transformation matrices it is important to explicitly set them to 4×4.

The following statement creates a matrix with four rows and columns. Each element is initialized to zero.

```
matrix $mat[4][4];
```

The $mat matrix's elements are as follows.

```
<< 0, 0, 0, 0;
   0, 0, 0, 0;
   0, 0, 0, 0;
   0, 0, 0, 0>>
```

To set the matrix to an identity matrix, use the following procedure.

```
proc identity( matrix $m )
{
 int $i, $j;
```

```
for( $i=0; $i < 4; $i++ )
{
 for( $j=0; $j < 4; $j++ )
 {
  if( $i==$j )
   $m[$i][$j] = 1.0;
  else
   $m[$i][$j] = 0.0;
 }
 }
}
```

Matrix concatenation is done using multiplication of the two matrices.

```
matrix $matA[4][4];
matrix $matB[4][4];
identity( $matA );
identity( $matB );
matrix $matC[4][4] = $matA * $matB;
```

It is important to initialize the matrices before multiplication, as not doing so can cause Maya to crash. Unfortunately, when the matrix attribute of an object is requested the result is an array of 16 floating-point values rather than a matrix. For instance, requesting the matrix of a transform node via

```
getAttr transform1.matrix;
```

results in the following array.

```
// Result: 1 0 0 0 0 1 0 0 0 0 1 0 1 2 3 1 //
```

To convert a single array of 16 floats into a 4×4 matrix, use the following procedure.

```
proc matrix toMatrix( float $values[] )
{
 matrix $mat[4][4];
 int $i, $ii, $jj;
```

```
for( $i=0; $i < 16; $i++ )
{
 $ii = $i / 4;
 $jj = $i % 4;
 $mat[$ii][$jj] = $values[$i];
}
return $mat;
}
```

5.1.6 C++ API

The **MMatrix** class is used to represent a 4×4 matrix of doubles. There is another class, **MFloatMatrix**, which provides the same functionality but uses floats rather than doubles. For the purpose of the following explanation, **MMatrix** and **MFloatMatrix** are synonymous.

The **MMatrix** is a simple class used to perform basic matrix operations. It doesn't provide any higher-level functions for translating, scaling, and so on. When an **MMatrix** instance is created it is set to the identity matrix.

```
MMatrix mat;
```

If at any time the matrix needs to be explicitly set to the identity matrix, use the setToIdentity function.

```
mat.setToIdentity();
```

Individual elements in the matrix are accessed by row and column index. The **MMatrix** class has overloaded the function call operator () to handle this. In this example the element at row index 1 and column index 2 is retrieved.

```
double value = mat(1,2);
```

Matrices are concatenated with other matrices via the multiplication operator.

```
MMatrix final = mat1 * mat2;
```

To convert between an **MFloatMatrix** and an **MMatrix**, use the `get` function.

```
MFloatMatrix fm;
MMatrix dm;
fm.get( dm.matrix );
```

The opposite conversion works similarly.

```
MMatrix dm;
MFloatMatrix fm;
dm.get( fm.matrix );
```

To get the inverse of a matrix, use the `inverse` function.

```
MMatrix mat;
MMatrix inv = mat.inverse();
```

The transpose of the matrix is calculated using the `transpose` function.

```
MMatrix mat;
MMatrix trans = mat.transpose();
```

5.2 TRANSFORMING POINTS

Points are transformed using matrix multiplication. The 3D point (x, y, z) is converted to a 4D homogeneous point (x, y, z, 1) before it is multiplied by the matrix. This point is treated as a row of four elements, and thus it has a matrix dimension of 1×4. This is now compatible with matrix multiplication of a 4×4 matrix: 1×4 matrix $* 4 \times 4$ matrix $= 1 \times 4$ matrix.

5.2.1 MEL

Maya doesn't have direct support for transforming vectors or float arrays in MEL. There is no multiply operator (*) overloading, as there is in the C++ API. There is a `pointMatrixMult` procedure, though it appears to not function as advertised. Instead, a custom `transformPoint` procedure is outlined that will transform a point using a matrix. Both the point and the matrix are arrays of floats.

```
proc float[] transformPoint( float $p[], float $m[] )
{
   // Transform 3D point (x,y,z) as a 4D homogeneous
   // point (x,y,z,1), since the matrix is 4 x 4
   //
   float $r[4];
   $r[0] = $p[0]*$m[0] + $p[1]*$m[4] + $p[2]*$m[8] + $m[12];
   $r[1] = $p[0]*$m[1] + $p[1]*$m[5] + $p[2]*$m[9] + $m[13];
   $r[2] = $p[0]*$m[2] + $p[1]*$m[6] + $p[2]*$m[10] + $m[14];
   $r[3] = $p[0]*$m[3] + $p[1]*$m[7] + $p[2]*$m[11] + $m[15];
   float $res[3] = { 0.0, 0.0, 0.0 };
   if($r[3] != 0.0) // Non-degenerate point
   {
      // Convert from homogeneous to cartesian
      $res[0] = $r[0] / $r[3];
      $res[1] = $r[1] / $r[3];
      $res[2] = $r[2] / $r[3];
   }

   return $res;
}
```

VECTOR

Because Maya will automatically convert a `vector` into a `float` array, the `transformPoint` procedure can be used directly.

```
float $m[] = `getAttr transform1.matrix`;
vector $p = << 1.0, 0.0, 0.0 >>;
vector $p2 = transformPoint( $p, $m );
```

FLOAT ARRAY

The `transformPoint` procedure will transform float arrays without any need for implicit Maya conversions.

```
float $m[] = `getAttr transform1.matrix`;
float $p[3] = { 1.0, 0.0, 0.0 };
float $p2[] = transformPoint( $p, $m );
```

5.2.2 C++ API

To transform a point by a matrix, the multiplication operator is used.

```
MMatrix mat;
MPoint p0, p1;
p1 = p0 * mat;
```

This works similarly for vectors.

```
MMatrix mat;
MVector v0, v1;
v1 = v0 * mat;
```

An in-place multiplication operator also exists. The point will be transformed by the matrix and the result will be stored in the original point.

```
MMatrix mat;
MPoint p0;
p0 * = mat; // In-place multiplication
```

Note that the **MPoint** and **MVector** classes are transformed using the **MMatrix** class. It is illegal to transform them using the **MFloatMatrix** class because this class is designed for the float variants of points and vectors (**MFloatPoint** and **MFloatVector**).

5.3 TRANSFORMING VECTORS

Because vectors and points are mathematically different, they need to be treated differently when transforming. Once a vector is converted to its homogeneous representation $(x, y, z, 0)$ it can be transformed using the standard matrix multiplication. The significance of having the $w = 0$ is that the bottom row and right column of the 4×4 matrix have no effect. The vector is transformed by the remaining 3×3 matrix.

5.3.1 MEL

The transformVector procedure is designed to transform a vector using a matrix. Both the vector and matrix are float arrays.

```
proc float [] transformVector(float $v[], float $m[])
{
 float $res[3];
 $res[0] = $v[0]*$m[0] + $v[1]*$m[4] + $v[2]*$m[8];
 $res[1] = $v[0]*$m[1] + $v[1]*$m[5] + $v[2]*$m[9];
 $res[2] = $v[0]*$m[2] + $v[1]*$m[6] + $v[2]*$m[10];
 return $res;
}
```

VECTOR

Because Maya will automatically convert `vector` to a `float` array, the `transformVector` procedure can be used directly.

```
float $m[] = `getAttr transform1.matrix`;
vector $v = << 1.0, 0.0, 0.0 >>;
vector $v2 = transformVector( $v, $m );
```

FLOAT ARRAY

A float array can be transformed using the same procedure.

```
float $m[] = `getAttr transform1.matrix`;
float $v[] = { 1.0, 0.0, 0.0 };
float $v2[] = transformVector( $v, $m );
```

5.3.2 C++ API

Because the C++ API makes the mathematical distinction between points and vectors, the **MVector**'s multiplication operator (*) has been overloaded to perform vector transformations correctly.

```
MMatrix mat;
MVector v0, v1;
v1 = v0 * mat;
```

5.4 TRANSFORMING NORMALS

Special care must be taken when transforming normals. This may at first seem unintuitive, in that a normal is a vector so why can't it be transformed like other vectors?

Although it is true that a normal is a vector, it is actually derived from the surface. The normal is calculated as the cross product of two tangent vectors on the surface. As such, each of the tangents ($t0$ and $t1$) is perpendicular to the normal. Taking a closer look at just $t0$, the following relationship exists.

$$\mathbf{n} \cdot \mathbf{t0} = 0$$

The same constraint applies to the other tangent, $t1$. When the normal and tangent are transformed ($\mathbf{n'}$ and $\mathbf{t0'}$) by the transformation matrix $\mathbf{M}$, the same relationship must exist.

$$\mathbf{n'} \cdot \mathbf{t0'} = 0$$

Otherwise, the normal isn't perpendicular to the transformed surface. The transformation of $t0$ is completed as expected.

$$\mathbf{t0'} = \mathbf{t} * \mathbf{M}$$

The transformation of $\mathbf{n}$ needs to be done with a matrix $\mathbf{G}$ (as yet unknown).

$$\mathbf{n'} = \mathbf{n} * \mathbf{G}$$

Substituting these equations into the original equation gives

$$(\mathbf{n} * \mathbf{G}) \cdot (\mathbf{t0} * \mathbf{M}) = 0$$

The complete derivation isn't given, but let it suffice that the final $\mathbf{G}$ matrix is

$$\mathbf{G} = (\mathbf{M^{-1}})^{\mathbf{T}}$$

This is the inverse transpose of the original $\mathbf{M}$ matrix. When this matrix is used to transform the normal, the resulting vector is guaranteed to be perpendicular to the transformed surface. Vectors that are tranformed in this fashion are called *covariant*, and vectors that are transformed in the usual fashion are called *contravariant*.

   If the matrix $\mathbf{M}$ is known to be orthogonal, the $\mathbf{M^{-1}} = \mathbf{M^T}$ and thus $(\mathbf{M^{-1}})^{\mathbf{T}} = \mathbf{M}$. As such, the normal can be transformed directly by $\mathbf{M}$ without needing to first calculate the inverse transpose matrix.

5.4.1 MEL

The `transformNormal` procedure is used to transform a normal via an inverse transpose matrix. The matrix, $m, that is passed to the procedure is assumed to already be inverted. The procedure doesn't perform a transpose on the matrix but instead completes the matrix multiplication as if it were. The elements in the matrix are referenced as if it were transposed.

```
proc float [] transformNormal( float $n[], float $m[] )
{
 float $res[3];
 $res[0] = $n[0]*$m[0] + $n[1]*$m[1] + $n[2]*$m[2];
 $res[1] = $n[0]*$m[4] + $n[1]*$m[5] + $n[2]*$m[6];
 $res[2] = $n[0]*$m[8] + $n[1]*$m[9] + $n[2]*$m[10];
 return $res;
}
```

VECTOR

```
float $m[] = `getAttr transform1.inverseMatrix`;
vector $n = << 1.0, 0.0, 0.0 >>;
vector $n2 = transformNormal( $n, $m );
```

FLOAT ARRAY

```
float $m[] = `getAttr transform1.inverseMatrix`;
float $n[] = { 1.0, 0.0, 0.0 };
float $n2[] = transformNormal( $n, $m );
```

5.4.2 C++ API

The **MVector**'s `transformAsNormal` function can be used to transform any vector as though it were a normal.

```
MMatrix mat;
MVector v0, v1;
v1 = v0.transformAsNormal( mat );
```

There is no need to perform any explicit matrix inversions or transposes. These are all handled by the `transformAsNormal` function.

CHAPTER 6

Transform Nodes

The transform node is responsible for positioning and orienting its child shape node in 3D. Figure 6.1 shows the relationship between the child shape node and transform node.

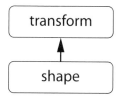

FIGURE 6.1 Shape's relationship to transform.

The transform node holds the translation, scale, shear, and rotation values that are then used to generate a transformation matrix. It is this transformation matrix that is applied to the geometry in the child shape node to place it in its final 3D position. The transform node provides a lot of options with regard to how the shape will be positioned. These include axis limits, pivot points, rotation order, and so on. All of these must be accounted for in the final transformation matrix.

6.1 PIVOT POINTS

The standard transformations that are applied to a point include scale, rotation, and translation. Figure 6.2 shows a simple 2D shape. Suppose that the points that make up the shape are in local coordinates; that is, the basic points of the shape with no transformations applied.

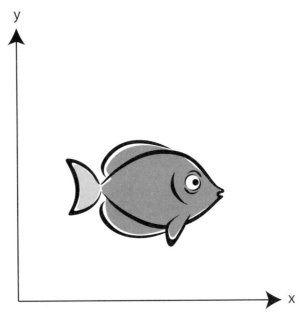

FIGURE 6.2 Basic 2D shape.

The shape is scaled by 150% (x 1.5), resulting in that shown in Figure 6.3.

Note that the scaling happened about the origin *(0,0,0)*. This is because the scaling transformation is simply a multiplication.

$$p' = p * 1.5$$
$$= (x * 1.5, y* 1.5)$$

What if the intention was to scale the shape about its center? In this case, it would be convenient to specify a point in 2D space that all scaling happens around. In Maya, this point is referred to as the *scale pivot point*. To understand how it works, consider again that all scaling happens about the origin *(0,0,0)* because the scaling transform just multiplies a scaling factor to each point. All points will expand inward or outward from the origin. This is an unchangeable rule. So how can this be circumvented to allow for arbitrary pivot points?

The trick is to move the shape to the origin, apply the scaling, and then move it back. For example, the scale pivot point is placed in the center of the shape, as shown in Figure 6.4.

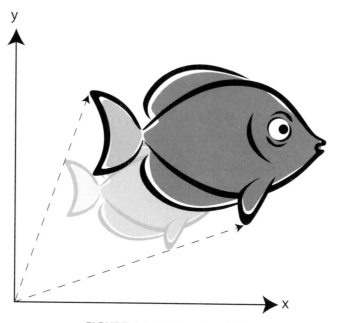

FIGURE 6.3 150% scale applied.

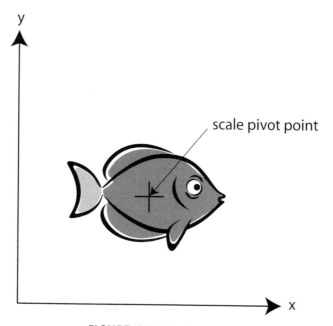

FIGURE 6.4 Scale pivot point.

It is then moved to the origin. The distance and direction is the exact opposite of the vector from the origin to the scale pivot point. Therefore, the shape undergoes the following translation.

p' = p + −scalePivotPoint
**   = p − scalePivotPoint**

Figure 6.5 shows the shape after the translation.

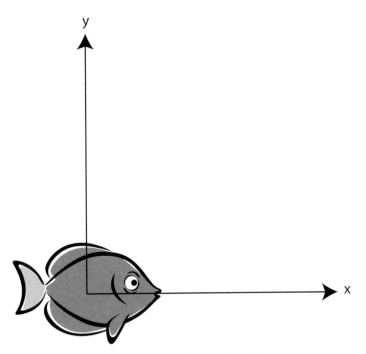

FIGURE 6.5 Translation to the origin.

The scale of 150% is then applied, as shown in Figure 6.6.

Adding the scaling to the original translation results in the following transformation.

p' = (p − scalePivotPoint) * scale

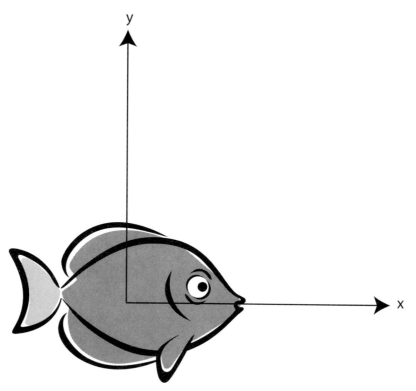

FIGURE 6.6 Scale applied.

Finally, the shape has to be returned to its original position. The shape is then translated by the vector from the origin to the scale pivot point. The final shape is shown in Figure 6.7.

Adding this translation to the end of the operations results in a final transformation of

p' = (p − scalePivotPoint) * scale + scalePivotPoint

The same flexibility of specifying arbitrary scale pivot points extends to rotations in the form of *rotation pivot points*. The same series of operations is applied. The shape is translated back by the vector from the pivot point to the origin. The rotation is then applied. Finally, the shape is translated forward by the vector from the origin to the pivot point.

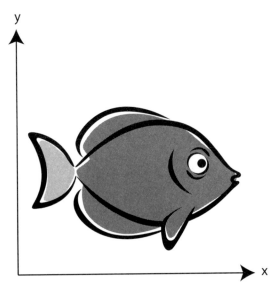

FIGURE 6.7 After final translation.

6.2 TRANSFORMATION MATRICES

The transformation matrix is built one matrix at a time. These are then concatenated into the final transformation matrix. The main parts to be constructed are the scale, rotation, and translation matrices. The values that drive these matrices come from the transform node. For instance, the translation matrix is generated from the transform node's **translateX**, **translateY**, and **translateZ** attributes. The order of the matrix concatenations is scale, shear, rotation, and translation.

Because a shear can be considered a specialized form of scaling, it shares the scale pivot point. To scale about the scale pivot point, the object must be translated back to the origin. The scale pivot point is given as (spx, spy, spz). Figure 6.8 shows the transformation matrix that encodes this "reverse" translation (i.e., the inverse of the scale pivot translation).

$$
\mathbf{SP^{-1}} = \begin{bmatrix} 1 & 0 & 0 & 0 \\ 0 & 1 & 0 & 0 \\ 0 & 0 & 1 & 0 \\ -spx & -spy & -spz & 1 \end{bmatrix}
$$

FIGURE 6.8 Scale pivot translation.

The scale is then applied. The scale is given as (sx, sy, sz). The transformation matrix that encodes this scale is shown in Figure 6.9.

$$
S = \begin{bmatrix} sx & 0 & 0 & 0 \\ 0 & sy & 0 & 0 \\ 0 & 0 & sz & 0 \\ 0 & 0 & 0 & 1 \end{bmatrix}
$$

FIGURE 6.9 Scale transformation matrix.

The shear is then applied to the object. It is given as (xy, yz, xz). Figure 6.10 shows the resulting shear transformation matrix.

$$
SH = \begin{bmatrix} 1 & 0 & 0 & 0 \\ xy & 1 & 0 & 0 \\ xz & yz & 1 & 0 \\ 0 & 0 & 0 & 1 \end{bmatrix}
$$

FIGURE 6.10 Shear transformation matrix.

With the scale and shear now complete, the object needs to be returned to its original position. This is achieved using the scale pivot point translation. This matrix is shown in Figure 6.11.

$$
SP = \begin{bmatrix} 1 & 0 & 0 & 0 \\ 0 & 1 & 0 & 0 \\ 0 & 0 & 1 & 0 \\ spx & spy & spz & 1 \end{bmatrix}
$$

FIGURE 6.11 Inverse scale pivot translation.

The final stage of the scaling and shearing involves the application of the scale translation. This translation isn't accessible to users, in that it is automatically recalculated by Maya whenever the scale pivot point is moved. A movement in the scale pivot point will change any existing scale. This translation compensates for the change in the scale pivot point, thereby preventing the object from inadvertently moving when the scale pivot point is moved. Figure 6.12 shows the matrix for this transformation.

$$\mathbf{ST} = \begin{bmatrix} 1 & 0 & 0 & 0 \\ 0 & 1 & 0 & 0 \\ 0 & 0 & 1 & 0 \\ \text{stx} & \text{sty} & \text{stz} & 1 \end{bmatrix}$$

FIGURE 6.12 Scale translation.

Concatenating all scale- and shear-related transformations results in the following matrix.

SCALE = SP^{-1} * S * SH * SP * ST

When applied to the points, this matrix would apply the scaling and shearing. The next step is to calculate and apply the rotation. Like the scaling, the rotation also has a pivot point that needs to be taken into account. As such, the first step is to translate the object to the origin by moving it by the inverse direction of the rotation pivot point (rpx, rpy, rpz). This translation is encoded in the matrix shown in Figure 6.13.

$$\mathbf{RP^{-1}} = \begin{bmatrix} 1 & 0 & 0 & 0 \\ 0 & 1 & 0 & 0 \\ 0 & 0 & 1 & 0 \\ -\text{rpx} & -\text{rpy} & -\text{rpz} & 1 \end{bmatrix}$$

FIGURE 6.13 Rotation pivot translation.

It is possible to set the orientation of the rotation space. By default, the axes of this rotation space are aligned with the local x, y, and z axes. These axes can be reoriented, thereby creating a new rotation space in which the final rotations will be performed. The series of rotation values (rox, roy, roz) reorients the local rotation axes. These rotations are converted to matrices as shown in Figure 6.14.

$$
ROX = \begin{bmatrix} 1 & 0 & 0 & 0 \\ 0 & \cos(rox) & \sin(rox) & 0 \\ 0 & -\sin(rox) & \cos(rox) & 0 \\ 0 & 0 & 0 & 1 \end{bmatrix}
$$

$$
ROY = \begin{bmatrix} \cos(roy) & 0 & -\sin(rox) & 0 \\ 0 & 1 & 0 & 0 \\ \cos(roy) & 0 & \cos(roy) & 0 \\ 0 & 0 & 0 & 1 \end{bmatrix}
$$

$$
ROZ = \begin{bmatrix} \cos(roz) & \sin(roz) & 0 & 0 \\ -\sin(roz) & \cos(roz) & 0 & 0 \\ 0 & 0 & 1 & 0 \\ 0 & 0 & 0 & 1 \end{bmatrix}
$$

FIGURE 6.14 Rotation orientation parts.

The final rotation orientation matrix is created by concatenating the three individual rotations.

RO = ROX * ROY * ROZ

With the rotation axes now oriented correctly, the actual rotation can take place. There are three rotations (rx, ry, and rz) about the three main axes (*X*, *Y*, and *Z*), respectively. Note that the rotation values are given in radians and not degrees. The three rotations are divided into three transformation matrices. Figure 6.15 shows the final transformation matrix for the x-axis rotation.

$$RX = \begin{bmatrix} 1 & 0 & 0 & 0 \\ 0 & \cos(rx) & \sin(rx) & 0 \\ 0 & -\sin(rx) & \cos(rx) & 0 \\ 0 & 0 & 0 & 1 \end{bmatrix}$$

FIGURE 6.15 *X*-axis rotation.

The *Y*-axis rotation matrix is shown in Figure 6.16.

$$RY = \begin{bmatrix} \cos(ry) & 0 & -\sin(ry) & 0 \\ 0 & 1 & 0 & 0 \\ \sin(ry) & 0 & \cos(ry) & 0 \\ 0 & 0 & 0 & 1 \end{bmatrix}$$

FIGURE 6.16 *Y*-axis rotation.

Finally, the *Z*-axis rotation matrix is shown in Figure 6.17.

$$RZ = \begin{bmatrix} \cos(rz) & \sin(rz) & 0 & 0 \\ -\sin(rz) & \cos(rz) & 0 & 0 \\ 0 & 0 & 1 & 0 \\ 0 & 0 & 0 & 1 \end{bmatrix}$$

FIGURE 6.17 *Z*-axis rotation.

The transform node has an attribute, **rotationOrder**, that specifies the order in which these rotations will be applied. By default, the ordering is XYZ, which means that the x-axis rotation is applied first, the y-axis rotation second, and then the z-axis rotation. There are six different combinations of ordering: XYZ, YZX, ZXY, XZY,

YXZ, and ZYX. Given a particular ordering, for instance YXZ, the final rotation matrix is calculated by concatenation.

R = RY * RX * RZ

With the rotation now complete, the object is then translated away from the origin to its original position. The transformation matrix for doing this is shown in Figure 6.18.

$$RP = \begin{bmatrix} 1 & 0 & 0 & 0 \\ 0 & 1 & 0 & 0 \\ 0 & 0 & 1 & 0 \\ rpx & rpy & rpz & 1 \end{bmatrix}$$

FIGURE 6.18 Inverse rotation pivot translation.

Analogous to the scale translation, there is an additional translation that compensates for any changes to the position of rotation pivot point. It prevents the object from inadvertently being moved as a result of the pivot point change. This translation is given as (rtx, rty, rtz). Figure 6.19 shows the matrix for this translation.

$$RT = \begin{bmatrix} 1 & 0 & 0 & 0 \\ 0 & 1 & 0 & 0 \\ 0 & 0 & 1 & 0 \\ rtx & rty & rtz & 1 \end{bmatrix}$$

FIGURE 6.19 Rotation translation.

Concatenating all rotation-related matrices into a single matrix results in

ROTATE = RP^{-1} * RO * R * RP * RT

Where **R** is the concatenation of **RX**, **RY**, and **RZ** in the user-specified order. With the scale and rotation matrices now calculated, the final transformation is the translation. The translation along the axes is given as (tx, ty, tz). The matrix for the translation is shown in Figure 6.20.

$$T = \begin{bmatrix} 1 & 0 & 0 & 0 \\ 0 & 1 & 0 & 0 \\ 0 & 0 & 1 & 0 \\ tx & ty & tz & 1 \end{bmatrix}$$

FIGURE 6.20 Translation.

Unlike the other operations, the translation doesn't need any moving back and forth around the origin. The translation is applied directly. Its final transformation matrix is then

TRANSLATE = T

The final transformation matrix is generated by concatenating the three main matrices just presented.

M = SCALE * ROTATION * TRANSLATE

The matrix, **M**, is applied to each point in the shape node to transform it.

6.2.1 QUERYING TRANSFORMATION MATRICES

MEL

The xform command is the principal means of querying the transformation settings for a transform node. The translation is queried as follows.

```
xform -query -translate;
```

This will return the translation in object space. To get the translation in world space, use the following.

```
xform -query -worldSpace -translation;
```

The scale and shear are retrieved as follows.

```
xform -query -relative -scale;
xform -query -relative -shear;
```

Note that the -relative flag is given, in that the absolute scale or shear can't be retrieved. The absolute value is the default setting for the xform command. The rotation is retrieved using the -rotation flag.

```
xform -query -rotation;
```

The rotation orientation is retrieved as follows.

```
xform -query -rotateAxis;
```

The order of the axis rotations is retrieved using the following.

```
xform -query -rotateOrder;
```

The result is a string set to one of the values xyz, yzx, zxy, xzy, yxz, or zyx. The scale and rotation pivot points are retrieved as follows.

```
xform -query -scalePivot;
xform -query -rotatePivot;
```

The translation offset for the scale and rotation pivot points is retrieved in a similar manner.

```
xform -query -scaleTranslation;
xform -query -rotateTranslation;
```

To retrieve the transformation matrix of the transform node, use the following.

```
xform -query -matrix;
```

To get the object-to-world space transformation matrix, use the following.

```
xform -query -worldSpace -matrix;
```

C++ API

Given a DAG path, dagPath, to a transform node or its child, the transformation matrix can be queried using the **MFnTransform** class. The scale is retrieved using the getScale function.

```
MFnTransform transformFn( dagPath );
double s[3];
transformFn.getScale( s );
```

The shear is retrieved using the getShear function.

```
double sh[3];
transformFn.getShear( s );
```

The rotation can be retrieved using a variety of functions.

```
MQuaternion qr;
transformFn.getRotation( qr );

MEulerRotation er;
transformFn.getRotation( er );

double r[3];
MTransformationMatrix::RotationOrder ro;
transformFn.getRotation( r, ro );
```

The translation is retrieved using the translation function.

```
MVector t;
t = transformFn.translation( MSpace::kTransform );
```

The orientation of the rotation axes is returned by the rotateOrientation function. The result is a quaternion.

```
MQuaternion ror;
ror = transformFn.rotateOrientation( MSpace::kTransform );
```

The order of the axis rotations is given by the rotationOrder function.

```
MTransformationMatrix::RotationOrder roto;
roto = transformFn.rotationOrder();
```

The scale and rotation pivots are retrieved using the scalePivot and rotatePivot functions, respectively.

```
MPoint sp;
sp = transformFn.scalePivot( MSpace::kTransform );
MPoint rp;
rp = transformFn.rotatePivot( MSpace::kTransform );
```

The scale and rotation pivot point translations can also be retrieved.

```
MVector spt;
spt = transformFn.scalePivotTranslation( MSpace::kTransform );
MVector rpt;
rpt = transformFn.rotatePivotTranslation( MSpace::kTransform );
```

Rather than use the **MFnTransform** class, the **MTransformationMatrix** class can be used instead. The **MTransformationMatrix** has very similar functionality. To get the transformation matrix for the transform node, use the following.

```
MTransformationMatrix tx;
tx = transformFn.transformation();
```

6.2.2 EDITING TRANSFORMATION MATRICES

MEL

To set the translation of an object, the xform command is used.

```
xform -translation 2 3 4;
```

By default, the translation will be an absolute movement in object space. To do a relative movement, use the following.

```
xform -relative -translation 1 0 0;
```

To do a translation in world space, use the -worldSpace flag. The following command will position the object at (4, 3, 1) in world space, irrespective of the number of parents and their locations.

```
xform -worldSpace -translation 4 3 1;
```

To move the object in local space, use the move command. The following statement will move the object by one unit along the parent's x-axis.

```
move -relative -localSpace 1 0 0;
```

The rotation can be set as follows.

```
xform -rotation 10 30 50;
```

The scale is applied also with the xform command. The values are given as fractions rather than as percentages.

```
xform -scale 0.8 0.9 1;
```

To reset the transformation back to its defaults, use the following.

```
makeIdentity -apply false;
```

To reset the transformation but have the object maintain its current orientation, size, and position, use the following.

```
makeIdentity -apply true;
```

This applies the current transformation to the points/vectors in the shape node, and then resets the transformation matrix. A **transformGeometry** node is inserted into the object's construction history. Its **transform** attribute is set to the original transformation matrix. The original geometry data is fed into its **inputGeometry** attribute. The node will then transform the input geometry by the transformation matrix and store the result in its **outputGeometry** attribute. This **outputGeometry** attribute then connects into the shape node. By using a separate node to perform this operation, the **makeIdentity** command can be undone or edited later.

C++ API

The **MFnTransform** class is used to set the various components of the transformation. An absolute or relative translation is set using the `setTranslation` and `translateBy` functions, respectively. The final result is a translation setting of (0, 2, 3).

```
MFnTransform transformFn( dagPath );
transformFn.setTranslation( MVector( 1.0, 2.0, 3.0 ),
                            MSpace::kTransform);
transformFn.translateBy( MVector( -1.0, 0.0, 0.0 ),
                         MSpace::kTransform );
```

Scaling is done via similar functions. The final scale is (0.5, 0.25, 0.4) because relative scaling is performed via multiplication.

```
double s[3] = {1.0, 0.5, 0.8 };
double s2[3] = { 0.5, 0.5, 0.5 };
transformFn.setScale( s );
transformFn.scaleBy( s2 );
```

A shearing is performed and the final shear vector is (1.5, 0, 0).

```
double sh[3] = { 0.5, 0.0, 0.0 };
double sh2[3] = { 3.0, 0.0, 0.0 };
transformFn.setShear( sh );
transformFn.shearBy( sh2 );
```

Rotations can be set in a variety of ways. The first is using a quaternion. The resulting rotation is (80°, 0°, 0°).

```
MQuaternion q( degToRad(45), MVector( 1.0, 0.0, 0.0 ) );
MQuaternion q2( degToRad(35), MVector( 1.0, 0.0, 0.0 ) );
transformFn.setRotation( q );
transformFn.rotateBy( q2 );
```

There are also the `setRotationQuaternion` and `rotateByQuaternion` functions that take the individual components of the quaternion (x, y, z, w).

The rotation can also be set using Euler angles. The final rotation is (50°, 0°, 0°).

```
MEulerRotation er( degToRad( 20.0 ), 0.0, 0.0 );
MEulerRotation er2( degToRad( 30.0 ), 0.0, 0.0 );
transformFn.setRotation( er );
transformFn.rotateBy( er2 );
```

The functions `setRotation` and `rotateBy` are overloaded to allow the setting of the rotation explicitly with Euler angles: `double[3]` and `MTransformation Matrix::RotationOrder`. To reset the transformation back to its defaults, use the following.

```
MTransformationMatrix tm;
transformFn.set( tm );
```

TRANSFORM SPACES

The **MSpace** class contains an enumerated type **Space** that includes all possible named spaces in Maya.

```
kInvalid
kTransform
kPreTransform
kPostTransform
kWorld
kObject
```

Not all of the named spaces are available in all function sets. The `kWorld` and `kObject` spaces can be used by function sets that work on shapes: **MFnMesh**, **MFnNurbsSurface**, and so on. The `kInvalid` space isn't a space but is used to identify an invalid space. The `kTransform`, `kPreTransform`, and `kPostTransform` spaces can only be used in the **MFnTransform** and **MFnTransformationMatrix** classes. As covered earlier, the final transformation matrix is the result of concatenating the following matrices.

M = SCALE * ROTATION * TRANSLATE

The kPreTransform space corresponds to

$$M = I$$

Because the matrix is the identity matrix, no transformation is applied. The kTransform space depends on whether the operation is being done to the transform's scale, rotation, or translation. If it is a scale operation, the kTransform space corresponds to

$$M = SCALE$$

This is the space after the scaling has been applied. If it is a rotation operation, the kTransform space corresponds to

$$M = SCALE * ROTATION$$

This is the space after the scaling and rotation have been applied but before the translation. If it is a translation operation, the kTransform space corresponds to

$$M = SCALE * ROTATION * TRANSLATE$$

This is the space after the translation has been completed. The kPostTransform corresponds to the entire transformation matrix

$$M = SCALE * ROTATION * TRANSLATE$$

6.3　HIERARCHIES OF TRANSFORMATIONS

The material to this point has dealt with a single transform node. After calculating the individual scale, rotation, and translation matrices for the node, a final transformation matrix was created. This transformation matrix represents the transformation points will undergo from this single transform node. Given a hierarchy of transform nodes, as in Figure 6.21, a point in the shape node will undergo a series of transformations.

The geometry will initially be created in the shape node. Each of the points will be first transformed by the direct parent, **transformC**. The remaining parents, **transformB** and **transformA**, will then transform the point. The process continues until there are no longer any parents. Note how the transformation begins at the

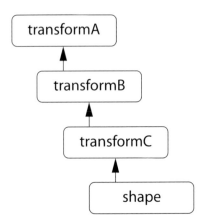

FIGURE 6.21 Hierarchy of transform nodes.

bottom of the hierarchy and works it way up. Thus, the complete transformation of a point will be as follows.

p' = p * transformC * transformB * transformA

It is possible to disable a set of parent transformations by turning off the **inheritTransform** attribute of the **transform** node. Turning this off effectively prunes all parents above the node. If the **transformC** node has its **inheritTransform** attribute set to *false*, all parent transformations above it will be ignored. In this case, all points in the shape node will only be transformed by the **transformC**'s transformation matrix.

6.3.1 TRANSFORMATION SPACES

There may be times when a point's position at a particular place in the hierarchy is needed. These different places are called *named spaces*. The series of transformations that are applied to a point determines which space it is in. Named spaces are just a convenient method of naming a series of concatenated transformations. The various named spaces in Maya are as follows.

- **Object Space**

   This is the space where no transformations have been applied. When a point is created in a shape node, it is implicitly in object space. No transformations, including any pivot point offsets, are taken into account.

   p' = p

- **Local/Parent Space**

  It is important to understand that a transform is used specifically to place an object relative to its parent. The transform **transformC** is used to place the object relative to the **transformB** space. The **transformB** space is used to place the object relative to **transformA** space. The **transformA** space is used to place the object relative to the world space. As such, to move an object in its local/parent space, the transform below the space is changed. To move the object in **transformB**'s space, the **transformC** is altered. The following will return the point **p** in **transformB**'s object space (the **transformC**'s parent space).

  p' = p * transformC

- **World Space**

  A point is in world space when all parent transforms have been applied to the object space point. This corresponds to the point

  p' = p * transformC * transformB * transformA.

6.3.2 MEL

When retrieving or setting the matrices of objects, it is important to use the complete DAG path to the object: the object's complete name preceded by the pipe character (|). This prevents confusion when objects with the same name exist in different hierarchies. It also ensures that the correct instance of an object is used, and therefore that the resulting world transformation matrices will be correct. To get the object-to-world space transformation of an object, use the following.

```
xform -query -worldSpace -matrix;
```

Alternatively, the following can be used.

```
getAttr |transform1.worldMatrix;
```

The world-to-object space transformation is the inverse of the object-to-world space transformation. Unfortunately, the `xform` command can't retrieve this information and thus the following must be used instead.

```
getAttr |transform1.worldInverseMatrix;
```

The object-to-world space of the parent transform of the current transform is retrieved using the following.

```
getAttr |transform1.parentMatrix;
```

The inverse of this matrix is retrieved similarly.

```
getAttr |transform1.parentInverseMatrix;
```

6.3.3 C++ API

If only the local transformation of a transform node is needed, the **MFnTransform** class can be used. If the object is part of a hierarchy (has more than one transform node parent), the **MDagPath** class should be used. The **MDagPath** class contains a variety of methods for getting the transformation matrix. When an object has been instanced multiple times, it is the DAG path that uniquely identifies a particular object instance. As such, a DAG path is necessary if the world space position of a point/vector is needed. The DAG path defines the series of parent transform nodes needed to build the object-to-world space transformation matrix. To get the object-to-world space transformation matrix, use the following.

```
MMatrix matObjToWorld = dagPath.inclusiveMatrix();
```

The world-to-object space transformation matrix is simply the inverse of the object-to-world space transformation matrix. It can be retrieved using the following.

```
MMatrix matWorldToObj = dagPath.inclusiveMatrixInverse();
```

The parent space is the transform above the current transform. To get the object-to-world transformation matrix for the parent transform, use the following.

```
MMatrix matParentObjToWorld = dagPath.exclusiveMatrix();
```

This creates a transformation matrix that includes all transforms in the hierarchy, except the current one, which is excluded. The inverse of this matrix is retrieved in a similar manner as before.

```
MMatrix matParentObjtoWorldInv = dagPath.exclusiveMatrixInverse();
```

Given these functions, it is possible to calculate the current transform node's transformation matrix without taking into account any of the parents.

```
MMatrix mat = matObjToWorld * matParentObjtoWorldInv;
```

The concatenation of the inverse parent matrix removes all parent transformations, thereby leaving just the current transform's transformation. Alternatively, the transformation could be retrieved directly using the **MFnDagNode** class.

```
MFnDagNode dagFn( dagPath );
MMatrix m = dagFn.transformationMatrix();
```

The transformation matrix can be retrieved from an **MFnTransform** using the following.

```
MFnTransform transformFn( dagPath );
MTransformationMatrix tm;
tm = transformFn.transformation();
MMatrix mat = tm.asMatrix();
```

To determine the object space coordinates of a point given any other space, use the following.

```
MSelectionList selection;
selection.add( "objA" );
selection.add( "objB" );

MDagPath a;
selection.getDagPath( 0, a );
MMatrix mAObjToWorld = a.inclusiveMatrix();

MDagPath b;
selection.getDagPath( 1, b );
MMatrix mBWorldToObj = b.inclusiveMatrixInverse();

MPoint p( 0.0, 0.0, 0.0 );
p *= mAObjToWorld * mBWorldToObj;
MGlobal::displayInfo( MString( "p: " ) + p.x + ", " + p.y + ", " + p.z );
```

To place any child of **objB** at the same physical location as **objA**, it needs to have its object position set to **p**. As an aside, it is interesting to understand how the **MDagPath** works internally. Each particular instance of an object has a unique DAG path. Each instance has a unique index. This is retrieved using the `instanceNumber` function. Although it may appear that the **worldMatrix** is a single matrix attribute, it is in fact an array of matrices. There are as many array elements as there are instances. To retrieve the matrix for a given instance, the `instanceNumber` is used as the index into the **worldMatrix** array. Similarly, the **worldInverseMatrix**, **parentMatrix**, and **parentInverseMatrix** attributes are arrays of matrices.

CHAPTER 7

Coordinate Frames

Mathematically, a coordinate system is referred to as a *coordinate frame*. Coordinate frames provide a frame of reference for points and vectors to be defined in. The Cartesian coordinate system, in 3D space, is defined by three axis vectors (*X, Y, Z*) and the origin *(0,0,0)*. If a rigid adherence to mathematics is followed, the three axis vectors don't need to be perpendicular to one another. Instead, they need only be linearly independent. This means that each axis vector can't be defined as a scaling of any of the others. Although this fulfills the mathematical constraints of linear independence, axis vectors that aren't orthogonal (90 degrees) are of little or no use in defining practical coordinate frames. As such, the *X, Y,* and *Z* axis vectors are defined to be orthogonal to one another.

A coordinate frame that has basis vectors of unit length that are pairwise perpendicular to each other is said to have an *orthonormal basis*. This is an important property, and one that will be exploited further in the section on transformations.

7.1 UP AXIS

In Maya, the up axis (the axis pointing vertically) is by default the *Y* axis. It is possible to switch this with the *Z* axis. Note that this doesn't mean that the *y* coordinates of all points are not swapped with their *z* coordinates. Internally, Maya doesn't change the interpretation of *x* and *y* coordinates. The up axis is just a visual aid. Changing the up axis simply rotates the ground plane and, optionally, the camera. If the *Z* axis is the up axis, the camera undergoes an additional 90-degree view rotation (applied to OpenGL view transformation matrix).

7.1.1 MEL

To get the current up axis, use the `upAxis` command.

```
upAxis -q -axis
// Result: y //
```

To set the current up axis, use the `setUpAxis` command.

```
setUpAxis "z";
```

7.1.2 C++ API

The **MGlobal** class contains a variety of functions for setting and querying the up axis. The `isYAxisUp` and `isZAxisUp` functions will return `true` or `false`, depending on which of the axes is the up axis.

```
bool yIsUp = MGlobal::isYAxisUp();
bool zIsUp = MGlobal::isZAxisUp();
```

To get the actual direction of the up axis vector, use the `upAxis` function.

```
MVector up = MGlobal::upAxis();
```

To set the up axis, use the `setZAxisUp` or the `setYAxisUp` function. These functions take an optional `rotateView` parameter. This defines whether the camera will also be rotated along with the ground plane.

```
MGlobal::setZAxisUp(true);
```

7.2 HANDEDNESS

The handedness of a coordinate system determines in which direction rotations will happen. There are two types of handedness: left and right. Maya uses a right-handed system. There is a simple method for determining the handedness of a coordinate system. Using your right hand, point your fingers along the positive X axis and your thumb along the positive Z axis. Now curl your fingers. In a right-handed system, your fingers will point toward the positive Y axis. If they don't point toward the Y axis, it is a left-handed system. Try the same exercise, but this time with your left hand.

This same method can be used to determine the direction of a positive rotation around any of the axes. With your right hand, point your thumb along the axis about which the rotation will happen. Curl your fingers. The direction of the curl will be the direction of positive rotations. Figure 7.1 shows the positive rotation directions for a right-handed coordinate system. Figure 7.2 shows the positive rotation directions for a left-handed coordinate system. Note that the Z axis is flipped to convert from a right-handed to a left-handed coordinate system.

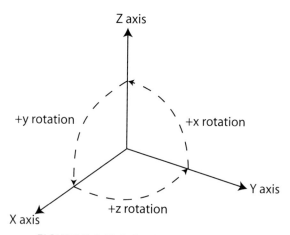

FIGURE 7.1 Right-handed coordinate system.

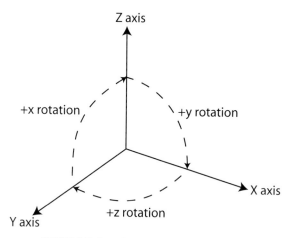

FIGURE 7.2 Left-handed coordinate system.

A more formal method of determining the handedness of a given set of axes (basis vectors) **a**, **b**, and **c** is to use the *scalar triple product*.

$$\mathbf{a} \cdot (\mathbf{b} \times \mathbf{c})$$

The scalar triple product produces a scalar result. If the result is > 0, the coordinate system is right-handed. If the result is < 0, the coordinate system is left-handed. If the result is 0, the vector **c** lies on the plane defined by vectors **a** and **b**. In this case, the axes are not perpendicular to each other. Note that this use of the scalar triple product only works for 3D vectors. As an aside, another formulation of the scalar triple product is

$$\mathbf{a} \cdot (\mathbf{b} \times \mathbf{c}) = \|\mathbf{a}\| \, \|\mathbf{b} \times \mathbf{c}\| \, \cos(\theta).$$

This is the volume of the parallelopiped formed by the three vectors, **a**, **b**, and **c**.

7.3 CUSTOM COORDINATE FRAMES

As mentioned previously, the Cartesian coordinate system is the most commonly used coordinate system. Cartesian coordinates are a specific instance of a general coordinate frame. For a 3D space, a coordinate frame is defined with an origin and three perpendicular vectors (*basis vectors*). For Cartesian coordinates, the coordinate frame is defined as follows.

origin = (0,0,0)
i = (1,0,0)
j = (0,1,0)
k = (0,0,1)

The **i**, **j**, and **k** vectors correspond respectively to the X, Y, and Z axes. Note that they are unit vectors (have a length of 1). The point (2, 4, 6) is intuitively understood to be at a position two units along the X axis, four units along the Y axis, and six units along the Z axis. Mathematically, the position is calculated based on the coordinate frame.

p = (x, y, z)
  = origin + x * i + y * j + z * k

This is referred to as a linear combination. The final position **p** is calculated as on offset from the frame's origin. The x coordinate is a scalar that is multiplied by the

i vector. The resulting vector is added to the origin given a new position along the **i** vector (X axis). The **j** vector (Y axis) is scaled by the y coordinate and then added to this position. The **k** vector (Z axis) is scaled by the z coordinate and then added to the position. The result is the final position. Note that the x, y, and z coordinates are used to scale the basis vectors. They are not offsets along the axes but are instead scaling factors. Mathematically, the x, y, and z coordinates are coefficients of the linear combination. For Cartesian coordinates, the final position is the familiar (x, y, z) position.

$$\textbf{p} = (0,0,0) + x * (1,0,0) + y * (0,1,0) + z * (0,0,1)$$
$$= (x, y, z)$$

With an understanding of what constitutes a general coordinate frame, it is possible to define custom coordinate frames. A custom coordinate system can be used to define a frame of reference with its own origin and axis directions. Say you had modeled an eye and wanted it to point at another object. The eye is modeled such that it stares along the X axis (the pupil is perpendicular to the X axis). The Y axis is the up axis and the Z axis runs along the width of the eye. Therefore, each point in the eye has an x, y, and z coordinate. By using a custom coordinate system, the eye can be repositioned and oriented to point at another object. Say the eye socket is located at position **es** and the object it needs to point at is at position **obj**. A custom coordinate frame, **eyeFrame**, will be defined with origin (**eyeFrameOrigin**) and with three basis vectors that will form the three axes: **eyeFrameU**, **eyeFrameV**, and **eyeFrameW**. The origin of the frame is the eye socket, in that this is where the eye will finally be positioned.

eyeFrameOrigin = es

The first axis, **eyeFrameU**, is chosen to point from the eye socket to the object. The direction of the vector is therefore calculated as the vector from the eye socket to the object. The final vector needs to be unit vector and is thus normalized.

eyeFrameU = normalize(obj − es)

The second axis, **eyeFrameV**, is initially chosen to point upward. Note that this vector may not be perpendicular to the **eyeFrameU** vector; a major oversight. Fortunately, there is an easy fix for this, which will be applied later.

eyeFrameV = (0, 1, 0)

The third vector needs to be perpendicular to the first two (i.e., perpendicular to the **eyeFrameU-eyeFrameV** plane). The right-hand rule defines on which side of the **eyeFrameU-eyeFrameV** plane the perpendicular vector will be.

eyeFrameW = normalize(crossProduct(eyeFrameU, eyeFrameV))

As mentioned previously, the **eyeFrameV** axis wasn't necessarily perpendicular to the **eyeFrameU** axis. The **eyeFrameV** axis will now be made perpendicular to the **eyeFrameU-eyeFrameW** plane. This is the last step in ensuring that all axes are perpendicular to one another, an important requirement for a coordinate frame. All axes must be linearly independent.

eyeFrameV = crossProduct(eyeFrameW, eyeFrameU)

With the custom coordinate frame in place, all points in the eye can be repositioned an oriented. Recall that the x, y, and z coordinates of the eye's vertices are defined in the Cartesian coordinate frame as follows.

p = (x, y, z)
**   = origin + x * i + y * j + z * k**

The eye coordinates are converted to the **eyeFrame** coordinates using the **eyeFrame**'s origin and basis vectors in place of the Cartesian coordinate frame's origin and basis vectors.

p = (x, y, z)
pEye = eyeFrameOrigin + x * eyeFrameU + y * eyeFrameV +
**   z * eyeFrameW**

Generating the coordinate frame using the methods just described works in 99% of all cases. The only time it doesn't work is when the direction the eye is pointing is exactly the same as the up vector (0, 1, 0). Because the eye direction corresponds to the **eyeFrameU** vector and the **eyeFrameV** vector is initialized to the up vector, the two vectors will be colinear. The problem is that the calculation of the initial **eyeFrameW** vector will be incorrect. To see why, set the **eyeFrameU** and **eyeFrameV** vectors to the up vector.

eyeFrameU = (0, 1, 0)
eyeFrameV = (0, 1, 0)

The cross product of these vectors is undefined because the two vectors don't define a plane but instead a line. There are an infinite number of perpendicular vectors to a line. Fortunately, there is a simple solution. When the eye direction is close to the up vector direction, another axis can be chosen as the up direction.

if(dotProduct(eyeFrameU, eyeFrameV) > 0.99)
     eyeFrameV = (1, 0, 0)

Recall that the dot product of two unit vectors is the cosine of the angle between them. When two vectors are close together, the cosine gets closer to 1. It is exactly 1 when the two vectors are identical. By testing within a small tolerance, such as 0.01 (1 − 0.99), numerical inaccuracies can be avoided. Thus, when the two vectors are found to be close to each other the X axis is used as the up axis. Thus, the X axis is guaranteed to not be colinear with the **eyeFrameU** axis. This new initial **eyeFrameV** axis can then be used in the remainder of the calculations.

Unfortunately, this solution isn't entirely perfect if used for animating the direction of the eye. When the eye is pointing in any direction but up, the eye's orientation will vary smoothly. When the eye points upward, its orientation will be immediately set so that the **eyeFrameU** axis points along the X axis. If the **eyeFrameU** axis were not already close to X axis, there would be a large rotation about the eye direction. This will show up as a telltale "popping" as the object suddenly reorients itself. A possible solution is to store the last valid **eyeFrameU** axis before the eye pointed upward and use it as the initial **eyeFrameU** axis.

7.3.1 C++ API

The following source code calculates the eye coordinate frame in world space. The coordinate frame will point in the direction of the object **obj** from the position of the object **es**.

```
MSelectionList sel;
sel.add("es");
sel.add("obj");

MDagPath esPath;
sel.getDagPath( 0, esPath );
MMatrix mEsObjToWorld = esPath.inclusiveMatrix();
MPoint esPos = MPoint::origin * mEsObjToWorld;
```

```
MDagPath objPath;
sel.getDagPath( 1, objPath );
MMatrix mObjToWorld = objPath.inclusiveMatrix();
MPoint objPos = MPoint::origin * mObjToWorld;

MPoint eyeOrigin( esPos );
MVector eyeU( objPos - eyeOrigin );
eyeU.normalize();
MVector eyeV( MVector::yAxis );
if( eyeU * eyeV > 0.99 )
    eyeV = MVector::xAxis;
MVector eyeW = eyeU ^ eyeV;
eyeW.normalize();
eyeV = eyeW ^ eyeU;

... use eye coordinate frame
```

The coordinate frame is currently represented using an origin and three direction vectors. To convert Cartesian coordinates into the coordinate frame, it is easier to represent the coordinate frame using matrices. The conversion is then the point/vector multiplied by the matrix. The matrix contains the various rotations and translation to reposition and reorient a point/vector in Cartesian coordinates to the coordinate frame. The rotations are calculated as a series of quaternions that are successively concatenated. The result of executing this code is that the selected object(s) will point in the eye direction and be repositioned at the eye socket.

```
... calculate eye coordinate frame

MQuaternion q;
MQuaternion qx( MVector::xAxis, eyeU );
q = qx;

MVector yRotated = MVector::yAxis.rotateBy( q );
double angle = acos(yRotated * eyeV);
MQuaternion qy( angle, eyeU );
if( !eyeV.isEquivalent( yRotated.rotateBy(qy), 1.0e-5 ) )
{
    angle = 2 * M_PI - angle;
    qy = MQuaternion( angle, eyeU );
}
q *= qy;
```

```
MGlobal::getActiveSelectionList( sel );

MDagPath dagPath;
MObject component;

MItSelectionList iter( sel );
for ( ; !iter.isDone(); iter.next() )
{
    iter.getDagPath( dagPath, component );
    MFnDagNode dagFn( dagPath );

    MFnTransform transformFn( dagPath );
    transformFn.setRotation( q );
    transformFn.setTranslation( eyeOrigin, MSpace::kTransform );
}
```

The calculation of the quaternion merits closer inspection. The final quaterion needs to rotate the Cartesian axes (X, Y, and Z) so that they are aligned respectively with **eyeU**, **eyeV**, and **eyeW**. First, the X axis is rotated to align with the **eyeU** axis. The **MQuaternion**'s constructor takes two vectors and sets the quaternion to the rotation needed to rotate the first vector (MVector::xAxis) onto the second vector (eyeU).

```
MQuaternion q;
MQuaternion qx( MVector::xAxis, eyeU );
q = qx;
```

Because the X axis is now aligned with the **eyeU** axis, the Y and Z axes simply need to be rotated around the **eyeU** axis so that they align respectively with the **eyeV** and **eyeW** axes. Once the **eyeV** axis is aligned, the **eyeW** axis is guaranteed to be aligned because both coordinate systems are the same handedness (right-handed). The Y axis is first rotated by the quaterion applied to align the **eyeU** axis.

```
MVector yRotated = MVector::yAxis.rotateBy( q );
```

The angle between the rotated Y axis and the **eyeV** is then calculated, and a quaternion is generated that will rotate around the **eyeU** axis by the amount of the angle.

```
double angle = acos(yRotated * eyeV);
MQuaternion qy( angle, eyeU );
```

The problem is that we don't know in which direction the quaternion will rotate. The quaternion is applied to the rotated Y axis to see if it will align with the **eyeV** axis. If it doesn't, the opposite angle is used.

```
if( !eyeV.isEquivalent( yRotated.rotateBy(qy), 1.0e-5 ) )
{
    angle = 2 * M_PI - angle;
    qy = MQuaternion( angle, eyeU );
}
```

The quaternion for aligning the Y axis is concatenated with the quaternion for aligning the X axis.

```
q *= qy;
```

If the three basis vectors of the coordinate frame are guaranteed to be orthogonal to one another and have a unit length (*orthonormal basis*), the vector components can be used to directly set the rotation part (top-left 3×3 matrix) of the matrix. There is no need for quaternions. The calculation of the matrix can then be replaced by the following.

```
... calculate eye coordinate frame
MMatrix m;
m(0,0) = eyeU.x; m(0,1) = eyeU.y; m(0,2) = eyeU.z;
m(1,0) = eyeV.x; m(1,1) = eyeV.y; m(1,2) = eyeV.z;
m(2,0) = eyeW.x; m(2,1) = eyeW.y; m(2,2) = eyeW.z;

MTransformationMatrix tm( m );
tm.setTranslation( eyeOrigin, MSpace::kTransform );

MGlobal::getActiveSelectionList( sel );

MDagPath dagPath;
MObject component;

MItSelectionList iter( sel );
for ( ; !iter.isDone(); iter.next() )
{
    iter.getDagPath( dagPath, component );
    MFnDagNode dagFn( dagPath );

    MFnTransform transformFn( dagPath );
    transformFn.set( tm );
}
```

CHAPTER 8

Polygonal Meshes

Meshes provide a simple and effective geometry type whereby you can easily specify objects of arbitrary complexity and topology. A mesh contains the following components: vertices, edges, and faces. Different types of data can be associated with each component, including colors, normals, *uv* texture coordinates, and blind data.

It is important to understand that the mesh architecture presented through Maya's MEL command and C++ API isn't the same internal mesh architecture Maya uses. It has its own internal representation of meshes that can be quite different from that presented through MEL and the API. Anecdotally, Maya's internal mesh architecture went through extensive changes in version 3.0, yet the external C++ API and MEL commands didn't change at all. Having the interface to the internal mesh architecture abstracted from the internal works means that Maya's architecture can change without breaking the interface.

Maya's internal representation of polygonal meshes is very compact. In addition, it will only compute information when it is requested. Such deferred evaluation of data includes connectivity information, normals, triangles, and so on. Maya's internal representation of meshes uses a completely different form from that shown in the API when changes to the topology are made. The topology changing operation is performed in its new internal form and then a final "normal" mesh is generated as a result.

8.1 DISPLAYING MESHES

The following sections describe how to query, create, and edit meshes. It is important to understand how to visualize the various components that make up a mesh. Some of the components can be displayed in the 3D viewports, whereas others are only visible in specific editors (**UV Texture Editor**, **Blind Data Editor**, and so on).

8.1.1 GENERAL

The `polyOptions` command is used to set and query the various display options for a mesh object.

1. Open the **BoxMeshes.ma** scene.

2. Select **Shading | Wireframe** from the **persp** view's menu.

3. Select the **box** object.

   ```
   polyOptions -activeObjects -displayTriangle true;
   ```

   The triangles of the **box** object are displayed. With the `-activeObjects` flag included, all display changes will only apply to the selected objects. This is the default behavior of the `polyOptions` command, and thus `-activeObjects` can be omitted.

4. Execute the following.

   ```
   polyOptions -displayTriangle false;
   ```

   This turns off the display of triangles for the selected objects.

5. Execute the following.

   ```
   polyOptions -global -displayTriangle true;
   ```

   All mesh objects now display their triangles. The `-global` flag indicates that the display changes should be applied to all existing mesh objects.

6. Execute the following.

   ```
   polyCube;
   ```

   A new cube is created. Note that it doesn't have its triangles displayed. Because the `-global` flag applies to all existing mesh objects, any new objects will not have the display setting applied.

7. Execute the following.

   ```
   undo;
   ```

This removes the new cube. To have all future meshes use a particular display setting, the -newPolymesh flag is needed.

8. Execute the following.

```
polyOptions -newPolymesh -displayTriangle true;
polyCube;
```

When the new cube is created, it automatically has its triangles displayed. Exercise caution with the -newPolymesh option because its display options will apply to all future mesh objects. If a Maya scene with meshes were opened, the -newPolymesh display options would apply to them all. In addition, the display options are saved between Maya sessions and thus they will apply to all new meshes created in future sessions. As such, this flag should only be used if really necessary.

9. Execute the following.

```
polyOptions -newPolymesh -displayTriangle false;
```

This restores the -newPolymesh display option to its previous setting.

8.1.2 COMPONENTS

1. Open the **BoxMesh.ma** scene.

2. Select the **box** object.

3. Select **Shading | Wireframe** from the **persp** view's menu.

4. Execute the following.

```
polyOptions -displayVertex true;
```

This displays the vertices of the mesh. Even though the vertices are in a different color, it is difficult to see them. Turning off the geometry should help.

5. Execute the following.

```
polyOptions -displayGeometry false;
```

This turns off display of the geometry. To toggle a display setting, simply use the -relative flag.

6. Execute the following.

```
polyOptions -relative -displayGeometry true;
```

This toggles the display of geometry. Because the display of geometry was turned off, it was toggled to now be on.

7. Execute the following.

```
polyOptions -displayCenter true;
```

This displays the center of each face in the mesh.

8. Execute the following.

```
polyOptions -displayTriangle true;
```

The mesh is triangulated and the resulting triangles are displayed.

9. Execute the following.

```
polyOptions -displayBorder true;
```

The top edges of the box are displayed with a thicker line. The border edges are those edges that are shared by only one face. If an edge had two faces that shared it, the edge would be an internal rather than a border edge. It would be easier to see the border edge if the line thickness were increased.

10. Execute the following.

```
polyOptions -q -sizeBorder;
```

The current border size is 2. This is the thickness of the line in pixels. This will now be doubled.

11. Execute the following.

```
polyOptions -relative -sizeBorder 2;
```

The border size is now set to 4 pixels, making it more distinct. Using the -relative flag when setting the size will multiply the current value rather than set an explicit value.

12. Execute the following.

```
polyOptions -displayItemNumbers true false false false;
```

This turns on the display of vertex indices. The Boolean parameters to the -displayItemNumbers flag are for turning on or off the vertices, edges, faces, and uvs, respectively.

8.1.3 NORMALS

1. Execute the following.

```
polyOptions -displayNormal true;
```

The face normals are displayed. This is the equivalent of executing polyOptions -facet -displayNormal true. Because the display of face normals is the default, the -facet flag can be omitted.

2. Execute the following.

```
polyOptions -sizeNormal 0.25;
```

The length of the normals is reduced to 0.25.

3. Execute the following.

```
polyOptions -point -displayNormal true;
```

The face-vertex normals are now displayed. When the face-vertex normals are displayed, the face normals are hidden. To have them both visible at the same time, the -pointFacet is used.

4. Execute the following.

```
polyOptions -pointFacet -displayNormal true;
```

Both the face and face-vertex normals are displayed.

8.1.4 BACK-FACE CULLING

1. Select **Shading | Smooth Shade All** in the **persp** view's menu.

2. Rotate the view so that the inside of the box is visible.

3. Execute the following.

```
polyOptions -fullBack;
```

The faces whose normals are not pointing toward the viewer are not displayed. This is referred to as *back-face culling* because all faces that point backward are culled from being displayed.

4. Execute the following.

```
polyOptions -backCullVertex false;
```

The vertices of faces that have been culled are now displayed. By setting the `-backCullVertex` flag to `false`, these vertices are not culled and are therefore displayed.

5. Execute the following.

```
polyOptions -wireBackCulling;
```

The edges of culled faces are now displayed.

6. Execute the following.

```
polyOptions -backCulling;
```

This turns back-face culling off, so that all faces are now visible.

8.1.5 UV TEXTURE COORDINATES

1. Select **Window | UV Texture Editor** from the main menu.

   Many of the uv display options are easier to see in the **UV Texture Editor** than they are in the 3D viewports.

2. Execute the following.

```
polyOptions -displayUVs true;
```

The uv coordinates are displayed.

3. Execute the following.

```
polyOptions -displayItemNumbers false false false true;
```

The uv indices are displayed in the **UV Texture Editor**.

4. Execute the following.

```
polyOptions -displayMapBorder true;
```

The edges of the uvs that are not shared are displayed with thicker lines. The `-sizeBorder` setting determines the width of the lines.

5. Execute the following.

```
polyOptions -displayUVTopology true;
```

The uv texture coordinates that are shared are drawn as a dot at their corresponding vertex. Face-vertex uvs that are separate are drawn as a dot near the corner of the face. In this display mode it is clear which uv texture coordinates are shared and which are not.

8.1.6 VERTEX COLORS

1. Open the **BoxMesh.ma** scene.

2. Select the **box** object.

3. Execute the following.

```
polyOptions -colorShadedDisplay true;
```

Even though vertex color display is turned on, the vertex colors are not displayed. The vertex color will be determined by the current setting of the mesh's color material channel.

4. Execute the following.

```
polyOptions -q -colorMaterialChannel;
```

The current color material channel is returned.

```
// Result: ambientDiffuse //
```

To see the vertex colors, the color material channel must be set to "none".

5. Execute the following.

```
polyOptions -colorMaterialChannel "none";
```

The vertex colors are displayed. Because no vertex colors have been assigned, the box is displayed using black.

6. Execute the following.

```
select -r box.vtx[3];
polyColorPerVertex -rgb 1 1 0;
```

The fourth vertex (index 3) is assigned the color yellow. The vertex color is interpolated across the faces that share it. This is the equivalent of *Gouraud shading*.

8.1.7 NONPLANAR FACES

1. Open the **BoxMesh.ma** scene.

2. Execute the following.

```
select -r box.vtx[3];
move -r 0.5 0.5 0.5 ;
select -r box ;
```

These commands move one of the top corner vertices, thereby making all faces that share this vertex nonplanar.

3. Execute the following.

```
polyOptions -displayWarp true;
```

All nonplanar faces in the mesh are now displayed in a different color.

8.2 QUERYING MESHES

This section describes how you can access the various mesh components and data using both MEL and the C++ API.

8.2.1 VERTICES

The vertices of a mesh are stored as a series of points. Figure 8.1 shows the vertex array for a triangle mesh. Each point has its own x-y-z coordinate.

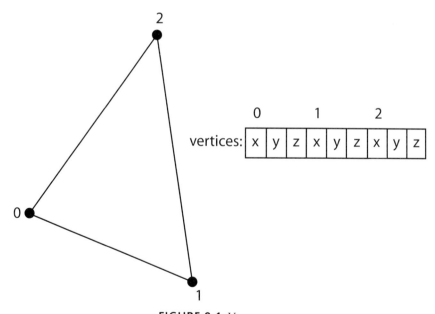

FIGURE 8.1 Vertex array.

Because there are only three vertices in a triangle, the vertex array contains only three points. An element in an array is accessed by its index. All indices are base 0, meaning that rather than starting from 1, like natural numbers, they start from 0. For this mesh there are three vertices, and their indices are 0, 1, and 2. In general, an array has indices from 0 to one less than the total number of elements; that is, `0 <= index <= size(array)-1`. To access the first vertex, use the following.

```
vertices[0]
```

The x component of the first vertex is accessed using the following.

```
vertices[0].x
```

Similarly, use the for the y and z components.

```
vertices[0].y
vertices[0].z
```

To access any given vertex, all that is needed is its index. Because the index is just the location of the vertex in the array, a simple integer can be used. Thus, anytime Maya wants to refer to a vertex an integer value is used. Because it is an index into the mesh's vertex array, it is more precisely described as a *mesh-relative vertex ID*, though more often referred to simply as a *vertex ID*. This is distinct from a *face-relative vertex ID*, described in material to follow.

Because the array will have a finite number of elements, it is important to note that only integer indices between 0 and size(array)-1 are valid. Any integer index outside this range isn't referring to a valid element in the array.

You will often see diagrams in which there are arrows pointing from one array to another. This can cause some confusion because you may think this represents a pointer to an element. A pointer doesn't refer to a position within a list but instead an address in the computer's memory. It is important to note that all references from one array to another are done simply by index. Pointers are not used for this purpose.

MEL

1. Open the **BasicPolygon.ma** scene.

2. Select the **square** object.

3. Execute the following.

```
polyEvaluate -vertex;
```

The number of vertices in the mesh is returned.

```
// Result: 4 //
```

4. To print out all vertices in the mesh, execute the following.

```
int $res[] = `polyEvaluate -vertex`;
int $nVerts = $res[0];
float $pos[3];
int $i;
for( $i=0; $i < $nVerts; $i += 1 )
{
    $pos = `getAttr square.vrts[$i]`;
    print ($pos[0] + ", " + $pos[1] + ", " + $pos[2] + "\n");
}
```

The vertices are then listed.

```
-2.5, -5.551115123e-016, 2.5
2.5, -5.551115123e-016, 2.5
-2.5, 5.551115123e-016, -2.5
2.5, 5.551115123e-016, -2.5
```

Note that the y coordinate is a very small number, rather than exactly 0. This is most likely due to some small amount of floating-point error when the points were being calculated.

The first line retrieves the number of vertices in the mesh. The result of the polyEvaluate command is an array, and thus the result must be stored in an array even though only the vertex count was requested.

```
int $res[] = `polyEvaluate -vertex`;
```

The first element is the vertex count. It is retrieved from the array.

```
int $nVerts = $res[0];
```

The array of vertices is then iterated over.

```
int $i;
for( $i=0; $i < $nVerts; $i += 1 )
{
```

Vertices are stored in the mesh's vrts attribute. The vertex with index $i is retrieved and stored in the array of three floats $pos.

```
    $pos = `getAttr square.vrts[$i]`;
```

Finally, the vertex position is then printed out.

```
    print ($pos[0] + ", " + $pos[1] + ", " + $pos[2] + "\n");
```

Alternatively, the polyEvaluate command could be circumvented entirely. Knowing that the vrts attribute holds all vertex positions means that it can be accessed directly. The size of the returned array, divided by 3, will give the number of vertices in the array.

5. Execute the following.

```
float $coords[] = `getAttr square.vrts["*"]`;
int $nVerts = size( $coords) / 3;
int $i;
for( $i=0; $i < $nVerts*3; $i += 3 )
    print ($coords[$i] + ", " +
            $coords[$i+1] + ", " +
            $coords[$i+2] + "\n");
```

The vertex coordinates are printed out as before. The entire array of vertices is retrieved using the "*" index into the array. This signifies that all array indices are to be used, not just a single one.

```
float $coords[] = `getAttr square.vrts["*"]`;
```

Because the `$coords` array holds all vertex coordinates for the mesh, its total length is the number of vertices multiplied by the number of coordinates. The number of coordinates is known to be three (x, y, and z), and thus to calculate the number of vertices divide the total length by 3.

```
int $nVerts = size( $coords) / 3;
```

Iterate over each coordinate (x, y, and z) in sequence. Note that the `$i` variable is incremented by 3 at the end of each loop. This ensures that $i is set to the next vertex in the array.

```
int $i;
for( $i=0; $i < $nVerts*3; $i += 3 )
```

The `$i` index refers to the x coordinate, the $i+1 to the y coordinate, and the $i+2 to the z coordinate. These coordinates are printed out as before.

```
print ($coords[$i] + ", " +
       $coords[$i+1] + ", " +
       $coords[$i+2] + "\n");
```

In the previous examples, the position of the vertices were in local space. This is the space the geometry is initially defined in, with no further transforms applied. To get the vertex positions in world space, the `pointPosition` command is used.

6. Open the **BasicPolygon.ma** scene.

7. Select the **square** object.

8. Open the **Attribute Editor**.

The **square** transform object currently has the default settings, and thus there is no translation, rotation, or scale. As such, there is effectively no transformation. If the world space position of a vertex were queried it would be the same as its local position.

9. Execute the following.

```
print `pointPosition -local square.vtx[0]`;
```

The local position of the first vertex (index 0) is printed out.

```
-2.5
0
2.5
```

10. Execute the following.

```
print `pointPosition -world square.vtx[0]`;
```

The world position of the first vertex is printed out.

```
-2.5
0
2.5
```

The local and world space positions are the same because there is effectively no transformation.

11. Execute the following.

```
setAttr square.translateY 3.0;
```

The plane is moved up three units along the y axis.

12. Execute the following.

```
print `pointPosition -world square.vtx[0]`;
```

The world space position of the first vertex now reflects the transformation applied to the plane; it has a y coordinate of 3.

```
-2.5
3
2.5
```

By default, the `pointPosition` command will return the world space position of the requested point, and thus the explicit use of -world isn't necessary (but helps for clarity).

13. Execute the following.

```
int $res[] = `polyEvaluate -vertex`;
int $nVerts = $res[0];
float $pos[3];
int $i;
for( $i=0; $i < $nVerts; $i += 1 )
  {
  $pos = `pointPosition -world ("square.vtx[" + $i + "]")`;
  print ($pos[0] + ", " + $pos[1] + ", " + $pos[2] + "\n");
  }
```

The world space positions of all vertices are printed out.

```
-2.5, 3, 2.5
2.5, 3, 2.5
-2.5, 3, -2.5
2.5, 3, -2.5
```

C++ API

The series of **MeshInfo** plug-ins will access and print out the various components (vertices, edges, faces, and so on) of a mesh. The **MeshInfo1** plug-in demonstrates the following.

- Retrieving current selected meshes and mesh vertices
- Printing out mesh vertex information

This section demonstrates the usage of the `meshInfo1` command.

1. Open the **MeshInfo1** workspace.

2. Compile it and load the resulting `meshInfo1` plug-in file in Maya.

3. Open the **BasicPolygon.ma** scene.

4. Execute the following.

```
select -r square;
```

This selects the **square** object.

5. Execute the following.

```
meshInfo1;
```

All vertices of the mesh are printed out.

```
// |square
# Vertices: 4
0: -2.5, 0, 2.5
1: 2.5, 0, 2.5
2: -2.5, 0, -2.5
3: 2.5, 0, -2.5
```

6. Execute the following.

```
select -r square.vtx[1];
```

This selects the second vertex of the square object.

7. Execute the following.

```
meshInfo1;
```

The second vertex in the square object is printed out.

```
// |square|squareShape
# Vertices: 1
  1: 2.5, 0, 2.5
```

The source code for the command is covered in detail in the following.

Source Code

Plug-in: MeshInfo1
File: MeshInfo1Cmd.cpp

```cpp
DeclareSimpleCommand( meshInfo1, "David Gould", "1.0" );

MStatus meshInfo1::doIt( const MArgList& args )
{
    MStatus stat = MS::kSuccess;

    MSelectionList selection;
    MGlobal::getActiveSelectionList( selection );

    MDagPath dagPath;
    MObject component;
    int vertCount, vertIndex;

    MString txt;
    MItSelectionList iter( selection );
    for ( ; !iter.isDone(); iter.next() )
    {
        iter.getDagPath( dagPath, component );

        MItMeshVertex meshIter( dagPath, component, &stat );
        if( stat == MS::kSuccess )
        {
            txt += dagPath.fullPathName() + "\n";

            vertCount = meshIter.count();
            txt += MString("# Vertices: ") + vertCount + "\n";

            for( ; !meshIter.isDone(); meshIter.next() )
            {
                MPoint pt = meshIter.position( MSpace::kWorld );

                vertIndex = meshIter.index();

                txt += MString(" ") + vertIndex + ": " +
                        pt.x + ", " + pt.y + ", " + pt.z + "\n";
            }
        }
    }

    MGlobal::displayInfo( txt );

    return MS::kSuccess;
}
```

SOURCE CODE EXPLANATION

Because the goal of the **meshInfo1** command is to simply print out the name, number, and coordinates of the mesh vertices, it can be considered a non-undoable command. This is a command that doesn't change Maya in any way. These can be thought of as read-only commands, in that they will often retrieve information about the current state of Maya but not alter or edit it in any way.

Because the **meshInfo1** command is quite simple, it can be defined using the `DeclareSimpleCommand` macro. This is a convenient macro that defines all necessary classes and plug-in initialization/deinitialization functions for the command.

```
DeclareSimpleCommand( meshInfo1, "David Gould", "1.0" );
```

The **meshInfo**'s `doIt` function is called when the command is executed. It performs the actual work.

```
MStatus meshInfo1::doIt( const MArgList& args )
{
```

The list of currently selected objects is retrieved.

```
MSelectionList selection;
MGlobal::getActiveSelectionList( selection );
```

The items in the selection list are iterated over using the **MItSelectionList** class. Note that no object type filter is specified in the constructor. Because the command works on meshes, it may be tempting to set the iterator's filter to **MFn::kMesh**. If this were done, only whole mesh objects would be considered. If a mesh vertex were selected, it would be ignored because it is of object type **MFn::kMeshVertComponent**. Because there is no filtering of the selection list, all currently selected items are iterated over.

```
MItSelectionList iter( selection );
for ( ; !iter.isDone(); iter.next() )
{
```

The DAG path and any possible components are retrieved for the current object. If no component is selected, the component object returned will be a null object.

```
iter.getDagPath( dagPath, component );
```

The **MItMeshVertex** class is used to iterate over the vertices of a mesh object. It is initialized using the DAG path and components of the current object. If the component object is null, all of the mesh's vertices are iterated over. The status of the constructor is stored in the stat variable.

```
MItMeshVertex meshIter( dagPath, component, &stat );
```

If the selected object and component are compatible with the **MItMeshVertex** class, the stat variable will be sent to **MS::kSuccess**. Currently, meshes (**MFn::kMesh**) and mesh vertices (**MFn::kMeshVertComponent**) are compatible with the class. If the selection is compatible (not a mesh or mesh vertex) with the **MItMeshVertex** class, the stat variable will be set to **MS::kFailure**.

```
if( stat == MS::kSuccess )
{
```

The DAG path of the currently selected object is then added to the output text.

```
txt += dagPath.fullPathName() + "\n";
```

The vertex count of the current item is then determined using the count function. If a mesh is selected, the count will return the number of vertices in the mesh. If a component is selected, the number of vertex components will be returned.

```
vertCount = meshIter.count();
txt += MString("# Vertices: ") + vertCount + "\n";
```

Fortunately, all iterator classes use a similar approach to iterating over a particular object or data. As such, the MItMeshVertex class, like the MItSelectionList class, has iteration functions isDone(), next(), and so on to iterate over the list of vertices.

```
for( ; !meshIter.isDone(); meshIter.next() )
{
```

The position of the current vertex is retrieved using the `position()` function. The function takes the coordinate space the position should be in as its first argument. By default, the `position()` function will return the vertex position in the local coordinate space. In this example, the vertex position in the world coordinate space is requested.

```
MPoint pt = meshIter.position( MSpace::kWorld );
```

The index of the vertex (vertex ID) is retrieved. This is the index of the vertex in the vertex array.

```
vertIndex = meshIter.index();
```

The vertex ID and vertex coordinates are formatted and added to the final text.

```
txt += MString(" ") + vertIndex + ": " +
       pt.x + ", " + pt.y + ", " + pt.z + "\n";
```

The final text contains the formated coordinates of all vertices. It is then printed out using the `displayInfo` function.

```
MGlobal::displayInfo( txt );
```

8.2.2 EDGES

An edge is a straight line between vertices. Any straight line can be identified by its start and end points. For an edge in a mesh, these points are the vertices. Thus, to uniquely identify a particular edge you simply need to give the vertex at its start and end. An edge is therefore defined as two vertices. As shown in the previous section, the vertices of the mesh are stored in an array. To refer to a particular vertex we simply need its index in the vertex array. This index is a number that can be stored as an integer. Thus, to uniquely identify an edge we need just two integers: one for the start vertex index and one for the end vertex index.

The list of edges is a single array, wherein each element consists of two integers. The vertex array and the edge array for a triangle are shown in Figure 8.2.

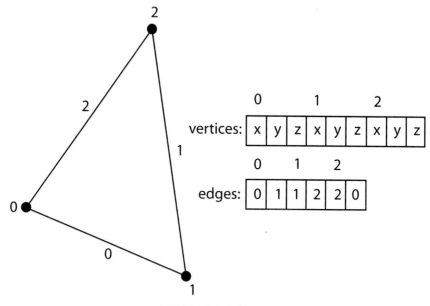

FIGURE 8.2 Edge array.

Given both the edge and vertex arrays, it is possible to retrieve the vertex coordinates. The start and end vertex indices of the first edge (index 0) are given, respectively, by the following.

```
edges[0][0]
edges[0][1]
```

These return an index into the vertex array. Thus, to get the vertex of the start of the first edge, use the following.

```
vertices[ edges[0][0] ]
```

As before, the coordinates of the vertex can be accessed using .x, .y, and .z. To access the x coordinate, use the following.

```
vertices[ edges[0][0] ].x
```

MEL

1. Open the **BasicPolygon.ma** scene.

2. Select the **square** object.

3. Execute the following.

```
polyEvaluate -edge;
```

The number of edges in the mesh is returned.

```
// Result: 4 //
```

4. To print out all vertices in the mesh, execute the following.

```
string $sel[] = `ls -long -dag -selection -geometry`;
int $i, $j;
for( $i=0; $i < size($sel); $i++ )
{
  string $node = $sel[$i];
  int $res[] = `polyEvaluate -edge $node`;
  int $nEdges = $res[0];
  print ($node + " has " + $nEdges + " edges:\n");
  for( $j=0; $j < $nEdges; $j++ )
  {
    string $pi[] = `polyInfo -edgeToVertex ($node + ".e[" + $j + "]")`;
    string $piParts[];
    tokenize $pi[0] $piParts;

    int $v0 = int( $piParts[2] );
    int $v1 = int( $piParts[3] );
    print ($v0 + ", " + $v1 + "\n");
  }
}
```

The edges are listed.

```
|square|squareShape has 4 edges:
0, 1
0, 2
1, 3
2, 3
```

This MEL code is more sophisticated than the last. It starts by getting the currently selected geometry objects, rather than using the hardcoded **square** object as in the previous example. It gets the full DAG path to the geometry nodes.

```
string $sel[] = `ls -long -dag -selection -geometry`;
```

The selected objects are then iterated over.

```
for( $i=0; $i < size($sel); $i++ )
{
```

The number of edges in the geometry node is then retrieved. As before, the `polyEvaluate` command returns an array of values. In this example, only the first element of the array is used.

```
int $res[] = `polyEvaluate -edge $node`;
int $nEdges = $res[0];
```

The geometry node name is printed out, along with its number of edges.

```
print ($node + " has " + $nEdges + " edges:\n");
```

The edges in the geometry node are then iterated over.

```
for( $j=0; $j < $nEdges; $j++ )
{
```

Because it isn't possible to directly access the edges attribute of the node using MEL, the `polyInfo` command is used to retrieve the edge information.

```
string $pi[] = `polyInfo -edgeToVertex ($node+".e["+$j+"]")`;
```

The result of the `polyInfo` command is an array of strings of the following form.

```
"EDGE 0: 0 1 Hard"
```

This string is broken down into its pieces using the `tokenize` command. This command will split the string into pieces using white space as the separator.

```
string $piParts[];
tokenize $pi[0] $piParts;
```

The `$piParts` array will now contain elements of the following form.

```
[ "EDGE", "0:", "0", "1", "Hard" ]
```

Because the start and end vertices of the edge are needed, the second (index 1) and third (index 2) elements of the array are retrieved.

```
int $v0 = int( $piParts[2] );
int $v1 = int( $piParts[3] );
```

These vertex indices are then printed out.

```
print ($v0 + ", " + $v1 + "\n");
```

C++ API

The **MeshInfo2** plug-in demonstrates the following.

- Retrieving the selected mesh and mesh edges
- Accessing edge connectivity (faces, vertices, and so on) information
- Printing out edge information

The command handles both mesh objects as well as components of meshes. For a given selected mesh, if there are no components selected all edges in the mesh will be output. If the selection contained, for instance, just

```
polyPlane1
```

all edges in the `polyPlane1` object would be output. If there are selected edges, those edges will be output. Given the edge selection

```
polyPlane1.e[3:5]
```

the fourth, fifth, and sixth edges of `polyPlane1` will be output. The command can also handle components that are not explicitly edges. If a mesh vertex is selected, all edges connected to this vertex will be output. If

```
polyPlane1.vtx[3]
```

were the current selection, all edges connected to the fourth vertex would be output. Similarly, if a mesh face is selected, all edges associated with the face will be output. Given the selected mesh face

```
polyPlane1.f[1]
```

all edges of the second face will be output. The command supports all of these various selection types because it uses the **MItMeshEdge** class to iterate over the current selection.

1. Open the **MeshInfo2** workspace.

2. Compile it and load the resulting `meshInfo2` plug-in file in Maya.

3. Open the **BasicPolygon.ma** scene.

4. Execute the following.

```
select -r square;
```

This selects the **square** object.

5. Execute the following.

```
meshInfo2;
```

Information about the mesh edges is printed out. In addition to the name of the mesh object and its number of edges, for each edge the vertex index and coordinates of the start and end vertices are printed out.

```
// |square
# Edges: 4
Edge 0: 0 (-2.5, 0, 2.5) 1 (2.5, 0, 2.5)
Edge 1: 0 (-2.5, 0, 2.5) 2 (-2.5, 0, -2.5)
Edge 2: 1 (2.5, 0, 2.5) 3 (2.5, 0, -2.5)
Edge 3: 2 (-2.5, 0, -2.5) 3 (2.5, 0, -2.5)
```

6. Execute the following.

```
select -r square.e[1];
```

This selects the second edge.

7. Execute the following.

```
meshInfo2;
```

The information about the second edge is printed out.

```
// |square|squareShape
# Edges: 1
Edge 1: 0 (-2.5, 0, 2.5) 2 (-2.5, 0, -2.5)
```

The source code for the command is covered in detail in the following.

SOURCE CODE

Plug-in: MeshInfo2
File: MeshInfo2Cmd.cpp

```
DeclareSimpleCommand( meshInfo2, "David Gould", "1.0" );

MStatus meshInfo2::doIt( const MArgList& args )
{
    MStatus stat = MS::kSuccess;

    MSelectionList selection;
    MGlobal::getActiveSelectionList( selection );
```

```
MDagPath dagPath;
MObject component;

int edgeCount, v0Index, v1Index, edgeIndex;
MPoint v0, v1;

MString txt;
MItSelectionList iter( selection );
for ( ; !iter.isDone(); iter.next() )
{
    iter.getDagPath( dagPath, component );

    MItMeshEdge edgeIter( dagPath, component, &stat );
    if( stat == MS::kSuccess )
    {
        txt += dagPath.fullPathName() + "\n";

        edgeCount = edgeIter.count();
        txt += MString("# Edges: ") + edgeCount + "\n";

        for( ; !edgeIter.isDone(); edgeIter.next() )
        {
            edgeIndex = edgeIter.index();

            v0Index = edgeIter.index(0);
            v1Index = edgeIter.index(1);

            v0 = edgeIter.point( 0, MSpace::kWorld );
            v1 = edgeIter.point( 1, MSpace::kWorld );

            txt = txt + "Edge " + edgeIndex + ": " +
                    v0Index + " (" +
                    v0.x + ", " + v0.y + ", " + v0.z + ") " +
                    v1Index + " (" +
                    v1.x + ", " + v1.y + ", " + v1.z + ")\n";
        }
    }
}

MGlobal::displayInfo( txt );
return MS::kSuccess;
}
```

SOURCE CODE EXPLANATION

Like the meshInfo1 command, the meshInfo2 command is non-undoable and thus can be defined using the DeclareSimpleCommand macro.

```
DeclareSimpleCommand( meshInfo2, "David Gould", "1.0" );
```

All currently selected objects are iterated through.

```
MItSelectionList iter( selection );
for ( ; !iter.isDone(); iter.next() )
{
```

The DAG path and component of the current selection are retrieved.

```
iter.getDagPath( dagPath, component );
```

The **MItMeshEdge** class is used to iterate through mesh edges. It is intialized with the DAG path and component of the currently selected item. The result of the initialization is stored in the stat variable.

```
MItMeshEdge edgeIter( dagPath, component, &stat );
```

If the DAG path and component are compatible with the mesh edge iterator, the stat variable will be set to **MS::kSuccess**. Otherwise, it will be set to **MS::kFailure**. Currently, the types **MS::kMesh**, **MS::kMeshVertComponent**, **MS::kMeshEdgeComponent**, and **MS::kMeshPolygonComponent** are compatible with **MItMeshEdge**.

```
if( stat == MS::kSuccess )
{
```

The full DAG path of the object is included in the output text.

```
txt += dagPath.fullPathName() + "\n";
```

The total number of edges is retrieved and included in the output text.

```
edgeCount = edgeIter.count();
txt += MString("# Edges: ") + edgeCount + "\n";
```

The edges are iterated over in a similar fashion to the mesh vertices.

```
for( ; !edgeIter.isDone(); edgeIter.next() )
{
```

The edge index of the current edge is retrieved. The edge indices are from 0 to edgeCount-1.

```
edgeIndex = edgeIter.index();
```

The vertex index of the start and end vertices of the edge are retrieved.

```
v0Index = edgeIter.index(0);
v1Index = edgeIter.index(1);
```

The world space vertex positions of the start and end vertices are retrieved.

```
v0 = edgeIter.point( 0, MSpace::kWorld );
v1 = edgeIter.point( 1, MSpace::kWorld );
```

Given the retrieved data, it is formatted and included in the output text.

```
txt = txt + "Edge " + edgeIndex + ": " +
    v0Index + " (" +
    v0.x + ", " + v0.y + ", " + v0.z + ") " +
    v1Index + " (" +
    v1.x + ", " + v1.y + ", " + v1.z + ")\n";
```

Finally, the output text is displayed.

```
MGlobal::displayInfo( txt );
```

8.2.3 POLYGONS

A polygon is a flat surface whose border is defined by a series of connected edges. Figure 8.3 shows a mesh with two polygons. For this example, both polygons have three edges and three vertices, though Maya places no limit on the number of edges or vertices in a polygon. It even allows polygons with multiple holes.

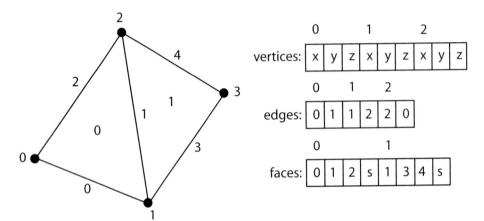

FIGURE 8.3 Polygons.

The terms *faces* and *polygons* can be used interchangeably. Maya defines a face in terms of edges. The **faces** array contains a list of edge indices that make up the face. Because an edge can be shared by multiple faces, an edge may not be unique to a particular face. The **faces** array is a long continuous array of edge indices. Only when Maya encounters a face-terminating index (shown as **s**, for "stop") does it know it has reached the end of a face and the beginning of a new one. Put another way, the process of iterating through all faces is done by starting at the first element of the **faces** array and then iterating through all elements until the special edge index is found. This marks the end of the current face. The element immediately following the face-terminating index is the first edge of the next face. The iteration of this face continues until the next face-terminating index is found. This process is repeated for all faces. It is pretty clear from this description that finding a particular face in a mesh with a lot of faces will take a long time, in that the iterator has to start at the beginning of the **faces** array each time.

Rather than employ this slow method for finding faces, another array is generated that is used to look up faces. This array is the **faceIndices** array. It has as many elements as there are faces. Each element is an index into the **faces** array. The element specifies the index of the start of a given face. The **faceIndices** array for the mesh is shown in Figure 8.4.

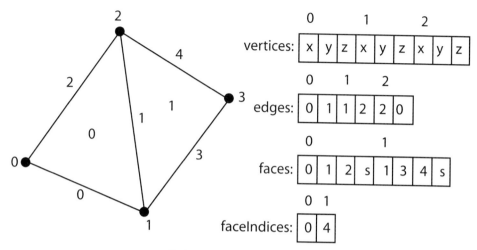

FIGURE 8.4 *faceIndices* array.

The **faceIndices** array has an index element for each face. The first element (index 0) contains the index 0. This indicates that the start of the first face is at index 0 in the **faces** array. The second element (index 1) contains the index 4. This indicates that the start of the second face is at index 4 in the **faces** array. Accessing faces is far faster now that this array has been built.

To get the second face in the mesh, rather than iterate through all elements in the **faces** array until reaching the second face, the start edge index can be accessed immediately using the **faceIndices** array. Although not shown here, Maya also stores the last edge index of each face in the **faceIndices** array. Being able to quickly determine the start and end indices of a given face in the **faces** array means that such calculations as the order (number of edges and vertices) can be done very quickly.

Fortunately, Maya hides the intricacies of these arrays from the developer, but instead provides conveniently more intuitive functions for manipulating faces. Each face is referenced by its face ID, which is simply its index in the total number of faces.

MEL

1. Open the **TwoPolygonMesh.ma** scene.

2. Select the **square** object.

3. To print out the mesh polygon data, execute the following.

```
string $sel[] = `ls -long -dag -selection -geometry`;
int $i, $j, $k;
for( $i=0; $i < size($sel); $i++ )
{
    string $node = $sel[$i];
    int $res[] = `polyEvaluate -face $node`;
    int $nFaces = $res[0];
    float $pos[3];
    int $vIndex;
    print ($node + " has " + $nFaces + " faces:\n");
    for( $j=0; $j < $nFaces; $j++ )
    {
        string $pi[] = `polyInfo -faceToVertex ($node + ".f[" + $j + "]")`;
        string $piParts[];
        tokenize $pi[0] $piParts;

        print ("Poly " + $j + "\n");
        print (" # Verts: " + (size($piParts)-2) + "\n");
        for( $k=2; $k < size($piParts); $k++ )
        {
            $vIndex = $piParts[$k];
            $pos = `pointPosition -world ($node + ".vtx[" + $vIndex + "]")`;
            print ( "  " + $vIndex + ": (" + $pos[0] + ", " + $pos[1] +
                        ", " + $pos[2] + ")\n");
        }
    }
}
```

The polygon data is printed out.

```
|square|squareShape has 2 faces:
Poly 0
 # Verts: 4
  0: (-7.502504913, -5.551115123e-016, -2.216297667)
  1: (-5.002504913, -5.551115123e-016, -2.216297667)
  4: (-5.002504913, 5.551115123e-016, -7.216297667)
  3: (-7.502504913, 5.551115123e-016, -7.216297667)
```

```
Poly 1
 # Verts: 4
 1: (-5.002504913, -5.551115123e-016, -2.216297667)
 2: (-2.502504913, -5.551115123e-016, -2.216297667)
 5: (-2.502504913,  5.551115123e-016, -7.216297667)
 4: (-5.002504913,  5.551115123e-016, -7.216297667)
```

As each selected mesh object is iterated over, its total number of faces is retrieved using the `polyEvaluate` command.

```
int $res[] = `polyEvaluate -face $node`;
int $nFaces = $res[0];
```

The faces in the mesh are looped over.

```
for( $j=0; $j < $nFaces; $j++ )
{
```

Using the `polyInfo` command, the indices of the vertices that make up the face are retrieved.

```
string $pi[] = `polyInfo -faceToVertex ($node + ".f[" + $j + "]")`;
```

The result of the `polyInfo` command is a string array of the following format:

```
"FACE 0: 0 1 4 3"
```

This string is tokenized using white-space delimiters into the `$piParts` array.

```
string $piParts[];
tokenize $pi[0] $piParts;
```

This results in an array of strings of the following form. It is clear that the first two elements of the array are not needed. All remaining elements (2 to size(array)-1) contain the vertex indices of the polygon.

```
["FACE", "0:", "0", "1", "4", "3"]
```

The polygon index (face ID) is then printed out.

```
print ("Poly " + $j + "\n");
```

The number of vertices in the polygon is calculated.

```
print (" # Verts: " + (size($piParts)-2) + "\n");
```

Each of the vertices in the polygon are then iterated over.

```
for( $k=2; $k < size($piParts); $k++ )
{
```

The index of the current vertex is retrieved.

```
$vIndex = $piParts[$k];
```

The world space position of the vertex is then calculated using the pointPosition command.

```
$pos = `pointPosition -world ($node + ".vtx[" + $vIndex + "]")`;
```

The vertex index and position are then printed out.

```
print ( " " + $vIndex + ": (" + $pos[0] + ", " + $pos[1] +
              ", " + $pos[2] + ")\n");
```

C++ API

The **MeshInfo3** plug-in demonstrates the following.

- Retrieving the selected mesh and mesh faces
- Accessing face information
- Printing out face information

The following section explores an example of its usage.

1. Open the **MeshInfo3** workspace.

2. Compile it and load the resulting meshInfo3 plug-in file in Maya.

3. Open the **TwoPolygonMesh.ma** scene.

4. Execute the following.

    ```
    select -r square;
    ```

    This selects the **square** object.

5. Execute the following.

    ```
    meshInfo3;
    ```

    The mesh faces are printed out.

    ```
    // Object: |square
    # Polygons: 2
    Poly 0
     # Verts: 4
     (-2.5, 0, 2.5) (0, 0, 2.5) (0, 0, -2.5) (-2.5, 0, -2.5)
    Poly 1
     # Verts: 4
     (0, 0, 2.5) (2.5, 0, 2.5) (2.5, 0, -2.5) (0, 0, -2.5)
    ```

6. Execute the following.

    ```
    select -r square.f[1];
    ```

    This selects the second face.

7. Execute the following.

    ```
    meshInfo3;
    ```

    The information about the second face is printed out.

    ```
    // Object: |square|squareShape
    # Polygons: 1
    Poly 1
     # Verts: 4
     (-5.002505, 0, -2.216298) (-2.502505, 0, -2.216298) (-2.502505, 0,
     -7.216298) (-5.002505, 0, -7.216298)
    ```

SOURCE CODE

Plug-in: `MeshInfo3`
File: `MeshInfo3Cmd.cpp`

```cpp
DeclareSimpleCommand( meshInfo3, "David Gould", "1.0" );

MStatus meshInfo3::doIt( const MArgList& args )
{
    MStatus stat = MS::kSuccess;

    MSelectionList selection;
    MGlobal::getActiveSelectionList( selection );

    MDagPath dagPath;
    MObject component;

    int i, polyCount, polyIndex, vertCount;
    MPoint p;

    MString txt;
    MItSelectionList iter( selection );
    for( ; !iter.isDone(); iter.next() )
    {
        iter.getDagPath( dagPath, component );

        MItMeshPolygon polyIter( dagPath, component, &stat );
        if( stat == MS::kSuccess )
        {
            txt += MString( "Object: " ) + dagPath.fullPathName() +
                    "\n";

            polyCount = polyIter.count();
            txt += MString("# Polygons: ") + polyCount + "\n";

            for( ; !polyIter.isDone(); polyIter.next() )
            {
                polyIndex = polyIter.index();
                txt += MString("Poly ") + polyIndex + "\n";

                vertCount = polyIter.polygonVertexCount();
                txt += MString(" # Verts: ") + vertCount + "\n";
```

```
                for( i=0; i < vertCount; i++ )
                {
                    p = polyIter.point( i, MSpace::kWorld );

                    txt += MString(" (") + p.x + ", " +
                            p.y + ", " + p.z + ")";
                }
                txt += "\n";
            }
        }
    }
    MGlobal::displayInfo( txt );

    return MS::kSuccess;
}
```

SOURCE CODE EXPLANATION

As with the previous **meshInfo** commands, the **meshInfo3** command is declared and its doIt function is then defined. The list of selected objects is iterated over and the dagPath and component variables are set to the currently selected object and any selected components.

The **MItMeshPolygon** class is used to iterate over a mesh's polygons. Like other mesh iterator classes it is initialized using the DAG path and component. The stat variable stores the result of the initialization.

```
        MItMeshPolygon polyIter( dagPath, component, &stat );
```

The stat variable is checked to determine if the currently selected item is compatible with the **MItMeshPolygon** class. Currently, objects of type **MS::kMesh** and **MS::kMeshPolygonComponent** are compatible with the class.

```
            if( stat == MS::kSuccess )
            {
```

The DAG path of the selected mesh is added to the output text.

```
            txt += MString( "Object: " ) + dagPath.fullPathName() +
                    "\n";
```

The total number of polygons in the mesh is retrieved using the `count` function. It is then formatted and included in the output text.

```
polyCount = polyIter.count();
txt += MString("# Polygons: ") + polyCount + "\n";
```

All polygons in the mesh are then iterated over.

```
for( ; !polyIter.isDone(); polyIter.next() )
{
```

The index of the polygon (face ID) is retrieved using the `index` function. It is important to remember that the index into the `point` function is the polygon-relative vertex index and not the vertex index into the mesh's vertex array. To convert a polygon-relative index into a mesh vertex index, use the `MItMeshPolygon::vertexIndex` function.

```
polyIndex = polyIter.index();
txt += MString("Poly ") + polyIndex + "\n";
```

The `polyVertexCount` function is used to determine the total number of vertices in the current polygon.

```
vertCount = polyIter.polygonVertexCount();
txt += MString(" # Verts: ") + vertCount + "\n";
```

Each vertex in the polygon is then iterated over.

```
for( i=0; i < vertCount; i++ )
{
```

The world space position of the ith vertex is retrieved and then added to the output text.

```
p = polyIter.point( i, MSpace::kWorld );
txt += MString(" (") + p.x + ", " +
       p.y + ", " + p.z + ")";
}
```

Once all selected items have been iterated over, the output text is then printed out.

```
MGlobal::displayInfo( txt );
```

8.2.4 FACE VERTICES

It is common to associate various data with a vertex. Each vertex can have an associated color, normal, uv coordinates, and so on. In Figure 8.5, an individual color is associated with each vertex. For simplicity of explanation, a `colors` array is shown. Maya doesn't store colors in this way but it helps to understand conceptually how data can be associated with vertices.

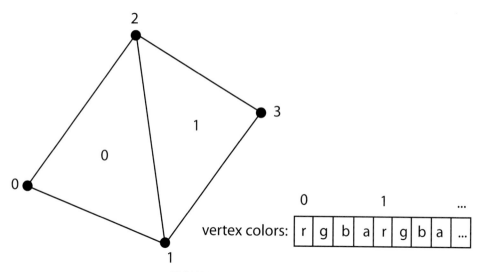

FIGURE 8.5 Per-vertex color.

To retrieve the color associated with a vertex, the **color** array is indexed using the vertex index. Thus, the color of the second vertex is retrieved as follows.

```
vertex_colors[1]
```

A similar array would be created for associating normals, uv coordinates, and any other data with the mesh vertices. If the mesh were rendered using the colors at the vertices, both face 0 and face 1 would share the colors at vertex 1 and vertex 2.

Changing the color for vertex 2 would change the color of both faces because they both share this same vertex. Because this vertex has only a single color associated with it, both faces automatically use this single color.

What if you wanted each face to be rendered with its own separate color? With the current structure, it isn't possible to render face 0 in red and face 1 in green. What is needed is a way of associating a color with both the face and its vertices. There needs to be a distinction between data associated with a given vertex and data associated with a face and its vertices. This distinction is created using *face vertices*. A face vertex is a means of uniquely referencing a vertex within a face.

The same mesh is now presented in Figure 8.6 with the vertex colors shown in face-vertex format. It is important to note that although the faces appear in the figure as separate distinct faces they are still attached, as before. They are conceptually separate but not physically separate.

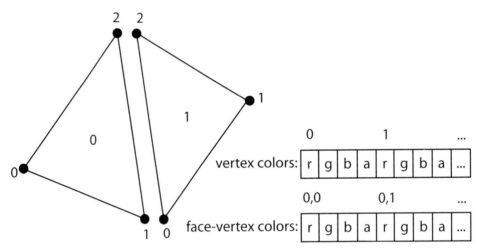

FIGURE 8.6 Face-vertex colors.

The vertex colors are still available, and thus it is still possible to associate a single color with a vertex and thereby have all faces around the vertex use it. With the **face-vertex colors** array, it is now possible to associate an individual color with a given vertex within a face.

As before, there are two faces, 0 and 1. Each face has its own separate sequences of vertices 0 to 2. Indices into these vertex arrays are referred to as *face-relative vertex*

IDs. These are distinct from vertex IDs that have been described so far. Those vertex IDs are indices into the mesh's vertex array.

The range of mesh-relative vertex IDs is 0 to `numberOfVerticesInMesh-1`. The range of face-relative vertexIDs depends on the face being referenced. Its range is 0 to `numberOfVerticesInFace-1`. To retrieve the color of the third vertex in the mesh, the mesh-relative vertex ID of 2 would be used.

```
vertex_colors [2]
```

To retrieve the color of the second vertex (index 1) in the second face (index 1), the face-vertex index of 1, 1 is first converted into a mesh-relative vertex ID and face pair. The face-relative vertex ID (1) is mapped to its mesh-relative vertex ID (3). The face index remains the same.

```
face_vertex_colors[ (3,1) ]
```

As such, any data associated with a face vertex is referenced using both the mesh-relative vertex ID and the face ID. It is important to note that internally Maya doesn't keep track of colors per vertex. When setting the color of a vertex, all face-relative vertices associated with the vertex have their color set.

MEL

1. Open the **TwoPolygonMesh.ma** scene.

   The following steps will display the colors assigned to the vertices.

2. Select **Shading | Smooth Shading All** from the **persp** viewport's menu.

3. Select the **square** object.

4. Select the option box next to **Display | Custom Polygon Display**.

   The **Custom Polygon Display Option** dialog box is displayed.

5. In the **Color** section, turn on the **Color In Shaded Display** option.

6. Set the **Color Material Channel** to **None**.

7. Click on the **Apply and Close** button.

   The mesh is now displayed in black because all the vertices are assigned a color (0,0,0), which is alpha 1 by default.

8. Execute the following.

```
select -r square.vtx[4];
```

The fifth vertex is selected. This is a common vertex to both faces.

9. Execute the following.

```
polyColorPerVertex -rgb 1 1 0;
```

The vertex's color is set to yellow. Because this vertex is shared by both faces, they are both colored yellow around this common vertex. To have the faces use distinct colors, the color will have to be assigned to the face vertex and not the vertex.

10. Right click in the **square** object, and then select **Vertex Faces** from the marking menu.

11. Execute the following.

```
select -r square.vtxFace[4][1] ;
```

This selects the vertex in the top left-hand corner of the second face.

12. Execute the following.

```
polyColorPerVertex -rgb 1 0 1;
```

This sets the face-vertex color to magenta.

13. Right click in the **square** object, and then select **Object Mode**.

The **square** object is now displayed with distinct colors for the two faces. To query the face-vertex colors, use the `polyColorPerVertex` command in query mode.

14. Execute the following.

```
select -r square.vtxFace["*"]["*"];
polyColorPerVertex -q -r -g -b -a;
```

This selects all face vertices in the **square** object. The red, green, blue, and alpha channels are then queried. An array of floats is returned containing the face-vertex colors.

```
// Result: 0 0 0 1 0 0 0 1 1 1 0 1 1 1 0 1 1 1 0 1 1 1 0 1 1 1 0 1 1
0 1 1 //
```

15. Execute the following.

```
select -r square.vtx["*"];
polyColorPerVertex -q -r -g -b -a;
```

This selects all vertices in the **square** object. The result of querying of the colors follows.

```
// Result: 0 0 0 0 0 0 0 0 0 0 0 0 0 0 1 0.5 0.5 1 0 0 0 0 //
```

Note that the colors are different from the face-vertex colors.

C++ API

The **MeshInfo4** plug-in demonstrates the following.

- Retrieving the selected mesh-face vertices
- Accessing face-vertex information (mesh-relative vertex IDs, face-relative vertex IDs, color, and so on)
- Printing out face-vertex information

1. Open the **MeshInfo4** workspace.
2. Compile it and load the resulting `meshInfo4` plug-in file in Maya.
3. Open the **TwoPolygonMesh.ma** scene.

   The next set of steps will display the colors assigned to the vertices.

4. Select **Shading | Smooth Shading All** from the **persp** viewport's menu.
5. Select the **square** object.
6. Select the option box next to **Display | Custom Polygon Display**.

   The **Custom Polygon Display Option** dialog box is displayed.

7. In the **Color** section, turn on the **Color In Shaded Display** option.

8. Set the **Color Material Channel** to **None**.

9. Click on the **Apply and Close** button.

    The mesh is now displayed in black because all vertices are assigned a color (0,0,0), which is alpha 1 by default.

10. Execute the following.

```
select -r square.vtxFace[4][0];
polyColorPerVertex -rgb 1 1 0;
select -r square.vtxFace[4][1];
polyColorPerVertex -rgb 1 0 1;
```

    This sets the first face vertex's color to yellow and the second face vertex's color to magenta.

11. Execute the following.

```
select -r square.f["*"];
```

    This selects all faces in the **square** object. The individual faces of the mesh need to be selected for the command to work. The reason for this limitation is explained in material to follow.

12. Execute the following.

```
meshInfo4;
```

    The face-vertex information is printed out. The complete DAG path of the selected object is printed first. For each face vertex the mesh-relative vertex ID and face-relative vertex ID are printed out. If the face vertex has a color, it is also printed out.

```
// Object: |square|squareShape
 Face 0: mesh-relative-vertexID (0), face-relative-vertexID (0)
 no color
 Face 0: mesh-relative-vertexID (1), face-relative-vertexID (1)
 no color
```

```
Face 0: mesh-relative-vertexID (4), face-relative-vertexID (2)
Color: 1, 1, 0
Face 0: mesh-relative-vertexID (3), face-relative-vertexID (3)
no color
Face 1: mesh-relative-vertexID (1), face-relative-vertexID (0)
no color
Face 1: mesh-relative-vertexID (2), face-relative-vertexID (1)
no color
Face 1: mesh-relative-vertexID (5), face-relative-vertexID (2)
no color
Face 1: mesh-relative-vertexID (4), face-relative-vertexID (3)
Color: 1, 0, 1
```

Note that where a face-vertex color wasn't explicitly set there is no color. In addition, all face-relative vertex IDs vary from 0 to 3, as you would expect given that each face has four vertices.

SOURCE CODE

Plug-in: MeshInfo4
File: MeshInfo4Cmd.cpp

```cpp
DeclareSimpleCommand( meshInfo4, "David Gould", "1.0" );

MStatus meshInfo4::doIt( const MArgList& args )
{
    MStatus stat = MS::kSuccess;

    MSelectionList selection;
    MGlobal::getActiveSelectionList( selection );

    MDagPath dagPath;
    MObject component;

    MColor c;

    MString txt;
    MItSelectionList iter( selection );
    for( ; !iter.isDone(); iter.next() )
    {
        iter.getDagPath( dagPath, component );
```

```
MItMeshFaceVertex fvIter( dagPath, component, &stat );
if( stat == MS::kSuccess )
{
      txt += MString( "Object: " ) + dagPath.fullPathName() +
            "\n";
      for( ; !fvIter.isDone(); fvIter.next() )
      {
            int vertId = fvIter.vertId();
            int faceId = fvIter.faceId();
            int faceVertId = fvIter.faceVertId();

            txt += MString(" Face ") + faceId +
                  ": mesh-relative-vertexID (" + vertId +
                  "), face-relative-vertexID (" + faceVertId +
                  ")\n";

            if( fvIter.hasColor() )
            {
                  fvIter.getColor( c );
                  txt += MString(" Color: ") +
                        c.r + ", " + c.g + ", " + c.b + "\n";
            }
            else
                  txt += MString(" no color\n");
      }
}
MGlobal::displayInfo( txt );

return MS::kSuccess;
}
```

SOURCE CODE EXPLANATION

The command follows the same methods as the other **meshInfo** commands. Once the DAG path and component of the currently selected object are retrieved, they are used to intialize the **MItMeshFaceVertex** class. This class is used to iterate over all face vertices in a mesh. Maya's current implementation of **MItMeshFaceVertex** doesn't allow a mesh with no components to be passed to the constructor. An **MS::kFailure** results. Only face components (**MFn::kMeshPolygonComponent**) are supported by this class. As such, all faces in the mesh must be selected before the command is run. This limitation may be removed in later versions of Maya.

```
MItMeshFaceVertex fvIter( dagPath, component, &stat );
if( stat == MS::kSuccess )
{
```

The complete DAG path of the selected object is added to the output text.

```
txt += MString( "Object: " ) + dagPath.fullPathName() +
       "\n";
```

All face vertices are iterated over.

```
for( ; !fvIter.isDone(); fvIter.next() )
{
```

The mesh-relative vertex ID is retrieved using the `vertId` function.

```
int vertId = fvIter.vertId();
```

The `faceId` function is used to retrieve the face ID of the current face.

```
int faceId = fvIter.faceId();
```

The face-relative vertex ID is retrieved using the `faceVertID` function.

```
int faceVertId = fvIter.faceVertId();
```

The data is formatted and then added to the output text.

```
txt += MString(" Face ") + faceId +
       ": mesh-relative-vertexID (" + vertId +
       "), face-relative-vertexID (" + faceVertId +
       ")\n";
```

Because a face vertex will not have a color unless it has been explicitly assigned one, it is necessary to test if a color exists.

```
if( fvIter.hasColor() )
{
```

The face-vertex color is retrieved.

```
fvIter.getColor( c );
```

The color data is formatted and then appended to the output text.

```
txt += MString(" Color: ") +
    c.r + ", " + c.g + ", " + c.b + "\n";
```

If there is no face-vertex color, "no color" is output.

```
}
else
    txt += MString(" no color\n");
```

8.2.5 NORMALS

A normal is, traditionally, a vector that is perpendicular to a surface. It often has a unit length. It is often used to determine the sidedness of a face; that is, which side of a face is inside and which is outside. The most common use of normals is for the shading of a surface. A polygonal sphere, though having a faceted geometric surface, can be rendered as a smooth surface by assigning smooth normals to the surface.

Maya extends the concept of normals to allow them to be set to any direction. In addition, normals can be associated with different components: faces, vertices, and face vertices. Figure 8.7 shows the face normal for the faces of a polygonal cube. Face normals are also called *geometric normals* because they are calculated by determining the vector that is perpendicular to the face.

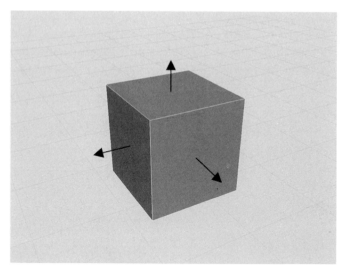

FIGURE 8.7 Face normal.

It is also possible to associate a normal with each vertex. These normals are referred to as vertex normals. The vertex normals for a cube are shown in Figure 8.8. Because the normal is associated with a vertex, all faces that share the vertex can use the normal.

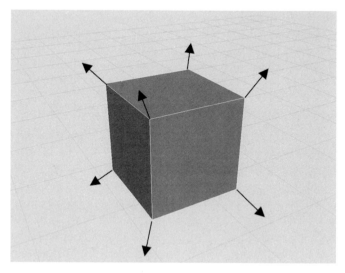

FIGURE 8.8 Vertex normal.

The last type of normal supported by meshes is the face-vertex normal. This allows a normal to be associated with a given vertex in a face. Because these normals are specific to a face, they allow for precise control of lighting and shading per face. The face-vertex normals shown in Figure 8.9 are color coded based on the color of the face they are associated with.

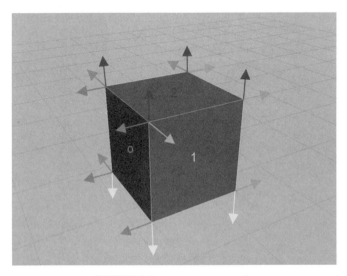

FIGURE 8.9 Face-vertex normals.

By default, the various types of normals are calculated automatically by Maya. If the mesh vertices are moved, the normals are automatically recalculated.

Face normals are calculated to be perpendicular to the underlying face surface. If the face is nonplanar, an average face normal is used. Vertex normals are calculated as the average of the face normals for all faces that share the vertex. As a result, vertex normals point directly outward from vertices in an average direction to all surrounding faces. Face-vertex normals are automatically set to the vertex normal of the face they are associated with.

There may be circumstances in which the normals will need to point in a specific direction. Both vertex normals and face-vertex normals can be set to an explicit direction. This can be done to simulate hard or soft edges when rendering the surface. Face normals can't be set but always point outward perpendicularly from the face. Alternatively, a vertex normal or face-vertex normal can be locked. If either type of normal is set to an explicit direction or is locked, Maya no longer automatically recalculates its direction.

MEL

1. Open the **CubeMesh.ma** scene.

   To better understand the various types of normals, the cube will be displayed with its face and face-vertex normals.

2. Select the **cube** object.

3. Select the option box in **Display | Custom Polygon Display.**

   The **Custom Polygon Display Options** dialog box is displayed.

4. In the **Vertices** section, turn on the **Normals** option.

5. In the **Face** section, turn on the **Normals** option.

6. Click on the **Apply and Close** button.

   The face normals are displayed in the center of the faces. The face-vertex normals are displayed outward from their respective associated vertex.

7. Execute the following.

   ```
   select -r cube.f[0];
   ```

   This selects the first face of the cube.

8. Execute the following.

   ```
   polyInfo -faceNormals;
   ```

   This calculates the face normal for the selected face. The result is returned as a string.

   ```
   // Result: FACE_NORMAL 0: 0.000000 0.000000 1.000000
   ```

9. Right click on the **cube** object, and then select **Vertex Faces** from the marking menu.

   This last step isn't strictly necessary, in that the selection will be done with MEL. Being able to see the face vertices helps in visualizing which vertex is being selected.

10. Execute the following.

```
select -r cube.vtxFace[3][0];
```

This selects the fourth vertex (3) of the first face, 0. Note that the fourth face-relative vertex ID (3) corresponds to the fourth mesh-relative vertex ID, 3.

11. Execute the following.

```
polyNormalPerVertex -q -xyz;
```

The face-vertex normal is retrieved.

```
// Result: 0 0 1 //
```

12. Right click on the **cube** object, and then select **Vertex** from the marking menu.

13. Execute the following.

```
select -r cube.vtx[3];
```

This selects the fourth vertex in the cube.

14. Execute the following.

```
polyNormalPerVertex -q -xyz;
```

This queries the face-vertex normals of the selected vertex. An array of floats with the x-y-z coordinates of the face-vertex normals is returned.

```
// Result: 1 0 0 0 0 1 0 1 0 //
```

Even though the vertex was selected and not the face vertex, the polyNormalPerVertex command returns all face-vertex normals. There is currently no MEL command to directly retrieve the vertex normal for a given vertex. However, it is possible to calculate it. The vertex normal is the result of adding all face normals of the faces that share the vertex and then averaging the sum.

15. Execute the following.

```
string $pi[] = `polyInfo -vertexToFace`;
string $piParts[];
tokenize $pi[0] $piParts;
int $i;
int $faceID;
vector $vNorm = 0;
vector $fNorm;
string $pi2[], $piParts2[];
for( $i=2; $i < size($piParts); $i++)
{
    $faceID = $piParts[$i];
    $pi2 = `polyInfo -faceNormals ("cube.f[" + $faceID +"]")`;
    tokenize $pi2[0] $piParts2;
    $fNorm = << float($piParts2[2]),
                float($piParts2[3]),
                float($piParts2[4]) >>;
    $vNorm += $fNorm;
}
$vNorm = `unit $vNorm`;
print $vNorm;
```

The vertex normal of the selected vertex is calculated and then printed out.

```
0.57735 0.57735 -0.57735
```

Given the selected vertex, the faces that share the vertex are determined.

```
string $pi[] = `polyInfo -vertexToFace`;
```

The resulting string from the polyInfo command has the following format.

```
"VERTEX 3: 1 0 4"
```

This string is broken down into its parts.

```
string $piParts[];
tokenize $pi[0] $piParts;
```

The $vNorm vector is initialized to 0. This vector will keep the sum of all face normals.

```
vector $vNorm = 0;
```

Each of the parts is then iterated over. Because the first and second elements are not needed, the loop starts from the third element (index 2).

```
for( $i=2; $i < size($piParts); $i++)
{
```

The index of the face is retrieved from the $piParts array.

```
$faceID = $piParts[$i];
```

The face normal for the given face is then calculated using the polyInfo command.

```
$pi2 = `polyInfo -faceNormals ("cube.f[" + $faceID +"]")`;
```

The resulting string is of the following format.

```
"FACE_NORMAL 1: 0.000000 1.000000 0.000000"
```

This string is broken into parts.

```
tokenize $pi2[0] $piParts2;
```

The last three elements of the $parts2 array are used to create the face-normal vector.

```
$fNorm = << float($piParts2[2]),
    float($piParts2[3]),
    float($piParts2[4]) >>;
```

The face-normal vector is added to the current sum of face-normal vectors.

```
    $vNorm += $fNorm;
}
```

The `$vNorm` contains the sum of all face-normal vectors. It now needs to be normalized to produce the final average vector.

```
    $vNorm = `unit $vNorm`;
```

The final vertex normal is printed out.

```
    print $vNorm;
```

C++ API

The **MeshInfo5** plug-in demonstrates the following.

- Retrieving the selected mesh vertices and face vertices
- Accessing face-vertex information
- Accessing face-normal, vertex-normal, and face-relative normal information
- Printing out normal information

1. Open the **MeshInfo5** workspace.
2. Compile it and load the resulting `meshInfo5` plug-in file in Maya.
3. Open the **CubeMesh.ma** scene.

   To better understand the various types of normals, the cube will be displayed with its face and face-vertex normals.

4. Select the **cube** object.
5. Select the option box in **Display | Custom Polygon Display**.

   The **Custom Polygon Display Options** dialog box is displayed.

6. In the **Vertices** section, turn on the **Normals** option.

7. In the **Face** section, turn on the **Normals** option.

8. Click on the **Apply and Close** button.

   The face normals are displayed in the center of the faces. The face-vertex normals are displayed outward from their respective associated vertex.

9. Execute the following.

```
select -r cube.vtx[3];
```

   This selects the fourth vertex in the cube.

10. Execute the following.

```
meshInfo5;
```

The various normals associated directly and indirectly with the vertex are printed out. All faces connected to the vertex are taken into consideration. First, the face ID, vertex ID, and face-relative vertex ID are printed. Next, the face normal for the face (face ID), the vertex normal for the vertex (vertex ID), and the face-vertex normal (face-relative vertex ID) are printed out. These printouts are repeated for all faces that share this vertex.

```
// Object: |cube|cubeShape
 Face: 4 Vertex: 3 Face-Vertex: 3
 Face Normal: (1, 0, 0)
 Vertex Normal: (0.57735, 0.57735, 0.57735)
 Face-Vertex Normal: (1, 0, 0)
 Face: 0 Vertex: 3 Face-Vertex: 2
 Face Normal: (0, 0, 1)
 Vertex Normal: (0.57735, 0.57735, 0.57735)
 Face-Vertex Normal: (0, 0, 1)
 Face: 1 Vertex: 3 Face-Vertex: 1
 Face Normal: (0, 1, 0)
```

```
Vertex Normal: (0.57735, 0.57735, 0.57735)
Face-Vertex Normal: (0, 1, 0)
```

The command also prints out the normal data if one or more meshes and/or mesh faces are selected.

SOURCE CODE

Plug-in: `MeshInfo5`
File: `MeshInfo5Cmd.cpp`

```cpp
void addData( MString &txt,
                const int fIndex,
                const int vIndex,
                const int fvIndex,
                const MVector &fNormal,
                const MVector &vNormal,
                const MVector &fvNormal
                )
{
    txt += MString(" Face: ") + fIndex + " Vertex: " + vIndex +
        " Face-Vertex: " + fvIndex + "\n";
    txt += MString(" Face Normal: (") +
        fNormal.x + ", " + fNormal.y + ", " + fNormal.z + ")\n";
    txt += MString(" Vertex Normal: (") +
        vNormal.x + ", " + vNormal.y + ", " + vNormal.z + ")\n";
    txt += MString(" Face-Vertex Normal: (") +
        fvNormal.x + ", " + fvNormal.y + ", " + fvNormal.z + ")\n";
}

DeclareSimpleCommand( meshInfo5, "David Gould", "1.0" );

MStatus meshInfo5::doIt( const MArgList& args )
{
    MStatus stat = MS::kSuccess;

    MSelectionList selection;
    MGlobal::getActiveSelectionList( selection );

    MDagPath dagPath;
    MObject component;
```

```
unsigned int i, nVerts;
int fIndex, vIndex, fvIndex;
MVector fNormal, vNormal, fvNormal;

MString txt;
MItSelectionList iter( selection );
for( ; !iter.isDone(); iter.next() )
{
    iter.getDagPath( dagPath, component );

    MFnMesh meshFn( dagPath );

    MItMeshPolygon faceIter( dagPath, component, &stat );
    if( stat == MS::kSuccess )
    {
        txt += MString( "Object: " ) + dagPath.fullPathName() +
            "\n";

        for( ; !faceIter.isDone(); faceIter.next() )
        {
            nVerts = faceIter.polygonVertexCount();

            for( i=0; i < nVerts; i++ )
            {
                fvIndex = i;
                fIndex = faceIter.index();
                vIndex = faceIter.vertexIndex( i );

                faceIter.getNormal( fNormal );
                meshFn.getVertexNormal( vIndex, vNormal );
                faceIter.getNormal( fvIndex, fvNormal );

                addData( txt, fIndex, vIndex,
                    fvIndex, fNormal, vNormal,
                    fvNormal );
            }
        }
    }
    else
    {
        MItMeshVertex vertIter( dagPath, component, &stat );
```

```
                    if( stat == MS::kSuccess )
                    {
                        txt += MString( "Object: " )
                            + dagPath.fullPathName() + "\n";

                    MIntArray faceIds;
                    MIntArray vertIds;

                    for( ; !vertIter.isDone(); vertIter.next() )
                    {
                        vIndex = vertIter.index();

                        vertIter.getNormal( vNormal );
                        vertIter.getConnectedFaces( faceIds );

                        for( i=0; i < faceIds.length(); i++ )
                        {
                            fIndex = faceIds[i];

                            meshFn.getPolygonNormal( fIndex, fNormal );
                            meshFn.getFaceVertexNormal( fIndex,
                                                vIndex, fvNormal );
                            meshFn.getPolygonVertices( fIndex,
                                                            vertIds );

                            for( fvIndex = 0;
                                fvIndex < int(vertIds.length());
                                fvIndex++ )
                            {
                                if( vertIds[fvIndex] == vIndex )
                                    break;
                            }
                            addData( txt, fIndex, vIndex, fvIndex,
                                    fNormal, vNormal, fvNormal );
                        }
                    }
                }
            }

        MGlobal::displayInfo( txt );

        return MS::kSuccess;
}
```

SOURCE CODE EXPLANATION

The **meshInfo5** command is implemented in a manner similar to that for the other **meshInfo** commands. The addData function is defined to take a series of indices and normals and add them to the text string.

```
void addData( MString &txt,
               const int fIndex,
               const int vIndex,
               const int fvIndex,
               const MVector &fNormal,
               const MVector &vNormal,
               const MVector &fvNormal
)
{
    txt += MString(" Face: ") + fIndex + " Vertex: " + vIndex +
        " Face-Vertex: " + fvIndex + "\n";
    txt += MString(" Face Normal: (") +
        fNormal.x + ", " + fNormal.y + ", " + fNormal.z + ")\n";
    txt += MString(" Vertex Normal: (") +
        vNormal.x + ", " + vNormal.y + ", " + vNormal.z + ")\n";
    txt += MString(" Face-Vertex Normal: (") +
        fvNormal.x + ", " + fvNormal.y + ", " + fvNormal.z + ")\n";
}
```

Once the DAG path and component of the currently selected object are stored, an instance of the **MFnMesh** class is constructed. The **MFnMesh** class is the main class for creating and editing meshes. Because there is some mesh data that can't be retrieved using the mesh iterators alone, this class will be used to retrieve that data.

```
MFnMesh meshFn( dagPath );
```

The **MItMeshPolygon** class is instantiated with the current DAG path and components. Its constructor will return a successful status if the DAG path is a mesh or mesh face.

```
MItMeshPolygon faceIter( dagPath, component, &stat );
if( stat == MS::kSuccess )
{
```

The complete path to the selected object is added to the output text.

```
txt += MString( "Object: " ) + dagPath.fullPathName() +
    "\n";
```

All selected faces are then iterated over.

```
for( ; !faceIter.isDone(); faceIter.next() )
{
```

The number of vertices in the face is retrieved.

```
nVerts = faceIter.polygonVertexCount();
```

All face vertices are then iterated over.

```
for( i=0; i < nVerts; i++ )
{
```

The face-relative vertex ID is the index in the face's list of vertices.

```
fvIndex = i;
```

The face ID is retrieved using the `index` function.

```
fIndex = faceIter.index();
```

The mesh-relative vertex ID is determined using the `vertexIndex` function. It takes the face-relative vertex ID and returns the mesh-relative vertex ID.

```
vIndex = faceIter.vertexIndex( i );
```

The face normal is calculated using the `getNormal` function.

```
faceIter.getNormal( fNormal );
```

The **MItMeshPolygon** iterator class doesn't have a function to get the vertex normal for a given vertex. The **MFnMesh** class is used instead because it has access to the entire mesh. The getVertexNormal function returns the vertex normal given the mesh-relative vertex ID.

```
meshFn.getVertexNormal( vIndex, vNormal );
```

The face-vertex normal is retrieved using the face-relative vertex ID.

```
faceIter.getNormal( fvIndex, fvNormal );
```

With all of the various normal data now retrieved, it can be added to the text string using the addData function.

```
addData( txt, fIndex, vIndex, fvIndex,
         fNormal, vNormal, fvNormal );
```

If the selection wasn't a mesh or mesh face, the next section of code is run.

```
else
{
```

If the selection is a mesh vertex, the **MItMeshVertex** class will iterate over it.

```
MItMeshVertex vertIter( dagPath, component, &stat );
if( stat == MS::kSuccess )
{
```

The complete path to the selected object is appended to the text string.

```
txt += MString( "Object: " )
       + dagPath.fullPathName() + "\n";
```

A list of all faces associated with the selected vertex and a list of all mesh-relative vertex IDs in the face will be needed. The two arrays, faceIds and vertIds, will provide storage for these lists.

```
MIntArray faceIds;
MIntArray vertIds;
```

Each vertex in the selection is iterated over.

```
for( ; !vertIter.isDone(); vertIter.next() )
{
```

The mesh-relative vertex ID of the vertex is retrieved.

```
vIndex = vertIter.index();
```

The vertex normal is retrieved using the `getNormal` function.

```
vertIter.getNormal( vNormal );
```

Because the **MItMeshVertex** class is designed to iterate over vertices, it doesn't have explicit functions for working with the faces associated with the vertex. Instead, the list of all faces that share the vertex is retrieved using the `getConnectedFaces` function. This list will be used later by the **MFnMesh** class.

```
vertIter.getConnectedFaces( faceIds );
```

All associated faces are iterated over.

```
for( i=0; i < faceIds.length(); i++ )
{
```

The face ID is simply the face index of the current face.

```
fIndex = faceIds[i];
```

The **MFnMesh**'s `getPolygonNormal` function is used to retreive the face normal.

```
meshFn.getPolygonNormal( fIndex,
                         fNormal );
```

The **MFnMesh** class is used to get the face-vertex normal. The **MFnMesh**'s getFaceVertexNormal function is used to retrieve the face-vertex normal using the face ID and mesh-relative vertex ID.

```
meshFn.getFaceVertexNormal( fIndex,
                  vIndex, fvNormal );
```

Although the mesh-relative vertex ID is known, what is the face-relative vertex ID? Because the **MItMeshVertex** class iterates across all vertices without regard to faces, this vertex ID has to be calculated. The getPolygonVertices function returns a list of mesh-relative vertex IDs for the given face. For each mesh-relative vertex ID in the array, its array position is the face-relative vertex ID.

```
meshFn.getPolygonVertices( fIndex,
                  vertIds );
```

The mesh-relative vertex ID for the current vertex is already known. It is now just a simple process of iterating through the vertIds list and determining the index of the matching vertex ID. The index of the matching vertex ID in the vertIds list is the face-relative vertex ID.

```
for( fvIndex=0;
     fvIndex < int(vertIds.length());
     fvIndex++ )
{
    if( vertIds[fvIndex] == vIndex )
        break;
}
```

With the data now calculated, it is passed to the addData function for formatting and inclusion in the output text.

```
addData( txt, fIndex, vIndex,
         fvIndex, fNormal, vNormal,
         fvNormal );
```

As always, the final output string is displayed using the displayInfo function.

```
MGlobal::displayInfo( txt );
```

8.2.6 UV TEXTURE COORDINATES

A mesh can be assigned uv texture coordinates. Texture coordinates have a u and v coordinate that provide a 2D mapping onto a surface. The u and v coordinates are synonymous with x and y coordinates. They are named differently to easily distinguish between a texture coordinate (u, v) and a cartesian coordinate (x, y). Because the texture coordinates are 2D, they specify a location within a 2D image. By assigning a region of uv coordinates to a surface, a region of an image can be mapped to the surface.

The texture coordinates are stored as in a single **uvs** array. Figure 8.10 shows the texture coordinates array for a mesh with four vertices.

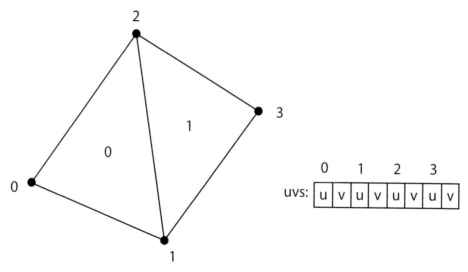

FIGURE 8.10 Vertex uv texture coordinates.

Each uv coordinate has an index in the **uvs** array. This index is referred to as the uv coordinate's *uvID*. Because each vertex has a single uv coordinate, their associated faces will use these shared uv coordinates when mapping an image onto their surface. This is fine if a continuous mapping across the surface is required, but there are cases in which separate faces may require their own individual mappings. *Face-vertex uv coordinates* are used to assign a distinct uv coordinate to a given vertex in a face.

The face-vertex uv coordinates use the same **uvs** array as the vertex uvs. In fact, this single **uvs** array is used for all uv coordinates in the mesh. As the face-vertex uv coordinates are created they are simply appended to the **uvs** array, as shown in Figure 8.11. The first four elements of the array were used by the vertex uvs, and thus the first face-vertex uv is the fifth element (index 4). A **faceUVIDs** array holds the uv IDs for the individual face vertices. This array has the same layout as the **faces** array, except that rather than storing edge indices it stores uv indices (uv IDs). Because it has the same layout as the **faces** array, it can use the **faceIndices** lookup array to quickly determine the start of each face list.

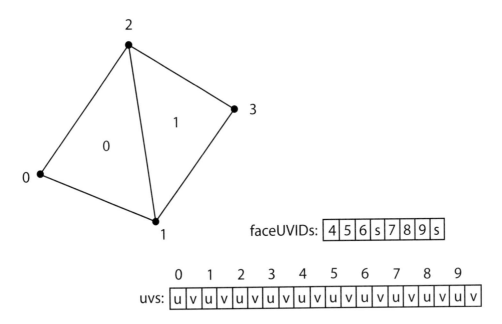

FIGURE 8.11 Face-vertex uv texture coordinates.

Not all meshes will have vertex uvs, and thus the **uvs** array could contain just face-vertex uvs, and vice versa. If a mesh-vertex is assigned a uv ID, all face vertices associated with the mesh vertex are also assigned the same uv ID. It is possible for different face vertices to refer to the same uv coordinate by having the same uv ID. Fortunately, Maya hides these details and allows access of various uvs via convenience functions.

It is possible that a face needs multiple uv mappings. Take for instance a face that is rendered with a landscape image. On top of this image there needs to be overlaid an image with some text. The way the landscape image is placed on the face may be different from how the text image is placed on the face. The text may need to be smaller and placed at the top. What is needed is a set of uv mappings for the landscape image and another set for the text image. Maya supports different sets of mappings by using *uv sets*. A mesh can contain any number of uv sets. Each uv set contains a separate series of uv coordinates. Although there may be multiple uv sets in a mesh, a single uv set is set to be the active one. All texturing operations operate on the active uv set of a mesh.

MEL

1. Open the **TwoPolygonMesh.ma** scene.

2. Select the **square** object.

3. Execute the following.

```
polyUVSet -q -allUVSets;
```

The list of uv sets in the mesh is printed out.

```
// Result: map1 map2 //
```

4. Execute the following.

```
polyUVSet -q -currentUVSet;
```

The currently active uv set is returned.

```
// Result: map1 //
```

5. Execute the following.

```
select -r square.map["*"] ;
polyEditUV -q -u -v;
```

This selects all uv coordinates and prints them out. The `polyEditUV` command only works on selected uvs. It doesn't operate on entire meshes or other components (vertices, faces, edges, and so on).

```
// Result: 0 0 0.5 0 1 0 0 1 0.5 1 1 1 //
```

C++ API

The **MeshInfo6** plug-in demonstrates the following.

- Retrieving the selected meshes and mesh vertices
- Accessing uv texturing information (uv sets, current uv set, face-vertex uvs, vertex uvs)
- Printing out the uv texturing information

1. Open the **MeshInfo6** workspace.
2. Compile it and load the resulting `meshInfo6` plug-in file in Maya.
3. Open the **TwoPolygonMesh.ma** scene.
4. Select the **square** object.
5. Execute the following.

```
meshInfo6;
```

All uv set information and uv texture coordinates for each of the mesh vertices are printed out. Note that the vertex indices are face relative.

```
// Object: |square
UV Set: map1 # UVs: 6
UV Set: map2 # UVs: 0
Current UV Set: map1
Vertex: 0
Vertex UV: (0, 0)
Face-vertex UV: face,vertex: (0, 0) uv: (0, 0)
Vertex: 1
Vertex UV: (0.5, 0)
Face-vertex UV: face,vertex: (0, 1) uv: (0.5, 0)
Face-vertex UV: face,vertex: (1, 0) uv: (0.5, 0)
```

```
Vertex: 2
Vertex UV: (1, 0)
Face-vertex UV: face,vertex: (1, 1) uv: (1, 0)
Vertex: 3
Vertex UV: (0, 1)
Face-vertex UV: face,vertex: (0, 3) uv: (0, 1)
Vertex: 4
Vertex UV: (0.5, 1)
Face-vertex UV: face,vertex: (1, 3) uv: (0.5, 1)
Face-vertex UV: face,vertex: (0, 2) uv: (0.5, 1)
Vertex: 5
Vertex UV: (1, 1)
Face-vertex UV: face,vertex: (1, 2) uv: (1, 1)
```

The **square** plane has six vertices. Because vertices, indexed by 3 and 4, are common to both faces they have two face-vertex uvs. For instance, vertex 4 shares the same uv texture coordinate as face-vertices (1, 3) and (0, 2). More precisely, they share the same uv ID and therefore all refer to the same uv in the **uvs** array.

6. Execute the following.

```
polyUVSet -currentUVSet -uvSet "map2";
```

This sets the current uv set to **map2**.

7. Execute the following.

```
meshInfo6;
```

The uv coordinates for the mesh are printed out once again. Because the current uv set doesn't have any uv coordinates, there are no uv coordinates assigned to any of the vertices.

```
// Object: |square
 UV Set: map1 # UVs: 6
 UV Set: map2 # UVs: 0
 Current UV Set: map2
 Vertex: 0
 No assigned uv
```

```
Vertex: 1
No assigned uv
Vertex: 2
No assigned uv
Vertex: 3
No assigned uv
Vertex: 4
No assigned uv
Vertex: 5
No assigned uv
```

SOURCE CODE

Plug-in: `MeshInfo6`
File: `MeshInfo6Cmd.cpp`

```cpp
DeclareSimpleCommand( meshInfo6, "David Gould", "1.0" );

MStatus meshInfo6::doIt( const MArgList& args )
{
    MStatus stat = MS::kSuccess;

    MSelectionList selection;
    MGlobal::getActiveSelectionList( selection );

    MDagPath dagPath;
    MObject component;

    unsigned int i;
    int fIndex, vIndex;

    MString txt;
    MItSelectionList iter( selection );
    for( ; !iter.isDone(); iter.next() )
    {
        iter.getDagPath( dagPath, component );

        MFnMesh meshFn( dagPath, &stat );
        if( !stat )
            continue;

        txt += MString( "Object: " ) + dagPath.fullPathName() + "\n";
```

```
MStringArray uvSetNames;
meshFn.getUVSetNames( uvSetNames );

for( i=0; i < uvSetNames.length(); i++ )
{
    txt += MString(" UV Set: " ) + uvSetNames[i];
    txt += MString(" # UVs: " ) + meshFn.numUVs(uvSetNames[i])
        + "\n";
}

MString cUVSetName;
meshFn.getCurrentUVSetName( cUVSetName );

txt += MString(" Current UV Set: ") + cUVSetName + "\n";

MItMeshVertex vertIter( dagPath, component, &stat );
if( !stat )
    continue;

float2 vUV;
MFloatArray fvUs;
MFloatArray fvVs;
MIntArray faceIds;
MIntArray vertIds;
unsigned int fvIndex;

for( ; !vertIter.isDone(); vertIter.next() )
{
    vIndex = vertIter.index();
    txt += MString(" Vertex: ") + vIndex + "\n";

    bool hasUV = false;

    stat = vertIter.getUV( vUV, &cUVSetName );
    if( stat )
    {
        txt += MString(" Vertex UV: (") +
            vUV[0] + ", " +
            vUV[1] + ")\n";
        hasUV = true;
    }
```

```
            stat = vertIter.getUVs( fvUs, fvVs, faceIds, &cUVSetName );
            if( stat )
            {
                for( i=0; i < faceIds.length(); i++ )
                {
                    fIndex = faceIds[i];

                    meshFn.getPolygonVertices( fIndex, vertIds );

                    for( fvIndex=0; fvIndex < vertIds.length();
                        fvIndex++ )
                    {
                        if( vertIds[fvIndex] == vIndex )
                            break;
                    }

                    txt+=MString(" Face-vertex UV: face,vertex:\
                        (") + fIndex + ", "+
                        fvIndex + ") uv: (" +
                        fvUs[i] + ", " +
                        fvVs[i] + ")\n";
                }
                hasUV = true;
            }

            if( !hasUV )
                txt += " No assigned uv\n";
        }
    }

    MGlobal::displayInfo( txt );

    return MS::kSuccess;
}
```

SOURCE CODE EXPLANATION

The **MFnMesh** function set is initialized to the currently selected DAG path.

```
    MFnMesh meshFn( dagPath, &stat );
```

Rather than compare `stat` against **MS::kSuccess**, it is possible to use it in a Boolean comparison directly because the **MStatus** class has overloaded the `bool()` operator.

```
if( !stat )
        continue;
```

The full path to the DAG object is added to the output text string.

```
txt += MString( "Object: " ) + dagPath.fullPathName() + "\n";
```

The complete list of uv set names for the mesh is retrieved using the `getUVSetNames` function.

```
MStringArray uvSetNames;
meshFn.getUVSetNames( uvSetNames );
```

The list of uv sets is iterated over.

```
for( i=0; i < uvSetNames.length(); i++ )
{
```

The uv set name and number of uv coordinates in the set are formatted and added to the output text.

```
txt += MString(" UV Set: " ) + uvSetNames[i];
txt += MString(" # UVs: " ) + meshFn.numUVs(uvSetNames[i])
        + "\n";
}
```

The name of the active uv set is retrieved using the `getCurrentUVSetName` function.

```
MString cUVSetName;
meshFn.getCurrentUVSetName( cUVSetName );
```

The current uv set name is added to the output text.

```
txt += MString(" Current UV Set: ") + cUVSetName + "\n";
```

An instance of the **MItMeshVertex** class is initialized.

```
MItMeshVertex vertIter( dagPath, component, &stat );
if( !stat )
       continue;

float2 vUV;
MFloatArray fvUs;
MFloatArray fvVs;
MIntArray faceIds;
MIntArray vertIds;
unsigned int fvIndex;
```

Each vertex in the selection is iterated over.

```
for( ; !vertIter.isDone(); vertIter.next() )
{
```

The vertex ID of the current vertex is retrieved and added to the output text.

```
vIndex = vertIter.index();
txt += MString(" Vertex: ") + vIndex + "\n";
```

It is possible that a uv texture coordinate hasn't been assigned to a vertex. There are many possible reasons for this. One is that the uv coordinate was deleted for the current vertex or the current uv set doesn't have a uv coordinate for the vertex. A flag hasUV indicating whether the vertex has a uv coordinate is initialized to be false.

```
bool hasUV = false;
```

The vertex uv coordinate is retrieved using the getUV function. If there is a vertex uv coordinate, the stat variable is set to **MS::kSuccess**.

```
stat = vertIter.getUV( vUV, &cUVSetName );
if( stat )
{
```

The vertex uv coordinate is output to the text string.

```
txt += MString(" Vertex UV: (") +
        vUV[0] + ", " +
        vUV[1] + ")\n";
```

The hasUV flag is updated to reflect the fact that the vertex has been assigned a uv coordinate.

```
hasUV = true;
    }
```

Now that the vertex uv coordinate has been output, the vertex is checked to determine if it has any face-vertex uv coordinates. The getUVs function will fill in the arrays of u, v, and face IDs passed into it. If no face-vertex uv coordinates have been assigned, the stat variable is set appropriately.

```
stat = vertIter.getUVs( fvUs, fvVs, faceIds, &cUVSetName );
if( stat )
{
```

Each face that shares the vertex is iterated over.

```
for( i=0; i < faceIds.length(); i++ )
{
```

The face index (face ID) of the current face is stored.

```
fIndex = faceIds[i];
```

Because the face-vertex index isn't known, the list of vertex IDs for the current face is retrieved.

```
meshFn.getPolygonVertices( fIndex, vertIds );
```

Each vertex ID in the current face is compared against the current vertex to determine if there is a match. If there is, the fvIndex reflects the face-relative vertex ID of the current vertex.

```
for( fvIndex=0; fvIndex < vertIds.length();
     fvIndex++ )
{
      if( vertIds[fvIndex] == vIndex )
            break;
}
```

The face-vertex data is added to the output text.

```
txt+=MString(" Face-vertex UV: face,vertex:\
    (") + fIndex + ", " +
    fvIndex + ") uv: (" +
    fvUs[i] + ", " +
    fvVs[i] + ")\n";
}
```

Because the face vertex has uv coordinates, the hasUV flag is now set to true.

```
hasUV = true;
    }
```

If the vertex has no uv coordinates, the output text will indicate this.

```
if( !hasUV )
     txt += " No assigned uv\n";
  }
}
```

Now that the text string is complete, it is printed out.

```
MGlobal::displayInfo( txt );
```

8.2.7 **BLIND DATA**

Blind data is any custom data a user may want to associate with a given polygonal mesh and/or its components. For example, a game may want to define certain faces as having particular properties. When a character touches the faces, a door may open or their energy may be drained. A custom value may be assigned to these faces. When the geometry is exported to the game, the custom values can be retrieved and sent to the game engine.

The advantage of using blind data over managing the information yourself is that Maya will ensure that the data is consistent. If blind data is assigned to several faces and some of the faces are deleted, the blind data assigned to the surviving faces will still be there. Likewise, when new faces are added they will be assigned the blind data's default values.

Blind data can be associated with any object node. However, in terms of assigning blind data to components only mesh vertices, edges, and faces are supported. Blind data can be assigned to NURBS patches using the face association type. Component blind data is stored internally within the polygonal mesh or NURBS patch. For blind data associated with an object, the values are stored as compound dynamic attributes in the object node.

In the context of an imaginary game, an object may be mortal or beneficial to a character. Within the object each of its faces can be separately defined as having a healing property. The level of healing property can be defined with a value between 0 and 1. Were a character to touch an object, its mortal setting would determine if the character dies. If the object isn't mortal, the healing value of the face touched would be added to the character's overall health level.

The following instructions cover how to create a blind data template and then assign blind data values to a simple cube. The template will specify two types of blind data. The first is the **mortal** blind data, which is a single Boolean value associated with the object. The second is a **healing** blind data that is a single floating-point value associated with each face of the object.

1. Select **File | New Scene** from the main menu.

2. Select **Create | Polygonal Primitives | Cube** from the main menu.

   The **pCube1** object is created.

3. Press the **f** key or select **View | Frame Selection** from the viewport menu.

4. Press the **5** key or select **Shading | Smooth Shade All** from the viewport menu.

5. Select **Window | General Editors | Blind Data Editor** from the main menu.

6. Click on the **Type Editor** tab.

   Before blind data can be assigned to an object, the type of data and how it is going to be associated with the object must be defined. This is done using a template. Templates are created in the **Type Editor**.

7. Resize the **Blind Data Editor** window so that the entire **Type Editor** interface can be seen.

8. Click on the **New** button on the left side, below the list box.

   The **Id** field defines the ID of the template. It has to be unique for each template. Leave it at 0.

9. Set the **Name** field to

   `mortalTemplate`.

   This is the name of the blind data template.

10. Set the **Association** type to `object`.

    The first blind data will be assigned per object.

11. Set the **Long name** field to `mortal`.

12. Set the **Short name** field to `mor`.

13. Set the **Data type** option to `boolean`.

14. Click on the **New Preset** button.

    This creates a new preset. These are the values that will be automatically assigned to the attribute by default.

15. Set the **Preset name** to `mortalPreset`.

16. Set the `mortal` field just below the **Preset name** field to **0**.

    The **mortal** blind data template is now set up.

17. Click on the **Save** button below the list box.

    The template, **mortalTemplate(0)**, is shown in the list box. The number in parentheses indicates the ID of the template. A template will now be created for the **healing** blind data.

18. Click on the **New** button below the list box.

19. Set the **Id** field to **1**.

20. Set the **Name** field to healingTemplate.

21. Set the **Association type** to face.

22. Set the **Long name** field to healing.

23. Set the **Short name** field to hel. Leave the **Data type** set to double.

24. Click on the **New Preset** button.

25. Set the **Preset name** field to healingPreset.

26. Set the **healing** field, just below the **Preset name** field, to **0.0**.

27. Click on the **Save** button below the list box.

    The template, **healingTemplate(1)**, is created and shown in the list box. Now that both templates have been created they can be used to apply blind data to the cube.

28. Click on the **Apply** tab.

29. Click on the mortalTemplate(0) item in the list box.

30. Click on the **Apply** button at the bottom left of the **Blind Data Editor** window.

31. Click on the healingTemplate(1) in the list box.

32. Click on the **Apply** button.

33. Execute the following.

```
select -r pCube1.f[4];
```

    This selects the front face of the cube.

34. Set the **healing** field to **0.5**.

35. Click on the **Apply** button.

    The face's blind data attribute, **healing**, is set to 0.5.

36. Execute the following.

```
select -r pCube1.f[1];
```

    The top face of the cube is selected.

37. Set the **healing** field to **1.0**.

38. Click on the **Apply** button.

   The top face's blind data attribute, **healing**, is set to 1.0.

39. Execute the following.

```
select -r pCube1;
```

   This selects the entire cube. Although it is possible to view the blind data value(s) of a single component using the **View** tab, it isn't very practical. Instead, the cube will be displayed with its faces drawn using different colors to indicate their blind data values.

40. Click on the **Color/View** tab.

41. Right click in the first **Tag/Id** field. It is the first text box below the **Tag/Id** label.

42. Select **mortalTemplate** from the pop-up list.

43. Click on the check box to the right of the **mortalTemplate** text field.

44. Click on the radio button next to the **mortalPreset** label.

45. Click on the **Set Color** button at the bottom of the **Blind Data Editor** window.

   The cube is now displayed in black. This is the color used when the blind data is set to "none". In this case, the value is 0. If the mortal blind data were set to 1, the cube would be displayed in red.

46. Click on the check box next to the **mortalTemplate** field to turn off coloring of the mortal blind data.

47. Right click in the second **Tag/Id** field.

48. Select **healingTemplate** from the pop-up list.

49. Click on the check box to the right of the **healingTemplate** text field.

50. Select **continuous** from the combo box below the **Select Value** label.

   This allows a unique color to be assigned to the minimum and maximum blind data values. All values between will be a mix of the minimum and maximum colors.

51. Click on the color swatch next to the **Min** label.

52. Set the color to pure black (r = 0, g = 0, b = 0).

53. Click on the **Accept** button.

54. Click on the color swatch next to the **Max** label.

55. Set the color to pure green (r = 0, g = 1, b = 0).

56. Click on the **Accept** button.

57. Click on the **Set Color** button at the bottom of the **Blind Data Editor** window.

    The cube is now displayed with its faces in colors varying from black to green, depending on their **healing** blind data values.

58. To remove the blind data coloring, click on the **Remove Color** button at the bottom of the **Blind Data Editor** window.

    This doesn't remove the blind data but just the false coloring displayed in the viewports.

BLIND DATA TYPES/TEMPLATES

This is a template for creating blind data. A single template can hold the specification of many different types of blind data. A template may, for example, define two int blind data types.

ID

The ID uniquely identifies a given template. A subdivision surface's hierarchical edit information can be stored as blind data on a polygonal mesh. ID numbers between 65119000 and 65119999 are reserved for this purpose.

Data Type

The following are the various types of blind data.

- int
- float
- double
- boolean

- string

- binary

The data types are the standard ones found in MEL and the C++ API. Binary can be any arbitrary data. The float data type is a 32-bit floating-point number, whereas a double data type is a 64-bit floating-point number. The MEL language only supports one type of floating-point number, `float`. MEL's `float` type is actually a 64-bit floating-point number, and thus to store and retrieve blind data values correctly the double data type should be used.

Names

A long and short name must be specified for the blind data. The long name can be any length, whereas the short name should be three or fewer characters. The names must be different from any current attributes in the object. If an object already has the attribute **powerUp**, then blind data named **powerUp** can't be assigned to the object.

When blind data is assigned to object components, it will create one of the following attributes, shown with their long and short names: **vertexBlindData/vbd**, **faceBlindData/fbd**, or **edgeBlindData/ebd**.

When the blind data is being assigned to the object, the blind data is stored in a compound dynamic attribute. The parent attribute of the compound attribute is named **BlindData$x$**, where x is the ID of the blind data template.

Association Type

There are currently four different possible association types: object, vertex, edge, and face.

MEL

The same series of operations shown in the preceding section are performed in the following, but this time using just MEL commands. The attributes and nodes created along the way are discussed.

1. Select **File | New Scene** from the main menu.

2. Select **Create | Polygonal Primitives | Cube** from the main menu.

   The **pCube1** object is created.

3. Press the **f** key or select **View | Frame Selection** from the viewport menu.

4. Press the **5** key or select **Shading | Smooth Shade All** from the viewport menu.

5. The template for the **mortal** blind data is created. Execute the following.

```
blindDataType -id 0 -dataType "boolean" -longDataName "mortal" -
shortDataName "mor";
// Result: blindDataTemplate1 //
```

The **blindDataTemplate** node named **blindDataTemplate1** is created. The `blindDataType` command is used to create and query blind data templates. The `-id` flag specifies the ID of the template. It must be unique within the scene.

6. To retrieve all data type information from a template, use the following.

```
blindDataType -query -id 0 -typeNames;
// Result: mortal mor boolean //
```

The long name, short name, and data type of each blind data are output.

7. The template for the healing blind data is now created. Execute the following.

```
blindDataType -id 1 -dataType "double" -longDataName "healing" -
shortDataName "hel";
// Result: blindDataTemplate2 //
```

The **blindDataTemplate** node named **blindDataTemplate2** is created. With the two templates now created they can be used to assign blind data to the cube.

8. The cube is assigned the **mortal** blind data.

```
polyBlindData -id 0 -associationType "object" -shape -longDataName
"mortal" -booleanData 0;
```

The `polyBlindData` command is used to assign blind data to objects and/or their components. The blind data template ID of 0 is specified using the `-id` flag. The `-associationType` flag defines which level, object, or specific component type the data is going to be assigned to. The `-shape` flag specifies that the blind data should be assigned to the object's shape node and not the transform node. The mortal blind data value of 0 is assigned to the object.

When the `polyBlindData` command is executed, a new dynamic attribute named **BlindData0** is added to the cube's shape node **pCubeShape1**. The **BlindData0** attribute is the parent of a compound attribute. The children of the attribute contain the actual blind data. The attribute name is constructed from the text "`Blind Data`" appended with the ID of the blind data template.

9. To query the blind data value, use the following.

```
polyQueryBlindData -id 0 -showComp pCubeShape1;
// Result: mor 0 //
```

The ID of the blind data template is specified using the `-id` flag. Because there is only blind data associated with the object and not its components, the `-showComp` flag indicates that the attribute name should be printed out before the blind data value. Note that the shape node's name, **pCubeShape1**, was used and not the transform node's name, **pCube1**. This is because the blind data has been assigned to the shape node.

10. The front face of the cube is assigned the **healing** blind data by executing the following.

```
select -r pCube1.f[4];
polyBlindData -id 1 -associationType "face" -longDataName "healing" -
doubleData 0.5;
```

A **polyBlindData** node named **polyBlindData1** is created. The node contains a dynamic attribute named **faceBlindData** that holds the blind data value. The node is inserted into the construction history of the cube, as shown in Figure 8.12. The **polyCube1**'s **output** mesh attribute is connected to the **inMesh** attribute of the **polyBlindData1** node. The node produces an output mesh with the blind data applied and stores it in its **outMesh** attribute. This mesh attribute is then connected to the **inMesh** attribute of the **pCubeShape1** node.

FIGURE 8.12 Inserted *polyBlindData1* node.

11. The top face of the cube is assigned another **healing** value by executing the following.

```
select -r pCube1.f[1];
polyBlindData -id 1 -associationType "face" -longDataName "healing" -
doubleData 1;
```

12. To get a list of all blind data for the faces, execute the following.

```
select -r pCubeShape1.f["*"];
polyQueryBlindData -showComp;
// Result: pCube1.f[1].hel::1 1.000000 pCube1.f[4].hel::1 0.500000 //
```

Because the -showComp flag is set, the output is of the following form.

object.component.attribute::typeId value

13. To only get the blind data value of the top face, execute the following.

```
polyQueryBlindData -id 1 -associationType "face" -longDataName
"healing" pCubeShape1.f[1];
// Result: 1 //
```

The healing blind data value is returned. Note that the -showComp flag wasn't used.

14. To use false coloring for the **mortal** blind data, execute the following.

```
select -r pCube1;
polyColorBlindData -id 0 -numIdTypes 1 -mode 1 -dataType "boolean" -
attrName "mortal" -noColorRed 0 -noColorGreen 0 -noColorBlue 0 -
clashColorRed 0 -clashColorGreen 1 -clashColorBlue 1 -value "1"
-colorRed 1 -colorGreen 0 -colorBlue 0;
```

The cube is displayed in black. This is the color assigned to the "no color" setting.

The polyColorBlindData command is used to display blind data using false colors. The ID of the blind data template is specified using the -id flag. The -mode is set to 1 to indicate that a discrete value is being displayed. If the value were 1, the cube would be displayed in red because -value "1" is specified along with its assigned color.

15. To use false color for the **healing** blind data, execute the following.

```
select -r pCube1.f["*"];
polyColorBlindData -id 1 -numIdTypes 1 -mode 6 -dataType "double" -
attrName "healing" -noColorRed 0 -noColorGreen 0 -noColorBlue 0 -
clashColorRed 0 -clashColorGreen 1 -clashColorBlue 1 -minColorRed 0 -
minColorGreen 0 -minColorBlue 0 -maxColorRed 0 -maxColorGreen 1 -
maxColorBlue 0 -minValue 0 -maxValue 1;
```

The mode is set to 6 to indicate that the color will be interpolated between the minimum and maximum colors assigned to the minimum and maximum values, respectively.

16. To turn off the false coloring, execute the following.

```
polyColorBlindData -enableFalseColor false;
```

This turns off false coloring for all objects in the scene.

At first glance it would appear that the **Blind Data Editor** has more features than are available using the MEL commands. There is an option to set the **Data type** to hex. This is the same as int and isn't treated any differently. The any option in the **Data type** combo box should be avoided and an explicit type specified.

C++ API

The **meshBlindData** plug-in demonstrates the following.

- Creating object and face blind data templates
- Assigning object and face blind data
- Retrieving template and blind data information
- Printing out template and blind data information

1. Select **File | New Scene** from the main menu.

2. Select **Create | Polygonal Primitives | Cube** from the main menu.

   The **pCube1** object is created.

3. Press the **f** key or select **View | Frame Selection** from the viewport menu.

4. Press the **5** key or select **Shading | Smooth Shade All** from the viewport menu.

5. Execute the following.

```
meshBlindData;
```

The result is as follows.

```
meshBlindData;
//
Blind Data Template: 0
 mortal mor boolean
Blind Data Template: 1
 healing hel double
Blind Data: |pCube1
 Mortal: 0
 Healing: face[0] 0
 Healing: face[1] 1
 Healing: face[2] 0
 Healing: face[3] 0
 Healing: face[4] 0.5
 Healing: face[5] 0
```

SOURCE CODE

Plug-in: `MeshBlindData`
File: `MeshBlindDataCmd.cpp`

```
DeclareSimpleCommand( meshBlindData, "David Gould", "1.0" );

int newTemplateId()
{
    MFnMesh meshFn;
    static int templateId = 0;
    while( meshFn.isBlindDataTypeUsed( templateId ) )
        templateId++;
    return templateId;
}
```

```
MStatus meshBlindData::doIt( const MArgList& args )
{
    MStatus stat = MS::kSuccess;

    MSelectionList selection;
    MGlobal::getActiveSelectionList( selection );

    MDagPath dagPath;
    MObject component;

    MString txt;
    MItSelectionList iter( selection );
    for( ; !iter.isDone(); iter.next() )
    {
        iter.getDagPath( dagPath, component );

        MFnMesh meshFn( dagPath, &stat );
        if( stat )
        {
            MStringArray longNames;
            MStringArray shortNames;
            MStringArray dataTypes;
            longNames.append( "mortal" );
            shortNames.append( "mor" );
            dataTypes.append( "boolean" );

            int id0 = newTemplateId();
            meshFn.createBlindDataType( id0, longNames, shortNames,
                                        dataTypes );

            longNames[0] = "healing";
            shortNames[0] = "hel";
            dataTypes[0] = "double";

            int id1 = newTemplateId();
            meshFn.createBlindDataType( id1, longNames, shortNames,
                                        dataTypes );

            MGlobal::executeCommand( MString( "polyBlindData -id " ) +
                        id0 + " -associationType \"object\" -shape
                        -longDataName \"mortal\" -booleanData 0" );
```

```
double healingData;
int i;
for( i=0; i < meshFn.numPolygons(); i++ )
{
    switch( i )
    {
        case 4:
            healingData = 0.5;
            break;

        case 1:
            healingData = 1.0;
            break;

        default:
            healingData = 0.0;
            break;
    }

    meshFn.setDoubleBlindData( i,
            MFn::kMeshPolygonComponent,
            id1, "healing", healingData );
}

int id;
unsigned int j;
for( i=0; i < 2; i++ )
{
    id = (i == 0) ? id0 : id1;
    txt += MString( "\nBlind Data Template: " ) + id;

    meshFn.getBlindDataAttrNames( id, longNames,
                            shortNames, dataTypes );
    for( j=0; j < longNames.length(); j++ )
        txt += MString( "\n " ) + longNames[j] + " " +
                shortNames[j] + " " + dataTypes[j];
}

txt += MString( "\nBlind Data: " )+dagPath.fullPathName();
MDagPath shapePath = dagPath;
```

```
            shapePath.extendToShape();
            MIntArray mortalData;
            MGlobal::executeCommand(
                    MString( "polyQueryBlindData -id " ) + id0 +
                    " " + shapePath.fullPathName(), mortalData );
            txt += MString( "\n Mortal: " ) + mortalData[0];

            for( i=0; i < meshFn.numPolygons(); i++ )
            {
                meshFn.getDoubleBlindData( i,
                                MFn::kMeshPolygonComponent, id1,
                                "healing", healingData );
                txt += MString( "\n Healing: face[") + i + "] " +
                                healingData;
            }
        }
    }

    MGlobal::displayInfo( txt );

    clearResult();

    return MS::kSuccess;
}
```

SOURCE CODE EXPLANATION

The meshBlindData command is defined as a simple command. Because the command changes the Maya scene, it should implement undoing. However, this command serves no purpose other than to demonstrate creating and assigning blind data and is thus not really necessary.

```
DeclareSimpleCommand( meshBlindData, "David Gould", "1.0" );
```

The newTemplateId function returns the next unused blind data template ID.

```
int newTemplateId()
{
    MFnMesh meshFn;
```

The `templateId` is a static variable, and thus its value persists between function calls. The variable keeps a record of the last unused blind data template ID. Starting from this ID avoids having to start the search at the first ID (0) each time.

```
static int templateId = 0;
```

The `isBlindDataTypeUsed` function returns `true` if the given blind data template ID is already used in the scene.

```
while( meshFn.isBlindDataTypeUsed( templateId ) )
    templateId++;
return templateId;
}
```

The `doIt` function demonstrates creating and assigning blind data to the selected meshes.

```
MStatus meshBlindData::doIt( const MArgList& args )
{
```

If the current object is a mesh, the **MFnMesh** instance is initialized.

```
...
    MFnMesh meshFn( dagPath, &stat );
    if( stat )
    {
```

The **mortal** blind data template's attribute name and type are defined.

```
MStringArray longNames;
MStringArray shortNames;
MStringArray dataTypes;
longNames.append( "mortal" );
shortNames.append( "mor" );
dataTypes.append( "boolean" );
```

A new ID for the **mortal** template is created.

```
int id0 = newTemplateId();
```

The `createBlindDataType` function is called to create the template.

```
meshFn.createBlindDataType( id0, longNames, shortNames,
                                        dataTypes );
```

The **healing** blind data template is created.

```
longNames[0] = "healing";
shortNames[0] = "hel";
dataTypes[0] = "double";

int id1 = newTemplateId();
meshFn.createBlindDataType( id1, longNames, shortNames,
                                        dataTypes );
```

The **MFnMesh** class doesn't have functions for assigning blind data to objects. The `polyBlindData` MEL command is used instead.

```
MGlobal::executeCommand( MString( "polyBlindData -id " ) +
                id0 + " -associationType \"object\" -shape
                -longDataName \"mortal\" -booleanData 0" );
```

Each of the faces in the mesh is assigned a **healing** blind data value. If the data for each face isn't initialized, the faces will contain random values. The front face (index 4) is assigned 0.5 and the top face (index 1) is assigned 1.

```
    ...
    for( i=0; i < meshFn.numPolygons(); i++ )
    {
        switch( i )
        {
            case 4:
                    healingData = 0.5;
                    break;
```

```
                    case 1:
                        healingData = 1.0;
                        break;

                default:
                        healingData = 0.0;
                        break;
            }
```

The setDoubleBlindData function is used to assign the value to the face.

```
                    meshFn.setDoubleBlindData( i,
                            MFn::kMeshPolygonComponent,
                            id1, "healing", healingData );
            }
```

With the templates created and the blind data assigned, the mesh is now queried. The templates associated with the mesh are retrieved.

```
            ...
            for( i=0; i < 2; i++ )
            {
                    id = (i == 0) ? id0 : id1;
                    txt += MString( "\nBlind Data Template: " ) + id;
```

The getBlindDataAttrNames function retrieves the long names, short names, and data types of the blind data in the template.

```
                    meshFn.getBlindDataAttrNames( id, longNames,
                                            shortNames, dataTypes );
```

The template data is included in the output text.

```
                    for( j=0; j < longNames.length(); j++ )
                        txt += MString( "\n " ) + longNames[j] + " " +
                                shortNames[j] + " " + dataTypes[j];
            }
```

The blind data assigned to the mesh is now retrieved. Because the object blind data has been assigned to the shape node and not the transform node, the DAG path to the shape node is retrieved.

```
txt += MString( "\nBlind Data: " )+dagPath.fullPathName();
MDagPath shapePath = dagPath;
shapePath.extendToShape();
```

The **MFnMesh** class doesn't have any functions for retrieving the blind data values associated with an object. The polyQueryBlindData MEL command is used instead.

```
MIntArray mortalData;
MGlobal::executeCommand(
            MString( "polyQueryBlindData -id ") + id0 +
            " " + shapePath.fullPathName(), mortalData );
    ...
```

The blind data for each of the faces is retrieved.

```
for( i=0; i < meshFn.numPolygons(); i++ )
{
```

The getDoubleBlindData function retrieves the floating-point value assigned to the face.

```
meshFn.getDoubleBlindData( i,
                MFn::kMeshPolygonComponent, id1,
                "healing", healingData );
        ...
    }
}
}
```

The text is then output.

```
MGlobal::displayInfo( txt );
    ...
}
```

8.3 CREATING MESHES

The process of creating meshes consists of preparing all necessary mesh data: vertices, faces, and so on. Although vertices and faces are fundamental to a mesh, they can optionally be assigned uv texture coordinates, colors, blind data, and so on.

8.3.1 PROBLEMATIC MESHES

Because a mesh consists principally of vertices that are connected to form faces, it is possible to create connectivity information that generates problematic meshes. Problematic meshes are not guaranteed to work with all of Maya's modeling tools. A valid mesh has 2-manifold topology. This basically means that if the connected faces of the mesh were spread out flat there would be no overlapping pieces. Considering the 2-manifold topology constraint, it is easy to demonstrate cases of problematic meshes.

Figure 8.13 shows three faces that all share a common edge. This scenario is known as multiple connected geometry. Typical edges should have a maximum of two faces sharing them.

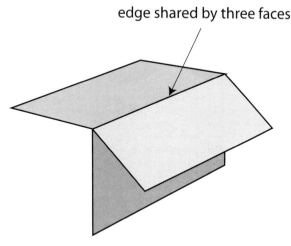

edge shared by three faces

FIGURE 8.13 More than two faces share an edge.

Another problematic mesh is where two or more faces share a common vertex but not an edge. This is shown in Figure 8.14.

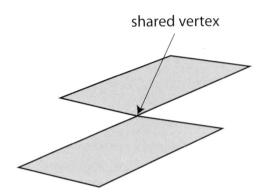

FIGURE 8.14 Faces share vertex but not edge.

Even though the faces of the mesh may satifsy the topology constraint, it is possible that the normals don't. Figure 8.15 shows such a case, where two adjoining faces have normals pointing in the opposite direction. This may be due to the face vertices being specified in the opposite order or the user explicitly flipping a normal without detaching the face.

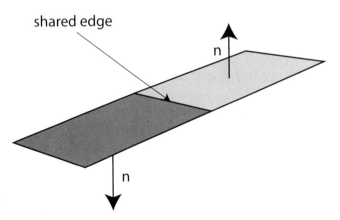

FIGURE 8.15 Flipped adjacent normals.

Although not strictly invalid, a mesh that has faces that are not planar should be avoided. A face with three vertices (a triangle) is always planar. If a face with four or more sides has one or more of its vertices that don't lie on the same plane, it is considered nonplanar. The face is not flat but is instead curved. In addition, there is no single perpendicular normal. An average normal is used instead.

Lamina faces are also considered irregular. A lamina face folds over onto itself. A lamina face can be easily created by duplicating a face and then merging all vertices. The poly count now shows two faces. These two faces share identical vertices. The surface can be thought of as being "two faces thick." The normals of both faces can point in the same or opposite directions.

Although meshes that don't satisfy the 2-manifold topology constraint still work with many of Maya's tools, though not all, any mesh that has "floating" vertices (not part of any edge) or edges (not part of any face) is strictly considered invalid.

8.3.2 CREATION CHECKS

The creation of a mesh is done using one of **MFnMesh**'s various `create` functions. These functions all have one goal: to ensure that the mesh generated is valid. Maya performs additional checking on the vertices and faces that are given to the creation functions. The following are some of these checks.

- **Repeated Vertices**

  If the same vertex appears contiguously in the face list, the duplicate is thrown away. If the face list were (1, 2, 3, 3, 4), the final face list would be (1, 2, 3, 4). This behavior can be changed by using the **MFnMesh**'s `setCheckSamePointTwice` function. By default, duplicate vertices are removed, unless this is set to `false`. To check the current status of duplicate removal, use the **MFnMesh**'s `getCheckSamePointTwice` function.

- **Unused Vertices**

  If a vertex isn't referenced in any of the faces, it is removed.

- **Shared Vertices**

  If a face uses the same vertex more than once, a duplicate of the vertex is created. This ensures that faces don't loop back on themselves. Given the face list (1, 2, 3, 1, 4), the fourth vertex would be duplicated, producing vertex 5. The final face list would be (1, 2, 3, 5, 4).

- **Noncontiguous Normals**

  It is possible that two adjoining faces have different orientations. If the first face has its vertices specified in a clockwise order and the neighboring face has its vertices in a counterclockwise order, the common edge is duplicated. This edge duplication is done by making copies of the common vertices in the edge and having the second face reference them. This effectively separates the two faces because they have normals pointing in different directions yet share a common edge.

Although it is possible in Maya to model meshes with lamina faces and faces with holes, it isn't possible to directly generate these using the create functions.

8.3.3 MOLECULE1 PLUG-IN

The **Molecule1** plug-in demonstrates the following.

• Creation of complex meshes using other meshes as guides

A **molecule** command takes an input mesh and generates a series of balls and rods that make up the mesh. The result resembles the ball-and-rod models used in science classes to show the structure of molecules. Figure 8.16 shows the result of applying the **molecule** command to a sphere mesh.

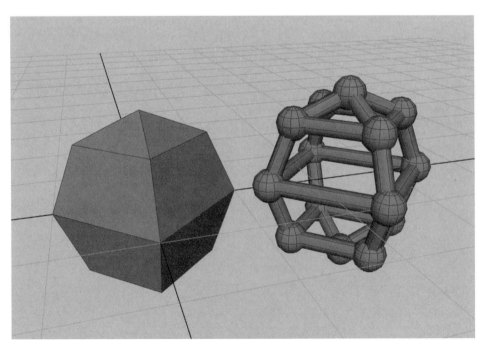

FIGURE 8.16 Result of molecule command.

Given the selected mesh(es), an entirely separate mesh is created that contains a rod for each edge and a ball for each vertex. Each ball and rod is a separate shell within a single mesh object. The first version of the command, **molecule1**, is used as follows.

1. Open the **Molecule1** workspace.

2. Compile it and load the resulting molecule1 plug-in file in Maya.

3. Open the **SphereMesh.ma** scene.

4. Select the **sphere** object.

5. Execute the following.

```
molecule1;
```

A new mesh, **polySurface1**, is created. It has used the sphere object as a basis for creating a ball-and-rod model of the sphere.

SOURCE CODE

Plug-in: Molecule1
File: Molecule1Cmd.cpp

```
class Molecule1Cmd : public MPxCommand
{
public:
   virtual MStatus  doIt  ( const MArgList& );
   static void *creator() { return new Molecule1Cmd; }
};

MStatus Molecule1Cmd::doIt ( const MArgList & )
{
   double radius = 0.1;
   int segs = 6;
   double ballRodRatio = 2.0;

   MStatus stat;

   MSelectionList selection;
   MGlobal::getActiveSelectionList( selection );
```

```
MDagPath dagPath;
MFnMesh meshFn;

int nBallPolys;
MPointArray ballVerts;
MIntArray ballPolyCounts;
MIntArray ballPolyConnects;
genBall( MPoint::origin, ballRodRatio * radius,
        segs, nBallPolys, ballVerts, ballPolyCounts,
          ballPolyConnects );

unsigned int i, j, vertOffset;
MPointArray meshVerts;
MPoint p0, p1;
MObject objTransform;

int nRodPolys;
MPointArray rodVerts;
MIntArray rodPolyCounts;
MIntArray rodPolyConnects;

int nNewPolys;
MPointArray newVerts;
MIntArray newPolyCounts;
MIntArray newPolyConnects;

MItSelectionList iter( selection, MFn::kMesh );
for( ; !iter.isDone(); iter.next() )
{
    iter.getDagPath( dagPath );
    meshFn.setObject( dagPath );

    nNewPolys = 0;
    newVerts.clear();
    newPolyCounts.clear();
    newPolyConnects.clear();

    meshFn.getPoints( meshVerts );
    for( i=0; i < meshVerts.length(); i++ )
    {
        vertOffset = newVerts.length();
```

```
        nNewPolys += nBallPolys;

        for( j=0; j < ballVerts.length(); j++ )
            newVerts.append( meshVerts[i] + ballVerts[j] );

        for( j=0; j < ballPolyCounts.length(); j++ )
            newPolyCounts.append( ballPolyCounts[j] );

        for( j=0; j < ballPolyConnects.length(); j++ )
            newPolyConnects.append( vertOffset +
                                        ballPolyConnects[j] );
    }

    MItMeshEdge edgeIter( dagPath );
    for( ; !edgeIter.isDone(); edgeIter.next() )
        {
        p0 = edgeIter.point( 0 );
        p1 = edgeIter.point( 1 );

        genRod( p0, p1, radius, segs, nRodPolys, rodVerts,
                rodPolyCounts, rodPolyConnects );

        vertOffset = newVerts.length();

        nNewPolys += nRodPolys;

        for( i=0; i < rodVerts.length(); i++ )
            newVerts.append( rodVerts[i] );

        for( i=0; i < rodPolyCounts.length(); i++ )
            newPolyCounts.append( rodPolyCounts[i] );

        for( i=0; i < rodPolyConnects.length(); i++ )
            newPolyConnects.append( vertOffset +
                                        rodPolyConnects[i] );
    }

    objTransform = meshFn.create( newVerts.length(),
                                  nNewPolys, newVerts,
                                  newPolyCounts, newPolyConnects,
                                  MObject::kNullObj, &stat );
    if( !stat )
        stat.perror( "Unable to create mesh" );
```

```
        meshFn.updateSurface();

        MString cmd( "sets -e -fe initialShadingGroup " );
        cmd += meshFn.name();
        MGlobal::executeCommand( cmd );
    }

    return MS::kSuccess;
}

MStatus initializePlugin( MObject obj )
{
    MFnPlugin plugin( obj, "David Gould", "1.0" );

    MStatus stat;
    stat = plugin.registerCommand( "molecule1", Molecule1Cmd::creator );
    if ( !stat )
        stat.perror( "registerCommand failed");

    return stat;
}

MStatus uninitializePlugin( MObject obj )
{
    MFnPlugin plugin( obj );

    MStatus  stat;
    stat = plugin.deregisterCommand( "molecule1" );
    if ( !stat )
        stat.perror( "deregisterCommand failed" );

    return stat;
}
```

Plug-in: Molecule1
File: MoleculeUtils.cpp

The genBall and genRod functions are defined in the **MoleculeUtils.cpp** file. This
file contains any utility functions needed by the molecule plug-in.

```
    int linearIndex(
        const int r,
        const int c,
```

```
      const int nRows,
      const int nCols
   )
   {
      return ((r % nRows) * nCols) + (c % nCols);
   }

MStatus genBall(
   const MPoint &centre,
   const double radius,
   const unsigned int nSegs,

   int &nPolys,
   MPointArray &verts,
   MIntArray &polyCounts,
   MIntArray &polyConnects
)
{
   verts.clear();
   polyCounts.clear();
   polyConnects.clear();

   int nAzimuthSegs = nSegs * 2;
   int nZenithSegs = nSegs;

   int nAzimuthPts = nAzimuthSegs;
   int nZenithPts = nZenithSegs + 1;

   double azimIncr = 2.0 * M_PI / nAzimuthSegs;
   double zenIncr = M_PI / nZenithSegs;

   MPoint p;
   double azimuth, zenith;
   double sinZenith;
   int azi, zeni;

   zenith = 0.0;
   for( zeni=0; zeni < nZenithPts; zeni++, zenith += zenIncr )
   {
      azimuth = 0.0;
      for( azi=0; azi < nAzimuthPts; azi++, azimuth += azimIncr )
      {
         sinZenith = sin(zenith);
```

```
                p.x = radius * sinZenith * cos(azimuth);
                p.y = radius * cos(zenith);
                p.z = radius * sinZenith * sin(azimuth);

                verts.append( p );
            }
        }

    nPolys = nAzimuthSegs * nZenithSegs;

    polyCounts.setLength( nPolys );
    int i;
    for( i=0; i < nPolys; i++ )
            polyCounts[i] = 4;

    for( zeni = 0; zeni < nZenithSegs; zeni++ )
    {
        for( azi=0; azi < nAzimuthSegs; azi++ )
        {
            polyConnects.append( linearIndex( zeni, azi,
                                 nZenithPts, nAzimuthPts ) );
            polyConnects.append( linearIndex( zeni, azi+1,
                                 nZenithPts, nAzimuthPts ) );
            polyConnects.append( linearIndex( zeni+1, azi+1,
                                 nZenithPts, nAzimuthPts ) );
            polyConnects.append( linearIndex( zeni+1, azi,
                                 nZenithPts, nAzimuthPts ) );
        }
    }

    return MS::kSuccess;
}

MStatus genRod(
    const MPoint &p0,
    const MPoint &p1,
    const double radius,
    const unsigned int nSegs,

    int &nPolys,
    MPointArray &verts,
```

```
        MIntArray &polyCounts,
        MIntArray &polyConnects
    )
    {
        verts.clear();
        polyCounts.clear();
        polyConnects.clear();

        unsigned int nCirclePts = nSegs;
        unsigned int nVerts = 2 * nCirclePts;

        MVector vec( p1 - p0 );
        MVector up( 0.0, 1.0, 0.0 );
        MVector xAxis, yAxis, zAxis;

        yAxis = vec.normal();
        if( up.isParallel( yAxis, 0.1 ) )
                up = MVector( 1.0, 0.0, 0.0 );
        xAxis = yAxis ^ up;
        zAxis = (xAxis ^ yAxis).normal();
        xAxis = (yAxis ^ zAxis ).normal();

        verts.setLength( nVerts );
        double angleIncr = 2.0 * M_PI / nSegs;
        double angle;
        MPoint p;
        double x, z;
        unsigned int i;
        for( i=0, angle=0; i < nCirclePts; i++, angle += angleIncr )
        {
            x = radius * cos( angle );
            z = radius * sin( angle );

            p = p0 + x * xAxis + z * zAxis;

            verts[ i ] = p;

            p += vec;

            verts[ i + nCirclePts ] = p;
        }
```

```
    nPolys = nSegs;

    polyCounts.setLength( nPolys );
    for( i=0; i < polyCounts.length(); i++ )
        polyCounts[i] = 4;

    polyConnects.setLength( nPolys * 4 );
    polyConnects.clear();
    for( i=0; i < nSegs; i++ )
    {
        polyConnects.append( linearIndex( 0, i, 2, nCirclePts ) );
        polyConnects.append( linearIndex( 0, i+1, 2, nCirclePts ) );
        polyConnects.append( linearIndex( 1, i+1, 2, nCirclePts ) );
        polyConnects.append( linearIndex( 1, i, 2, nCirclePts ) );
    }

    return MS::kSuccess;
}
```

SOURCE CODE EXPLANATION

Plug-in: `Molecule1`
File: `Molecule1Cmd.cpp`

The **Molecule1Cmd** class is defined first. It is derived from **MPxCommand** and
defines some of the minimal functions. The first item to note is that it doesn't
support undoing. This shortcoming will be remedied in the next version of the
command.

```
class Molecule1Cmd : public MPxCommand
{
public:
    virtual MStatus  doIt  ( const MArgList& );
    static void *creator() { return new Molecule1Cmd; }
};
```

Because the command doesn't support undoing, the `doIt` function does the major
work.

```
MStatus Molecule1Cmd::doIt ( const MArgList & )
{
```

The command options include the radius of the rods (radius), the number of segments in the rods and balls (segs), and the ratio of the ball size to the rod size (ballRodRatio). Currently, these options are hard coded.

```
double radius = 0.1;
int segs = 6;
double ballRodRatio = 2.0;
```

The list of currently selected objects is retrieved.

```
MSelectionList selection;
MGlobal::getActiveSelectionList( selection );
```

A single ball is created by using the genBall function. This function generates the vertices, faces, and face connection data for the ball. This function is explained in greater detail in the next section.

```
int nBallPolys;
MPointArray ballVerts;
MIntArray ballPolyCounts;
MIntArray ballPolyConnects;
genBall( MPoint::origin, ballRodRatio * radius,
        segs, nBallPolys, ballVerts, ballPolyCounts,
          ballPolyConnects );
```

The data needed to generate the new mesh is declared. The total number of polygons in the mesh is initialized to 0.

```
int nNewPolys=0;
```

The vertices of the new mesh are stored in an **MPointArray**. As such there is one **MPoint** element for each vertex.

```
MPointArray newVerts;
```

Each polygon in the mesh can have an arbitrary number of vertices. To determine how many vertices each polygon has, an **MIntArray** is created. This array has as many elements as there are polygons in the mesh. Each integer element specifies the number of vertices for the given polygon. Thus, the number of vertices in the *i*th polygon is newPolyCounts[i].

```
MIntArray newPolyCounts;
```

The list of vertices that make up each polygon is stored in the newPolyConnects array. The vertex ID of each vertex in the polygon is listed from the first polygon to the last.

```
MIntArray newPolyConnects;
```

All meshes in the selection are iterated over.

```
MItSelectionList iter( selection, MFn::kMesh );
for ( ; !iter.isDone(); iter.next() )
{
```

The DAG path to the current object is retrieved. The **MFnMesh** function set is bound to the current object.

```
iter.getDagPath( dagPath );
meshFn.setObject( dagPath );
```

All balls are now generated. A ball is created at each vertex in the source mesh. The complete list of vertices in the source mesh is retrieved using the getPoints function.

```
meshFn.getPoints( meshVerts );
```

Each vertex in the list is then iterated over.

```
for( i=0; i < meshVerts.length(); i++ )
{
```

The current vertex index in the new mesh's list of vertices is recorded in the vertOffset variable.

```
vertOffset = newVerts.length();
```

The ball is added to the new mesh. The total number of polygons is increased by the number of polygons in the ball.

```
nNewPolys += nBallPolys;
```

All vertices in the ball are added to the new vertices.

```
for( j=0; j < ballVerts.length(); j++ )
```

The ball's vertices are specified around the origin. To have the new ball centered around the vertex, the ball vertices are added to the source mesh vertex.

```
newVerts.append( meshVerts[i] + ballVerts[j] );
```

The polygon counts for all new ball polygons are added to the new mesh's newPolyCounts list.

```
for( j=0; j < ballPolyCounts.length(); j++ )
    newPolyCounts.append( ballPolyCounts[j] );
```

The list of vertices per polygon is added to the new mesh's list. Because the new ball vertices were added to the new mesh, their indices are relative to the end of the old list. As such, each new polygon references the new vertex indices.

```
for( j=0; j < ballPolyConnects.length(); j++ )
    newPolyConnects.append( vertOffset +
                                 ballPolyConnects[j] );
}
```

A rod is created for each edge in the source mesh. Each edge is iterated over.

```
MItMeshEdge edgeIter( dagPath );
for( ; !edgeIter.isDone(); edgeIter.next() )
{
```

The start and end point of the edge is calculated.

```
p0 = edgeIter.point( 0 );
p1 = edgeIter.point( 1 );
```

The genRod function is called to create a rod between the two points.

```
genRod( p0, p1, radius, segs, nRodPolys, rodVerts,
            rodPolyCounts, rodPolyConnects );
```

The rod mesh data is added to the end of the new mesh data in a manner similar to the way in which the ball mesh data was added.

```
vertOffset = newVerts.length();

nNewPolys += nRodPolys;

for( i=0; i < rodVerts.length(); i++ )
    newVerts.append( rodVerts[i] );

for( i=0; i < rodPolyCounts.length(); i++ )
    newPolyCounts.append( rodPolyCounts[i] );

for( i=0; i < rodPolyConnects.length(); i++ )
    newPolyConnects.append( vertOffset +
                            rodPolyConnects[i] );
}
```

Now that the new mesh data has been prepared, the create function is called to actually create the mesh. Because MObject::kNullObj is passed to the function as the parent/owner of the mesh, a new mesh shape and parent transform are created. The parent transform is returned and stored in the objTransform variable.

```
objTransform = meshFn.create( newVerts.length(),
                            nNewPolys, newVerts,
                            newPolyCounts, newPolyConnects,
                            MObject::kNullObj, &stat );
if( !stat )
    stat.perror( "Unable to create mesh" );
```

Because the mesh has changed, the updateSurface function needs to be called.

```
meshFn.updateSurface();
```

The new mesh shape node is added to the `initialShadingGroup` set. If the shape isn't included in a shading group, it will not display correctly in a viewport when shading is turned on.

```
MString cmd( "sets -e -fe initialShadingGroup " );
cmd += meshFn.name();
MGlobal::executeCommand( cmd );
```

The **molecule1** command is registered and unregistered in the `initializePlugin` and `uninitializePlugin` functions, respectively.

```
MStatus initializePlugin( MObject obj )
{
    MFnPlugin plugin( obj, "David Gould", "1.0" );

    MStatus stat;
    stat = plugin.registerCommand( "molecule1", Molecule1Cmd::creator );
    if ( !stat )
            stat.perror( "registerCommand failed");

    return stat;
}

MStatus uninitializePlugin( MObject obj )
{
    MFnPlugin plugin( obj );

    MStatus  stat;
    stat = plugin.deregisterCommand( "molecule1" );
    if ( !stat )
            stat.perror( "deregisterCommand failed" );

    return stat;
}
```

Plug-in: `Molecule1`
File: `MoleculeUtils.cpp`

The `linearIndex` function is used to calculate the index into a 1D array using a row and column index. This simulates a 2D array using a 1D array. The row and column index is calculated to wrap around at the arrays. If the row or column

index is beyond the extents of the simulated 2D array, the wrapped-around indices
will be used.

```
int linearIndex(
    const int r,
    const int c,
    const int nRows,
    const int nCols
)
{
    return ((r % nRows) * nCols) + (c % nCols);
}
```

The genBall function generates a mesh in the form of a sphere. The ball mesh data
is stored in the arrays passed into the function.

```
MStatus genBall(
    const MPoint &centre,
    const double radius,
    const unsigned int nSegs,

    int &nPolys,
    MPointArray &verts,
    MIntArray &polyCounts,
    MIntArray &polyConnects
)
{
```

Because the passed-in arrays could have been used in other calls, it is important to reset
their size. It is important to not make the assumption that they are already empty.

```
    verts.clear();
    polyCounts.clear();
    polyConnects.clear();
```

A sphere is constructed from two angles, the azimuth and zenith angles. These
two angles define the spherical coordinates of a point on the sphere. The azimuth
angle can be thought of as the longtitude around the sphere, which varies from

0 to 360 degrees (0 to 2*π in radians). The zenith angle is equivalent to the latitude, except that in this example the angle varies from 0 to 180 degrees (0 to π radians) rather than 90 degrees South to 90 degrees North.

The number of segments is the same as the number of polygons around the azimuth and zenith. The number of segments around the azimuth is twice that of its zenith because the azimuth covers twice the angle as the zenith.

```
int nAzimuthSegs = nSegs * 2;
int nZenithSegs = nSegs;
```

The number of points in the azimuth is the same as the number of azimuth segments. Because the last point around the azimuth is the same as the first, it doesn't have to be explicitly stored.

```
int nAzimuthPts = nAzimuthSegs;
```

The zenith varies from the southern pole to the northern pole. Because the first and last points are not the same, they have to be explicitly stored.

```
int nZenithPts = nZenithSegs + 1;
```

The azimuth's angular increment, in radians, from one segment to the next is calculated.

```
double azimIncr = 2.0 * M_PI / nAzimuthSegs;
```

The zenith's angular increment is calculated.

```
double zenIncr = M_PI / nZenithSegs;
```

The sphere vertices are constructed by iterating through the azimuth and zenith ranges.

```
zenith = 0.0;
for( zeni=0; zeni < nZenithPts; zeni++, zenith += zenIncr )
{
    azimuth = 0.0;
    for( azi=0; azi < nAzimuthPts; azi++, azimuth += azimIncr )
    {
```

The spherical coordinates, `azimuth` and `zenith`, are converted into the Cartesian coordinates p.x, p.y, and p.z.

```
sinZenith = sin(zenith);

p.x = radius * sinZenith * cos(azimuth);
p.y = radius * cos(zenith);
p.z = radius * sinZenith * sin(azimuth);
```

The resulting point is added to the vertex list.

```
verts.append( p );
        }
    }
```

The total number of polygons in the mesh will be the product of the number of azimuth segments and zenith segments.

```
nPolys = nAzimuthSegs * nZenithSegs;
```

Each face in the sphere has four points. An obvious extension to this function is to have the faces at the south and north poles use just three points.

```
polyCounts.setLength( nPolys );
int i;
for( i=0; i < nPolys; i++ )
        polyCounts[i] = 4;
```

The zenith angles are considered the rows in the simulated 2D array. The azimuth angles are considered the columns in the simulated 2D array.

```
for( zeni=0; zeni < nZenithSegs; zeni++ )
{
        for( azi=0; azi < nAzimuthSegs; azi++ )
        {
```

Each polygon in the sphere is defined by defining the vertices that make it up. Because the vertices have been constructed in a consistent fashion, the polygons are defined using the simulated 2D array's row and column indices. Because the polygons are to be displayed in a right-handed coordinate system, the vertices are specified in a counterclockwise order. This also ensures that the normals point in the correct direction.

```
            polyConnects.append( linearIndex( zeni, azi,
                                 nZenithPts, nAzimuthPts ) );
            polyConnects.append( linearIndex( zeni, azi+1,
                                 nZenithPts, nAzimuthPts ) );
            polyConnects.append( linearIndex( zeni+1, azi+1,
                                 nZenithPts, nAzimuthPts ) );
            polyConnects.append( linearIndex( zeni+1, azi,
                                 nZenithPts, nAzimuthPts ) );
        }
    }
```

The genRod function generates the mesh data for a cylinder that has its main axis running from point p0 to point p1. The number of polygons making up the entire circumference of the cylinder is defined by the nSegs variable. There is only one segment along its length. The radius of the cylinder is defined by the radius variable. The cylinder isn't capped.

```
MStatus genRod(
    const MPoint &p0,
    const MPoint &p1,
    const double radius,
    const unsigned int nSegs,

    int &nPolys,
    MPointArray &verts,
    MIntArray &polyCounts,
    MIntArray &polyConnects
)
{
```

The mesh data arrays are reset to be empty.

```
    verts.clear();
    polyCounts.clear();
    polyConnects.clear();
```

The number of points around the rod's circumference is the same as the number of segments because the last and first points are coincident.

```
unsigned int nCirclePts = nSegs;
```

The total number of vertices is twice the number of vertices around the base.

```
unsigned int nVerts = 2 * nCirclePts;
```

Because the cylinder is aligned along the vector from p0 to p1, a local axis is created.

```
MVector vec( p1 - p0 );
```

The up direction vector is initially set to the world Y axis.

```
MVector up( 0.0, 1.0, 0.0 );
```

The local y axis runs from p0 to p1. Because each axis needs to be of unit length, the axes are normalized.

```
yAxis = vec.normal();
```

The x axis is going to be calculated by using the cross product of the up vector and the y axis. If both vectors are effectively (within a certain tolerance) colinear, the resulting perpendicular vector will not be valid. If this is the case, the world X axis is used as the up vector.

```
if( up.isParallel( yAxis, 0.1 ) )
        up = MVector( 1.0, 0.0, 0.0 );
```

The initial x-axis vector is calculated as the cross product of the y axis and up vector. Note that this isn't the final x axis because there is no guarantee that the x axis is orthogonal to the final y and z axes.

```
xAxis = yAxis ^ up;
```

The z axis is calculated as the cross product of the x and y axes. As always, the axis vector is normalized.

```
zAxis = (xAxis ^ yAxis).normal();
```

The final x-axis vector is calculated as the cross product of the y and z axes. Because the y and z axes are guaranteed to be orthogonal, the x axis is also guaranteed to be orthogonal. This means that all axes are guaranteed to be perpendicular to one another.

```
xAxis = (yAxis ^ zAxis ).normal();
```

The local axes xAxis, yAxis, and zAxis are now calculated. The vertex positions of the cylinder will lie along these axes.

```
verts.setLength( nVerts );
```

The vertices in the cylinder follow around two circles: one at the base and one at the top. The 360-degree circumference is divided into the number of segments.

```
double angleIncr = 2.0 * M_PI / nSegs;
```

Each point around the circumference is calculated.

```
for( i=0, angle=0; i < nCirclePts; i++, angle += angleIncr )
{
```

The x and z Cartesian coordinates are calculated from the angle (polar coordinate).

```
x = radius * cos( angle );
z = radius * sin( angle );
```

The position of each vertex on the base of the cylinder is calculated as the offset from position p0 to the circular location on the local x and z axes.

```
p = p0 + x * xAxis + z * zAxis;
```

The newly calculated position is added to the vertices.

```
verts[ i ] = p;
```

The corresponding position of each vertex on the top of the cylinder is simply the base position offset by the vector (p1 - p0). This is the vector running through the center of the cylinder from its base to its top.

```
p += vec;
```

The top vertex position is added to the vertex list. Because all top vertices will follow the base vertices, the beginning index of the top vertices is nCirclePts.

```
    verts[ i + nCirclePts ] = p;
}
```

The number of polygons in the cylinder is the same as the number of segments. The cylinder isn't capped.

```
nPolys = nSegs;
```

Each polygon has four vertices.

```
polyCounts.setLength( nPolys );
for( i=0; i < polyCounts.length(); i++ )
    polyCounts[i] = 4;
```

Preallocate the size of the array for holding the polygon vertex lists. Calling the setLength function will preallocate the given number of elements. By calling the clear function, the length is set to zero but the array isn't deallocated.

```
polyConnects.setLength( nPolys * 4 );
polyConnects.clear();
```

The layout of the vertices in the cylinder can be simulated as a 2D array with two rows (base and top) and nCirclePts columns. The polygons are constructed by iterating around the points that make up the circumference. As with the ball, the vertices are listed in a counterclockwise fashion.

```
for( i=0; i < nSegs; i++ )
{
    polyConnects.append( linearIndex( 0, i, 2, nCirclePts ) );
    polyConnects.append( linearIndex( 0, i+1, 2, nCirclePts ) );
    polyConnects.append( linearIndex( 1, i+1, 2, nCirclePts ) );
    polyConnects.append( linearIndex( 1, i, 2, nCirclePts ) );
}
```

8.3.4 MOLECULE2 PLUG-IN

The **Molecule2** plug-in builds on the **Molecule1** plug-in and demonstrates the following.

- Support for undoing
- Automatic generation of uv texture coordinates for each vertex
- Support for command arguments
- World space positioning

1. Open the **SphereMeshTextured.ma** scene.

   The **sphere** object has a checker texture. This texture helps show the uv texture coordinates.

2. Load the **molecule1** plug-in file in Maya.

3. Select the **sphere** object.

4. Execute the following.

```
molecule1;
```

   The ball-and-rod mesh is created but doesn't display correctly because it doesn't have any uv coordinates.

5. Select the **polySurface1** object and then delete it.

6. Open the **Molecule2** workspace.

7. Compile it and load the resulting **molecule2** plug-in file in Maya.

8. Select the **sphere** object.

9. Execute the following.

```
molecule2;
```

The molecule mesh is created but this time it has uv texture coordinates. The different meshes generated by **molecule1** and **molecule2** are shown in Figure 8.17.

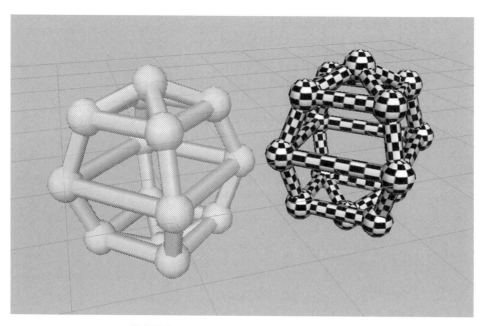

FIGURE 8.17 *molecule1* and *molecule2* meshes.

10. Open the **ConeAndSphereMeshTextured.ma** scene.

11. Select the **cone** and **sphere** objects.

12. Execute the following.

```
molecule1;
```

The molecule meshes are created but they are located around the origin. This is because the `molecule1` command retreived the vertices and edges of the source meshes in local coordinates. The **molecule1** command doesn't support undoing, and thus the molecule meshes must be explicitly deleted.

13. Execute the following.

```
select -r "polySurface*";
delete;
```

The molecule meshes are deleted.

14. Select the **cone** and **sphere** objects.

15. Execute the following.

```
molecule2;
```

The molecule meshes are created using the world-space vertices and edges of the source meshes.

16. Execute the following.

```
undo;
```

The molecule meshes are automatically removed.

17. Select the **cone** and **sphere** objects.

18. Execute the following.

```
molecule2 -radius 0.05;
```

The radii of the rods in the molecule mesh are smaller.

19. Execute the following.

```
undo;
select -r cone sphere;
molecule2 -ballRatio 3;
```

The balls are now larger.

SOURCE CODE

Plug-in: `Molecule2`
File: `Molecule2Cmd.cpp`

```
class Molecule2Cmd : public MPxCommand
{
public:
   virtual MStatus  doIt( const MArgList& );
   virtual MStatus  redoIt();
   virtual MStatus  undoIt();
   virtual bool isUndoable() const { return true; }

   static void *creator() { return new Molecule2Cmd; }
   static MSyntax newSyntax();

private:
   MDistance radius;
   int segs;
   double ballRodRatio;
   MDagPathArray selMeshes;

   MObjectArray objTransforms;
};

const char *radiusFlag = "-r", *radiusLongFlag = "-radius";
const char *segsFlag = "-s", *segsLongFlag = "-segments";
const char *ballRatioFlag = "-br", *ballRatioLongFlag = "-ballRatio";

MSyntax Molecule2Cmd::newSyntax()
{
 MSyntax syntax;

 syntax.addFlag( radiusFlag, radiusLongFlag, MSyntax::kDistance );
 syntax.addFlag( segsFlag, segsLongFlag, MSyntax::kLong );
 syntax.addFlag( ballRatioFlag, ballRatioLongFlag, MSyntax::kDouble );

   syntax.enableQuery( false );
   syntax.enableEdit( false );

   return syntax;
}
```

```
MStatus Molecule2Cmd::doIt( const MArgList &args )
{
    MStatus stat;

    radius.setValue( 0.1 );
    segs = 6;
    ballRodRatio = 2.0;
    selMeshes.clear();

    MArgDatabase argData( syntax(), args, &stat );
    if( !stat )
        return stat;

    if( argData.isFlagSet( radiusFlag ) )
        argData.getFlagArgument( radiusFlag, 0, radius );

    if( argData.isFlagSet( segsFlag ) )
        argData.getFlagArgument( segsFlag, 0, segs );

    if( argData.isFlagSet( ballRatioFlag ) )
        argData.getFlagArgument( ballRatioFlag, 0, ballRodRatio );

    MSelectionList selection;
    MGlobal::getActiveSelectionList( selection );

    MDagPath dagPath;
    MItSelectionList iter( selection, MFn::kMesh );
    for( ; !iter.isDone(); iter.next() )
    {
        iter.getDagPath( dagPath );
        selMeshes.append( dagPath );
    }

    if( selMeshes.length() == 0 )
    {
        MGlobal::displayWarning( "Select one or more meshes" );
        return MS::kFailure;
    }

    return redoIt();
}
```

```
MStatus Molecule2Cmd::redoIt()
{
    MStatus stat;
    MDagPath dagPath;
    MFnMesh meshFn;

    int nBallPolys;
    MPointArray ballVerts;
    MIntArray ballPolyCounts;
    MIntArray ballPolyConnects;
    MFloatArray ballUCoords;
    MFloatArray ballVCoords;
    MIntArray ballFvUVIDs;
    genBall( MPoint::origin, ballRodRatio * radius.value(),
             segs, nBallPolys,
           ballVerts, ballPolyCounts, ballPolyConnects,
           true, ballUCoords, ballVCoords, ballFvUVIDs );

    unsigned int i, j, vertOffset;
    MPointArray meshVerts;
    MPoint p0, p1;
    MObject objTransform;

    int nRodPolys;
    MPointArray rodVerts;
    MIntArray rodPolyCounts;
    MIntArray rodPolyConnects;
    MFloatArray rodUCoords;
    MFloatArray rodVCoords;
    MIntArray rodFvUVIDs;

    int nNewPolys;
    MPointArray newVerts;
    MIntArray newPolyCounts;
    MIntArray newPolyConnects;
    MFloatArray newUCoords;
    MFloatArray newVCoords;
    MIntArray newFvUVIDs;

    int uvOffset;
    MDagModifier dagMod;
    MFnDagNode dagFn;
```

```
objTransforms.clear();

unsigned int mi;
for( mi=0; mi < selMeshes.length(); mi++ )
{
     dagPath = selMeshes[mi];
     meshFn.setObject( dagPath );

     uvOffset = 0;
     nNewPolys = 0;
     newVerts.clear();
     newPolyCounts.clear();
     newPolyConnects.clear();
     newUCoords.clear();
     newVCoords.clear();
     newFvUVIDs.clear();

     meshFn.getPoints( meshVerts, MSpace::kWorld );
     for( i=0; i < meshVerts.length(); i++ )
     {
          vertOffset = newVerts.length();

          nNewPolys += nBallPolys;

          for( j=0; j < ballVerts.length(); j++ )
               newVerts.append( meshVerts[i] + ballVerts[j] );

          for( j=0; j < ballPolyCounts.length(); j++ )
               newPolyCounts.append( ballPolyCounts[j] );

          for( j=0; j < ballPolyConnects.length(); j++ )
               newPolyConnects.append( vertOffset +
                                       ballPolyConnects[j] );

          if( i == 0 )
          {
               for( j=0; j < ballUCoords.length(); j++ )
               {
                    newUCoords.append( ballUCoords[j] );
                    newVCoords.append( ballVCoords[j] );
               }
          }
     }
```

```
          for( j=0; j < ballFvUVIDs.length(); j++ )
          {
                newFvUVIDs.append( uvOffset + ballFvUVIDs[j] );
          }
    }

    uvOffset = newUCoords.length();

    int nRods = 0;
    MItMeshEdge edgeIter( dagPath );
    for( ; !edgeIter.isDone(); edgeIter.next(), nRods++ )
    {
        p0 = edgeIter.point( 0, MSpace::kWorld );
        p1 = edgeIter.point( 1, MSpace::kWorld );

        genRod( p0, p1,
                radius.value(), segs, nRodPolys,
                rodVerts, rodPolyCounts, rodPolyConnects,
                nRods == 0, rodUCoords, rodVCoords,
                rodFvUVIDs );

        vertOffset = newVerts.length();

        nNewPolys += nRodPolys;

        for( i=0; i < rodVerts.length(); i++ )
            newVerts.append( rodVerts[i] );

        for( i=0; i < rodPolyCounts.length(); i++ )
            newPolyCounts.append( rodPolyCounts[i] );

        for( i=0; i < rodPolyConnects.length(); i++ )
            newPolyConnects.append( vertOffset +
                                          rodPolyConnects[i] );

        if( nRods == 0 )
        {
            for( i=0; i < rodUCoords.length(); i++ )
            {
                newUCoords.append( rodUCoords[i] );
                newVCoords.append( rodVCoords[i] );
            }
        }
```

```
            for( i=0; i < rodFvUVIDs.length(); i++ )
            {
                    newFvUVIDs.append( uvOffset + rodFvUVIDs[i] );
            }
        }

        objTransform = meshFn.create( newVerts.length(),
                                      nNewPolys, newVerts,
                                      newPolyCounts, newPolyConnects,
                                      newUCoords, newVCoords,
                                      MObject::kNullObj, &stat );
        if( !stat )
        {
            MGlobal::displayError( MString( "Unable to create mesh: " )
                                   + stat.errorString() );
            return stat;
        }

        objTransforms.append( objTransform );

        meshFn.assignUVs( newPolyCounts, newFvUVIDs );

        meshFn.updateSurface();

        dagFn.setObject( objTransform );
        dagFn.setName( "molecule" );

        dagMod.commandToExecute(
            MString( "sets -e -fe initialShadingGroup " ) +
            meshFn.name() );
    }
    MString cmd( "select -r" );
    for( i=0; i < objTransforms.length(); i++ )
    {
        dagFn.setObject( objTransforms[i] );
        cmd += " " + dagFn.name();
    }
    dagMod.commandToExecute( cmd );

    return dagMod.doIt();
}
```

```
MStatus Molecule2Cmd::undoIt()
{
    MDGModifier dgMod;
    MFnDagNode dagFn;
    MObject child;

    unsigned int i;
    for( i=0; i < objTransforms.length(); i++ )
    {
        dagFn.setObject( objTransforms[i] );
        child = dagFn.child( 0 );
        dgMod.deleteNode( child );

        dgMod.deleteNode( objTransforms[i] );
    }

    return dgMod.doIt();
}

MStatus initializePlugin( MObject obj )
{
    MFnPlugin plugin( obj, "David Gould", "1.0" );

    MStatus stat;
    stat = plugin.registerCommand( "molecule2",
                                   Molecule2Cmd::creator,
                                   Molecule2Cmd::newSyntax );
    if ( !stat )
        MGlobal::displayError( MString( "registerCommand failed: " ) +
                                       stat.errorString() );

    return stat;
}

MStatus uninitializePlugin( MObject obj )
{
    MFnPlugin plugin( obj );

    MStatus stat;
    stat = plugin.deregisterCommand( "molecule2" );
```

```
        if ( !stat )
            MGlobal::displayError( MString( "deregisterCommand failed: " ) +
                                  stat.errorString() );

        return stat;
    }
```

Plug-in: `Molecule2`
File: `MoleculeUtils.cpp`

```
    ...

    MStatus genBall(
        const MPoint &centre,
        const double radius,
        const unsigned int nSegs,

        int &nPolys,
        MPointArray &verts,
        MIntArray &polyCounts,
        MIntArray &polyConnects,

        const bool genUVs,
        MFloatArray &uCoords,
        MFloatArray &vCoords,
        MIntArray &fvUVIDs
    )
    {
        verts.clear();
        polyCounts.clear();
        polyConnects.clear();

        if( genUVs )
        {
            uCoords.clear();
            vCoords.clear();
            fvUVIDs.clear();
        }

        int nAzimuthSegs = nSegs * 2;
        int nZenithSegs = nSegs;
```

```
int nAzimuthPts = nAzimuthSegs;
int nZenithPts = nZenithSegs + 1;

double azimIncr = 2.0 * M_PI / nAzimuthSegs;
double zenIncr = M_PI / nZenithSegs;

MPoint p;
double azimuth, zenith;
double sinZenith;
int azi, zeni;

for( zeni=0, zenith=0.0;
  zeni < nZenithPts;
  zeni++, zenith += zenIncr )
{
    for( azi=0, azimuth=0.0;
            azi < nAzimuthPts;
            azi++, azimuth += azimIncr )
    {
        sinZenith = sin(zenith);

        p.x = radius * sinZenith * cos(azimuth);
        p.y = radius * cos(zenith);
        p.z = radius * sinZenith * sin(azimuth);

        verts.append( p );
    }
}

int nUCols = nAzimuthSegs + 1;
int nVRows = nZenithSegs + 1;

if( genUVs )
{
    int nUVCoords = nUCols * nVRows;
    uCoords.setLength( nUVCoords );
    uCoords.clear();
    vCoords.setLength( nUVCoords );
    vCoords.clear();

    float uIncr = 1.0f / nAzimuthSegs;
    float vIncr = 1.0f / nZenithSegs;
```

```
        float u, v;
        int ui, vi;

        for( vi=0, v=0.0; vi < nVRows; vi++, v += vIncr )
        {
            for( ui=0, u=0.0; ui < nUCols; ui++, u += uIncr )
            {
                uCoords.append( u );
                vCoords.append( v );
            }
        }
    }

    nPolys = nAzimuthSegs * nZenithSegs;

    polyCounts.setLength( nPolys );
    int i;
    for( i=0; i < nPolys; i++ )
        polyCounts[i] = 4;

    for( zeni=0; zeni < nZenithSegs; zeni++ )
    {
        for( azi=0; azi < nAzimuthSegs; azi++ )
        {
            polyConnects.append( linearIndex( zeni, azi,
                                    nZenithPts, nAzimuthPts ) );
            polyConnects.append( linearIndex( zeni, azi+1,
                                    nZenithPts, nAzimuthPts ) );
            polyConnects.append( linearIndex( zeni+1, azi+1,
                                    nZenithPts, nAzimuthPts ) );
            polyConnects.append( linearIndex( zeni+1, azi,
                                    nZenithPts, nAzimuthPts ) );

            if( genUVs )
            {
                fvUVIDs.append( linearIndex( zeni, azi,
                                    nVRows, nUCols ) );
                fvUVIDs.append( linearIndex( zeni, azi+1,
                                    nVRows, nUCols ) );
```

```
                    fvUVIDs.append( linearIndex( zeni+1, azi+1,
                                 nVRows, nUCols ) );
                    fvUVIDs.append( linearIndex( zeni+1, azi,
                                 nVRows, nUCols ) );
            }
        }
    }

    return MS::kSuccess;
}

MStatus genRod(
    const MPoint &p0,
    const MPoint &p1,
    const double radius,
    const unsigned int nSegs,

    int &nPolys,
    MPointArray &verts,
    MIntArray &polyCounts,
    MIntArray &polyConnects,

    const bool genUVs,
    MFloatArray &uCoords,
    MFloatArray &vCoords,
    MIntArray &fvUVIDs
)
{
    verts.clear();
    polyCounts.clear();
    polyConnects.clear();
    if( genUVs )
    {
        uCoords.clear();
        vCoords.clear();
        fvUVIDs.clear();
    }

    unsigned int nCirclePts = nSegs;
    unsigned int nVerts = 2 * nCirclePts;
```

```
MVector vec( p1 - p0 );
MVector up( 0.0, 1.0, 0.0 );
MVector xAxis, yAxis, zAxis;

yAxis = vec.normal();
if( up.isParallel( yAxis, 0.1 ) )
     up = MVector( 1.0, 0.0, 0.0 );
xAxis = yAxis ^ up;
zAxis = (xAxis ^ yAxis).normal();
xAxis = (yAxis ^ zAxis ).normal();

verts.setLength( nVerts );
double angleIncr = 2.0 * M_PI / nSegs;
double angle;
MPoint p;
double x, z;
unsigned int i;
for( i=0, angle=0.0; i < nCirclePts; i++, angle += angleIncr )
{
     x = radius * cos( angle );
     z = radius * sin( angle );

     p = p0 + x * xAxis + z * zAxis;

     verts[ i ] = p;

     p += vec;

     verts[ i + nCirclePts ] = p;
}

int nUCols = nSegs + 1;
int nVRows = 2;

if( genUVs )
{
     int nUVCoords = nUCols * nVRows;
     uCoords.setLength( nUVCoords );
     uCoords.clear();
     vCoords.setLength( nUVCoords );
     vCoords.clear();
```

```
        float uIncr = 1.0f / nSegs;
        float u, v;
        int ui, vi;

        for( vi=0, v=0.0; vi < nVRows; vi++, v += 1.0 )
        {
            for( ui=0, u=0.0; ui < nUCols; ui++, u += uIncr )
            {
                uCoords.append( u );
                vCoords.append( v );
            }
        }
    }

    nPolys = nSegs;

    polyCounts.setLength( nPolys );
    for( i=0; i < polyCounts.length(); i++ )
        polyCounts[i] = 4;

    polyConnects.setLength( nPolys * 4 );
    polyConnects.clear();
    for( i=0; i < nSegs; i++ )
    {
        polyConnects.append( linearIndex( 0, i, 2, nCirclePts ) );
        polyConnects.append( linearIndex( 0, i+1, 2, nCirclePts ) );
        polyConnects.append( linearIndex( 1, i+1, 2, nCirclePts ) );
        polyConnects.append( linearIndex( 1, i, 2, nCirclePts ) );

        if( genUVs )
        {
            fvUVIDs.append( linearIndex( 0, i, nVRows, nUCols ) );
            fvUVIDs.append( linearIndex( 0, i+1, nVRows, nUCols ) );
            fvUVIDs.append( linearIndex( 1, i+1, nVRows, nUCols ) );
            fvUVIDs.append( linearIndex( 1, i, nVRows, nUCols ) );
        }
    }

    return MS::kSuccess;
}
```

SOURCE CODE EXPLANATION

Plug-in: `Molecule2`
File: `Molecule2Cmd.cpp`

The **molecule2** command class is declared. Because it supports undoing, it includes the following additional functions.

```
virtual MStatus redoIt();
virtual MStatus undoIt();
virtual bool isUndoable() const { return true; }
```

The command has command options, and thus it creates an **MSyntax** object.

```
static MSyntax newSyntax();
```

The various options for the command are now declared. The radius is defined as an **MDistance** variable because the radius can be defined in different units.

```
MDistance radius;
```

The number of segments in the ball and rods is declared next.

```
int segs;
```

The ratio of the ball to the rod size is declared.

```
double ballRodRatio;
```

The list of DAG paths to the currently selected meshes is stored in the `selMeshes` variable.

```
MDagPathArray selMeshes;
```

The command records the parent transforms of the resulting mesh shapes in the `objTransforms` array.

```
MObjectArray objTransforms;
};
```

The short and long flags for the various command options are defined.

```
const char *radiusFlag = "-r", *radiusLongFlag = "-radius";
const char *segsFlag = "-s", *segsLongFlag = "-segments";
const char *ballRatioFlag = "-br", *ballRatioLongFlag = "-ballRatio";
```

The syntax object, returned by the newSyntax function, contains the list of flags and arguments the command supports.

```
MSyntax Molecule2Cmd::newSyntax()
{
 MSyntax syntax;

 syntax.addFlag( radiusFlag, radiusLongFlag, MSyntax::kDistance );
 syntax.addFlag( segsFlag, segsLongFlag, MSyntax::kLong );
 syntax.addFlag( ballRatioFlag, ballRatioLongFlag, MSyntax::kDouble );
```

Because this command simply creates static meshes, it doesn't support editing or querying of the command afterward. As such, the querying and editing options are disabled for the command.

```
syntax.enableQuery( false );
syntax.enableEdit( false );
```

Unlike the doIt function in the **molecule1** command that did all the work, this function simply records all flag options and the currently selected meshes. It then calls the redoIt function to perform the real work.

```
MStatus Molecule2Cmd::doIt( const MArgList &args )
{
```

The command options are set to their default values. If these options are not overridden by flags given with the command, these will be the values used.

```
radius.setValue( 0.1 );
segs = 6;
ballRodRatio = 2.0;
selMeshes.clear();
```

If the **MArgDatabase** instance couldn't be initialized correctly, the command exits immediately.

```
MArgDatabase argData( syntax(), args, &stat );
if( !stat )
    return stat;
```

The various flags are queried, and if they are present their associated arguments are stored.

```
if( argData.isFlagSet( radiusFlag ) )
    argData.getFlagArgument( radiusFlag, 0, radius );

if( argData.isFlagSet( segsFlag ) )
    argData.getFlagArgument( segsFlag, 0, segs );

if( argData.isFlagSet( ballRatioFlag ) )
    argData.getFlagArgument( ballRatioFlag, 0, ballRodRatio );
```

The list of currently selected objects is retrieved.

```
MSelectionList selection;
MGlobal::getActiveSelectionList( selection );
```

All meshes in the selection are iterated over.

```
MDagPath dagPath;
MItSelectionList iter( selection, MFn::kMesh );
for ( ; !iter.isDone(); iter.next() )
{
```

The DAG path to the currently selected mesh is retrieved and added to the selMeshes array.

```
    iter.getDagPath( dagPath );
    selMeshes.append( dagPath );
}
```

If the user didn't select any mesh objects, a warning message is displayed and the command exits with a failure.

```
if( selMeshes.length() == 0 )
{
        MGlobal::displayWarning( "Select one or more meshes" );
        return MS::kFailure;
}
```

With all the command options now retrieved, the actual work can begin by calling the redoIt function.

```
    return redoIt();
}
```

The redoIt command performs the actual work of the command.

```
MStatus Molecule2Cmd::redoIt()
{
```

The ball mesh data is created as before, except that it now generates uv data: uv texture coordinates (ballUCoords and ballVCoords) and face-vertex uv IDs for each face vertex (ballFvUVIDs). Because the genBall's genUVs parameter is set to true, uv data is generated. The details of the updated genBall function are covered in the next section.

```
int nBallPolys;
MPointArray ballVerts;
MIntArray ballPolyCounts;
MIntArray ballPolyConnects;
MFloatArray ballUCoords;
MFloatArray ballVCoords;
MIntArray ballFvUVIDs;
genBall( MPoint::origin, ballRodRatio * radius.value(),
        segs, nBallPolys,
     ballVerts, ballPolyCounts, ballPolyConnects,
     true, ballUCoords, ballVCoords, ballFvUVIDs );
```

Each of the selected meshes is iterated over.

```
unsigned int mi;
for( mi=0; mi < selMeshes.length(); mi++ )
{
        dagPath = selMeshes[mi];
        meshFn.setObject( dagPath );
```

The mesh data arrays are reset for each new mesh.

```
uvOffset = 0;
nNewPolys = 0;
newVerts.clear();
newPolyCounts.clear();
newPolyConnects.clear();
newUCoords.clear();
newVCoords.clear();
newFvUVIDs.clear();
```

The vertices of the mesh are retrieved in world space, rather than local space, as they were previously.

```
meshFn.getPoints( meshVerts, MSpace::kWorld );
```

Each of the mesh vertices is iterated over and the major mesh data is generated. Because all balls in the mesh will use the same uv texture coordinates, they are only added once to the newUCoords and newVCoords arrays.

```
if( i == 0 )
{
        for( j=0; j < ballUCoords.length(); j++ )
        {
                newUCoords.append( ballUCoords[j] );
                newVCoords.append( ballVCoords[j] );
        }
}
```

A uv coordinate is associated with each face vertex in the ball mesh. The ballFvUVIDs contains a uv ID for each face vertex in the mesh. The uvOffset defines where the uv coordinates for the ball start in the newUCoords and newVCoords arrays.

```
for( j=0; j < ballFvUVIDs.length(); j++ )
{
        newFvUVIDs.append( uvOffset + ballFvUVIDs[j] );
}
}
```

The uvOffset for the next set of uv coordinates is at the end of the current list.

```
uvOffset = newUCoords.length();
```

Each edge in the mesh is iterated over. The start and end points of the edge are now retrieved in world space, rather than the default object space.

```
p0 = edgeIter.point( 0, MSpace::kWorld );
p1 = edgeIter.point( 1, MSpace::kWorld );
```

The genRod function has been updated to generate uv data. The genRod function uses the genUVs parameter to determine if uv data should be generated. Only when the first rod is created (nRods == 0) will the uv data be generated. Like the balls, all rods use the same uv coordinates and thus need be generated just once.

```
genRod( p0, p1,
        radius.value(), segs, nRodPolys,
        rodVerts, rodPolyCounts, rodPolyConnects,
        nRods == 0, rodUCoords, rodVCoords,
        rodFvUVIDs );
```

The main mesh data for the rod is added to the final mesh data. If this is the first rod, the uv coordinate data is added to the final uv coordinate lists.

```
if( nRods == 0 )
{
        for( i=0; i < rodUCoords.length(); i++ )
        {
                newUCoords.append( rodUCoords[i] );
```

```
                          newVCoords.append( rodVCoords[i] );
                     }
               }
```

The face-vertex uv IDs for the rods are added to the final mesh data's face-vertex uv IDs list.

```
               for( i=0; i < rodFvUVIDs.length(); i++ )
               {
                     newFvUVIDs.append( uvOffset + rodFvUVIDs[i] );
               }
          }
```

The mesh is now created. The mesh's final uv coordinates array is created from the two newUCoords and newVCoords arrays.

```
          objTransform = meshFn.create( newVerts.length(),
                              nNewPolys, newVerts,
                              newPolyCounts, newPolyConnects,
                              newUCoords, newVCoords,
                              MObject::kNullObj, &stat );
```

Rather than print the error data to the standard error stream, the error data is output to the **Script Editor**.

```
          if( !stat )
          {
               MGlobal::displayError( MString( "Unable to create mesh: " )
                                   + stat.errorString() );
               return stat;
          }
```

The parent transform of the newly created mesh shape is added to the objTransforms list.

```
          objTransforms.append( objTransform );
```

The face-vertex uv coordinates are assigned to the mesh. The first parameter to the assignUVs function is a list of uv coordinates per polygon count. Because there is a uv coordinate for each face vertex, the number of uv coordinates per polygon is the same as the number of vertices per polygon. As such, the `newPolyCounts` array can be used as is for defining the number of uv coordinates per polygon. The second parameter to the function is the face-vertex uv IDs for each face vertex in the mesh.

```
meshFn.assignUVs( newPolyCounts, newFvUVIDs );
```

The mesh has been changed, and thus it needs to be updated.

```
meshFn.updateSurface();
```

The name of the parent transform node is changed to **molecule**. If there is another node with the same name, Maya will automatically rename it so that the name is unqiue.

```
dagFn.setObject( objTransform );
dagFn.setName( "molecule" );
```

The mesh shape node is included in the `initialShadingGroup` set so that it displays and renders correctly.

```
dagMod.commandToExecute(
        MString( "sets -e -fe initialShadingGroup " ) +
        meshFn.name() );
    }
```

With all molecule meshes now created, they are all selected.

```
MString cmd( "select -r" );
for( i=0; i < objTransforms.length(); i++ )
{
        dagFn.setObject( objTransforms[i] );
        cmd += " " + dagFn.name();
}
dagMod.commandToExecute( cmd );
```

With all DAG modifications now recorded, they are now executed.

```
    return dagMod.doIt();
}
```

The undoIt function will reverse all operations performed by the redoIt function.

```
MStatus Molecule2Cmd::undoIt()
{
```

Each of the parent transforms of the molecule meshes is iterated over.

```
unsigned int i;
for( i=0; i < objTransforms.length(); i++ )
{
```

The mesh shape node is retrieved as the first child of the transform node. It is important to delete the child shape node before the transform node. Failing to do this causes Maya to crash.

```
dagFn.setObject( objTransforms[i] );
child = dagFn.child( 0 );
dgMod.deleteNode( child );
```

The parent transform node is deleted after the child shape node.

```
dgMod.deleteNode( objTransforms[i] );
}
```

With all node deletions now recorded, they can be executed.

```
return dgMod.doIt();
}
```

The initializePlugin and uninitializePlugin functions are similar to those shown in the previous version of the command. Because the command now takes arguments, the custom syntax object needs to be registered.

```
stat = plugin.registerCommand( "molecule2",
                               Molecule2Cmd::creator,
                               Molecule2Cmd::newSyntax );
```

Plug-in: `Molecule2`
File: `MoleculeUtils.cpp`

The `genBall` and `genRod` functions have been updated to include the generation of uv texture coordinate data.

```
MStatus genBall(
    const MPoint &centre,
    const double radius,
    const unsigned int nSegs,

    int &nPolys,
    MPointArray &verts,
    MIntArray &polyCounts,
    MIntArray &polyConnects,
```

If the `genUVs` parameter is `true`, the uv texture coordinate data is calculated.

```
    const bool genUVs,
```

The `uCoords` and `vCoords` array hold the u and v coordinates of each of the texture coordinates, respectively. Because both arrays are paired to create the final uv coordinates, it follows logically that both arrays are of the same size.

```
    MFloatArray &uCoords,
    MFloatArray &vCoords,
```

The uv IDs of each face vertex are calculated and stored in the `fvUVIDs` array. There is an element for each face vertex in the ball mesh. Each element is an index (uv ID) into the `uCoords` and `vCoords` arrays.

```
    MIntArray &fvUVIDs
)
{
```

The main mesh data is first cleared. If the uv coordinate data is requested, the uv arrays are cleared.

```
if( genUVs )
{
      uCoords.clear();
      vCoords.clear();
      fvUVIDs.clear();
}
```

The mesh vertices are generated, followed by the uv texture coordinates. The number of rows and colums of uv coordinates is calculated. Note that the number of columns is one larger than the number of columns of vertices. Because the last column of vertices corresponds to the first column, the last column isn't needed. On the other hand, the uv coordinates of the last column of vertices are different from the first, and thus they need to be included.

```
int nUCols = nAzimuthSegs + 1;
int nVRows = nZenithSegs + 1;
```

The uv coordinates are generated if requested.

```
if( genUVs )
{
```

The total number of texture coordinates is the product of the number of rows and columns.

```
int nUVCoords = nUCols * nVRows;
```

The sizes of the u and v coordinate arrays are set and then cleared. By preallocating these arrays, they can be constructed faster than simply using the append function, which may require several array resizings as elements are added.

```
uCoords.setLength( nUVCoords );
uCoords.clear();
vCoords.setLength( nUVCoords );
vCoords.clear();
```

The u and v coordinates will cover the unit square (0 to 1). The rows will correspond to the v coordinates, whereas the columms will correspond to the u coordinates. Each row and column element is iterated over and uv coordinates generated for it.

```
float uIncr = 1.0f / nAzimuthSegs;
float vIncr = 1.0f / nZenithSegs;
float u, v;
int ui, vi;
for( vi=0, v=0.0; vi < nVRows; vi++, v += vIncr )
{
        for( ui=0, u=0.0; ui < nUCols; ui++, u += uIncr )
        {
                uCoords.append( u );
                vCoords.append( v );
        }
}
```

The faces for the ball mesh are calculated.

```
for( zeni=0; zeni < nZenithSegs; zeni++ )
{
        for( azi=0; azi < nAzimuthSegs; azi++ )
        {
                polyConnects.append( linearIndex( zeni, azi,
                                        nZenithPts, nAzimuthPts ) );
                polyConnects.append( linearIndex( zeni, azi+1,
                                        nZenithPts, nAzimuthPts ) );
                polyConnects.append( linearIndex( zeni+1, azi+1,
                                        nZenithPts, nAzimuthPts ) );
                polyConnects.append( linearIndex( zeni+1, azi,
                                        nZenithPts, nAzimuthPts ) );
```

For each face vertex, the corresponding uv ID of its uv coordinate is recorded in the fvUVIDs array. Note that when calculating the final linear index the nVRows and nUCols variables are used to determine the 2D array size. As mentioned earlier, the number of uv coordinates is different from the number of mesh vertices.

```
if( genUVs )
{
    fvUVIDs.append( linearIndex( zeni, azi,
                    nVRows, nUCols ) );
    fvUVIDs.append( linearIndex( zeni, azi+1,
                    nVRows, nUCols ) );
    fvUVIDs.append( linearIndex( zeni+1, azi+1,
                    nVRows, nUCols ) );
    fvUVIDs.append( linearIndex( zeni+1, azi,
                    nVRows, nUCols ) );
    }
}
}

return MS::kSuccess;
}
```

The genRod uses a technique similar to that of the genBall function to generate its uv coordinate data. Its differences are noted in the following. Like the ball, the number of uv columns is one more than the number of vertex columns because the last column of uv coordinates is unique. The number of rows is simply two because there are vertices at the base and top of the rod.

```
int nUCols = nSegs + 1;
int nVRows = 2;
```

The arrays for the u and v coordinates are preallocated.

```
if( genUVs )
{
    int nUVCoords = nUCols * nVRows;
    uCoords.setLength( nUVCoords );
    uCoords.clear();
```

```
vCoords.setLength( nUVCoords );
vCoords.clear();
```

The u and v coordinates of the rod cover the unit square (0 to 1). The v coordinate can be calculated explicitly. The u coordinate is calculated by dividing the unit width by the number of segments.

```
float uIncr = 1.0f / nSegs;
float u, v;
int ui, vi;
for( vi=0, v=0.0; vi < nVRows; vi++, v += 1.0 )
{
        for( ui=0, u=0.0; ui < nUCols; ui++, u += uIncr )
        {
                uCoords.append( u );
                vCoords.append( v );
        }
}
```

Each face vertex is assigned a uv ID.

```
for( i=0; i < nSegs; i++ )
{
        polyConnects.append( linearIndex( 0, i, 2, nCirclePts ) );
        polyConnects.append( linearIndex( 0, i+1, 2, nCirclePts ) );
        polyConnects.append( linearIndex( 1, i+1, 2, nCirclePts ) );
        polyConnects.append( linearIndex( 1, i, 2, nCirclePts ) );

        if( genUVs )
        {
                fvUVIDs.append( linearIndex( 0, i, nVRows, nUCols ) );
                fvUVIDs.append( linearIndex( 0, i+1, nVRows, nUCols ) );
                fvUVIDs.append( linearIndex( 1, i+1, nVRows, nUCols ) );
                fvUVIDs.append( linearIndex( 1, i, nVRows, nUCols ) );
        }
}
```

8.3.5 MOLECULE3 PLUG-IN

The **Molecule3** plug-in builds on the **Molecule2** plug-in and demonstrates the following.

- Making a command available in the main menu
- Using option variables to store values between sessions
- Creating a custom window for editing command options

With the major functionality now in place, it is time to include a graphical user interface (GUI) for the plug-in.

1. The **molecule3** MEL scripts are in the same directory as the source code for the **molecule3** plug-in. Set the `$moleculeScripts` string to that directory.

   ```
   string $moleculeScripts = <molecule3_source_code_directory>;
   ```

   For example:

   ```
   string $moleculeScripts = "C:/DavidGould/molecule3";
   ```

   When specifying a path in Windows with backslashes, be sure to use two backslashes. A single backslash will be interpreted as an escape sequence. The same path with backslashes would therefore be written as follows.

   ```
   string $moleculeScripts = "C:\\DavidGould\\molecule3";
   ```

   Maya will automatically convert all directory paths with backslashes to forward slashes.

2. Execute the following.

   ```
   string $newScriptPath = $moleculeScripts + ";"
   + `getenv "MAYA_SCRIPT_PATH"`;
   putenv "MAYA_SCRIPT_PATH" $newScriptPath;
   ```

   For Maya to find the **molecule3**'s MEL scripts, their directory needs to be listed in the MAYA_SCRIPT_PATH. The first line initializes the `$newScriptPath` variable to the molecule's script path and then appends the current setting for the

MAYA_SCRIPT_PATH variable. The second line uses the putenv command to set the MAYA_SCRIPT_PATH variable to the path. With the MAYA_SCRIPT_PATH environment variable now updated, the plug-in can be compiled and loaded.

3. Open the **Molecule3** workspace.

4. Compile it and load the resulting molecule3 plug-in file in Maya.

5. Open the **SphereMesh.ma** scene.

6. Select the **sphere** object.

7. Select **Polygons | Molecule3** from the main menu. The **Molecule3** menu item is at the bottom of the **Polygons** menu list.

   The molecules model is created around the sphere.

8. Select **Edit | Undo**.

9. Select the options box next to the **Polygons | Molecule3** menu item.

   The **Molecule3 Options** dialog box is presented. It has sliders and fields for changing the radius, number of segments, and the ratio of the ball to the rod.

10. Set the **Segments** field to 10.

11. Click on the **Create** button.

    The dialog box is closed and the molecule model is created. It now has more segments than before.

12. Select **File | New Scene**. When prompted, don't save the changes.

13. Execute the following.

```
unloadPlugin molecule3;
```

    This unloads the **molecule3** plug-in.

14. Click on the **Polygons** item in the main menu.

    Note that the **Molecule3** menu item is no longer present. Because the plug-in has been unloaded, it removes its custom interface.

This version of the plug-in contains custom scripts to define an option box and other interface items.

SOURCE CODE

Plug-in: `Molecule3`
File: `Molecule3Cmd.cpp`

The source code is the same as **Molecule2Cmd.cpp** but with some modifications to the `initializePlugin` function.

Plug-in: `Molecule3`
File: `molecule3CreateUI.mel`

```
global proc molecule3CreateUI()
{
    global string $gMainPolygonsMenu;

    if (`menu -exists $gMainPolygonsMenu`)
    {
        string $postMenuCmd = `menu -query -postMenuCommand
                                $gMainPolygonsMenu`;
        catch( eval( $postMenuCmd ) );

        setParent -menu $gMainPolygonsMenu;
        menuItem -divider true molecule3DividerItem;
        menuItem -label "Molecule3"
                    -command "molecule3MenuItemCallback 0"
                    -annotation "Molecule: Create ball-rod model"
                    molecule3Item;
        menuItem -optionBox true
                    -command "molecule3MenuItemCallback 1";
    }
    else
        error "molecule3: Unable to get the \"Polygons\" menu";
}

global proc molecule3SetupOptions( int $reset )
{
    if( $reset || !`optionVar -exists "molecule3Radius"` )
        optionVar -floatValue "molecule3Radius" 0.1;
    if( $reset || !`optionVar -exists "molecule3Segments"` )
        optionVar -intValue "molecule3Segments" 6;
    if( $reset || !`optionVar -exists "molecule3BallRatio"` )
        optionVar -floatValue "molecule3BallRatio" 2.0;
}
```

```
global proc molecule3MenuItemCallback( int $showOptions )
{
   molecule3SetupOptions(0);
   if( $showOptions )
        molecule3Window();
   else
        molecule3Execute();
}

global proc molecule3Execute()
{
   float $rad = `optionVar -q "molecule3Radius"`;
   int $segs = `optionVar -q "molecule3Segments"`;
   float $br = `optionVar -q "molecule3BallRatio"`;

   evalEcho( "molecule3 -radius " + $rad +
            " -segments " + $segs + " -ballRatio " + $br );
}
```

Plug-in: `Molecule3`
File: `molecule3DeleteUI.mel`

```
global proc molecule3DeleteUI()
{
   global string $gMainPolygonsMenu;

   if (`menu -exists $gMainPolygonsMenu`)
   {
        deleteUI -menuItem molecule3DividerItem;
        deleteUI -menuItem molecule3Item;
   }
}
```

Plug-in: `Molecule3`
File: `molecule3Window.mel`

```
global proc molecule3Window()
{
   string $layout = getOptionBox();
   setParent $layout;
   setUITemplate -pushTemplate DefaultTemplate;
   waitCursor -state 1;
```

```
    float $rad = `optionVar -q "molecule3Radius"`;
    int $segs = `optionVar -q "molecule3Segments"`;
    float $br = `optionVar -q "molecule3BallRatio"`;

    string $parent = `columnLayout -adjustableColumn 1`;
    floatSliderGrp -label "Radius" -value $rad -min 0.00001 -max 100
                   -fieldMinValue 0.00001 -fieldMaxValue 10000000
                   molecule3Radius;
    intSliderGrp -label "Segments" -value $segs -min 1 -max 60
                   -fieldMinValue 1 -fieldMaxValue 10000
                   molecule3Segments;
    floatSliderGrp -label "Ball-Rod Ratio" -value $br -min 0.00001 -max 10
                   -fieldMinValue 0.00001 -fieldMaxValue 10000000
                   molecule3BallRatio;

    waitCursor -state 0;
    setUITemplate -popTemplate;

    string $applyBtn = getOptionBoxApplyBtn();
    button -edit -label "Create"
        -command ("molecule3SaveOptions( \"" + $parent + "\" );
                  molecule3Execute();")
        $applyBtn;
    string $saveBtn = getOptionBoxSaveBtn();
    button -edit
        -command ("molecule3SaveOptions( \"" + $parent + "\");")
        $saveBtn;
    string $resetBtn = getOptionBoxResetBtn();
    button -edit
        -command "molecule3SetupOptions(1); molecule3UpdateWindow();"
        $resetBtn;

    setOptionBoxTitle( "Molecule3 Options" );

    showOptionBox();
}

global proc molecule3SaveOptions( string $parent )
{
    setParent $parent;
    float $rad = `floatSliderGrp -query -value molecule3Radius`;
```

```
    int $segs = `intSliderGrp -query -value molecule3Segments`;
    float $br = `floatSliderGrp -query -value molecule3BallRatio`;

    optionVar -floatValue molecule3Radius $rad;
    optionVar -intValue molecule3Segments $segs;
    optionVar -floatValue molecule3BallRatio $br;
}

global proc molecule3UpdateWindow()
{
    float $rad = `optionVar -q "molecule3Radius"`;
    int $segs = `optionVar -q "molecule3Segments"`;
    float $br = `optionVar -q "molecule3BallRatio"`;

    floatSliderGrp -edit -value $rad "molecule3Radius";
    intSliderGrp -edit -value $segs "molecule3Segments";
    floatSliderGrp -edit -value $br "molecule3BallRatio";
}
```

SOURCE CODE EXPLANATION

Plug-in: `Molecule3`
File: `Molecule3Cmd.cpp`

The command only needs a small change to the `initializePlugin` function in order to support a custom interface. The `registerUI` function is called to specify an MEL command to be run when the plug-in is loaded and unloaded. This function specifies that the `molecule3CreateUI` and `molecule3DeleteUI` MEL procedures will be called upon plug-in intialization and uninitialization, respectively.

```
MStatus initializePlugin( MObject obj )
{
    ...
    stat = plugin.registerUI( "molecule3CreateUI", "molecule3DeleteUI");
    if( !stat )
    {
        MGlobal::displayError( MString( "registerUI failed: " ) +
                                 stat.errorString() );
        return stat;
    }
    return stat;
}
```

Note that no MEL scripts are specified. Instead, this example relies on Maya's automatic method for locating MEL scripts given a procedure name. Maya will automatically look for an MEL script with the same name as the procedure. Thus, for the creation procedure, `molecule3CreateUI`, Maya will try to locate the **molecule3CreateUI.mel** script file. If it finds it in the list of script paths, as defined by the MAYA_SCRIPT_PATH variable, it will load the MEL script file and source it. This same process is applied to the deletion procedure, `molecule3DeleteUI`.

Although this example sets up an interface for the plug-in, it is possible to perform any operations during the loading and unloading of the plug-in. As such, the `registerUI` function can be used to provide any additional plug-in loading and unloading functionality, independent of its typical use to create and remove the plug-in user interface. The user interface MEL scripts are covered in the material that follows.

Plug-in: `Molecule3`
File: `molecule3CreateUI.mel`

The `molecule3CreateUI` procedure sets up the user interface for the plug-in.

```
global proc molecule3CreateUI()
{
```

The global variable, `$gMainPolygonsMenu`, contains the name of the **Polygons** menu item.

```
global string $gMainPolygonsMenu;
```

The existence of the menu is first checked, and if it exists the plug-in's custom menu items are added to the **Polygons** menu.

```
if (`menu -exists $gMainPolygonsMenu`)
{
```

The **Polygons** menu isn't created until the user selects it, at which point its `postMenuCommand` is called and the submenu containing the polygon menu items is created. It is important to ensure that the **Polygons** menu items are created before this plug-in's menu items are added. The creation of the **Polygons** menu is forced by directly calling the `postMenuCommand`. First, the `postMenuCommand` is queried for the **Polygons** menu.

```
string $postMenuCmd = `menu -query -postMenuCommand
                      $gMainPolygonsMenu`;
```

Second, the postMenuCommand is executed. It is done inside a catch statement so that if the command produces an error it doesn't cause this MEL script to fail. The catch statement essentially prevents the error being propagated up the MEL execution stack.

```
catch( eval( $postMenuCmd ) );
```

To ensure that all future user interface calls know which menu item to refer to, the setParent command is called with the name of the **Polygons** menu.

```
setParent -menu $gMainPolygonsMenu;
```

A menu separator is added to the menu. This helps to distinguish the plug-in's custom menu items from Maya's standard items.

```
menuItem -divider true molecule3DividerItem;
```

A menu item labeled **Molecule3** is added to the end of the menu. When pressed, it will execute the molecule3MenuItemCallback procedure. This procedure takes a single parameter that determines if an options dialog box should be shown. Note that this menu item is explicitly named molecule3Item. This name will be used later to remove the menu item when the plug-in is unloaded.

```
menuItem -label "Molecule3"
         -command "molecule3MenuItemCallback 0"
         -annotation "Molecule: Create ball-rod model"
         molecule3Item;
```

An option box item is added to the menu item. When the user selects it, the molecule3MenuItemCallback procedure will be called with a value of 1, to indicate that the command's option dialog box should be displayed.

```
menuItem -optionBox true
         -command "molecule3MenuItemCallback 1";
    }
```

Should the procedure fail to locate the **Polygons** menu, an error message is emitted.

```
else
        error "molecule3: Unable to get the \"Polygons\" menu";
}
```

This procedure defines the various option variables the user interface will use. An option variable is a variable Maya stores so that it is always available, even between sessions. The `molecule3SetupOptions` procedure takes the single parameter `$reset`, which determines if the option variables need to be reset to their default values.

```
global proc molecule3SetupOptions( int $reset )
{
```

The user interface uses three option variables: `molecule3Radius`, `molecule3Segments`, and `molecule3BallRatio`. These hold, respectively, the current value for the rod radius, number of rod and ball segments, and ball-to-rod size ratio. Like global variables, these variable names need to be unique because they are shared between all MEL scripts.

If `$reset` is `true` or the option variable doesn't exist, it is created using the `optionVar` command. The radius value is a floating-point number and thus the command is called with the `-floatValue` flag. It is set to to a value of 0.1.

```
if( $reset || !`optionVar -exists "molecule3Radius"` )
        optionVar -floatValue "molecule3Radius" 0.1;
```

Because the number of segments is an integer, the `optionVar` command is called with the `-intValue` flag.

```
if( $reset || !`optionVar -exists "molecule3Segments"` )
        optionVar -intValue "molecule3Segments" 6;
```

The ball ratio variable is a floating-point number and is thus specified as such to the `optionVar` command.

```
if( $reset || !`optionVar -exists "molecule3BallRatio"` )
        optionVar -floatValue "molecule3BallRatio" 2.0;
}
```

When either the **Molecule3**'s menu item or its option box menu item is selected, the `molecule3MenuItemCallback` procedure is called.

```
global proc molecule3MenuItemCallback( int $showOptions )
{
```

The user's interface option variables are created if they don't already exist.

```
molecule3SetupOptions(0);
```

If the `$showOptions` parameter is set to `true`, the **Molecule3**'s window will be displayed. Otherwise, the **molecule3** command is called immediately.

```
if( $showOptions )
        molecule3Window();
else
        molecule3Execute();
}
```

The following procedure is called to actually execute the `molecule3` command.

```
global proc molecule3Execute()
{
```

The values of all option variables are retrieved.

```
float $rad = `optionVar -q "molecule3Radius"`;
int $segs = `optionVar -q "molecule3Segments"`;
float $br = `optionVar -q "molecule3BallRatio"`;
```

The `molecule3` command is called with the option variable values.

```
evalEcho( "molecule3 -radius " + $rad +
        " -segments " + $segs + " -ballRatio " + $br );
}
```

Plug-in: `Molecule3`
File: `molecule3DeleteUI.mel`

The `molecule3DeleteUI` procedure is called when the plug-in is unloaded. It will remove all interface elements the user interface creation procedure created.

```
global proc molecule3DeleteUI()
{
```

The **Polygons** menu item is retrieved.

```
    global string $gMainPolygonsMenu;

    if (`menu -exists $gMainPolygonsMenu`)
    {
```

The divider and **molecule3** menu items are deleted from the user interface.

```
        deleteUI -menuItem molecule3DividerItem;
        deleteUI -menuItem molecule3Item;
    }
}
```

Plug-in: `Molecule3`
File: `molecule3Window.mel`

This MEL script contains the procedures for the option dialog box. The `molecule3Window` procedure generates and displays the option box. Some of the procedures used are not documented in the MEL documentation. To locate the source code for a particular procedure, simply use the `whatIs` command.

```
global proc molecule3Window()
{
```

The `getOptionBox` procedure gets the standard option dialog box.

```
    string $layout = getOptionBox();
```

All future interface calls will use this layout as its parent.

```
setParent $layout;
```

The setUITemplate command is called to add the DefaultTemplate template to the template stack. This makes DefaultTemplate the current command template for future interface commands.

```
setUITemplate -pushTemplate DefaultTemplate;
```

Because the interface construction could be potentially time consuming, the mouse cursor is changed to reflect that a lengthy operation is underway.

```
waitCursor -state 1;
```

The values of the option variables are retrieved.

```
float $rad = `optionVar -q "molecule3Radius"`;
int $segs = `optionVar -q "molecule3Segments"`;
float $br = `optionVar -q "molecule3BallRatio"`;
```

A **columnLayout** is added to the window. All of **molecule3**'s command options will then be added to this layout.

```
string $parent = `columnLayout -adjustableColumn 1`;
```

A float slider group is created for the radius value. Note that the slider's range is smaller than that available for the field. It makes sense to use a limited number of values because the user will set the value by dragging the slider.

```
floatSliderGrp -label "Radius" -value $rad -min 0.00001 -max 100
               -fieldMinValue 0.00001 -fieldMaxValue 10000000
               molecule3Radius;
```

The number of segments is an integer and thus an integer slider group is created.

```
intSliderGrp -label "Segments" -value $segs -min 1 -max 60
             -fieldMinValue 1 -fieldMaxValue 10000
             molecule3Segments;
```

Finally, the ball-to-rod ratio value is added as a float slider group.

```
floatSliderGrp -label "Ball-Rod Ratio" -value $br -min 0.00001 -max 10
              -fieldMinValue 0.00001 -fieldMaxValue 10000000
                  molecule3BallRatio;
```

With the main work now completed, the mouse cursor is set back to its normal state.

```
waitCursor -state 0;
```

The construction of the interface is now completed, and thus the command template can be removed by popping it.

```
setUITemplate -popTemplate;
```

The standard option dialog box has an **Apply** button. The name of this button is retrieved.

```
string $applyBtn = getOptionBoxApplyBtn();
```

When the user clicks on this button, the `molecule3SaveOptions` procedure is called to save the current interface settings, and then `molecule3Execute` is called to actually execute the command.

```
button -edit -label "Create"
-command ("molecule3SaveOptions( \"" + $parent + "\" );
        molecule3Execute();")
    $applyBtn;
```

From the option dialog box it is possible to save the current settings by selecting **Edit | Save Settings** from the option dialog box's menu. The name of this menu item is retrieved.

```
string $saveBtn = getOptionBoxSaveBtn();
```

The save menu item is changed so that when it is clicked the molecule3SaveOptions procedure will be called.

```
button -edit
        -command ("molecule3SaveOptions( \"" + $parent + "\");")
        $saveBtn;
```

In addition to the menu item for saving the current settings, there is an **Edit | Reset Settings** menu item. The getOptionBoxResetBtn procedure is used to retrieve the name of this menu item.

```
string $resetBtn = getOptionBoxResetBtn();
```

When this menu item is selected, the molecule3SetupOptions procedure will be called with a value of 1 to ensure that the option variable values are reset to their defaults. To ensure that the user interface reflects these new values, the molecule3UpdateWindow procedure is called.

```
button -edit
        -command "molecule3SetupOptions(1); molecule3UpdateWindow();"
        $resetBtn;
```

The title of the option dialog box is set.

```
setOptionBoxTitle( "Molecule3 Options" );
```

With the dialog box construction now complete, it is shown.

```
showOptionBox();
}
```

This procedure is used to retrieve the current interface settings and store them in the option variables.

```
global proc molecule3SaveOptions( string $parent )
{
```

For the user interface command to know which control element is being worked on, it is necessary to specify the parent.

```
setParent $parent;
```

The values of the user interface elements are retrieved and stored in local variables.

```
float $rad = `floatSliderGrp -query -value molecule3Radius`;
int $segs = `intSliderGrp -query -value molecule3Segments`;
float $br = `floatSliderGrp -query -value molecule3BallRatio`;
```

The plug-in's option variables are updated with these new values.

```
optionVar -floatValue molecule3Radius $rad;
optionVar -intValue molecule3Segments $segs;
optionVar -floatValue molecule3BallRatio $br;
}
```

The `molecule3UpdateWindow` procedure will update the user interface with the current option variable values.

```
global proc molecule3UpdateWindow()
{
```

The current option variable values are retrieved.

```
float $rad = `optionVar -q "molecule3Radius"`;
int $segs = `optionVar -q "molecule3Segments"`;
float $br = `optionVar -q "molecule3BallRatio"`;
```

The user interface elements are updated to reflect the current option variable values.

```
floatSliderGrp -edit -value $rad "molecule3Radius";
intSliderGrp -edit -value $segs "molecule3Segments";
floatSliderGrp -edit -value $br "molecule3BallRatio";
}
```

8.3.6 MOLECULE4 PLUG-IN

The **Molecule4** plug-in builds on the **Molecule3** plug-in and demonstrates the following.

- Dynamic molecule mesh generation

Currently the molecule command generates a static molecule mesh. If the original mesh changes, the molecule mesh doesn't update. The rod radius, number of segments, and so on can't be changed once the moledule mesh is generated. To have the molecule mesh update automatically when the original mesh changes, a custom **MPxNode** is needed.

1. Ensure that the directory containing the **Molecule4** MEL scripts is listed in the MAYA_SCRIPT_PATH by executing the following.

   ```
   string $moleculeScripts = <molecule4_source_code_directory>;
   string $newScriptPath = $moleculeScripts + ";" +
                                        `getenv "MAYA_SCRIPT_PATH"`;
   putenv "MAYA_SCRIPT_PATH" $newScriptPath;
   ```

   The <molecule4_source_code_directory> should be replaced with the path to the **Molecule4** MEL scripts.

2. Open the **Molecule4** workspace.

3. Compile it and load the resulting molecule4 plug-in file in Maya.

4. Open the **SphereMesh.ma** scene.

5. Select the **sphere** object.

6. Set the main menu to the **Modeling** menu.

7. Select **Polygons | Molecule4** from the main menu.

   The molecule mesh is created from the sphere mesh.

8. Open the **Channel Box**.

   The **molecule41** node is automatically selected. This is the molecule node that generates the molecule mesh.

9. Set the **Radius** attribute to **0.15**.

   The molecule mesh is updated to have a wider radius for the rods and balls.

10. Execute the following.

```
select -r sphere.vtx[4];
move -r 0 0 -0.5;
```

One of the vertices on the sphere's equator is moved outward. The molecule mesh is automatically updated in response to the change in the sphere mesh.

Figure 8.18 shows the **sphere** object before the **molecule4** command is applied. Note that the shape doesn't have any history; it has been deleted, reducing the object to just a single mesh shape node. Although the **sphereShape** mesh node has many attributes, only the **worldMesh** attribute is displayed. It is an array of meshes, one for each DAG path instance.

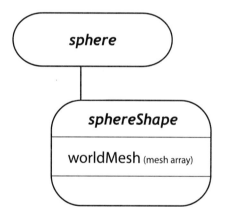

FIGURE 8.18 Sphere before *molecule4* command.

Having applied the **molecule4** command to the **sphere** object results in the dependency graph shown in Figure 8.19. An instance of the **molecule** node, **molecule41**, has been created. In addition, a new transform **molecule** with a mesh shape node **polySurfaceShape1** has been created. The first element of the **worldMesh** attribute, **worldMesh[0]**, is connected into the **inMesh** attribute of the **molecule41** node. The resulting ball-and-rod mesh generated by the **molecule41** node is output through its **outMesh** attribute. This attribute is then connected into the **inMesh** attribute of the new mesh shape, **polySurfaceShape1**.

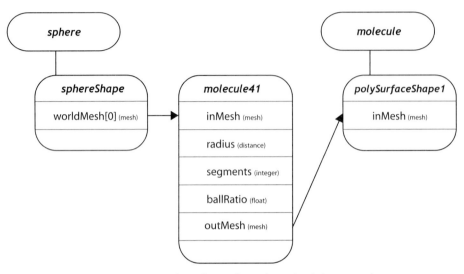

FIGURE 8.19 Sphere after applying the molecule4 command.

Having the output mesh of the sphere feed directly into the **molecule41** node means that any changes to the sphere object will cause the **molecule41** node to regenerate its output mesh. In addition, any changes to its other attributes (radius, segments, and so on) will cause a regeneration of its output mesh. As such, it is totally dynamic with regard to any of its inputs.

SOURCE CODE

Plug-in: `Molecule4`
File: `Molecule4Cmd.h`

```
class Molecule4Cmd : public MPxCommand
{
public:
   virtual MStatus  doIt( const MArgList& );
   virtual MStatus  redoIt();
   virtual MStatus  undoIt();
   virtual bool isUndoable() const { return true; }

   static void *creator() { return new Molecule4Cmd; }
   static MSyntax newSyntax();
```

```
private:
    MDistance radius;
    int segs;
    double ballRodRatio;

    MDagModifier dagMods[2];
    MObjectArray moleculeNodes;
    MObjectArray meshShapeNodes;
};
```

Plug-in: `Molecule4`
File: `Molecule4Cmd.cpp`

```
MStatus Molecule4Cmd::doIt( const MArgList &args )
{
    MStatus stat;

    radius = Molecule4Node::radiusDefault();
    segs = Molecule4Node::segmentsDefault();
    ballRodRatio = Molecule4Node::ballRatioDefault();

    moleculeNodes.clear();
    meshShapeNodes.clear();

    MArgDatabase argData( syntax(), args, &stat );
    if( !stat )
        return stat;

    if( argData.isFlagSet( radiusFlag ) )
        argData.getFlagArgument( radiusFlag, 0, radius );

    if( argData.isFlagSet( segsFlag ) )
        argData.getFlagArgument( segsFlag, 0, segs );

    if( argData.isFlagSet( ballRatioFlag ) )
        argData.getFlagArgument( ballRatioFlag, 0, ballRodRatio );

    MSelectionList selection;
    MGlobal::getActiveSelectionList( selection );

    MObject inMeshShape;
    MPlug outMeshPlug, inMeshPlug;
    MFnDependencyNode nodeFn, molecule4NodeFn;
```

```
MObject molecule4Node, newMeshTransform, newMeshShape;
MFnDagNode dagFn;

int nSelMeshes = 0;
MDagPath dagPath;
MItSelectionList iter( selection, MFn::kMesh );
for ( ; !iter.isDone(); iter.next() )
{
    nSelMeshes++;
    iter.getDagPath( dagPath );

    dagPath.extendToShape();
    inMeshShape = dagPath.node();

    dagFn.setObject( dagPath );
    unsigned int instanceNum = dagPath.instanceNumber();
    MPlug outMeshesPlug = dagFn.findPlug( "worldMesh" );
    outMeshPlug = outMeshesPlug.elementByLogicalIndex( instanceNum );

    molecule4Node = dagMods[0].MDGModifier::createNode(
                        Molecule4Node::id );
    moleculeNodes.append( molecule4Node );
    molecule4NodeFn.setObject( molecule4Node );

    MPlug inMeshPlug = molecule4NodeFn.findPlug( "inMesh" );
    dagMods[0].connect( outMeshPlug, inMeshPlug );

    newMeshTransform = dagMods[0].createNode( "transform" );
    newMeshShape = dagMods[0].createNode( "mesh", newMeshTransform );
    meshShapeNodes.append( newMeshShape );

    dagMods[0].renameNode( newMeshTransform, "molecule" );

    nodeFn.setObject( newMeshShape );

    outMeshPlug = molecule4NodeFn.findPlug( "outMesh", &stat );
    inMeshPlug = nodeFn.findPlug( "inMesh", &stat );
    stat = dagMods[0].connect( outMeshPlug, inMeshPlug );
}

if( nSelMeshes == 0 )
{
    MGlobal::displayWarning( "Select one or more meshes" );
    return MS::kFailure;
}
```

```
    dagMods[0].doIt();

    unsigned int i;
    for( i=0; i < moleculeNodes.length(); i++ )
    {
        nodeFn.setObject( moleculeNodes[i] );
        dagMods[1].commandToExecute( MString("setAttr ") +
                    nodeFn.name() + ".radius " + radius.value() );
        dagMods[1].commandToExecute( MString("setAttr ") +
                    nodeFn.name() + ".segments " + segs );
        dagMods[1].commandToExecute( MString("setAttr ") +
                    nodeFn.name() + ".ballRatio " + ballRodRatio );
    }

    for( i=0; i < meshShapeNodes.length(); i++ )
    {
        nodeFn.setObject( meshShapeNodes[i] );
        dagMods[1].commandToExecute( MString( "sets -e -fe
                            initialShadingGroup " ) + nodeFn.name() );
    }

    MString cmd( "select -r" );
    for( i=0; i < moleculeNodes.length(); i++ )
    {
        nodeFn.setObject( moleculeNodes[i] );
        cmd += " " + nodeFn.name();
    }

    dagMods[1].commandToExecute( cmd );

    dagMods[1].doIt();

    return MS::kSuccess;
}

MStatus Molecule4Cmd::redoIt()
{
    int i;
    for( i=0; i < 2; i++ )
        dagMods[i].doIt();

    return MS::kSuccess;
}
```

```
MStatus Molecule4Cmd::undoIt()
{
   int i;
   for( i=1; i >= 0; i-- )
         dagMods[i].undoIt();

   return MS::kSuccess;
}
```

Plug-in: `Molecule4`
File: `Molecule4Node.h`

```
class Molecule4Node : public MPxNode
{
public:
   virtual MStatus compute( const MPlug &plug, MDataBlock &data );
   static void *creator();
   static MStatus initialize();

   static MObject radius;
   static MObject segments;
   static MObject ballRatio;
   static MObject inMesh;
   static MObject outMesh;

   static MTypeId id;

   static MDistance radiusDefault();
   static int segmentsDefault();
   static double ballRatioDefault();
};
```

Plug-in: `Molecule4`
File: `Molecule4Node.cpp`

```
MTypeId Molecule4Node::id( 0x00337 );

MObject Molecule4Node::radius;
MObject Molecule4Node::segments;
MObject Molecule4Node::ballRatio;
MObject Molecule4Node::inMesh;
MObject Molecule4Node::outMesh;
```

```
MStatus Molecule4Node::compute( const MPlug &plug, MDataBlock &data )
{
    MStatus stat;

    MDataHandle stateHnd = data.inputValue( state );
    int state = stateHnd.asInt();
    if( state == 1 )
    {
        MDataHandle inMeshHnd = data.inputValue( inMesh );
        MDataHandle outMeshHnd = data.outputValue( outMesh );

        outMeshHnd.set( inMeshHnd.asMesh() );
        data.setClean( plug );

        return MS::kSuccess;
    }

    if( plug == outMesh )
    {
        MDataHandle radiusHnd = data.inputValue( radius );
        MDataHandle segmentsHnd = data.inputValue( segments );
        MDataHandle ballRatioHnd = data.inputValue( ballRatio );
        MDataHandle inMeshHnd = data.inputValue( inMesh );
        MDataHandle outMeshHnd = data.outputValue( outMesh );

        double radius = radiusHnd.asDouble();
        int segs = segmentsHnd.asInt();
        double ballRatio = ballRatioHnd.asDouble();

        MObject inMeshObj = inMeshHnd.asMeshTransformed();
        MFnMesh inMeshFn( inMeshObj );

        MFnMeshData meshDataFn;
        MObject newMeshData = meshDataFn.create();

        int nBallPolys;
        MPointArray ballVerts;
        MIntArray ballPolyCounts;
        MIntArray ballPolyConnects;
        MFloatArray ballUCoords;
        MFloatArray ballVCoords;
        MIntArray ballFvUVIDs;
```

```
genBall( MPoint::origin, ballRatio * radius, segs, nBallPolys,
         ballVerts, ballPolyCounts, ballPolyConnects,
         true, ballUCoords, ballVCoords, ballFvUVIDs );

unsigned int i, j, vertOffset;
MPointArray meshVerts;
MPoint p0, p1;

int nRodPolys;
MPointArray rodVerts;
MIntArray rodPolyCounts;
MIntArray rodPolyConnects;
MFloatArray rodUCoords;
MFloatArray rodVCoords;
MIntArray rodFvUVIDs;

int nNewPolys;
MPointArray newVerts;
MIntArray newPolyCounts;
MIntArray newPolyConnects;
MFloatArray newUCoords;
MFloatArray newVCoords;
MIntArray newFvUVIDs;

int uvOffset;

uvOffset = 0;
nNewPolys = 0;
newVerts.clear();
newPolyCounts.clear();
newPolyConnects.clear();
newUCoords.clear();
newVCoords.clear();
newFvUVIDs.clear();

inMeshFn.getPoints( meshVerts, MSpace::kWorld );
for( i=0; i < meshVerts.length(); i++ )
{
      vertOffset = newVerts.length();

      nNewPolys += nBallPolys;
```

```
        for( j=0; j < ballVerts.length(); j++ )
              newVerts.append( meshVerts[i] + ballVerts[j] );

        for( j=0; j < ballPolyCounts.length(); j++ )
              newPolyCounts.append( ballPolyCounts[j] );

        for( j=0; j < ballPolyConnects.length(); j++ )
              newPolyConnects.append( vertOffset +
                                    ballPolyConnects[j] );

        if( i == 0 )
        {
              for( j=0; j < ballUCoords.length(); j++ )
              {
                    newUCoords.append( ballUCoords[j] );
                    newVCoords.append( ballVCoords[j] );
              }
        }

        for( j=0; j < ballFvUVIDs.length(); j++ )
        {
              newFvUVIDs.append( uvOffset + ballFvUVIDs[j] );
        }
}

uvOffset = newUCoords.length();

int nRods = 0;
MItMeshEdge edgeIter( inMeshObj );
for( ; !edgeIter.isDone(); edgeIter.next(), nRods++ )
{
      p0 = edgeIter.point( 0, MSpace::kWorld );
      p1 = edgeIter.point( 1, MSpace::kWorld );

      genRod( p0, p1,
              radius, segs, nRodPolys,
              rodVerts, rodPolyCounts, rodPolyConnects,
              nRods == 0, rodUCoords, rodVCoords,
              rodFvUVIDs );

      vertOffset = newVerts.length();

      nNewPolys += nRodPolys;
```

```
            for( i=0; i < rodVerts.length(); i++ )
                    newVerts.append( rodVerts[i] );

            for( i=0; i < rodPolyCounts.length(); i++ )
                    newPolyCounts.append( rodPolyCounts[i] );

            for( i=0; i < rodPolyConnects.length(); i++ )
                    newPolyConnects.append( vertOffset +
                                            rodPolyConnects[i] );

            if( nRods == 0 )
            {
                    for( i=0; i < rodUCoords.length(); i++ )
                    {
                            newUCoords.append( rodUCoords[i] );
                            newVCoords.append( rodVCoords[i] );
                    }
            }

            for( i=0; i < rodFvUVIDs.length(); i++ )
            {
                    newFvUVIDs.append( uvOffset + rodFvUVIDs[i] );
            }
    }

    MFnMesh meshFn;
    meshFn.create( newVerts.length(), nNewPolys, newVerts,
                   newPolyCounts, newPolyConnects,
                   newUCoords, newVCoords,
                   newMeshData, &stat );
    if( !stat )
    {
        MGlobal::displayError( MString( "Unable to create mesh: " +
                               stat.errorString() ) );
        return stat;
    }

    meshFn.assignUVs( newPolyCounts, newFvUVIDs );
    meshFn.updateSurface();

    outMeshHnd.set( newMeshData );

    data.setClean( plug );
    }
```

```cpp
    else
        stat = MS::kUnknownParameter;

    return stat;
}

void *Molecule4Node::creator()
{
    return new Molecule4Node();
}

MStatus Molecule4Node::initialize()
{
    MFnUnitAttribute uAttr;
    MFnNumericAttribute nAttr;
    MFnTypedAttribute tAttr;

    radius = uAttr.create( "radius", "rad", MFnUnitAttribute::kDistance,
                           0.1 );
    uAttr.setKeyable( true );

    segments = nAttr.create( "segments", "seg", MFnNumericData::kLong, 6 );
    nAttr.setKeyable( true );

    ballRatio = nAttr.create( "ballRatio", "br", MFnNumericData::kDouble,
                              2.0 );
    nAttr.setKeyable( true );

    inMesh = tAttr.create( "inMesh", "im", MFnData::kMesh );

    outMesh = tAttr.create( "outMesh", "om", MFnData::kMesh );
    tAttr.setStorable( false );

    addAttribute( radius );
    addAttribute( segments );
    addAttribute( ballRatio );
    addAttribute( inMesh );
    addAttribute( outMesh );

    attributeAffects( radius, outMesh );
    attributeAffects( segments, outMesh );
    attributeAffects( ballRatio, outMesh );
    attributeAffects( inMesh, outMesh );

    return MS::kSuccess;
}
```

```
MDistance Molecule4Node::radiusDefault()
{
    MFnUnitAttribute uAttr( radius );
    MDistance d;
    uAttr.getDefault( d );
    return d;
}

int Molecule4Node::segmentsDefault()
{
    MFnNumericAttribute nAttr( segments );
    int d;
    nAttr.getDefault( d );
    return d;
}

double Molecule4Node::ballRatioDefault()
{
    MFnNumericAttribute nAttr( ballRatio );
    double d;
    nAttr.getDefault( d );
    return d;
}
```

SOURCE CODE EXPLANATION

Plug-in: Molecule4
File: Molecule4Cmd.h

This version of the molecule command relies more heavily on **MDagModifier**s for all processing and undoing than the previous version. As such, it includes two **MDagModifier** instances, embodied in the array dagMods[2]. An array for storing all molecule nodes, moleculeNodes, and another meshShapeNodes for storing each of the new mesh shapes are included in the class.

Plug-in: Molecule4
File: Molecule4Cmd.cpp

The newSyntax function remains unchanged from the previous version. The doIt function, however, has changed significantly. No longer does this function generate the molecule mesh directly but instead creates a molecule node that generates a mesh dynamically.

```
MStatus Molecule4Cmd::doIt( const MArgList &args )
{
```

The class member variables are initialized to the **molecule** node's default values.

```
radius = Molecule4Node::radiusDefault();
segs = Molecule4Node::segmentsDefault();
ballRodRatio = Molecule4Node::ballRatioDefault();

moleculeNodes.clear();
meshShapeNodes.clear();
```

The arguments to the command are retrieved and then analyzed.

```
MArgDatabase argData( syntax(), args, &stat );
if( !stat )
    return stat;

if( argData.isFlagSet( radiusFlag ) )
    argData.getFlagArgument( radiusFlag, 0, radius );

if( argData.isFlagSet( segsFlag ) )
    argData.getFlagArgument( segsFlag, 0, segs );

if( argData.isFlagSet( ballRatioFlag ) )
    argData.getFlagArgument( ballRatioFlag, 0, ballRodRatio );
```

The current selection is retrieved.

```
MSelectionList selection;
MGlobal::getActiveSelectionList( selection );
```

Each of the selected meshes is iterated over.

```
int nSelMeshes = 0;
MDagPath dagPath;
MItSelectionList iter( selection, MFn::kMesh );
```

```
for ( ; !iter.isDone(); iter.next() )
{
        nSelMeshes++;
        iter.getDagPath( dagPath );
```

The DAG path child shape node of the transform node is retrieved.

```
dagPath.extendToShape();
```

The child shape node is retrieved. This shape node will provide the input to the **molecule** node; that is, this mesh shape will be the source for the molecule node's ball-and-rod model.

```
inMeshShape = dagPath.node();
```

The DAG node function set is initialized to the mesh shape node.

```
dagFn.setObject( dagPath );
```

Each DAG path can be unique or an instance of one of many possible paths. To determine which instance of the DAG path is being used, the instanceNumber function is used.

```
unsigned int instanceNum = dagPath.instanceNumber();
```

A plug to the source mesh shape's **worldMesh** attribute is retrieved.

```
MPlug outMeshesPlug = dagFn.findPlug( "worldMesh" );
```

There can be multiple instances of this mesh shape if the shape has been instanced. The **worldMesh** attribute is an array of meshes for each of these instances. To retrieve the mesh for the current instance, elementByLogicalIndex is used. It is past the instance number of the DAG path. The result is a plug to the **worldMesh** element for the given DAG path instance.

```
outMeshPlug = outMeshesPlug.elementByLogicalIndex( instanceNum );
```

There are two **MDagModifier** instances: `dagMods[0]` and `dagMods[1]`. The first modifier is used for creating nodes and connecting them. (The second is explained in material to follow.) A **molecule** node is created.

```
molecule4Node = dagMods[0].MDGModifier::createNode(
                Molecule4Node::id );
```

The newly created **molecule** node is added to the list of molecule nodes.

```
moleculeNodes.append( molecule4Node );
```

The `molecule4NodeFn` dependency node function set is initialized so that it can operate on the new **molecule** node.

```
molecule4NodeFn.setObject( molecule4Node );
```

A plug to the **molecule** node's **inMesh** attribute is retrieved.

```
MPlug inMeshPlug = molecule4NodeFn.findPlug( "inMesh" );
```

The output mesh attribute **outMesh** of the source mesh is connected to the input mesh attribute **inMesh** of the **molecule** node.

```
dagMods[0].connect( outMeshPlug, inMeshPlug );
```

A **transform** and a **mesh** node are now created. The `createNode` function can automatically create the transform parent of the mesh shape node if requested, but unfortunately once the transform parent is returned, it is impossible to access the child shape node. This is simply because the `dag` modifier is storing the operations to be performed later. It isn't actually performing the operations just yet, which means that the shape node doesn't exist and is thus inaccessible at this point. To get around this, a **transform** and **mesh** node are created explicitly.

```
newMeshTransform = dagMods[0].createNode( "transform" );
```

The **mesh** node is created, with the newly created **transform** node specified as its parent.

```
newMeshShape = dagMods[0].createNode( "mesh", newMeshTransform );
```

The new **mesh** node is added to the list of mesh shape nodes.

```
meshShapeNodes.append( newMeshShape );
```

The **transform** node is given a more appropriate name that better indicates its purpose.

```
dagMods[0].renameNode( newMeshTransform, "molecule" );
```

The nodeFn function set now operates on the new mesh shape node.

```
nodeFn.setObject( newMeshShape );
```

A plug to the **molecule** node's resulting output mesh attribute, **outMesh**, is retrieved. This is the final ball-and-rod model generated by the **molecule** node.

```
outMeshPlug = molecule4NodeFn.findPlug( "outMesh", &stat );
```

The attribute containing the **mesh** shape's input mesh, **inMesh**, is retrieved into a plug.

```
inMeshPlug = nodeFn.findPlug( "inMesh", &stat );
```

The **molecule** node's output mesh attribute, **outMesh**, is connected into the **mesh** shape's input mesh attribute, **inMesh**.

```
stat = dagMods[0].connect( outMeshPlug, inMeshPlug );
    }
```

If there are no meshes in the current selection, a warning message is issued and the command exits, indicating a failure.

```
if( nSelMeshes == 0 )
{
    MGlobal::displayWarning( "Select one or more meshes" );
    return MS::kFailure;
}
```

Now that all node creations and connections have been recorded, the actual operations can be performed.

```
dagMods[0].doIt();
```

The preparation of the second **MDagModifier**, dagMods[1], now commences. It is impossible to perform all operations necessary in the first modifier because until all nodes are actually created by calling the doIt function, the final names of the nodes are not known. Where a node name conflicts with an existing node, Maya will rename it appropriately. As such, it is only after the doIt function of the first modifier is called that the final node names are known. The second **MDagModifier**, dagMods[1], can now record its own series of operations on these now known nodes.

All of the **molecule** node's attributes are updated to reflect the settings passed as flags to this command. The operation is recorded using the commandToExecute function, which allows a particular portion of MEL code to be executed.

```
unsigned int i;
for( i=0; i < moleculeNodes.length(); i++ )
{
        nodeFn.setObject( moleculeNodes[i] );
        dagMods[1].commandToExecute( MString("setAttr ") +
                    nodeFn.name() + ".radius " + radius.value() );
        dagMods[1].commandToExecute( MString("setAttr ") +
                    nodeFn.name() + ".segments " + segs );
        dagMods[1].commandToExecute( MString("setAttr ") +
                    nodeFn.name() + ".ballRatio " + ballRodRatio );
}
```

Because Maya doesn't automatically ensure that a shape node is included in the initialShadingGroup, it must be done explicitly by the command.

```
for( i=0; i < meshShapeNodes.length(); i++ )
{
        nodeFn.setObject( meshShapeNodes[i] );
        dagMods[1].commandToExecute( MString( "sets -e -fe
                            initialShadingGroup " ) + nodeFn.name() );
}
```

Last, all molecule nodes are selected.

```
MString cmd( "select -r" );
for( i=0; i < moleculeNodes.length(); i++ )
{
        nodeFn.setObject( moleculeNodes[i] );
        cmd += " " + nodeFn.name();
}

dagMods[1].commandToExecute( cmd );
```

Now that all operations on the final nodes are stored, they can be executed.

```
dagMods[1].doIt();
```

The command returns with success.

```
    return MS::kSuccess;
}
```

With the two **MDagModifiers** prepared in the doIt function, the redoIt function simply repeats them by calling their corresponding doIt functions in order.

```
MStatus Molecule4Cmd::redoIt()
{
    int i;
    for( i=0; i < 2; i++ )
        dagMods[i].doIt();

    return MS::kSuccess;
}
```

The undoIt function simply calls the dag modifier's undoIt functions, starting with the most recent dag modifier and finishing with the least recent.

```
MStatus Molecule4Cmd::undoIt()
{
    int i;
```

```
    for( i=1; i >= 0; i-- )
            dagMods[i].undoIt();

    return MS::kSuccess;
}
```

Plug-in: `Molecule4`
File: `Molecule4Node.h`

The **Molecule4Node** class defines a custom **MPxNode** that will generate a ball-and-rod model from the given input mesh attribute, **inMesh**, and its other various attributes: **radius**, **segments**, and **ballRatio**. It generates the final mesh and places it in its output mesh attribute, **outMesh**.

Plug-in: `Molecule4`
File: `Molecule4Node.cpp`

After the node's ID and attribute objects are defined, the `compute` function follows.

```
MStatus Molecule4Node::compute( const MPlug &plug, MDataBlock &data )
{
    MStatus stat;
```

If the node's **state** attribute is set to **HasNoEffect/Pass-Through**, the input mesh **inMesh** is passed directly into the output mesh **outMesh** without any modifications. The `compute` function then exits immediately with success.

```
        MDataHandle stateHnd = data.inputValue( state );
        int state = stateHnd.asInt();
        if( state == 1 )
        {
            MDataHandle inMeshHnd = data.inputValue( inMesh );
            MDataHandle outMeshHnd = data.outputValue( outMesh );

            outMeshHnd.set( inMeshHnd.asMesh() );
            data.setClean( plug );

            return MS::kSuccess;
        }
```

If the plug being requested for recomputation is the **outMesh**, it is now calculated.

```
if( plug == outMesh )
{
```

MDataHandles to all node attributes are initialized.

```
MDataHandle radiusHnd = data.inputValue( radius );
MDataHandle segmentsHnd = data.inputValue( segments );
MDataHandle ballRatioHnd = data.inputValue( ballRatio );
MDataHandle inMeshHnd = data.inputValue( inMesh );
MDataHandle outMeshHnd = data.outputValue( outMesh );
```

The radius is retrieved as a double floating-point number. Even though the radius attribute is of type **MDistance**, Maya will automatically convert it to a double.

```
double radius = radiusHnd.asDouble();
```

The number of segments and the ratio of the balls to the rods are then retrieved.

```
int segs = segmentsHnd.asInt();
double ballRatio = ballRatioHnd.asDouble();
```

The input mesh is retrieved using the asMeshTransformed function. This returns the mesh data in world coordinates rather than in local coordinates. This function only works if the input mesh includes a geometry transformation matrix. Because this node had its **inMesh** attribute connected to the source mesh's **worldMesh** attribute, the transformation matrix is known. To determine the local-to-world transformation matrix for a given mesh inside the compute function, simply use the **MDataHandle**'s geometryTransformMatrix function.

```
MObject inMeshObj = inMeshHnd.asMeshTransformed();
```

A **MFnMesh** function set is initialized to work on the input mesh.

```
MFnMesh inMeshFn( inMeshObj );
```

A new mesh data object is created. This is where the final mesh will be stored.

```
MFnMeshData meshDataFn;
MObject newMeshData = meshDataFn.create();
```

The balls-and-rods mesh data is generated exactly as explained in the previous version, and is not repeated here.

```
int nBallPolys;
...
```

Once the final mesh data is prepared, the actual mesh can be created. Unlike the previous version of the **molecule** command, this node calls the create function with the newMeshData as the parentOrOwner parameter. This specifies to the create function that the resulting mesh should be stored in the newMeshData object, rather than creating a mesh shape node.

```
MFnMesh meshFn;
meshFn.create( newVerts.length(), nNewPolys, newVerts,
            newPolyCounts, newPolyConnects,
            newUCoords, newVCoords,
            newMeshData, &stat );
```

The status of the create function is then tested.

```
if( !stat )
{
        MGlobal::displayError( MString( "Unable to create mesh: " +
                            stat.errorString() );

        return stat;
}
```

The uv texture coordinates are assigned, as before.

```
meshFn.assignUVs( newPolyCounts, newFvUVIDs );
```

Because the mesh has changed, the updateSurface function needs to be called.

```
meshFn.updateSurface();
```

The final mesh has been generated. The output mesh attribute, **outMesh**, is updated to use the mesh.

```
outMeshHnd.set( newMeshData );
```

With the plug now successfully updated, it can be marked as clean.

```
data.setClean( plug );
}
```

If any plug other than **outMesh** is being requested for recomputation, simply return MS::kUnknownParameter. The base class of this node will then attempt to process the recomputation request.

```
else
        stat = MS::kUnknownParameter;
```

The final status is returned.

```
    return stat;
}
```

The creator function simply returns a new instance of the node.

```
void *Molecule4Node::creator()
{
    return new Molecule4Node();
}
```

The initialize function is responsible for defining the blueprint for the node's attributes.

```
MStatus Molecule4Node::initialize()
{
    MFnUnitAttribute uAttr;
    MFnNumericAttribute nAttr;
    MFnTypedAttribute tAttr;
```

The **radius** attribute is a distance and is thus created using the **MFnUnitAttribute** class.

```
radius = uAttr.create( "radius", "rad", MFnUnitAttribute::kDistance,
                     0.1 );
```

The **radius** attribute should be visible in the **Channel Box** and is thus set to be keyable.

```
uAttr.setKeyable( true );
```

The **segments** attribute is a simple integer number and thus the **MFnNumericAttribute** class is used to create it.

```
segments = nAttr.create( "segments", "seg", MFnNumericData::kLong, 6 );
```

Like the **radius** attribute, the **segments** attribute is visible in the **Channel Box**.

```
nAttr.setKeyable( true );
```

The **ballRatio** attribute is a double floating-point number and is made to be visible in the **Channel Box**.

```
ballRatio = nAttr.create( "ballRatio", "br", MFnNumericData::kDouble,
                        2.0 );
nAttr.setKeyable( true );
```

The input mesh attribute, **inMesh**, is created using the **MFnTypedAttribute** class. This class allows the creation of a variety of more complex data types. In this case, the **inMesh** attribute is created as a **MFnData::kMesh** type.

```
inMesh = tAttr.create( "inMesh", "im", MFnData::kMesh );
```

Because the output mesh attribute, **outMesh**, is also a mesh it is created using the same method.

```
outMesh = tAttr.create( "outMesh", "om", MFnData::kMesh );
```

The output mesh doesn't need to be stored in the Maya scene file because it can be automatically regenerated from the input attributes.

```
tAttr.setStorable( false );
```

All attributes are added to the node.

```
addAttribute( radius );
addAttribute( segments );
addAttribute( ballRatio );
addAttribute( inMesh );
addAttribute( outMesh );
```

All input attributes affect the output mesh attribute.

```
attributeAffects( radius, outMesh );
attributeAffects( segments, outMesh );
attributeAffects( ballRatio, outMesh );
attributeAffects( inMesh, outMesh );
```

The node's attributes have been successfully initialized.

```
    return MS::kSuccess;
}
```

This function returns the default value for the node's **radius** attribute. Because it is of type **MDistance**, an instance of **MDistance** is returned.

```
MDistance Molecule4Node::radiusDefault()
{
    MFnUnitAttribute uAttr( radius );
    MDistance d;
```

The getDefault function returns the default value of the attribute, as it was specified during the attribute's creation in the initialize function previously.

```
    uAttr.getDefault( d );
    return d;
}
```

The `segmentsDefault` function returns the number of default segments for the node.

```
int Molecule4Node::segmentsDefault()
{
    MFnNumericAttribute nAttr( segments );
    int d;
    nAttr.getDefault( d );
    return d;
}
```

The `ballRatioDefault` function returns the default ratio of the ball to the rods.

```
double Molecule4Node::ballRatioDefault()
{
    MFnNumericAttribute nAttr( ballRatio );
    double d;
    nAttr.getDefault( d );
    return d;
}
```

8.4 EDITING MESHES

Editing a mesh consists of modifying the mesh data. This includes adding, removing, or editing vertices, faces, uv texture coordinates, and so on. It is possible to edit a mesh so that all changes are applied directly to the mesh data. This means that there is no way in a later session to reverse these changes. The mesh contains the final result of all successive edits. Another approach is to record all edits done to a mesh so that they can later be undone or tweaked. Maya maintains this record of mesh edits by using a *construction history*.

8.4.1 CONSTRUCTION HISTORY

Because Maya is based on an interconnected node architecture, it follows that in order to record the history of changes to a mesh that a series of mesh editing nodes should be joined. The original mesh is placed at the start of the list. It is then connected into the first node that will edit the mesh. The resulting mesh after its edit is then passed into the next node, and so on. At the end of the chain of mesh editing nodes is the final shape node that will hold the final mesh. The series of joined nodes constitutes the object's construction history.

This can be viewed conceptually as follows. Starting with a simple mesh object, as shown in Figure 8.20, this mesh shape node holds the final mesh. It has no construction history because there are no nodes feeding into it. It is important to note that when creating most Maya shapes they will automatically have construction history, and thus the history has to be removed to reduce it to the state shown in Figure 8.20.

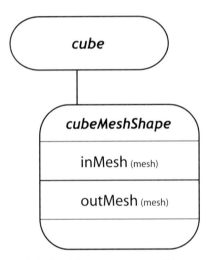

FIGURE 8.20 No construction history.

Suppose then that two hypothetical operations were applied to the **cube** object. The first is an **addFace** operation, which will add a face to the mesh. The second operation is an **extrudeFace** operation that will extrude a face outward. The **cube** object now has the construction history shown in Figure 8.21.

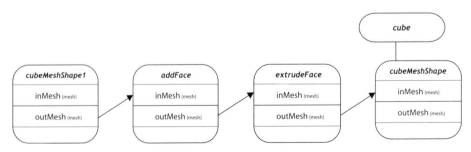

FIGURE 8.21 With construction history.

The first node in the series, **cubeMeshShape1**, is a duplicate of the orignal mesh shape, **cubeMeshShape**. This is the source mesh to the construction chain. It feeds the original mesh into the first editing node, **addFace**. This node adds a face to the incoming mesh attribute, **inMesh**, and then stores the result in its outgoing mesh attribute, **outMesh**. This attribute is connected into the second editing node, **extrudeFace**. It extrudes a face from the incoming mesh and stores the resulting mesh in its **outMesh** attribute. Finally, the **outMesh** attribute of the last editing node (**extrudeFace**) is connected into the incoming mesh attribute (**inMesh**) for the mesh shape node **cubeMeshShape**. This final mesh shape is the one shown in Maya's viewports.

The process of creating a construction history for modeling is very similar to that used to deform objects using deformers. A similar series of nodes forms a linear chain, each node of which operates on incoming data and produces its own outgoing data.

Because the construction history maintains a record of all editing operations that have been performed on the mesh, it can easily become quite large. Once an object is deemed complete and the construction history is no longer needed, the history can be deleted. Deleting the construction history consists of evaluating the final mesh and then removing all nodes that feed into the final shape node. The final mesh object will then consist of a transform with a single shape node, as is the case shown in Figure 8.20. Once reduced to this state, additional editing operations can still be performed and a new construction history created.

It is important to understand that there is nothing special about a construction history. It is simply a series of interconnected nodes that feeds into the final shape node. As such, it is no different from any other interconnected part of the Dependency Graph.

1. Select **File | New Scene** from the main menu.

2. To ensure that Maya will generate construction histories if necessary, turn this feature on by executing the following.

```
constructionHistory -toggle true;
```

3. Select **Create | Polygonal Primitives | Cube** from the main menu.

4. Ensure that the **Modeling** menu is visible in the main menu.

5. Select **Edit Polygons | Extrude Faces** from the main menu.

6. Select **Edit Polygons | Bevel** from the main menu.

7. Execute the following.

```
select -r pCube1;
listHistory;
```

The nodes that make up the construction history of the object are listed in the reverse order of that in which they were applied.

```
// Result: pCubeShape1 polyBevel1 polyExtrudeFace1 polyCube1 //
```

INTERMEDIATE OBJECTS

All shape nodes must have a parent transform node. When the construction history was created, a duplicate of the original shape node was put at the head of the interconnected nodes. Referring to Figure 8.21, this results in the **cube** tranform having two child shape nodes, **cubeMeshShape1** and **cubeMeshShape**, under it.

So which of the two shape nodes will Maya display? It is clear that the final shape node is really the one at the end of the chain, the **cubeMeshShape** node. The duplicated shape node, **cubeMeshShape1**, is really just there to feed into the chain of nodes. It shouldn't be displayed. Maya refers to these types of shape nodes as *intermediate objects*. They are used in the construction of the final object but shouldn't be visible or rendered.

Because any object that has a construction history is likely to have more than one child shape node, it is important to take this into consideration when iterating through a transform's children. If the shape node of a transform node is needed, it is necessary to iterate through all children and return the node that is both a shape node and *not* an intermediate object. The **MFnDagNode** class has two functions relating to intermediate objects. The **MFnDagNode**'s `isIntermediateObject` function returns `true` if the current node is an intermediate object. A node can be flagged as being an intermediate object using the **MFnDagNode**'s `setIntermediateObject` function. Alternatively, this state can be determined by retrieving the **intermediateObject** attribute.

```
getAttr cubeMeshShape1.intermediateObject;
```

Changing an object's intermediate object status should only be done if absolutely necessary. Incorrectly setting it to the wrong value could cause unpredictable results.

VERTEX TWEAKS

In general computer graphics nomenclature, a *tweak* refers to a small change made to a model, image, or other object. Maya uses the term *tweak* to refer to the movement of vertices; more precisely, the relative displacement of vertices from their original positions. A vertex can be moved by a wide variety of means, including applying an **xform** to geometry components, attaching animation or deformers to vertices, or pretty well any operation that moves a vertex from its original location.

Given a mesh shape node with no construction history, when a vertex is moved the new vertex position isn't stored in the mesh vertices. Instead, the direction and distance from the original vertex is stored as a tweak. The tweaks to the mesh are stored in the **pnts** attribute of the mesh shape node. This is a hidden attribute that holds an array of **float3** attributes (**pntx**, **pnty**, and **pntz**) that hold the vertex displacement. This array is initialized to an array of zero vectors, indicating that no tweaks have been applied. A mesh node with no construction history but having tweaks actually stores the original mesh data in the **cachedInMesh** attribute, rather than in the usual **inMesh** attribute. Once again, this is a hidden attribute. When the output mesh attribute, **outMesh**, of the shape node is requested, the node will generate the output mesh vertex positions as follows.

outMesh_vertices = cachedInMesh_vertices + pnts

The final vertex positions are calculated by displacing the **cachedInMesh** vertices by the amount of the tweaks (**pnts** array). Because the mesh shape node automatically adds the tweak displacements to the mesh before outputting, this complicates matters if the object were to be edited and therefore have a construction history.

1. To ensure that Maya will generate construction histories if necessary, turn this feature on by executing the following.

```
constructionHistory -toggle true;
```

2. Open the **CubeMesh.ma** scene.

3. Select the **cube** object.

4. Select **Edit | Delete by Type | History**.

5. Open the **Hypergraph** window.

6. Click on the **Input and Output Connections** button in the **Hypergraph** toolbar.

   Under the **cube** transform node there is a single mesh shape node, **cubeShape**, with no construction history.

7. Execute the following.

   ```
   getAttr cube.pnts["*"];
   ```

   The array of tweaks is printed out. Recall that it is an array of 3D vectors.

   ```
   // Result: 0 0 0 0 0 0 0 0 0 0 0 0 0 0 0 0 0 0 0 0 0 0 0 0 //
   ```

   Because none of the vertices have been tweaked, the displacement vectors are all zero.

8. Execute the following.

   ```
   getAttr cube.vrts[0];
   ```

   The local position, without tweaks, of the first vertex is printed out.

   ```
   // Result: -0.5 -0.5 0.5 //
   ```

9. Execute the following.

   ```
   move -relative 0.5 0.5 0.5 cube.vtx[0];
   ```

   The first vertex is moved +0.5 along each of the axes.

10. Execute the following.

   ```
   getAttr cube.vrts[0];
   ```

   Once again, the local position is printed out.

   ```
   // Result: -0.5 -0.5 0.5 //
   ```

   Note that the position hasn't changed.

11. Execute the following.

```
getAttr cube.pnts["*"];
```

The tweak array is printed out.

```
// Result: 0.5 0.5 0.5 0 0 0 0 0 0 0 0 0 0 0 0 0 0 0 0 0 0 0 0 0 //
```

The first tweak vector in the array holds the relative movement applied to the first vertex. To get the tweak vector for the first vertex, execute the following.

```
getAttr cube.pnts[0];
```

The tweak vector is printed out.

```
// Result: 0.5 0.5 0.5 //
```

It follows from the previous discussion that the final local position of the first vertex is the result of adding the original local position (`vrts[0]`) to the tweak vectors (`pnts[0]`).

final = vrts[0] + pnts[0]
　　　= (−0.5 −0.5 0.5) + (0.5 0.5 0.5)
　　　= (0.0 0.0 1.0)

To determine if this calculation is correct, the local position is retrieved using the `pointPosition` command.

12. Execute the following.

```
pointPosition -local cube.vtx[0];
```

The resulting vector matches the previous calculation.

```
// Result: 0 0 1 //
```

The situation in which the mesh shape node has construction history is explored in the following.

1. If Maya's construction history feature isn't turned on, do so by executing the following.

    ```
    constructionHistory -toggle true;
    ```

2. Open the **CubeMesh.ma** scene.

3. Select the **cube** object.

4. Open the **Hypergraph** window.

5. Click on the **Input and Output Connections** button in the **Hypergraph** toolbar.

    The **cube** transform has a **cubeShape** mesh shape node as its child. The **polyCube1** node generates the cube mesh data and feeds it into the **cubeShape**'s **inMesh** attribute. As such, the **cube** object has a construction history, shown in Figure 8.22.

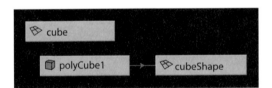

FIGURE 8.22 Construction history of **cube** object.

6. Execute the following.

    ```
    move -relative 0.5 0.5 0.5 cube.vtx[0];
    ```

    Maya moves the first vertex, but also issues the following warning.

    ```
    // Warning: line 1: cubeShape (Mesh Node): Tweaks can be undesirable on
    shapes with history. //
    ```

    The reason Maya issued this warning is that tweaks will always happen at the very end of all other operations. Because the tweaks are applied only when the **outMesh** attribute of the mesh shape node is requested, if there are any operations earlier in the construction history that depend on the tweaks having already been applied, the correct result will not be generated. The current final mesh is the result of the following operations.

**final_mesh = polyCube1_mesh ->
   (cubeShape_mesh + cubeShape_tweaks)**

The tweaks are applied automatically inside the mesh shape node and are thus not part of a separate editing node. If the face extrusion operation were now performed on the mesh, the result would logically look as follows.

**final_mesh = polyCube1_mesh -> faceExtrude_mesh ->
   (cubeShape_mesh + cubeShape_tweaks)**

The **faceExtrude** node would be inserted after the **polyCube1** node. It is quickly clear that the result isn't exactly what was intended. The problem is that the **faceExtrude** operation will be applied *before* the tweaks. What really needs to happen is that the tweaks be applied before the face extrusion. To get around this problem of the tweaks always occuring last, Maya will extract the tweaks from the mesh shape node and put them in a special **polyTweak** node further upstream in the construction history. This ensures that the tweaks are applied before the face extrusion. The resulting series of operations, in their now correct order, is as follows.

**final_mesh = polyCube1_mesh -> cubeShape_tweaks ->
   faceExtrude_mesh -> cubeShape_mesh**

7. Execute the following.

```
polyMergeVertex;
```

The new construction history is shown in Figure 8.23.

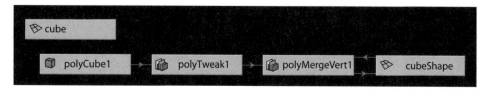

FIGURE 8.23 New construction history.

8. A new **polyTweak1** node is inserted directly after the **polyCube1** node. This tweak node contains a copy of the tweak vectors (**pnts** array attribute) from the original **cubeShape** shape node. The **cubeShape** node's **pnts** array is reset to zero vectors, in that the **polyTweak1** node now holds all necessary tweaks. The output of the **polyTweak1** node is a mesh with the tweaks applied. It is fed into the **polyMergeVert1** node, which performs the vertex merging. The mesh this node produces is fed into the **inMesh** attribute of the final mesh shape node, **cubeShape**. The construction order is now correct: the tweaks are applied to the mesh before the vertex merging operation.

9. Execute the following.

```
getAttr polyTweak1.tweak[0];
```

This gets the tweak node's displacement vector for the first vertex.

```
// Result: 0.5 0.5 0.5 //
```

This is the amount the first vertex was tweaked.

10. Execute the following.

```
getAttr cube.pnts[0];
```

This retrieves the tweak vector for the first vertex stored in the **cubeShape** node.

```
// Result: 0 0 0 //
```

As expected, it is a zero vector. Because the **polyTweak1** node now holds the original tweaks, the mesh shape node no longer applies any tweaks. With the construction history now in place, what happens now if the mesh vertices are moved?

11. Execute the following.

```
move -relative 0 0 1 cube.vtx[0];
```

The first vertex is moved further along the Z axis.

12. Execute the following.

```
getAttr cube.pnts[0];
```

The vertex tweak has been stored in the mesh shape node and not in the **polyTweak1** node. Whenever a tweak is performed it is always stored in mesh shape node's **pnts** array. This may not be what was intended. This is another reason Maya discourages tweaking mesh shapes with construction history by warning the user.

If another editing operation were now performed, the same set of steps would be carried out. The current **pnts** tweaks would be stored in a new **polyTweak** node, which would be inserted after the last operation. The mesh shape node's **pnts** array would then be reset. As such, there can be many tweak nodes in an object's construction history.

8.4.2 SUPPORTING CONSTRUCTION HISTORY

Any mesh-editing command must support construction history. Maya's internal mesh-editing commands (`polyExtrudeFacet`, `polyBevel`, `polyMergeVertex`, and so on) all support construction history. Unfortunately, Maya doesn't provide any framework for developers to easily create custom commands that support construction history. As such, it is up to developers to ensure that their commands will manage and maintain the construction history of the objects they work on. This can be a quite complex undertaking, and is further exacerbated by the need to support undoing.

Any new mesh-editing functionality will need to be implemented as two parts: a custom command and custom node. The custom command will create the custom node that is responsible for doing the actual editing of the mesh. The command will also manage the construction history of the object. This means that the command will create any necessary tweak nodes, create mesh duplicates, insert and reconnect nodes, collapse the history, and so on. It is important that the command take into account Maya's **Construction History** setting. This setting can be queried using the `constructionHistory` command.

```
constructionHistory -query -toggle;
```

When it is active, the new mesh-editing functionality must maintain the object's construction history. There are two states that need to be taken into account. Does the object already have a construction history? Is Maya's **Construction History** setting turned on? All combinations of these states need to be taken into account. Table 8.1 outlines all possible scenarios.

TABLE 8.1 CONSTRUCTION HISTORY SCENARIOS		
	Has History?	Create History?
Case A	Yes	Yes
Case B	Yes	No
Case C	No	Yes
Case D	No	No

Cases A and B are treated identically. If an object already has construction history, it must be maintained irrespective of Maya's current **Construction History** setting. The steps for both cases are as follows.

1. Create a mesh modifier node.

2. Get the node directly upstream of the mesh shape node.

3. Disconnect the upstream node.

4. Connect the upstream node to the mesh modifier node.

5. Connect the mesh modifier node to the mesh shape node.

For Case C, no history currently exists but one needs to be created. The steps for the history creation are as follows.

1. Create a mesh modifier node.

2. Duplicate the existing mesh shape node.

3. Connect the duplicate mesh shape node to the mesh modifier node.

4. Connect the mesh modifier node to the original mesh shape node.

The final scenario, Case D, requires that the mesh-editing operation be applied directly to the mesh with no residual construction history after the operation. It is possible to create a specific command that will operate on the mesh directly, but this would result in duplicate code because the mesh-editing operation is already encapsulated in the mesh modifier node. A far more simplistic solution is to actually create a construction history for the mesh and then collapse it afterward, thereby reducing it back to a single mesh shape node. The steps for Case D are therefore the same as those for Case C, with the exception that the construction history is collapsed at the end.

1. Perform all steps in Case C.

2. Delete the construction history.

8.4.3 SUPPORTING TWEAKS

In addition to supporting construction history, it is important that the command also support tweaks. Fortunately, the same procedure is used for tweaks in all possible construction history scenarios.

First, the object is checked to determine if it has any tweaks. If it does, the following steps are performed.

1. Create a **polyTweak** node.

2. Copy the tweak values from the mesh shape node to the **polyTweak** node.

3. Clear the tweak values in the mesh shape node.

These steps are done before the steps listed in the previous cases. This prevents a potential problem for Case C. If the mesh shape node were duplicated before the tweak values were cleared, the upstream duplicate node would contain the tweaks. Because the **polyTweak** node will also exist downstream of the duplicate node, the tweaks will effectively be applied twice. Clearing the tweaks on the original mesh shape node before it is duplicated ensures that the tweaks only exist in the **polyTweak** node.

8.4.4 MESH-EDITING FRAMEWORK

The process of creating and maintaining construction history and tweaks is complex. Because the burden is on the developer to perform this work, it can be quite difficult if many mesh-editing commands need to be implemented. To reduce this burden, a set of custom C++ classes has been developed by the author that hide a lot of the complexity and allow the developer to focus on the main functionality of the command and mesh modifier nodes. These are not Maya classes and thus their source code is only available with the source code associated with this book.

Two custom classes have been defined: **CmpMeshModifierCmd** and **CmpMeshModiferNode**. Both classes are prefixed by **Cmp** (Complete Maya Programming) to prevent conflicting with other possible class names.

The **CmpMeshModifierCmd** class defines a command that automatically handles construction history, tweaks, and undoing. The developer simply creates a new class derived from this class to create a custom command with all required construction history functionality. The **CmpMeshModifierNode** class defines a node that has attributes **inMesh** and **outMesh** that hold the incoming and outgoing meshes, respectively.

The following section describes these classes in detail. It isn't necessary to understand their internal workings to make use of them, and thus if the reader so desires this section can be skipped in favor of the next section that describes how to use them in a mesh-editing example.

It is important to note that the command operates on one mesh per instantiation. It doesn't support the selection of a series of meshes and application of the mesh modifier node to each of them. As such, if the command needs to be applied to multiple mesh objects it must be called once for each mesh object.

SOURCE CODE

File: `CmpMeshModifierNode.h`

```
class CmpMeshModifierNode : public MPxNode
{
public:
    static MStatus initialize();

protected:
    static MObject inMesh;
    static MObject outMesh;
};
```

File: `CmpMeshModifierNode.cpp`

```
MObject CmpMeshModifierNode::inMesh;
MObject CmpMeshModifierNode::outMesh;

MStatus CmpMeshModifierNode::initialize()
{
    MFnTypedAttribute tAttr;
    inMesh = tAttr.create( "inMesh", "im", MFnData::kMesh );

    outMesh = tAttr.create( "outMesh", "om", MFnData::kMesh );
    tAttr.setStorable( false );

    addAttribute( inMesh );
    addAttribute( outMesh );

    attributeAffects( inMesh, outMesh );
```

```
       return MS::kSuccess;
    }
```

File: `CmpMeshModifierCmd.h`

```
    class CmpMeshModifierCmd : public MPxCommand
    {
    public:
       CmpMeshModifierCmd();

       MStatus doIt( const MDagPath &dagPath,
                     const MTypeId &meshModType );
       virtual MStatus redoIt();
       virtual MStatus undoIt();
       virtual bool isUndoable() const { return true; }

       virtual MStatus initModifierNode( MObject &node,
                                         MDagModifier &dagMod ) = 0;

    private:
       MDagPath meshShapePath;
       MTypeId meshModifierNodeType;

       bool hasHistory;
       bool hasInternalTweaks;
       bool genHistory;

       enum { N_DAGMODIFIERS=3 };
       MDagModifier dagMods[N_DAGMODIFIERS];

       MStatus transferTweaks( const MDagPath &shapePath,
                               MObject &tweakNode,
                               MDagModifier &dagMod );

       MObject copyTransform;
       MObject origMeshData;
    };
```

File: `CmpMeshModifierCmd.cpp`

```
    CmpMeshModifierCmd::CmpMeshModifierCmd()
    {
       hasHistory = hasInternalTweaks = genHistory = false;
    }
```

```
MStatus CmpMeshModifierCmd::doIt( const MDagPath &dagPath,
                                  const MTypeId &meshModType )
{
   MStatus stat;

   meshShapePath = dagPath;
   if( !meshShapePath.isValid() )
   {
        displayError( "Invalid mesh shape path: " +
                      meshShapePath.fullPathName() );
        return MS::kFailure;
   }

   meshModifierNodeType = meshModType;

   MFnDagNode origShapeNodeFn( meshShapePath );

   MPlug inMeshOrigPlug = origShapeNodeFn.findPlug( "inMesh" );
   hasHistory = inMeshOrigPlug.isConnected();

   hasInternalTweaks = false;
   MPlug tweaksPlug = origShapeNodeFn.findPlug( "pnts" );
   if( !tweaksPlug.isNull() )
   {
        MObject obj;
        MPlug tweakPlug;
        MFloatVector tweak;
        unsigned int i;
        unsigned int nTweaks = tweaksPlug.numElements();
        for( i=0; i < nTweaks; i++ )
        {
             tweakPlug = tweaksPlug.elementByPhysicalIndex( i, &stat );
             if( stat && !tweakPlug.isNull() )
             {
                  tweakPlug.getValue( obj );
                  MFnNumericData numDataFn( obj );
                  numDataFn.getData( tweak[0], tweak[1], tweak[2] );

                  if( tweak[0] ! = 0.0f ||
                      tweak[1] ! = 0.0f ||
                      tweak[2] ! = 0.0f )
```

```
                    {
                            hasInternalTweaks = true;
                            break;
                    }
            }
       }
}

int res;

MGlobal::executeCommand( "constructionHistory -query -toggle", res );
genHistory = (res != 0);

if( !hasHistory )
{
       MPlug meshPlug = origShapeNodeFn.findPlug(
                       hasInternalTweaks ? "cachedInMesh" : "outMesh" );
       meshPlug.getValue( origMeshData );
}

MObject modNode = dagMods[0].MDGModifier::createNode(
                                 meshModifierNodeType, &stat );
MObject tweakNode = dagMods[0].MDGModifier::createNode(
                                 "polyTweak", &stat );
dagMods[0].doIt();

MFnDependencyNode nodeFn( modNode );
if( nodeFn.attribute( "inMesh" ).isNull() ||
    nodeFn.attribute( "outMesh" ).isNull() )
{
       displayError( "Invalid modifier node. It doesn't have
                       inMesh and/or outMesh attributes" );
       return MS::kFailure;
}

initModifierNode( modNode, dagMods[1] );
MFnDependencyNode modNodeFn( modNode );

MPlug newStreamInMeshPlug = modNodeFn.findPlug( "inMesh" );

MPlugArray inPlugs;
inMeshOrigPlug.connectedTo( inPlugs, true, false );
```

```
MPlug oldStreamOutMeshPlug;
if( inPlugs.length() )
{
      oldStreamOutMeshPlug = inPlugs[0];
      dagMods[1].disconnect( oldStreamOutMeshPlug, inMeshOrigPlug );
}

if( hasInternalTweaks )
{
      transferTweaks( meshShapePath, tweakNode, dagMods[1] );

      MFnDependencyNode tweakNodeFn( tweakNode );
      newStreamInMeshPlug = tweakNodeFn.findPlug( "inputPolymesh" );

      MPlug inMeshModPlug = modNodeFn.findPlug( "inMesh" );
      MPlug outMeshTweakPlug = tweakNodeFn.findPlug( "output" );
      dagMods[1].connect( outMeshTweakPlug, inMeshModPlug );
}

dagMods[1].doIt();

copyTransform = MObject::kNullObj;

if( !hasHistory )
{
      copyTransform = origShapeNodeFn.duplicate();
      MFnDagNode copyTransformFn( copyTransform );

      MObject copyShapeNode = copyTransformFn.child(0);
      MFnDagNode copyShapeNodeFn( copyShapeNode );

      dagMods[2].commandToExecute( "setAttr " +
              copyShapeNodeFn.fullPathName() +
              ".intermediateObject true" );

      oldStreamOutMeshPlug = copyShapeNodeFn.findPlug( "outMesh" );

      dagMods[2].renameNode( copyShapeNode,
                          copyShapeNodeFn.name() + "Orig" );

      MObject origTransform = meshShapePath.transform();
      dagMods[2].reparentNode( copyShapeNode, origTransform );
```

```
                dagMods[2].commandToExecute( "delete " +
                                             copyTransformFn.fullPathName() );
        }

        if( !oldStreamOutMeshPlug.isNull() )
            dagMods[2].connect( oldStreamOutMeshPlug, newStreamInMeshPlug );

        MPlug outMeshModPlug = modNodeFn.findPlug( "outMesh" );
        dagMods[2].connect( outMeshModPlug, inMeshOrigPlug );

        if( !hasHistory && !genHistory )
            dagMods[2].commandToExecute(
                        MString("delete -constructionHistory ") +
                        meshShapePath.fullPathName() );

        dagMods[2].doIt();

        return MS::kSuccess;
}

MStatus CmpMeshModifierCmd::transferTweaks( const MDagPath &shapePath,
                                            MObject &tweakNode,
                                            MDagModifier &dagMod )
{
    MFnDagNode shapeNodeFn( shapePath );
    MPlug srcTweaksPlug = shapeNodeFn.findPlug( "pnts" );

    MFnDependencyNode tweakNodeFn( tweakNode );
    MPlug dstTweaksPlug = tweakNodeFn.findPlug( "tweak" );

    MPlugArray plugs;
    MPlug srcTweakPlug;
    MPlug dstTweakPlug;
    MObject dataObj;
    MFloatVector tweak;
    unsigned int nTweaks = srcTweaksPlug.numElements();
    unsigned int i, j, ci, logicalIndex;
    for( i=0; i < nTweaks; i++ )
    {
        srcTweakPlug = srcTweaksPlug.elementByPhysicalIndex( i );
        if( !srcTweakPlug.isNull() )
        {
```

```
logicalIndex = srcTweakPlug.logicalIndex();

srcTweakPlug.getValue( dataObj );
MFnNumericData numDataFn( dataObj );
numDataFn.getData( tweak[0], tweak[1], tweak[2] );

dagMod.commandToExecute(
     MString( "setAttr " ) + tweakNodeFn.name() +
     ".tweak[" + logicalIndex + "] " +
     tweak[0] + " " + tweak[1] + " " + tweak[2] );

dstTweakPlug = dstTweaksPlug.elementByLogicalIndex(
                              logicalIndex);

if( srcTweakPlug.isConnected() )
{
     srcTweakPlug.connectedTo( plugs, false, true );
     for( j=0; j < plugs.length(); j++ )
     {
          dagMod.disconnect( srcTweakPlug, plugs[j] );
          dagMod.connect( dstTweakPlug, plugs[j] );
     }

     srcTweakPlug.connectedTo( plugs, true, false );
     if( plugs.length() == 1 )
     {
          dagMod.disconnect( plugs[0], srcTweakPlug );
          dagMod.connect( plugs[0], dstTweakPlug );
     }
}
else
{
     MPlug srcTweakChildPlug;
     MPlug dstTweakChildPlug;

     for( ci=0; ci < srcTweakPlug.numChildren(); ci++ )
     {
          srcTweakChildPlug = srcTweakPlug.child(ci);
          dstTweakChildPlug = dstTweakPlug.child(ci);
```

```
                          if( srcTweakChildPlug.isConnected() )
                          {
                          srcTweakChildPlug.connectedTo( plugs, false,
                                                         true );
                          for( j=0; j < plugs.length(); j++ )
                          {
                                  dagMod.disconnect( srcTweakChildPlug,
                                                     plugs[j] );
                                  dagMod.connect( dstTweakChildPlug,
                                                  plugs[j] );
                          }
                          srcTweakChildPlug.connectedTo( plugs, true,
                                                         false );
                          if( plugs.length() == 1 )
                          {
                                  dagMod.disconnect( plugs[0],
                                                     srcTweakChildPlug );
                                  dagMod.connect( plugs[0],
                                                  stTweakChildPlug );
                          }
                          }
                      }
              }

          dagMod.commandToExecute( MString( "setAttr " ) +
                  shapePath.fullPathName() + ".pnts[" +
                  logicalIndex + "] 0 0 0" );
      }
   }

   return MS::kSuccess;
}

MStatus CmpMeshModifierCmd::redoIt()
{
   dagMods[0].doIt();
   dagMods[1].doIt();
   if( !hasHistory )
   {
```

```
            MFnDagNode origShapeNodeFn( meshShapePath );
            copyTransform = origShapeNodeFn.duplicate();
        }
        dagMods[2].doIt();

        return MS::kSuccess;
    }

    MStatus CmpMeshModifierCmd::undoIt()
    {
        dagMods[2].undoIt();
        if( !copyTransform.isNull() )
            MGlobal::deleteNode( copyTransform );
        dagMods[1].undoIt();
        dagMods[0].undoIt();
        if( !hasHistory )
        {
            MFnDagNode origShapeNodeFn( meshShapePath );
            MPlug meshPlug = origShapeNodeFn.findPlug(
                        hasInternalTweaks ? "cachedInMesh" : "outMesh" );
            meshPlug.setValue( origMeshData );
        }

        return MS::kSuccess;
    }
```

SOURCE CODE EXPLANATION

File: `CmpMeshModifierNode.h`

The **CmpMeshModiferNode** is derived from the **MPxNode**. It declares two attributes: **inMesh** and **outMesh**. Because the node is so simple, it may be understandable to question why it is needed. The **CmpMeshModifierCmd** class relies on the mesh modifier node to have at least the **inMesh** and **outMesh** attributes. As such, it is possible that this class can be circumvented and another custom node used in its place. The only requirement is that the custom node have the **inMesh** and **outMesh** attributes.

File: `CmpMeshModifierNode.cpp`

The two attributes, **inMesh** and **outMesh**, are initialized.

File: `CmpMeshModifierCmd.h`

The **CmpMeshModifierCmd** is derived from the **MPxCommand**, and is an abstract class because it doesn't define the pure virtual `doIt` function inherited from **MPxCommand**. This function is left to the derived class to define. The class also has another pure virtual function, `initModifierNode`. The class implements most of the command functions, including `redoIt`, `undoIt`, `isUndoable`, and so on. It does define its own custom `doIt` function that takes the mesh shape the modifier will operate on as well as the **MTypeId** of the custom mesh modifier node that will do the mesh editing.

```
MStatus doIt( const MDagPath &dagPath,
            const MTypeId &meshModType );
```

The class declares the pure virtual `initModifierNode` function that must be defined in the derived class.

```
virtual MStatus initModifierNode( MObject &node,
                                  MDagModifier &dagMod ) = 0;
```

This function takes the newly created mesh modifier node and intializes it. It should record all changes it makes to the node in the supplied **dagMod** object. This ensures that the changes can be undone. The remaining functions are described in the `.cpp` implementation file.

File: `CmpMeshModifierCmd.cpp`

The constructor initializes the information about the node's state.

```
CmpMeshModifierCmd::CmpMeshModifierCmd()
{
    hasHistory = hasInternalTweaks = genHistory = false;
}
```

The custom `doIt` function (not to be confused with the **MPxCommand**'s virtual `doIt` function) prepares the various nodes and sets up the construction history and tweaks. It takes the DAG path, **dagPath**, of the mesh shape node the mesh modifier node will edit. The **MTypeId** of the mesh modifier node is also passed to the function, **meshModType**. The function uses this type of ID to create an instance of the mesh modifier node.

```
MStatus CmpMeshModifierCmd::doIt( const MDagPath &dagPath,
                                  const MTypeId &meshModType )
{
    MStatus stat;
```

The DAG path to the mesh shape node is recorded and tested.

```
meshShapePath = dagPath;
if( !meshShapePath.isValid() )
{
    displayError( "Invalid mesh shape path: " +
                    meshShapePath.fullPathName() );
    return MS::kFailure;
}
```

The **MTypeId** of the mesh modifier node is recorded.

```
meshModifierNodeType = meshModType;
```

The **inMesh** attribute is checked to see if it has any connections. If it does, the object has a construction history.

```
MFnDagNode origShapeNodeFn( meshShapePath );
MPlug inMeshOrigPlug = origShapeNodeFn.findPlug( "inMesh" );
hasHistory = inMeshOrigPlug.isConnected();
```

Whether the mesh shape node has tweaks is now determined. The **pnts** attribute holds the internal tweaks for the mesh shape node. If it has non-zero vectors, there are tweaks.

```
hasInternalTweaks = false;
MPlug tweaksPlug = origShapeNodeFn.findPlug( "pnts" );
if( !tweaksPlug.isNull() )
{
    MObject obj;
    MPlug tweakPlug;
```

```
MFloatVector tweak;
unsigned int i;
unsigned int nTweaks = tweaksPlug.numElements();
```

Each element in the **pnts** array is iterated over by using the physical index.

```
for( i=0; i < nTweaks; i++ )
{
        tweakPlug = tweaksPlug.elementByPhysicalIndex( i, &stat );
```

Because the array is sparse, the physical index may not hold a plug to an actual attribute and is thus tested.

```
if( stat && !tweakPlug.isNull() )
{
```

The numeric data object is retrieved for the tweak element. It is of type `MFnNumericData::k3Float` and is thus a vector of three floats.

```
tweakPlug.getValue( obj );
MFnNumericData numDataFn( obj );
numDataFn.getData( tweak[0], tweak[1], tweak[2] );
```

The tweak vector is checked to see if it isn't a zero vector. If it isn't, the node has internal tweaks and the `hasInternalTweaks` is updated to reflect this. The loop is then immediately exited.

```
if( tweak[0] != 0.0f ||
        tweak[1] != 0.0f ||
        tweak[2] != 0.0f )
{
        hasInternalTweaks = true;
        break;
}
    }
}
}
```

The global **Construction History** setting is retrieved.

```
int res;
MGlobal::executeCommand( "constructionHistory -query -toggle", res );
genHistory = (res != 0);
```

If the mesh shape node doesn't have a history, its original mesh data is stored in the origMeshData variable. This way, it can be restored later if the command is undone.

```
if( !hasHistory )
{
```

If the mesh shape node has internal tweaks, the actual input mesh is stored in the **cachedInMesh** attribute. If there are no internal tweaks, the **outMesh** attribute can be used to retrieve the final mesh.

```
MPlug meshPlug = origShapeNodeFn.findPlug(
                hasInternalTweaks ? "cachedInMesh" : "outMesh" );
meshPlug.getValue( origMeshData );
}
```

An instance of the mesh modifier node is created.

```
MObject modNode = dagMods[0].MDGModifier::createNode(
                            meshModifierNodeType, &stat );
```

An instance of the **polyTweak** node is created.

```
MObject tweakNode = dagMods[0].MDGModifier::createNode(
                            "polyTweak", &stat );
```

The first DAG modifier, dagMods[0], is executed. This ensures that the nodes it recorded for construction are actually created. This is important if there are later commands that need to use the node's actual names. In particular, this ensures that when the initModifierNode function is called later the mesh modifier node actually exists.

```
dagMods[0].doIt();
```

The mesh modifier node created must have **inMesh** and **outMesh** attributes.

```
MFnDependencyNode nodeFn( modNode );
if( nodeFn.attribute( "inMesh" ).isNull() ||
    nodeFn.attribute( "outMesh" ).isNull() )
{
    displayError( "Invalid modifier node. It doesn't have
                   inMesh and/or outMesh attributes" );
    return MS::kFailure;
}
```

The `initModifierNode` function is called. This function will be defined in the derived class. It takes the newly created mesh modifier node, `modNode`, as well as a DAG Modifier, `dagMods[1]`. The function intializes the mesh modifier node. Any changes it makes are stored in the supplied DAG modifier so that they can be undone later.

```
initModifierNode( modNode, dagMods[1] );
```

When the new nodes are inserted into the object's contruction history, they are referred to as the new stream. The mesh modifier node's **inMesh** attribute provides the insertion point of the new stream. The `newStreamInMeshPlug` variable records this insertion point.

```
MFnDependencyNode modNodeFn( modNode );
MPlug newStreamInMeshPlug = modNodeFn.findPlug( "inMesh" );
```

The connection to the mesh shape node's **inMesh** attribute is retrieved.

```
MPlugArray inPlugs;
inMeshOrigPlug.connectedTo( inPlugs, true, false );
MPlug oldStreamOutMeshPlug;
```

Only if the mesh shape node has construction history will there be an incoming connection.

```
if( inPlugs.length() )
{
```

The `oldStreamOutMeshPlug` variable stores the plug representing the end of the previous stream.

```
oldStreamOutMeshPlug = inPlugs[0];
```

Because the mesh modifier node will be inserted before the **inMesh** attribute, the old connection is broken.

```
        dagMods[1].disconnect( oldStreamOutMeshPlug, inMeshOrigPlug );
    }

    if( hasInternalTweaks )
    {
```

If the mesh shape node has its own tweaks, the `transferTweaks` function is called to transfer them to the tweak node. The function's actions are recorded in the supplied DAG modifier, `dagMods[1]`, so that they can be later undone.

```
        transferTweaks( meshShapePath, tweakNode, dagMods[1] );
```

Because the tweak node will be inserted ahead of the mesh modifier node, it is now the starting point of the new stream. The `newStreamInMeshPlug` is updated to refer to the tweak node's `inputPolymesh` attribute.

```
        MFnDependencyNode tweakNodeFn( tweakNode );
        newStreamInMeshPlug = tweakNodeFn.findPlug( "inputPolymesh" );
```

The output of the tweak node (**output**) is connected to the input (**inMesh**) of the mesh modifier node.

```
        MPlug inMeshModPlug = modNodeFn.findPlug( "inMesh" );
        MPlug outMeshTweakPlug = tweakNodeFn.findPlug( "output" );
        dagMods[1].connect( outMeshTweakPlug, inMeshModPlug );
    }
```

All actions recorded in the second DAG modifier, `dagMods[1]`, are now executed. The reason they are executed now is that the next section of code calls the `MFnDagNode::duplicate` function that can't be recorded in a DAG modifier. As such, it will have to be manually undone. Thus, whenever an undoable operation is performed it is done between new instances of the DAG modifiers. The need for this separation will become clearer when the `redoIt` and `undoIt` functions are covered.

```
dagMods[1].doIt();
```

The transform node, `copyTransform`, of the duplicate shape node is initialized to a null object. If the duplicate isn't created, the transform node will remain a null object.

```
copyTransform = MObject::kNullObj;
```

If the mesh shape node doesn't have a history, it needs to be created.

```
if( !hasHistory )
{
```

The original mesh shape node is duplicated using the `duplicate` function. This function returns the parent transform node of the duplicated shape.

```
copyTransform = origShapeNodeFn.duplicate();
MFnDagNode copyTransformFn( copyTransform );
```

The duplicate mesh shape node is the first child of the transform node.

```
MObject copyShapeNode = copyTransformFn.child(0);
MFnDagNode copyShapeNodeFn( copyShapeNode );
```

The duplicate mesh shape node will provide the source for the construction history. It will be at the start of the chain of nodes. Because it isn't the final shape node but instead part of the construction history, it is flagged as an intermediate object.

```
dagMods[2].commandToExecute( "setAttr " +
        copyShapeNodeFn.fullPathName() +
        ".intermediateObject true" );
```

The end of the "old stream" is now the **outMesh** attribute of this duplicate shape node. The new stream will connect to the old stream at this point.

```
oldStreamOutMeshPlug = copyShapeNodeFn.findPlug( "outMesh" );
```

The duplicate shape node is renamed to better reflect its origins. This is also consistent with how Maya names intermediate shape objects.

```
dagMods[2].renameNode( copyShapeNode,
                       copyShapeNodeFn.name() + "Orig" );
```

The duplicate shape node is still under its own parent. It needs to be reparented to be under the original mesh shape node's parent transform.

```
MObject origTransform = meshShapePath.transform();
dagMods[2].reparentNode( copyShapeNode, origTransform );
```

With its shape node now a child of another transform, the `copyTransform` transform node can be deleted. Note that the MEL command, `delete`, is called rather than using the **MDagModifier**'s `deleteNode` function. When the `deleteNode` function is called, it records information not only about the node being deleted but about its children. When the deletion action is actually executed it will delete the node and its children. It will do this even if the children have been reparented. As such, the `deleteNode` function can't be used in this circumstance.

```
dagMods[2].commandToExecute( "delete " +
                            copyTransformFn.fullPathName() );
}
```

If there is an old stream, connect it to the new stream.

```
if( !oldStreamOutMeshPlug.isNull() )
   dagMods[2].connect( oldStreamOutMeshPlug, newStreamInMeshPlug );
```

Connect the **outMesh** attribute of the mesh modifier node to the **inMesh** attribute of the original mesh shape node.

```
MPlug outMeshModPlug = modNodeFn.findPlug( "outMesh" );
dagMods[2].connect( outMeshModPlug, inMeshOrigPlug );
```

If the mesh shape node didn't have a construction history and Maya's **Construction History** setting is turned off, the construction history just created can be deleted.

```
if( !hasHistory && !genHistory )
    dagMods[2].commandToExecute(
              MString("delete -constructionHistory ") +
              meshShapePath.fullPathName() );
```

The last DAG modifier is executed.

```
dagMods[2].doIt();

return MS::kSuccess;
}
```

The `transferTweaks` function transfers the internal tweaks from the mesh shape node `shapePath` to the tweak node `tweakNode`. It records all of its actions in the **MDagModifier** variable `dagMod`.

```
MStatus CmpMeshModifierCmd::transferTweaks( const MDagPath &shapePath,
                                            MObject &tweakNode,
                                            MDagModifier &dagMod )
    {
```

The tweaks internal to the mesh shape node are stored in the **pnts** attribute. This provides the source of the tweaks.

```
MFnDagNode shapeNodeFn( shapePath );
MPlug srcTweaksPlug = shapeNodeFn.findPlug( "pnts" );
```

The **polyTweak** node stores its tweaks in the **tweak** attribute. This will be the destination of the tweak transfer.

```
MFnDependencyNode tweakNodeFn( tweakNode );
MPlug dstTweaksPlug = tweakNodeFn.findPlug( "tweak" );
```

Each of the elements in the **pnts** array attribute is iterated over.

```
MPlugArray plugs;
MPlug srcTweakPlug;
MPlug dstTweakPlug;
MObject dataObj;
```

```
MFloatVector tweak;
unsigned int nTweaks = srcTweaksPlug.numElements();
unsigned int i, j, ci, logicalIndex;
for( i=0; i < nTweaks; i++ )
{
        srcTweakPlug = srcTweaksPlug.elementByPhysicalIndex( i );
        if( !srcTweakPlug.isNull() )
        {
```

Even though the plugs are iterated by physical index, it is the logical index that will be used for assigning the tweak to the tweak node.

```
logicalIndex = srcTweakPlug.logicalIndex();
```

The tweak values are retrieved and stored in the tweak vector variable.

```
srcTweakPlug.getValue( dataObj );
MFnNumericData numDataFn( dataObj );
numDataFn.getData( tweak[0], tweak[1], tweak[2] );
```

The tweak values are set in the **tweakNode**'s corresponding tweak element.

```
dagMod.commandToExecute(
        MString( "setAttr " ) + tweakNodeFn.name() +
        ".tweak[" + logicalIndex + "] " +
        tweak[0] + " " + tweak[1] + " " + tweak[2] );
```

It is possible that the tweak element is being used as the source or destination of connections. If this is the case, all outgoing and incoming connections must be transferred to the **tweakNode**'s tweak element. This destination element and the source tweak element have the same logical index.

```
dstTweakPlug = dstTweaksPlug.elementByLogicalIndex(
                              logicalIndex);
```

Each element of the **tweak** array is a **MFnNumericData::float3** object. This means that a direct connection can be made to and from it. Otherwise, a direction connection can be made to any of its three child elements. It isn't possible to have connections to both the element and its children. This first section checks the connections to the element itself, whereas the later section checks the connections to its children.

```
if( srcTweakPlug.isConnected() )
{
```

If the original tweak is used as the source of connections, those connections are retrieved.

```
srcTweakPlug.connectedTo( plugs, false, true );
for( j=0; j < plugs.length(); j++ )
{
```

The original connection is broken.

```
dagMod.disconnect( srcTweakPlug, plugs[j] );
```

The tweak node's element now provides the source of the connection.

```
dagMod.connect( dstTweakPlug, plugs[j] );
}
```

If the original tweak is the destination of a connection, the connection is retrieved.

```
srcTweakPlug.connectedTo( plugs, true, false );
```

An attribute can have, at most, one incoming connection.

```
if( plugs.length() == 1 )
{
```

The original connection is disconnected.

```
dagMod.disconnect( plugs[0], srcTweakPlug );
```

The incoming connection is fed into the tweak node's element.

```
dagMod.connect( plugs[0], dstTweakPlug );
}
}
```

Because there are no connections to the parent tweak element, check the element's children. The same procedure is used as before. The only difference is that the `dstTweakChildPlug` is determined by using the `dstTweakPlug`'s child. It uses the same child index as the source tweak's child.

```
else
{
        MPlug srcTweakChildPlug;
        MPlug dstTweakChildPlug;

        for( ci=0; ci < srcTweakPlug.numChildren(); ci++ )
        {
                srcTweakChildPlug = srcTweakPlug.child(ci);
                dstTweakChildPlug = dstTweakPlug.child(ci);
                if( srcTweakChildPlug.isConnected() )
                {
                srcTweakChildPlug.connectedTo( plugs, false,
                                                true );
                for( j=0; j < plugs.length(); j++ )
                {
                        dagMod.disconnect( srcTweakChildPlug,
                                                plugs[j] );
                        dagMod.connect( dstTweakChildPlug,
                                                plugs[j] );
                }

                srcTweakChildPlug.connectedTo( plugs, true,
                                                false );
                if( plugs.length() == 1 )
                {
                        dagMod.disconnect( plugs[0],
                                                srcTweakChildPlug );
                        dagMod.connect( plugs[0],
                                                stTweakChildPlug );
                }
                }
        }
}
```

Now that the tweak has been successfully transfered to the tweak node, the tweak can be reset.

```
                dagMod.commandToExecute( MString( "setAttr " ) +
                    shapePath.fullPathName() + ".pnts[" +
                    logicalIndex + "] 0 0 0" );
        }
    }

    return MS::kSuccess;
}
```

The redoIt function will perform the same operations as the doIt function but will make use of the prerecorded DAG modifiers to do the main work.

```
    MStatus CmpMeshModifierCmd::redoIt()
    {
```

The first two DAG modifers are replayed.

```
        dagMods[0].doIt();
        dagMods[1].doIt();
```

If the mesh shape node doesn't have a history, a duplicate mesh shape node is created. This duplication must been done manually because it couldn't be recorded in a DAG modifier.

```
        if( !hasHistory )
        {
            MFnDagNode origShapeNodeFn( meshShapePath );
            copyTransform = origShapeNodeFn.duplicate();
        }
```

The remaining DAG modifer is executed.

```
        dagMods[2].doIt();

        return MS::kSuccess;
    }
```

The undoIt function undoes the DAG modifiers in the reverse order of that in which they were executed. This effectively unrolls the changes in reverse order.

```
MStatus CmpMeshModifierCmd::undoIt()
{
```

The last DAG modifier is undone.

```
dagMods[2].undoIt();
```

Because the duplication of the mesh shape node couldn't be recorded, it is deleted manually.

```
if( !copyTransform.isNull() )
    MGlobal::deleteNode( copyTransform );
```

The first two DAG modifiers are undone.

```
dagMods[1].undoIt();
dagMods[0].undoIt();
```

If the original mesh shape node didn't have a history, its mesh data would have been stored internally. Because a construction history was created and applied to the mesh, this original mesh data is now lost. To restore it, the saved mesh data, origMeshData, is stored in the mesh shape node.

```
if( !hasHistory )
{
    MFnDagNode origShapeNodeFn( meshShapePath );
```

If the mesh shape node has tweaks, the mesh data is stored in the **cachedInMesh** attribute. If there are no tweaks, the mesh data can be stored in the **outMesh** attribute.

Because it doesn't have any tweaks that are construction history, the **outMesh** will not be updated by a Dependency Graph evaluation.

```
        MPlug meshPlug = origShapeNodeFn.findPlug(
                    hasInternalTweaks ? "cachedInMesh" : "outMesh" );
        meshPlug.setValue( origMeshData );
    }

    return MS::kSuccess;
}
```

8.4.5 DISPLACEMESH PLUG-IN

The **DisplaceMesh** plug-in demonstrates the following.

- Using the **CmpMeshModifier** classes to support construction history

- Creating custom mesh-editing commands and nodes

- Displacing a mesh surface using a displacement image

Figure 8.24 shows the result of applying the `displaceMesh` command to a flat plane using the displacement image shown in Figure 8.25. The command allows

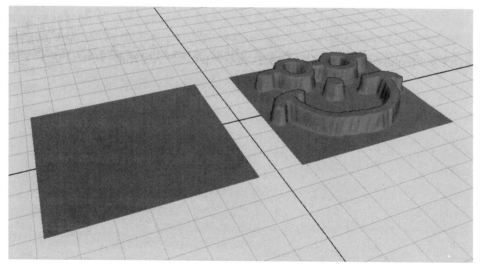

FIGURE 8.24 Before and after applying `displaceMesh`.

FIGURE 8.25 Displacement image.

the specification of a strength and displacement image. These values can be changed later, in the node that does the actual displacing. The mesh modifier operates as follows. Given a vertex, its uv texture coordinates are retrieved. This uv position is used to index a pixel in the displacement image. The luminance of this pixel is used to determine how much the vertex should be displaced. The vertex is then displaced along its average normal based on the strength attribute and pixel luminance.

1. Open the **DisplaceMesh** workspace.

2. Compile and load the resulting `displaceMesh` plug-in file in Maya.

3. Open the **PlaneMeshDetailed.ma** scene.

4. Select the plane object, **pPlane1**.

5. The displacement needs an image to define how much each vertex in the mesh is going to be displaced. The **smiley.jpg** file is located in the same directory as the source code for the **DisplaceMesh** plug-in. Define the following string variable that points to the image file.

```
string $displaceImage = <displaceMesh_source_code_directory> +
                        "/smiley.jpg";
```

Here, `<displaceMesh_source_code_directory>` is the directory containing the **DisplaceMesh** source code. Use forward slashes (/) rather than backward slashes (\) when specifying the directory. This ensures that Maya will not try to interpret them as escape characters.

6. Execute the following.

```
displaceMesh -strength 0.1 -image $displaceImage;
```

The surface of the plane is displaced based on the given image. The `displaceMesh` command created a **displaceMesh** node, **displaceMesh1**.

7. Open the **Attribute Editor**.

8. Click on the **displaceMesh1** tab.

9. Set the **Strength** field to -0.5.

The surface is now pushed in.

SOURCE CODE

Plug-in: `DisplaceMesh`
File: `DisplaceMeshCmd.h`

```
class DisplaceMeshCmd : public CmpMeshModifierCmd
{
public:
    virtual MStatus doIt( const MArgList &args );

    virtual MStatus DisplaceMeshCmd::initModifierNode( MObject &node,
                                        MDagModifier &dagMod );

    static void *creator();
    static MSyntax newSyntax();

private:
    double strength;
    MString imageFilename;
};
```

Plug-in: `DisplaceMesh`
File: `DisplaceMeshCmd.cpp`

```
const char *strengthFlag = "-s", *strengthLongFlag = "-strength";
const char *imageFilenameFlag = "-i", *imageFilenameLongFlag = "-image";
```

```
MSyntax DisplaceMeshCmd::newSyntax()
{
 MSyntax syntax;

 syntax.addFlag( strengthFlag, strengthLongFlag, MSyntax::kDouble );
 syntax.addFlag( imageFilenameFlag, imageFilenameLongFlag,
                 MSyntax::kString );

 syntax.enableQuery( false );
 syntax.enableEdit( false );

 return syntax;
}

MStatus DisplaceMeshCmd::doIt( const MArgList &args )
{
    strength = DisplaceMeshNode::strengthDefault();
    imageFilename = DisplaceMeshNode::imageFilenameDefault();

    MStatus stat;
    MArgDatabase argData( syntax(), args, &stat );
    if( !stat )
         return stat;

    if( argData.isFlagSet( strengthFlag ) )
         argData.getFlagArgument( strengthFlag, 0, strength );

    if( argData.isFlagSet( imageFilenameFlag ) )
         argData.getFlagArgument( imageFilenameFlag, 0, imageFilename );

    MSelectionList selection;
    MGlobal::getActiveSelectionList( selection );

    int nSelMeshes = 0;
    MDagPath dagPath;
    MItSelectionList iter( selection, MFn::kMesh );
    for ( ; !iter.isDone(); iter.next() )
    {
```

```
            nSelMeshes++;

            iter.getDagPath( dagPath );
            dagPath.extendToShape();

            break;
        }

        if( nSelMeshes == 0 )
        {
            MGlobal::displayWarning( "Select one or more meshes" );
            return MS::kFailure;
        }

        CmpMeshModifierCmd::doIt( dagPath, DisplaceMeshNode::id );

        return MS::kSuccess;
}


void *DisplaceMeshCmd::creator()
{
        return new DisplaceMeshCmd;
}


MStatus DisplaceMeshCmd::initModifierNode( MObject &node,
                                               MDagModifier &dagMod )
{
        MFnDependencyNode depFn( node );
        MString name = depFn.name();

    dagMod.commandToExecute( MString( "setAttr " ) + name + ".strength " +
                                strength );
    dagMod.commandToExecute( MString( "setAttr -type \"string\"" ) + name +
                                ".imageFilename \" " + imageFilename + "\" " );

        return MS::kSuccess;
}
```

Plug-in: `DisplaceMesh`
File: `DisplaceMeshNode.h`

```
class DisplaceMeshNode : public CmpMeshModifierNode
{
public:
    virtual MStatus compute( const MPlug &plug, MDataBlock &data );
    static void *creator();
    static MStatus initialize();

    static MTypeId id;

    static MObject strength;
    static MObject imageFilename;

    static double strengthDefault();
    static MString imageFilenameDefault();
};
```

Plug-in: `DisplaceMesh`
File: `DisplaceMeshNode.cpp`

```
MTypeId DisplaceMeshNode::id( 0x00338 );

MObject DisplaceMeshNode::strength;
MObject DisplaceMeshNode::imageFilename;

MStatus DisplaceMeshNode::compute( const MPlug &plug, MDataBlock &data )
{
    MStatus stat;
    bool hasNoEffect = false;

    MDataHandle inMeshHnd = data.inputValue( inMesh );
    MDataHandle outMeshHnd = data.outputValue( outMesh );

    MDataHandle stateHnd = data.inputValue( state );
    int state = stateHnd.asInt();
    if( state == 1 )
            hasNoEffect = true;

    if( !hasNoEffect && plug == outMesh )
    {
        MObject inMeshData = inMeshHnd.asMesh();
```

```
MDataHandle strengthHnd = data.inputValue( strength );
MDataHandle imageFilenameHnd = data.inputValue( imageFilename );

double strengthValue = strengthHnd.asDouble();
MString imageFilenameStr = imageFilenameHnd.asString();

hasNoEffect = strengthValue == 0.0 ||
              imageFilenameStr.length() == 0;

MImage image;
if( !hasNoEffect )
     hasNoEffect = !image.readFromFile( imageFilenameStr );

if( !hasNoEffect )
{
     MFnMeshData meshDataFn;
     MObject newMeshData = meshDataFn.create();
     MFnMesh inMeshFn( inMeshData );
     inMeshFn.copy( inMeshData, newMeshData );

     unsigned int width, height;
     image.getSize( width, height );

     unsigned char *pixs = image.pixels();
     unsigned int depth = image.depth();

     MFnMesh meshFn( newMeshData );
     MPointArray pts;
     meshFn.getPoints( pts );

     const unsigned int nPts = pts.length();
     bool *visited = new bool[ nPts ];
     unsigned int i;
     for( i=0; i < nPts; i++ )
          visited[i] = false;

     float2 uv;
     int vertId;
     MVector norm;
     double lum;
     int x, y;
     unsigned char *pix;
```

```
            MItMeshFaceVertex fvIter( newMeshData );
            for( ; !fvIter.isDone(); fvIter.next() )
            {
                    vertId = fvIter.vertId();

                    if( visited[ vertId ] )
                            continue;

                    if( !fvIter.hasUVs() )
                            continue;

                    fvIter.getUV( uv );

                    x = int( uv[0] * (width-1) );
                    y = int( uv[1] * (height-1) );

                    pix = pixs + (y * width * depth) + x * depth;

                    if( depth >= 3 )
                            lum = 0.29 * *pix + 0.59 * *(pix+1) +
                                    0.12 * *(pix+2);
                    else
                            lum = *pix;
                    lum / = 255.0;

                    meshFn.getVertexNormal( vertId, norm );

                    pts[ vertId ] += strengthValue * lum * norm;

                    visited[ vertId ] = true;
            }

            delete[] visited;

            meshFn.setPoints( pts );
            meshFn.updateSurface();

            outMeshHnd.set( newMeshData );
        }
    }
    else
        return MS::kUnknownParameter;

    if( hasNoEffect )
        outMeshHnd.set( inMeshHnd.asMesh() );
```

```
   data.setClean( plug );

   return stat;
}

void *DisplaceMeshNode::creator()
{
   return new DisplaceMeshNode();
}

MStatus DisplaceMeshNode::initialize()
{
   CmpMeshModifierNode::initialize();

   MFnNumericAttribute nAttr;
   strength = nAttr.create( "strength", "str", MFnNumericData::kDouble,
                            1.0 );
   nAttr.setKeyable( true );

   MFnTypedAttribute tAttr;
   imageFilename = tAttr.create( "imageFilename", "img",MFnData::kString );

   addAttribute( strength );
   addAttribute( imageFilename );

   attributeAffects( strength, outMesh );
   attributeAffects( imageFilename, outMesh );

   return MS::kSuccess;
}

double DisplaceMeshNode::strengthDefault()
{
   MFnNumericAttribute nAttr( strength );
   double d;
   nAttr.getDefault( d );
   return d;
}

MString DisplaceMeshNode::imageFilenameDefault()
{
   MFnTypedAttribute tAttr;
   MObject d;
```

```
        tAttr.getDefault( d );
        MFnStringData sd( d );
        return sd.string();
    }
```

Plug-in: `DisplaceMesh`
File: `PluginMain.cpp`

```
    MStatus initializePlugin( MObject obj )
    {
        MFnPlugin plugin( obj, "David Gould", "1.0" );

        MStatus stat;
        stat = plugin.registerCommand( "displaceMesh",
                                        DisplaceMeshCmd::creator,
                                        DisplaceMeshCmd::newSyntax );
        if( !stat )
        {
            MGlobal::displayError( MString( "registerCommand failed: " ) +
                                    stat.errorString() );
            return stat;
        }

        stat = plugin.registerNode( "displaceMesh",
                                     DisplaceMeshNode::id,
                                     DisplaceMeshNode::creator,
                                     DisplaceMeshNode::initialize );
        if( !stat )
        {
            MGlobal::displayError( MString( "registerNode failed: " ) +
                                    stat.errorString() );
            return stat;
        }

        return stat;
    }

    MStatus uninitializePlugin( MObject obj )
    {
        MFnPlugin plugin( obj );
```

```
    MStatus     stat;
    stat = plugin.deregisterCommand( "displaceMesh" );
    if ( !stat )
    {
        MGlobal::displayError( MString( "deregisterCommand failed: " ) +
                                    stat.errorString() );
        return stat;
    }

    stat = plugin.deregisterNode( DisplaceMeshNode::id );
    if ( !stat )
    {
        MGlobal::displayError( MString( "deregisterNode failed: " ) +
                                    stat.errorString() );
        return stat;
    }

    return stat;
}
```

SOURCE CODE EXPLANATION

Plug-in: `DisplaceMesh`
File: `DisplaceMeshCmd.h`

The **DisplaceMeshCmd** class is responsible for the `displaceMesh` command. It is
derived from the **CmpMeshModifierCmd** class, and thus it must define the superclass's
pure virtual functions `doIt` and `initModifierNode`.

```
    class DisplaceMeshCmd : public CmpMeshModifierCmd
    {
    public:
       virtual MStatus doIt( const MArgList &args );

       virtual MStatus DisplaceMeshCmd::initModifierNode( MObject &node,
                                            MDagModifier &dagMod );

       ...
    };
```

Plug-in: `DisplaceMesh`
File: `DisplaceMeshCmd.cpp`

The command has two command flags, `-strength` and `-image`, that define the strength of the displacement and the image used to control the amount of displacing per vertex, respectively.

```
const char *strengthFlag = "-s", *strengthLongFlag = "-strength";
const char *imageFilenameFlag = "-i", *imageFilenameLongFlag = "-image";
...
```

The `doIt` function prepares all input to the command and then calls the **CmpMeshModifierCmd**'s `doIt` function to do the actual work.

```
MStatus DisplaceMeshCmd::doIt( const MArgList &args )
{
```

The command options are initialized with the node's default values. Because it is the node that contains the **strength** and **imageFilename** attributes it is responsible for defining the default values.

```
strength = DisplaceMeshNode::strengthDefault();
imageFilename = DisplaceMeshNode::imageFilenameDefault();
...
```

The DAG path to the first selected mesh object is retrieved. The final DAG path extends to the shape node.

```
int nSelMeshes = 0;
MDagPath dagPath;
MItSelectionList iter( selection, MFn::kMesh );
for ( ; !iter.isDone(); iter.next() )
{
    nSelMeshes++;

    iter.getDagPath( dagPath );
    dagPath.extendToShape();

    break;
}
...
```

The **CmpMeshModifierCmd**'s `doIt` function is called to do the command's work. It is passed a DAG path to the object being modified, as well as the ID of the mesh-modifying node. The function uses this ID to create an instance of the node.

```
CmpMeshModifierCmd::doIt( dagPath, DisplaceMeshNode::id );
    ...
}
```

By the time the `initModifierNode` function is called, the mesh modifiying node (in this case an instance of **DisplaceMeshNode**) has already been created. This function is responsible for initializing the node. It records any changes it makes to the supplied **MDagModifier** instance, `dagMod`. This ensures that the changes can be undone.

```
MStatus DisplaceMeshCmd::initModifierNode( MObject &node,
                                           MDagModifier &dagMod )
{
    ...
```

The `commandToExecute` function is called rather than using the **MPlug** class because they can be undone. The **MPlug** class's functions can't be automatically undone.

```
dagMod.commandToExecute( MString( "setAttr " ) + name + ".strength " +
                         strength );
dagMod.commandToExecute( MString( "setAttr -type \"string\"" ) + name +
                         ".imageFilename \"" + imageFilename + "\"" );

    ...
}
```

Plug-in: `DisplaceMesh`
File: `DisplaceMeshNode.h`

The **DisplaceMeshNode** class is responsible for displacing the mesh. It will be automatically inserted into the construction history of the mesh being edited by the `displaceMesh` command. The class is derived from **CmpMeshModifierNode** and thus inherits the **inMesh** and **outMesh** attributes.

```
class DisplaceMeshNode : public CmpMeshModifierNode
{
    ...
```

The **strength** and **imageFilename** attributes store the scaling of the displacement and the name of the image that controls the individual vertex displacements, respectively.

```
static MObject strength;
static MObject imageFilename;
    ...
};
```

Plug-in: `DisplaceMesh`
File: `DisplaceMeshNode.cpp`

The `compute` function is responsible for calculating the final displaced mesh (**outMesh**) given the input mesh, **inMesh**.

```
MStatus DisplaceMeshNode::compute( const MPlug &plug, MDataBlock &data )
{
    ...
```

The `hasNoEffect` variable defines whether the node will process the input mesh.

```
bool hasNoEffect = false;
    ...
```

This section handles the case in which the **state** attribute is set to **No Effect/Pass Through**. The node is flagged as not having any effect.

```
MDataHandle stateHnd = data.inputValue( state );
int state = stateHnd.asInt();
if( state = 1 )
    hasNoEffect = true;
```

If the output mesh is requested, the following section is executed.

```
if( !hasNoEffect && plug == outMesh )
{
    ...
```

The values of the attributes are retrieved.

```
double strengthValue = strengthHnd.asDouble();
MString imageFilenameStr = imageFilenameHnd.asString();
```

If the strength is zero or there is no image file specified, the node will not have an effect.

```
hasNoEffect = strengthValue == 0.0 ||
              imageFilenameStr.length() == 0;
```

If the node still has some effect, the image file is loaded. The **MImage** class is used to read an image in any of Maya's supported raster file formats.

```
MImage image;
if( !hasNoEffect )
        hasNoEffect = !image.readFromFile( imageFilenameStr );
```

If the node still has an effect, the mesh is displaced.

```
if( !hasNoEffect )
{
        ...
```

A copy of the input mesh is created and stored in the newMeshData data object.

```
MFnMeshData meshDataFn;
MObject newMeshData = meshDataFn.create();
MFnMesh inMeshFn( inMeshData );
inMeshFn.copy( inMeshData, newMeshData );
...
```

A pointer to the image data is retrieved. The data is a block of memory containing the pixels.

```
unsigned char *pixs = image.pixels();
```

The depth of the image is the number of channels it contains. Each channel is 1 byte in size, and thus the range per channel is [0, 255]. A standard image with RGB channels will therefore have a depth of 3.

```
unsigned int depth = image.depth();
```

The positions of the vertices, in object space, are retrieved.

```
MFnMesh meshFn( newMeshData );
MPointArray pts;
meshFn.getPoints( pts );
```

A flag per vertex is allocated. When a vertex has been processed it is flagged in the visited array.

```
const unsigned int nPts = pts.length();
bool *visited = new bool[ nPts ];
unsigned int i;
for( i=0; i < nPts; i++ )
        visited[i] = false;
...
```

The uv texture coordinate of each vertex is needed. These texture coordinates are indexed by face vertex, and thus the **MItMeshFaceVertex** class is used to iterate over all face vertices.

```
MItMeshFaceVertex fvIter( newMeshData );
for( ; !fvIter.isDone(); fvIter.next() )
{
```

The mesh-relative vertex ID is retrieved using the vertId function.

```
vertId = fvIter.vertId();
```

If the face vertex has already been processed, it is skipped.

```
if( visited[ vertId ] )
        continue;
```

If the face vertex doesn't have any uv texture coordinates, it is skipped.

```
if( !fvIter.hasUVs() )
    continue;
```

The uv texture coordinates are retrieved.

```
fvIter.getUV( uv );
```

The uv texture coordinate is converted into a pixel location (x, y) in the image.

```
x = int( uv[0] * (width-1) );
y = int( uv[1] * (height-1) );
```

A pointer to the pixel at the position (x, y) is retrieved.

```
pix = pixs + (y * width * depth) + x * depth;
```

If the image has three or more channels, the luminance is based on the red, green, and blue channels.

```
if( depth >= 3 )
    lum = 0.29 * *pix + 0.59 * *(pix+1) +
          0.12 * *(pix+2);
else
```

If the image has less than three channels, the first channel is used.

```
lum = *pix;
```

Because the channel values are in the range [0, 255], this next step scales the luminance to the range [0, 1].

```
lum / = 255.0;
```

The mesh-relative vertex's normal is retrieved. If the user hasn't set this explicitly, it is the normal resulting from averaging all surrounding face normals. The normal is object space.

```
meshFn.getVertexNormal( vertId, norm );
```

The vertex is displaced.

```
                    pts[ vertId ] += strengthValue * lum * norm;
```

The vertex is flagged as processed.

```
                    visited[ vertId ] = true;
            }
            ...
```

The mesh data is updated with the new vertex positions.

```
                meshFn.setPoints( pts );
                meshFn.updateSurface();
```

The **outMesh** attribute is set to the new data.

```
                outMeshHnd.set( newMeshData );
        }
```

If the plug isn't known it is relegated to the superclass to handle.

```
        }
        else
            return MS::kUnknownParameter;
```

If the node doesn't have any effect, the output mesh is set to the input mesh.

```
        if( hasNoEffect )
            outMeshHnd.set( inMeshHnd.asMesh() );
```

The plug has been updated so that it is marked as clean.

```
        data.setClean( plug );
        ...
    }
```

The `initialize` function sets up the attributes for the node. It must call the following.

```
MStatus DisplaceMeshNode::initialize()
{
```

The **CmpMeshModifierNode**'s `initialize` function must be called first to ensure that the **inMesh** and **outMesh** attributes are created and registered.

```
CmpMeshModifierNode::initialize();
```

Once the **strength** and **imageFilename** attributes are created, it is important to register their effect on the **outMesh** attribute. Should they ever change, the **outMesh** will need to be updated.

```
...
attributeAffects( strength, outMesh );
attributeAffects( imageFilename, outMesh );
...
}
```

NURBS

Before discussing NURBSs, it is important to cover how curves are created in general. There are many different types of curves: Bezier, Hermite, Catmull-Rom, uniform B-splines, nonuniform B-splines, Kochanek-Bartels, and so on. All curves start out as a set of points (*control vertices*). Depending on its type, the curve will either go through these points (interpolate), get close to them (approximate), or a mix of both. Given a point on the curve, the fundamental question that is asked is how the control points near it will influence it. Some control points will pull the curve very close, whereas others will have only a small effect. All of these influences can be given as a series of weights. Each control vertex will be assigned a given weight. The higher the weight, the more influence. A weight of 0 will mean that the control vertex will have no influence whatsoever. A weight of 1 will mean that the control vertex will have all of the influence. In this case, none of the other control vertices have any influence. Because the control vertex has all of the influence, the curve will pass through the control vertex. Fundamentally, all that changes between the various types of curves is how they weight the control vertices.

Typically the weight of a control vertex should be stronger the closer the curve is. Thus, the part of the curve that is far from a control vertex should not be affected by the control vertex, but as the curve gets closer the control vertex should exercise a greater influence. The influence of a control vertex therefore varies. This variation in weight is defined using equations that take into account the "closeness" of the control vertex. These equations are called *basis functions*. This is where the B in B-splines comes from: basis spline. A basis function determines the weight of a given control vertex. Because the weight changes, these functions produce a different weight depending on what part of the curve is being evaluated. As such, these functions are often themselves curved; that is, they smoothly vary.

Take, for example, a curve with four control vertices. A point on the curve is calculated as follows. A location along the curve is chosen. This location is fed into the basis function for each of the control vertices. Each basis function will return a weight. These weights are multiplied by the control vertex. This results in a series of points. These points are then added together to produce a final position. This is the point on the curve.

It is important to note that the location chosen along the curve is a parametric location. A curve is just a series of points. Each point along the curve is calculated by entering a chosen parametric location. This parametric location is a scalar value that indicates where along the curve the position should be calculated. A curve will have a minimum and maximum parametric location. The minimum corresponds to the start of the curve and the maximum to the end of the curve. Values between produce points along the curve.

Although each curve is basically a weighting of control vertices along its length, some curves are more sophisticated than others. NURBS curves are the most general of all. NURBS is an acronym for nonuniform rational B-spline.

- *Nonuniform* refers to the fact that the parameterization of the curve isn't uniform. Because NURBSs use knots to define their parameterization, these can vary from one span to another.

- *Rational* refers to the fact that NURBSs are based on a ratio of sums of polynomials. This allows each control point to have a weight. These weights define how close the curve will come to its control vertex. A stronger weight will pull the curve closer to the control vertex. Although Maya supports rational curves, this functionality is rarely used and is currently inaccessible through Maya's user interface. As such, nonrational curves are the most common curves.

- *B-spline* is shorthand for "basis spline." A NURBS is a sum of simpler polynomial splines. These simpler splines are referred to as *basis functions*.

Mathematically, NURBSs are parametric polynomial curves. NURBSs are a superset of splines, conics (parabolics, arcs, circles, ellipses, and so on), and beziers. This means that NURBS curves can represent all of these types of curves and more. Figure 9.1 shows a simple NURBS curve. The four control vertices that define the final shape of the curve are numbered. The curve itself is shown in blue.

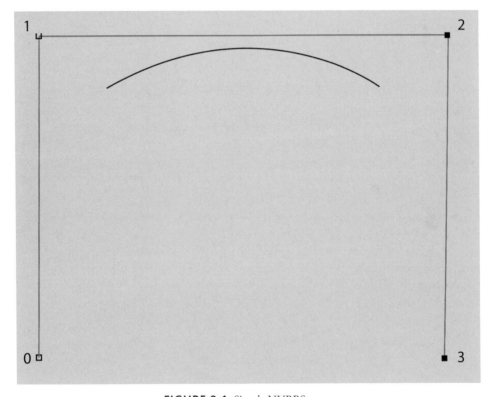

FIGURE 9.1 Simple NURBS curve.

First, the curve doesn't go through the control vertices. NURBS curves are approximative rather than interpolative, which means that the control vertices influence the curve segments by pulling them toward the control vertices. It is possible to force a curve segment to pass through a control vertex by changing the knot vector. Note that the curve doesn't go through the first and last control vertices. When a NURBS curve is created in Maya, the Multiple End Knots parameter is on by default. This generates additional knots that force the curve to go through the first and last control vertices.

A NURBS curve is actually a composite curve made up of smaller curves. Figure 9.2 shows the result of adding an additional control vertex to the previous curve. There are now two curve segments in the curve. Each segment is referred to as a *span*. The mathematical nature of NURBS curves ensures that where the two spans join the connection will be smooth.

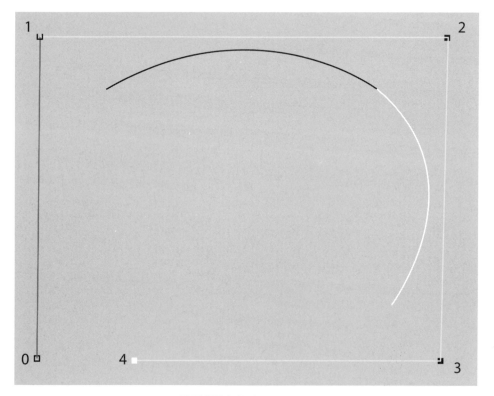

FIGURE 9.2 Curve pieces.

A NURBS curve and NURBS surface use the same underlying mathematical representation. As such, many of the concepts that are explained below using curves apply equally well to surfaces.

9.1 CONCEPTS

9.1.1 CONTROL VERTEX (CV)

The control vertices define the points a NURBS curve is generated from. The curve runs through the first and last vertices but only approaches the other vertices. The positions of the vertices influence the final shape of the curve. Figure 9.3 shows the second control vertex in the NURBS curve. Maya displays it as a U rather than the usual dot to indicate the direction of the *u* parameter.

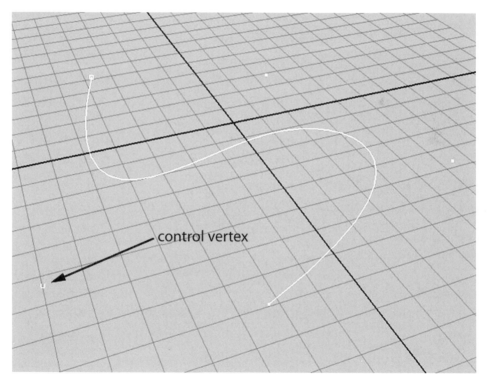

FIGURE 9.3 Control vertex.

9.1.2 HULL

A hull is the result of drawing a line through a curve's control vertices. Figure 9.4 shows the hull of the NURBS curve.

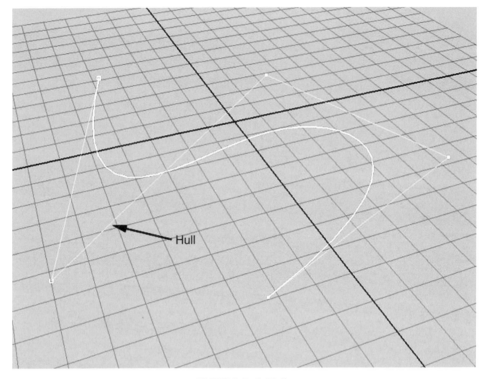

FIGURE 9.4 Hull.

An interesting property of approximative curves (NURBS, Bezier) is that in each case the curve is guaranteed to lie inside the *convex hull*. Intuitively, the convex hull is the shape that would be formed by wrapping a piece of string around the hull.

9.1.3 SPAN

A NURBS curve is actually made up of multiple smaller curves. Technically, these smaller curves are called *curve segments*, though Maya refers to them as *spans*. These smaller curves are joined to define the final curve. Two separate curve segments join smoothly because they have some control vertices in common. Figure 9.5 shows the first span in the NURBS curve.

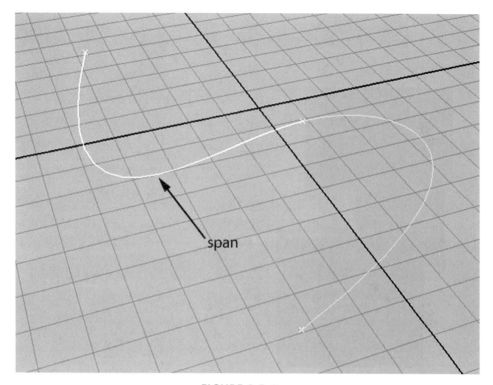

FIGURE 9.5 Span.

9.1.4 DEGREE

The number of control vertices that influence a span is defined by the curve's *degree* plus one.

control vertices per span = degree + 1

NURBS curves are typically of degree 3, and thus a span will be defined by four control vertices. The higher the degree of a curve, the more control vertices that influence a given span. This can also be thought of in terms of the control vertex's influence. The higher the degree of the curve, the more spans a given control vertex will influence. Moving such a control vertex will change a larger part of the overall curve. As such, curves of higher degrees tend to be smoother. A curve with degree 7 will be very smooth, whereas a curve of degree 1 will not be smooth at all. In fact, a curve with degree 1 results in straight line segments. As you may have guessed, a downside of higher-degree curves is a reduction in the local control of a given control vertex. Curves of degree 3 are the most common because they provide a good balance between smoothness and local control.

Maya supports curves of degrees 1, 2, 3, 5, and 7. Curves with degrees higher than 7 result in potentially erratic oscillations and thus are rarely used. It is better to join a series of degree-3 curves rather than create a single curve with a higher degree. This gives more localized control while allowing curves of arbitrary complexity. This also reduces the computation time required for higher-degree curves.

Mathematically, the degree of a curve defines the highest exponent in the polynomial equation. The polynomial equations are used to blend the control vertices to produce a point on the curve. A curve with degree 3 will use a *cubic polynomial* (highest polynomial exponent of 3):

$$x(u) = d*u^3 + c*u^2 + b*u^1 + a*u^0$$
$$= d*u^3 + c*u^2 + b*u + a$$

The other common polynomials, *quadratic* and *linear*, have degree of 2 and 1, respectively. The linear polynomial is simply the equation for a straight line. It is important to note that NURBS surfaces can have curves of different degree across their width and length.

9.1.5 ORDER

The *order* of a curve is its degree plus one. As such, the order is the number of control vertices per span.

$$order = degree + 1$$
$$\# \text{ control vertices per span} = degree + 1$$

Therefore,

$$\# \text{ control vertices per span} = order$$

A curve of order 4 will therefore have four control vertices per span. Such a curve would have degree 3.

9.1.6 EDIT POINTS

NURBS curves don't explicitly have *edit points*. They are an entirely Maya-centric concept. An edit point (see Figure 9.6) lies on the junction between two spans. When an edit point is moved, it isn't the edit point that changes. Instead, the control vertices that influence the edit point are moved. An edit point is therefore a more intuitive means of altering the curve by indirectly moving control vertices.

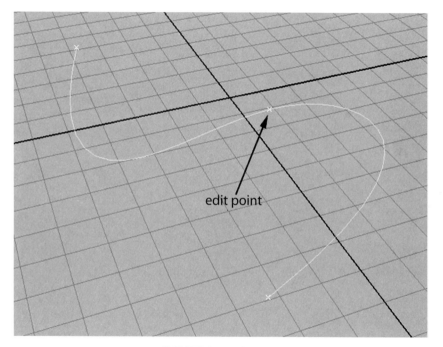

edit point

FIGURE 9.6 Edit point.

9.1.7 CURVE POINT

Each point on a NURBS curve has a parametric position. This parametric position is referred to as its u coordinate. Maya refers to this parametric position as the *curve point*. The parameteric positions of a typical curve vary from 0 to 1, and thus by varying the u coordinate from 0 to 1, all points along the curve are traced out.

Because the curve point is calculated from the control vertices, when they move the control point will also move. Figure 9.7 shows the curve whose u parameter varies from 0 to 2. The curve point at u = 0.5 is indicated.

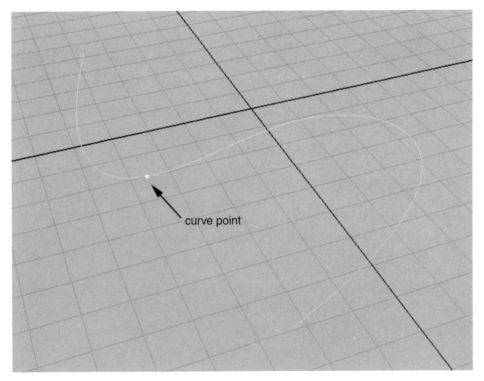

FIGURE 9.7 Curve point.

9.1.8 PARAMETERIZATION

The parameterization of a curve defines how the knots are distributed along the curve. A change in parameterization results in a change in the curve's knot vector. Maya supports two types of parameterizations: uniform and chord length. The uniform parameterization means that from one span to the next the parametric difference between them is the same. Typically, the spans are parameterized starting from 0 to the number of spans. This simply assigns an increasing whole value to each knot. Recall that there is a knot at the end of each span. Figure 9.8 shows an example of uniform parameterization.

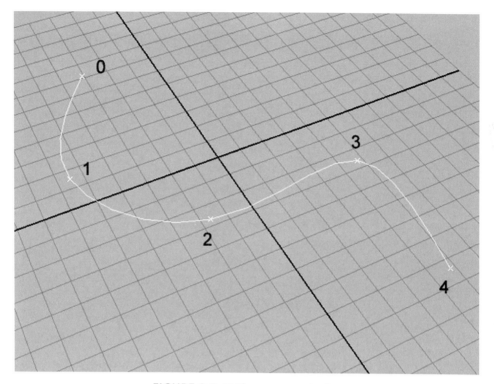

FIGURE 9.8 Uniform parameterization.

Although the default uniform parameterization is to assign a whole integer value to each knot, it is also possible to have a normalized uniform parameterization where a curve's parameterization varies from 0 to 1 rather than 0 to #spans. This parameterization can often be more intuitive. In all cases, as long as the difference between knot values is the same, the parameterization is uniform. It is important to note that it is the parameterization of the knots that is uniform. The actual distance between edit points can be widely varying.

The chord length parameterization assigns the parameter values to the knots by calculating the distance between each successive edit point (end of the span). This distance is the length of the straight line between edit points. It is important not to confuse the chord length with the arc length of a curve. The arc length is the actual length of the final curve. Figure 9.9 shows the same curve with a chord length parameterization. Each edit point's parameter is set to the chord length accumulated

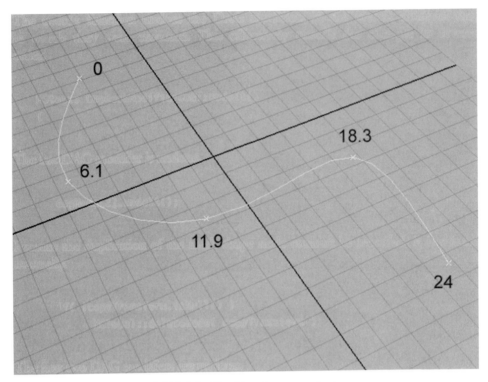

FIGURE 9.9 Chord length parameterization.

so far. Because the chord length is based on the actual distance, the parameterziation is more evenly spaced in physical space. This means that texture mapping will often be more even than if uniform parameterization were used.

It is important to understand that the chord length is only calculated once when the curve is created or rebuilt. If the control vertices are moved and the curve changes, the chord length parameterization isn't updated. The knots retain their previous chord length parameterization.

9.1.9 KNOTS

This discussion focuses on curves of degree 3, the most common, although the concepts apply equally well to curves of any degree. As mentioned previously, a NURBS curve is a parametric curve. Given a parametric location, u, a 3D position along the curve can be calculated. Assume the extent of the possible parametric locations is from u_{min} to u_{max}. When u is set to u_{min}, the first point on the curve is calculated. Likewise, when u is set to u_{max} the last point on the curve is calculated. All the other points along the curve are calculated by setting u to a value between u_{min} and u_{max}.

Most NURBS curves have more than four control vertices and thus contain more than one curve segment. Thus, the more typical NURBS curves have many curve segments. The entire parametric range for the curve varies from u_{min} to u_{max}, but because the curve is actually composed on curve segments, each segment is assigned a portion of this parametric range. A NURBS curve with two segments and a range of 0 to 1 will assign the first curve segment the parametric range 0 to 0.5 and the second segment the range above 0.5 to 1. The extents of the two curve segments form the following series of parametric locations: 0, 0.5, 1.

The end points of curve segments are called *knots*. These are the places where curve segments join. It is important to reiterate that a knot is not a physical location but instead a parametric location, u, along the curve. From the parametric location a physical location can be calculated.

Because a curve can have multiple curve segments it can have multiple knots. The series of knots is called a *knot vector* or *knot sequence*.

A curve segment is calculated by applying a set of basis functions to the control vertices. For Bezier curves these basis functions (Bernstein polynomials) are defined using fixed formulas; the basis functions don't change. For NURBS curves, the basis functions can change. The basis functions for a NURBS curve are controlled by the knot vector. The knot vector is fed into the basis functions to calculate the final weighting of a given control vertex. Their effect on the basis functions is somewhat more complex to understand. This is because they are closely tied to the mathematical formulation for NURBS curves. Such a closeness means that a truly complete understanding of their workings is only possible by studying the exact formulas for NURBS curves. These formulas include the recursive evaluation of higher-order functions from lower-order functions. See the Further Reading section for a listing of books that cover the NURBS formulas in great detail.

Figure 9.10 shows two curves that have four control vertices. Both curves have control vertices in exactly the same positions, and both have a parametric range from 0 to 1. Because they both have a single curve segment, this segment covers the entire parametric range [0, 1]. The only difference between them is their knot vector.

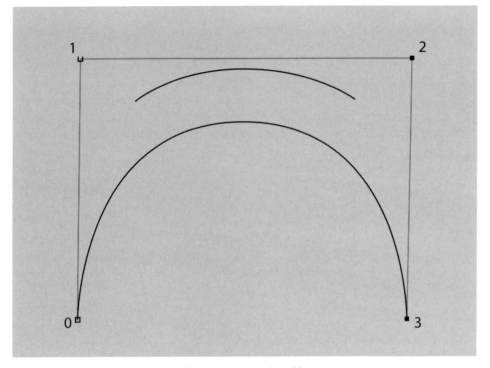

FIGURE 9.10 Multiple end knots.

The knot vector for the top curve is:

    -2 -1 0 1 2 3

The knot vector for the bottom curve is:

    0 0 0 1 1 1

A knot vector must be a nondecreasing sequence of numbers. Two consecutive knot values can be the same but the second one can't be less than the first. Note that the two knot values in the middle of the knot vectors are the same.

    -2 -1 **0 1** 2 3
     0 0 **0 1** 1 1

This covers the parametric range of the curve, 0 to 1. So why are there two additional knot values on both sides and why are they outside the parametric range? Each point along the curve is controlled by four control vertices. Each control vertex has its associated basis function. This means that there needs to be four overlapping basis functions for each point along the curve. The problem is that the control vertices at the start and end of the curves don't have enough overlapping basis functions if only four knot values were specified. Additional knot values are given to ensure that there are additional basis functions at both ends, so that when summed the end points of the curve have exactly four overlapping basis functions. The additional knot vectors at the start and ends of the knot vector are there for this reason. The knot values determine the extent of the control of the control points.

The top curve uses a uniform knot vector. This means that the difference between successive knots is the same. In this case, the difference is 1. The advantage of uniform knot vectors is that the curve will be smoothly varying. In fact, a uniform cubic B-spline is guaranteed to have C^2 continuity at all points along the curve.

The bottom curve uses a nonuniform knot vector. This means that the difference between successive knots values isn't the same. In fact, the second knot vector has *multiple knots*. This is a consecutive series of knots with the same value. The number of times a knot value is consecutively repeated is the *multiplicity* of a knot. The first knot value 0 has a multiplicity of 3 because there are three of them. The second knot value 1 also has a multiplicity of 3. All knots in the first knot vector have a multiplicity of 1 because they don't repeat. Multiplicity has an important effect on the continuity of the curve. A multiplicity of 2 will cause a curve segment to reduce to a single point. The curve segment will be degenerate and have a length of zero. A multiplicity of 3 will cause two curve segments to reduce to a single point. There will be a sharp cusp in the curve. A multiplicity of 4 will cause three curve segments to reduce and there will be gap in the curve. This is because the segments before and after that area don't have any control vertices in common.

Many other 3D applications support curves with multiple end knots, but don't support curves with duplicate knots other than at the ends. The same curve can be achieved by creating duplicate control vertices at the same locations as control vertices 0 and 3. This is called *CV multiplicity* because the duplicate control vertices are coincident. In both cases, multiple knots and CV multiplicity can cause degenerate spans in the curve. This results in shaper bends in the curve, and many of Maya's tools don't work with them. In addition, the resulting curve is impractical for animation because it doesn't flow smoothly.

9.1.10 FORM

The form of a NURBS geometry determines how the object deforms. There are three possible forms: open, closed, and periodic. Figure 9.11 shows an open curve. The first and last control vertices are not coincident, therefore creating a gap in the curve.

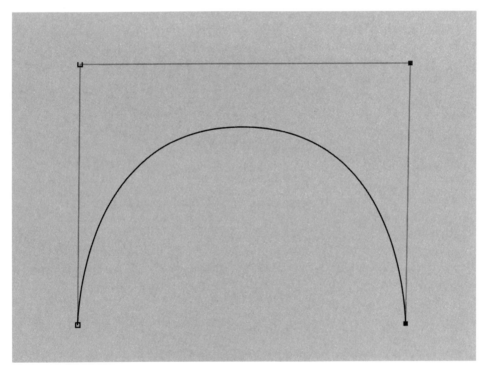

FIGURE 9.11 Open curve.

A closed curve is shown in Figure 9.12. Its first and last control vertices are coincident, resulting in a curve that is completely enclosed. The first and last control vertices are joined in such a way as to create a *seam*. A seam ensures that if the first control vertex is moved the last control vertex will also be moved to ensure that they are coincident.

The final form, periodic, is shown in Figure 9.13. A periodic curve is similar to a closed curve in that it has a seam between the start and end control vertices.

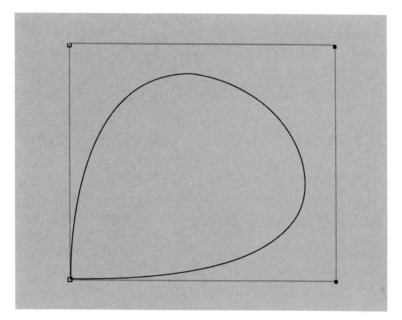

FIGURE 9.12 Closed curve.

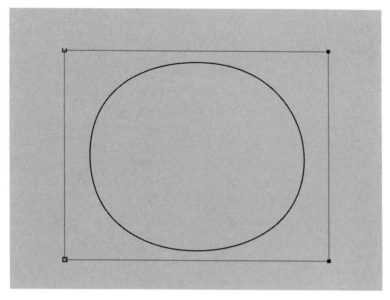

FIGURE 9.13 Periodic curve.

A periodic curve also has two hidden spans at the ends of the curve that overlap the first two visible spans. By adding two hidden spans to the end of the curve, continuity along the seam is maintained. Figure 9.14 shows the same periodic curve but with the spans numbered. There are actually six spans in the curve. The first four (spans 0 to 3) are visible, whereas the last two (spans 4 and 5) are invisible. Span 4 coincides with span 0, and span 5 coincides with span 1.

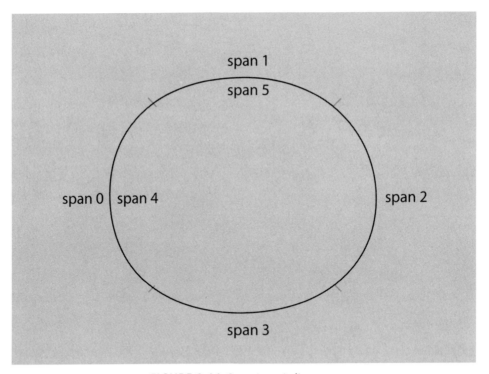

FIGURE 9.14 Spans in periodic curve.

9.1.11 SURFACE POINT

The surface point is the logical extension of a curve point to a 2D surface. A surface point is a parametric position on the NURBS surface. It has two coordinates: u and v. Because the parametric position is derived from the control vertices, when the control vertices move, the parametric position also moves. Figure 9.15 shows a NURBS curve with the surface point (u = 0.62, v = 0.36) indicated.

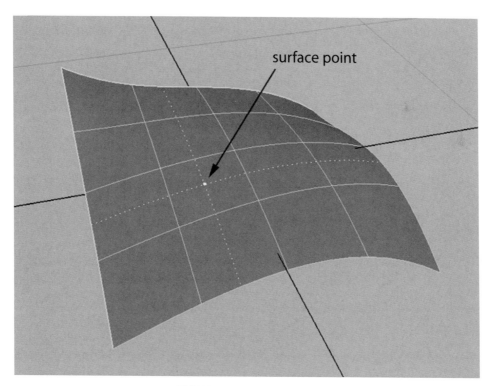

surface point

FIGURE 9.15 Surface point.

9.1.12 SURFACE ISOPARMS

More completely defined as *isoparametric curves*, isoparms are curves that run across a NURBS surface when you hold the u or v coordinate fixed and then let the other one vary. As the varying coordinate changes, it traces out a curve across the surface along the line of the fixed coordinate. Figure 9.16 shows the isoparametric curve of u = 0.38. The *u* parameter is held fixed at 0.38, whereas the v parameter is allowed to vary from 0 to 1. The curve traced out by these coordinates defines the isoparm.

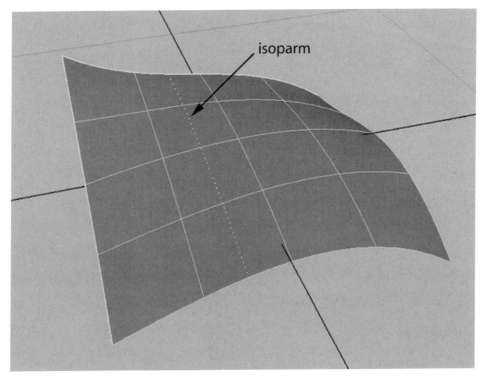

FIGURE 9.16 Isoparm.

9.1.13 SURFACE PATCHES

Given four separate isoparms, the area they enclose defines a *patch*. As such, a patch is defined by two u coordinates and two v coordinates. An example patch of a NURBS surface is shown in Figure 9.17.

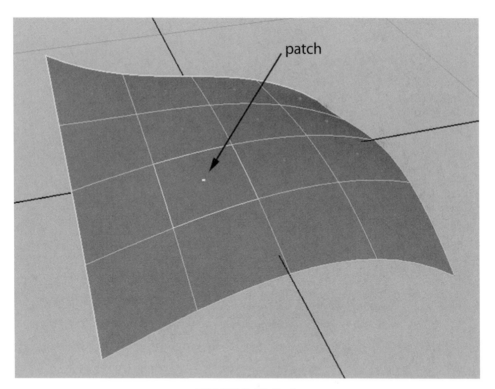

FIGURE 9.17 Patch.

9.1.14 SURFACE CURVES

Surface curves are curves stuck to the surface of a NURBS curve, as shown in Figure 9.18. Such curves, rather than defining their control vertices in 3D space, define them in the 2D parameteric space of the surface. Each of the control vertices is defined as u, v coordinates corresponding to a surface point. Because the control vertices are parametric, when the surface changes the control vertices move correspondingly. This way, the curve is always guaranteed to stay attached to the surface.

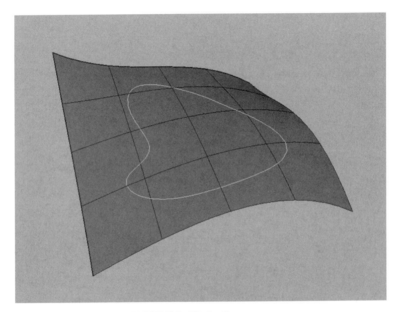

FIGURE 9.18 Surface curve.

It is important to note that the surface curve is located in the *underworld* of the dependency graph. The underworld is denoted using the arrow character (->). The DAG path to the NURBS surface is

| nurbsPlane1 | nurbsPlaneShape1

The DAG path to the curve on its surface is

| nurbsPlane1 | nurbsPlaneShape1-> | curve1

9.1.15 **TRIMMED SURFACES**

Because a NURBS surface is intrinsically a four-sided patch, there is no way to implicitly define holes. Holes and more complex slicing is achieved by using surface curves and trimming. The interior of the surface curve defines an enclosed space that is the hole in the NURBS surface, as shown in Figure 9.19. No actual hole is created because the underlying NURBS surface still exists. By removing the trimming surface curve, the original NURBS surface will be displayed.

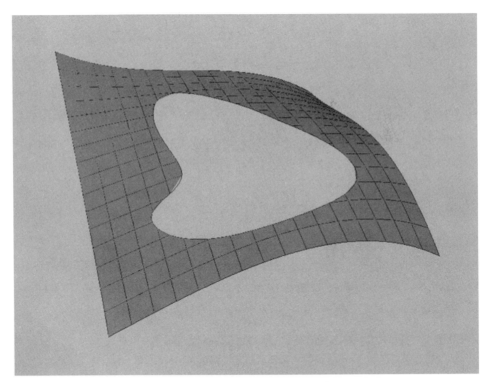

FIGURE 9.19 Trimmed interior surface.

Alternatively, the surface curve can define the part that should remain after trimming. An example of this is shown in Figure 9.20.

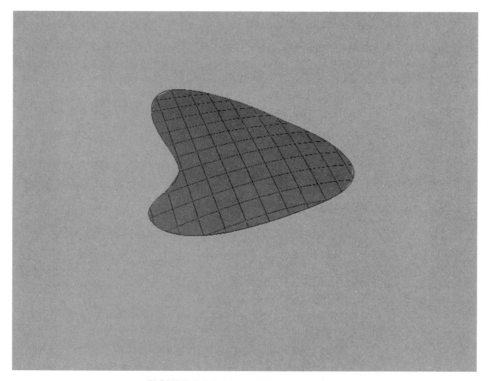

FIGURE 9.20 Trimmed exterior surface.

9.2 NURBS CURVES

The **nurbsCurve** shape node holds the NURBS curve information for a given curve. Each shape node can only hold a single curve, and thus it isn't possible to have multiple curves within a single shape node.

9.2.1 DISPLAYING CURVES

A NURBS curve can be displayed in a variety of ways, including whether its components (control vertices, hulls, edit points, and so on) are displayed.

1. Open the **TwoCurves.ma** scene.

2. Select the **curve1** object.

3. Execute the following.

```
toggle -geometry;
```

The curve is no longer displayed. It is important to note that the `curve1` object itself is visible but the curve itself is now hidden.

4. Execute the following.

```
toggle -geometry;
```

The curve is now displayed. The toggle command will toggle the visibility of the specified item. It will also be used to explicitly set the visibility of an item.

5. Execute the following.

```
toggle -controlVertex -state true;
```

The control vertices are now explicitly set to be visible.

6. Execute the following.

```
toggle -editPoint;
```

The edit points in the curve are now displayed. The display setting can be applied to all curves rather than the currently selected one.

7. Execute the following.

```
toggle -global -hull;
```

All curves now display their hulls. Because this toggles the current curve settings, those that already had their hulls displayed will now have them turned off. To explicitly display all of the curve's hulls, use the following.

```
toggle -global -hull -state true;
```

If a new curve is created it will not automatically have its hull displayed. To have a display state applied to new curves, the `-newCurve` flag must be used.

8. Execute the following.

```
toggle -newCurve -controlVertex -state true;
```

This sets the display state for curves created in the future.

9. Execute the following.

```
curve -p 0 0 0 -p 3 5 6 -p 5 6 7 -p 9 9 9;
```

A curve is created and its control vertices are automatically displayed. Note that the -newCurve state is maintained between sessions and thus all curves created later will use that state. If this isn't the intention, restore the -newCurve state.

10. Execute the following.

```
toggle -newCurve -controlVertex -state false;
```

Control vertices are no longer automatically displayed for newly created curves.

11. To reduce or increase the detail of the curve, use the displaySmoothness command.

```
displaySmoothness -pointsWire 2;
```

The -pointsWire flag sets the number of points per span that are drawn. The default setting is 5.

12. Because the displaySmoothness command isn't undoable, the command must be called again to restore the original setting.

```
displaySmoothness -pointsWire 5;
```

It is important to note that the displaySmoothness command controls the smoothness of the curve in the viewports. The underlying mathematical NURBS curve itself has a great deal more detail.

9.2.2 QUERYING CURVES

GENERAL

This section describes how to query the various components and attributes of a NURBS curve.

MEL

1. Open the **TwoCurves.ma** scene.

2. To get the total length of the curve, use the arclen command.

```
arclen curve1;
```

The result is shown.

```
// Result: 24.133793 //
```

3. Execute the following.

```
getAttr curve1.degree;
```

The degree of the curve is returned.

```
// Result: 3 //
```

4. The form of the curve can be determined by retrieving the `form` attribute:

```
getAttr curve1.form;
```

The form is returned.

```
// Result: 0 //
```

The form is stored as an integer with the following values: `0=Open`, `1=Closed`, and `2=Periodic`.

5. The number of spans is stored in the spans attribute.

```
getAttr curve1.spans; // Returns the number of spans
```

There are three spans in the curve.

```
// Result: 3 //
```

6. The parameter range of the curve is queried using the `minValue` and `maxValue` attributes.

```
getAttr curve1.minValue;
getAttr curve1.maxValue;
```

The results are:

```
// Result: 0 //
// Result: 3 //
```

7. The object space coordinates of the control vertices are queried as follows.

```
getAttr curve1.cv["*"];
```

The object space coordinates are output.

```
// Result: -8.551223 0 4.78932 -0.748818 0 10.077989 4.167374 0 7.754801
6.411612 0 4.375327 11.836032 0 4.084736 12.292791 0 6.662515 //
```

If the curve is a surface curve, the x, y, z coordinates retrieved will correspond respectively to the u, v, and 0 parametric coordinates.

8. The world space coordinates of the control vertices can't be retrieved directly. Instead, a curveInfo node is created. The curve whose control vertices are to be queried is connected into its inputCurve attribute. The control vertices are then retrieved by querying the curveInfo node's controlPoints attribute.

```
createNode curveInfo;
connectAttr curveShape1.worldSpace curveInfo1.inputCurve;
getAttr curveInfo1.controlPoints["*"];
```

The world space coordinates are displayed.

```
// Result: -8.551223 0 5.78932 -0.748818 0 11.077989 4.167374 0 8.754801
6.411612 0 5.375327 11.836032 0 5.084736 12.292791 0 7.662515 //
```

9. The knot vector for the curve is also retrieved using the curveInfo node.

```
getAttr curveInfo1.knots["*"];
```

The knot vector is output.

```
// Result: 0 0 0 1 2 3 3 3 //
```

10. The weights of the curve are queried using the curveInfo node.

```
getAttr curveInfo1.weights["*"];
```

A warning is issued.

```
// Warning: line 1: curveInfo1 (Curve Info Node): Curve is Non rational.
All weights are 1. //
```

NURBS curves are by default nonrational and thus don't have any associated weights. Only when the curve is rational can the weights be successfully retrieved.

11. The `curveInfo` node can also be used to retrieve the arc length of the curve.

```
getAttr curveInfo1.arcLength;
```

The result matches that returned by the `arclength` command.

```
// Result: 24.133793 //
```

Using the `curveInfo` node's `arcLength` attribute is a more dynamic way of retrieving the arc length because it could be connected into another attribute or expression so that whenever the length of the curve changed the connected attributes and/or expressions would be updated.

C++ API

The **CurveInfo1** plug-in demonstrates the following.

- Retrieving one or more selected curves
- Accessing curve information (length, degree, form, spans, parametric range, control vertices, and knots)
- Printing out curve information

1. Open the **CurveInfo1** workspace.

2. Compile it and load the resulting `curveInfo1` plug-in file in Maya.

3. Open the **TwoCurves.ma** scene.

4. Select the **curve1** object.

5. Execute the following.

```
curveInfo1;
```

A variety of information about the curve is output.

```
// |curve1
Length: 24.134094
Degree: 3
Form: Open
Spans: 3
MinValue: 0 MaxValue: 3
CVs: 6
 (-8.551223, 0, 5.78932) (-0.748818, 0, 11.077989) (4.167374,
 0, 8.754801) (6.411612, 0, 5.375327) (11.836032, 0, 5.084736)
 (12.292791, 0, 7.662515)
Knots: 8
 0 0 0 1 2 3 3 3
```

SOURCE CODE

Plug-in: `CurveInfo1`
File: `CurveInfo1Cmd.cpp`

```cpp
DeclareSimpleCommand( curveInfo1, "David Gould", "1.0" );

MStatus curveInfo1::doIt( const MArgList& args )
{
    MStatus stat = MS::kSuccess;

    MSelectionList selection;
    MGlobal::getActiveSelectionList( selection );

    MDagPath dagPath;
    MObject component;

    const char *formTxt[] = { "Invalid", "Open", "Closed",
                              "Periodic", "Last" };
    double start, end;
    int i, nCVs, nKnots;
    MPoint pt;
    double knot;
    MString txt;
    MItSelectionList iter( selection );
```

```
for( ; !iter.isDone(); iter.next() )
{
      iter.getDagPath( dagPath, component );

      MFnNurbsCurve curveFn( dagPath, &stat );
      if( stat )
      {
            txt += dagPath.fullPathName() + "\n";

            txt += MString("Length: ") + curveFn.length() + "\n";
            txt += MString("Degree: ") + curveFn.degree() + "\n";
            txt += MString("Form: ") +
                  formTxt[ curveFn.form() ] + "\n";
            txt += MString("Spans: ") +
                  curveFn.numSpans() + "\n";
            curveFn.getKnotDomain( start, end );
            txt += MString("MinValue: ") + start +
                     " MaxValue: " + end + "\n";

            nCVs = curveFn.numCVs();
            txt += MString("CVs: ") + nCVs + "\n";
            for( i=0; i < nCVs; i++ )
            {
                  curveFn.getCV( i, pt, MSpace::kWorld );
                  txt += MString(" (") + pt.x +
                        ", " + pt.y + ", " + pt.z + ")";
            }
            txt += "\n";

            nKnots = curveFn.numKnots();
            txt += MString("Knots: ") + nKnots + "\n";
            for( i=0; i < nKnots; i++ )
            {
                  knot = curveFn.knot( i );
                  txt += MString(" ") + knot;
            }
            txt += "\n";
      }
}
```

```
    MGlobal::displayInfo( txt );

    return MS::kSuccess;
}
```

SOURCE CODE EXPLANATION

Plug-in: `CurveInfo1`
File: `CurveInfo1Cmd.cpp`

The **curveInfo1**'s `doIt` function does the main work of outputting the curve information.

```
MStatus curveInfo1::doIt( const MArgList& args )
{
```

Each selected object is iterated over.

```
    MItSelectionList iter( selection );
    for ( ; !iter.isDone(); iter.next() )
    {
        iter.getDagPath( dagPath, component );
```

The `MFnNurbsCurve` function set is bound to the currently selected object. If its constructor succeeds, the current object is a NURBS curve.

```
        MFnNurbsCurve curveFn( dagPath, &stat );
        if( stat )
        {
```

The complete DAG path to the object is added to the output text.

```
            txt += dagPath.fullPathName() + "\n";
```

The length and degree of the curve are calculated using the `length` and `degree` functions, respectively.

```
            txt += MString("Length: ") + curveFn.length() + "\n";
            txt += MString("Degree: ") + curveFn.degree() + "\n";
```

The form of the curve is returned as an enumerated type from the `form` function. This is used to index into the `formTxt` array that has strings for each of the possible form values.

```
txt += MString("Form: ") +
        formTxt[ curveFn.form() ] + "\n";
```

The number of spans is retrieved using the numSpans function.

```
txt += MString("Spans: ") +
        curveFn.numSpans() + "\n";
```

The parametric range of the curve is retrieved using the getKnotDomain function.

```
curveFn.getKnotDomain( start, end );
txt += MString("MinValue: ") + start +
        " MaxValue: " + end + "\n";
```

The number of control vertices is retrieved using the numCVs function, and the getCV function is used to actually retrieve a given control vertex. The control vertex's coordinates are returned in world space coordinates because the MSpace::kWorld option is used.

```
nCVs = curveFn.numCVs();
txt += MString("CVs: ") + nCVs + "\n";
for( i=0; i < nCVs; i++ )
{
        curveFn.getCV( i, pt, MSpace::kWorld );
        txt += MString(" (") + pt.x +
                ", " + pt.y + ", " + pt.z + ")";
}
txt += "\n";
```

The number of knots in the knot vector is retrieved using the numKnots function. The parametric knot value is returned by the knot function.

```
nKnots = curveFn.numKnots();
txt += MString("Knots: ") + nKnots + "\n";
for( i=0; i < nKnots; i++ )
{
        knot = curveFn.knot( i );
        txt += MString(" ") + knot;
}
txt += "\n";
    }
}
```

The curve information is displayed as info text, and then the function returns successfully.

```
MGlobal::displayInfo( txt );

return MS::kSuccess;
}
```

SAMPLING CURVES

Each curve has a parametric range and it can be sampled at any location along the range. To sample a curve, a parametric location is given and then the position, tangent, and normal at the parametric location are calculated. Figure 9.21 shows the calculated position, tangent, and normal for the curve at the parametric location u = 1.6.

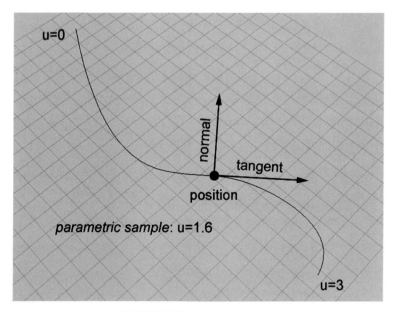

FIGURE 9.21 Curve sampling.

Maya provides two pieces of information regarding the *curvature* of a curve at a given parametric location: the center and radius of a circle that would fit tightly against the curve at the given location. Quantitatively, the resulting circle will have the same first- and second-order derivatives as the curve at the chosen parametric location. This circle is referred to as the osculating circle. Figure 9.22 shows the osculating circle for a curve at the parametric position 0.5.

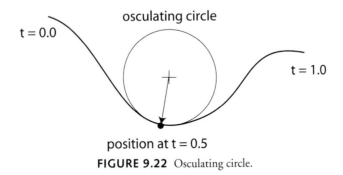

position at t = 0.5

FIGURE 9.22 Osculating circle.

Formally, the curvature is the reciprocal of the circle's radius.

curvature = 1 / circle_radius

If the radius is very large, the curvature will be small, which follows intuitively because a large circle would indicate only a slight bend in the curve. Likewise, if the radius is small the curvature will be larger, indicating a sharper bend in the curve.

Measure Tools

There are two measure tools that provide the parametric position and arc length along a curve: the **Parameter** and **Arc Length** tools. These tools provide for the interactive placement of the sample location along the curve.

1. Open the **TwoCurves.ma** scene.

2. Select **Create | Measure Tools | Parameter Tool**.

3. Click on the **curve1** object.

   A **paramDimension** object, **paramDimension1**, is created in the **curve1** object's underworld. This object displays the current parametric location along the curve.

4. Select the **Move Tool**.

5. Move the **paramDimension1** object along the curve and it will automatically display the parametric position.

6. Select **Edit | Delete** to remove the **paramDimension1** object.

7. Select **Create | Measure Tools | Arc Length Tool**.

8. Click on the **curve1** object.

   An **arcLengthDimension** object, **arcLengthDimension1**, is created in the **curve1** object's underworld. The arc length of the curve at the current position is displayed.

9. Select the **Move Tool**.

10. Move the **arcLengthDimension1** object along the curve. The current arc length is automatically updated.

This section describes how to sample a curve at a given parametric location. The sampled data includes the position on the curve, its normal, tangent, and so on.

MEL

1. Open the **TwoCurves.ma** scene.

2. To take several samples along the **curve1** object, execute the following.

```
float $start = `getAttr curve1.minValue`;
float $end = `getAttr curve1.maxValue`;
int $nSegs = 10;
float $tIncr = ($end - $start) / $nSegs;
float $t;
int $seg;
float $pt[], $norm[], $tang[], $cCenter[], $cRadius;
for( $seg=0, $t = $start; $seg < ($nSegs+1); $seg++, $t += $tIncr )
 {
 $pt = `pointOnCurve -parameter $t -position curve1`;
 $norm = `pointOnCurve -parameter $t -normalizedNormal curve1`;
 $tang = `pointOnCurve -parameter $t -normalizedTangent curve1`;
```

```
$cCenter = `pointOnCurve -parameter $t -curvatureCenter curve1`;
$cRadius = `pointOnCurve -parameter $t -curvatureRadius curve1`;

print ("Segment: " + $seg + "\n");
print ("Position: (" + $pt[0] + ", " + $pt[1] + ", " +
  $pt[2] + ")" + "\n");
print ("Normal: (" + $norm[0] + ", " + $norm[1] + ", " +
  $norm[2] + ")" + "\n");
print ("Tangent: (" + $tang[0] + ", " + $tang[1] + ", " +
  $tang[2] + ")" + "\n");
print ("CurvatureCenter: (" + $cCenter[0] + ", " + $cCenter[1] + ", " +
  $cCenter[2] + ")" + "\n");
print ("CurvatureRadius: " + $cRadius + "\n");
}
```

The various sampled information is printed out.

```
Segment: 0
Position: (-8.551223493, 0, 5.789319865)
Normal: (0.5610785259, 0, -0.8277625793)
Tangent: (0.8277625793, 0, 0.5610785259)
CurvatureCenter: (23.39451652, 0, -41.34042567)
CurvatureRadius: 56.93630845
Segment: 1
Position: (-2.85081106, 0, 8.98218181)
Normal: (0.3714981934, 0, -0.9284336768)
Tangent: (0.9284336768, 0, 0.3714981934)
CurvatureCenter: (3.130021677, 0, -5.964880186)
CurvatureRadius: 16.09922428
Segment: 2
...
```

The parametric range of the curve is retrieved.

```
float $start = `getAttr curve1.minValue`;
float $end = `getAttr curve1.maxValue`;
```

The curve will be divided into $nSegs segments. Change this value to have more or fewer segments.

```
int $nSegs = 10;
```

The $tIncr is set to the parametric increment per segment.

```
float $tIncr = ($end - $start) / $nSegs;
```

The various increment variables, $t (which holds the current parametric position), and $seg (which holds the current segment) are defined.

```
float $t;
int $seg;
```

The variety of sample data variables are defined.

```
float $pt[], $norm[], $tang[], $cCenter[], $cRadius;
```

The parameteric length of the curve is traversed.

```
for( $seg=0, $t = $start; $seg < ($nSegs+1); $seg++, $t += $tIncr )
  {
```

The current position sampled at the parameter location $t is retrieved using the pointOnCurve command. Note that it is also possible to use a percentage position along the curve rather than a parametric position by using the -turnOnPercentage true flag. The parametric position is still given by the -parametric flag but should be given as a value between 0 and 1 corresponding to 0% and 100%, respectively.

```
$pt = `pointOnCurve -parameter $t -position curve1`;
```

The normal vector at the current parametric location is retrieved using the same command but with the -normalizedNormal flag. It is also possible to get the unnormalized normal by using the -normal flag. The normal is the vector perpendicular to the curve at the given parametric position.

```
$norm = `pointOnCurve -parameter $t -normalizedNormal curve1`;
```

The tangent vector at the given parametric location $t is calculated by using the `-normalizedTangent` flag. The unnormalized tangent can be retrieved using the `-tangent` flag.

```
$tang = `pointOnCurve -parameter $t -normalizedTangent curve1`;
```

The center of the osculating circle is retrieved using the `-curvatureCenter` flag, whereas the radius of the osculating circle is retrieved using the `-curvatureRadius` flag.

```
$cCenter = `pointOnCurve -parameter $t -curvatureCenter curve1`;
$cRadius = `pointOnCurve -parameter $t -curvatureRadius curve1`;
```

With all relevant sample data now calculated, it is now output to the **Script Editor**.

```
print ("Segment: " + $seg + "\n");
print ("Position: (" + $pt[0] + ", " + $pt[1] + ", " +
  $pt[2] + ")" + "\n");
print ("Normal: (" + $norm[0] + ", " + $norm[1] + ", " +
  $norm[2] + ")" + "\n");
print ("Tangent: (" + $tang[0] + ", " + $tang[1] + ", " +
  $tang[2] + ")" + "\n");
print ("CurvatureCenter: (" + $cCenter[0] + ", " + $cCenter[1] + ", " +
  $cCenter[2] + ")" + "\n");
print ("CurvatureRadius: " + $cRadius + "\n");
}
```

C++ API

The **CurveInfo2** plug-in demonstrates the following.

- Retrieving one or more selected curves
- Sampling the curve at a given parametric position
- Accessing sampled information (segment, position, normal, tangent)
- Printing out sampled information

1. Open the **CurveInfo2** workspace.

2. Compile it and load the resulting `CurveInfo2` plug-in file in Maya.

3. Open the **TwoCurves.ma** scene.

4. Select the **curve1** object.

5. To sample the curve, execute the following.

```
curveInfo2;
```

Ten samples are taken along the curve's length. The various data retrieved per sample are output.

```
// |curve1
Segment: 0
Position: (-8.551223, 0, 5.78932)
Normal: (0.561079, 0, -0.827763)
Tangent: (0.827763, 0, 0.561079)
Segment: 1
Position: (-2.850811, 0, 8.982182)
Normal: (0.371498, 0, -0.928434)
Tangent: (0.928434, 0, 0.371498)
Segment: 2
...
```

SOURCE CODE
Plug-in: `CurveInfo2`
File: `CurveInfo2Cmd.cpp`

```
DeclareSimpleCommand( curveInfo2, "David Gould", "1.0" );

MStatus curveInfo2::doIt( const MArgList& args )
{
    MStatus stat = MS::kSuccess;

    MSelectionList selection;
    MGlobal::getActiveSelectionList( selection );

    MDagPath dagPath;
    MObject component;

    const int nSegs = 10;
    double start, end, t, tIncr;
```

```
int seg;
MPoint pt;
MVector norm, tang;

MString txt;
MItSelectionList iter( selection );
for ( ; !iter.isDone(); iter.next() )
{
      iter.getDagPath( dagPath, component );

      MFnNurbsCurve curveFn( dagPath, &stat );
      if( stat )
      {
            txt += dagPath.fullPathName() + "\n";

            curveFn.getKnotDomain( start, end );
            tIncr = (end - start) /nSegs;

            for( seg=0, t=start; seg < (nSegs+1); seg++, t+=tIncr )
            {
                  curveFn.getPointAtParam( t, pt, MSpace::kWorld );
                  norm = curveFn.normal( t, MSpace::kWorld );
                  tang = curveFn.tangent( t, MSpace::kWorld );

                  txt += MString("Segment: ") + seg + "\n";
                  txt += MString("Position: (") + pt.x + ", " +
                        pt.y + ", " + pt.z + ")\n";
                  txt += MString("Normal: (") + norm.x + ", " +
                        norm.y + ", " + norm.z + ")\n";
                  txt += MString("Tangent: (") + tang.x + ", " +
                        tang.y + ", " + tang.z + ")\n";
            }
      }
}

MGlobal::displayInfo( txt );

return MS::kSuccess;
}
```

SOURCE CODE EXPLANATION

Plug-in: `CurveInfo2`
File: `CurveInfo2Cmd.cpp`

Inside the `doIt` function, the number of segments to sample, `nSegs`, is defined. The actual number of sample points is this number plus one.

```
const int nSegs = 10;
```

Each object in the current selection list is iterated over.

```
MItSelectionList iter( selection );
for ( ; !iter.isDone(); iter.next() )
{
```

The **MFnNurbsCurve** function set is applied to the currently selected object. If the object is compatible with the function set, the status returned in the variable `stat` is `MS::kSuccess`.

```
MFnNurbsCurve curveFn( dagPath, &stat );
if( stat )
{
```

The current object's full DAG path is output.

```
txt += dagPath.fullPathName() + "\n";
```

The parametric range of the curve is determined.

```
curveFn.getKnotDomain( start, end );
```

The parametric increment is determined by dividing the parametric range into the number of requested segments. This increment will be added to the current parametric location for each segment.

```
tIncr = (end - start) / nSegs;
```

The curve's length is iterated over in increments.

```
for( seg=0, t=start; seg < (nSegs+1); seg++, t+=tIncr )
{
```

The `getPointAtParam` function retrieves the current position along the curve at parametric location t. In this case, the `MSpace::kWorld` option is used so that the returned position is in world space coordinates.

```
curveFn.getPointAtParam( t, pt, MSpace::kWorld );
```

The normal vector at the parametric location is retrieved using the `normal` function.

```
norm = curveFn.normal( t, MSpace::kWorld );
```

The tangent vector at the parametric location is retrieved using the `tangent` function.

```
tang = curveFn.tangent( t, MSpace::kWorld );
```

With all of the information about the current sample now retrieved, it is added to the output text.

```
txt += MString("Segment: ") + seg + "\n";
txt += MString("Position: (") + pt.x + ", " +
       pt.y + ", " + pt.z + ")\n";
txt += MString("Normal: (") + norm.x + ", " +
       norm.y + ", " + norm.z + ")\n";
txt += MString("Tangent: (") + tang.x + ", " +
       tang.y + ", " + tang.z + ")\n";
            }
        }
    }
```

The output text is then displayed.

```
MGlobal::displayInfo( txt );
return MS::kSuccess;
}
```

9.2.3 CREATING CURVES

This section covers the creation of NURBS curves.

GENERAL

1. Select **File | New Scene**.

2. Create a simple curve by executing the following.

    ```
    curve -degree 1 -p 0 0 0 -p 1 0 1;
    ```

    A straight line segment is created because the degree is set to 1. Smoother curves can be created by using a larger degree. The control vertices are specified by using the -p flag with the three coordinates of the vertex.

3. An additional point will be added to the curve.

    ```
    curve -append -p 0 0 1 curve1;
    ```

    An additional control vertex is appended to the curve.

4. A curve can be totally replaced with another.

    ```
    curve -replace -degree 2 -p 0 0 0 -p 1 0 1 -p 1 0 0 curve1;
    ```

    The original curve is replaced by the newly specified one.

5. A curve in the shape of a circle can be created using the circle command.

    ```
    circle;
    ```

6. Likewise, a square can be created.

    ```
    nurbsSquare;
    ```

7. Text can be created in Maya by using the textCurves command.

    ```
    textCurves -font "Times-Roman" -text "curve";
    ```

NURBS curves are generated for the different letters in the text. Note that separate NURBS curve shape nodes are created for each curve. For instance, the letter *e* consists of two separate curves.

CURVESWIRL

The first example defines the curveSwirl procedure that creates a curve with control vertices that twirl up and around the shape of a sphere. Figure 9.23 shows the result of calling the procedure with different curve degrees.

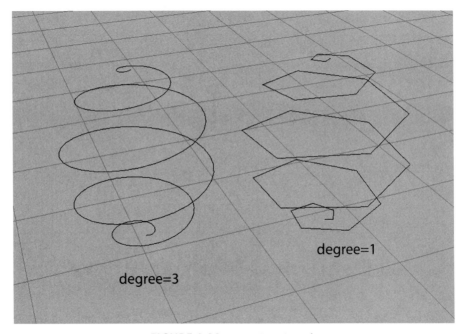

FIGURE 9.23 curveSwirl result.

MEL

1. Ensure that the MAYA_SCRIPT_PATH is set up correctly. (See Section 1.1.2 for further details.)

2. Execute the following.

```
source curveSwirl;
```

3. To create the curve, the `curveSwirl` procedure is called.

    ```
    curveSwirl( 1.0, 30, 5, 3 );
    ```

    A curve is created that follows the surface of a sphere. The `curveSwirl` procedure is called. It takes the following parameters.

    ```
    global proc curveSwirl(
        float $radius,      // Radius of sphere
        int $nSpans,        // Number of spans in curve
        int $nRevolutions,  // Number of revolutions around sphere
        int $degree         // Degree of the curve
    )
    ```

4. To create the same curve but of degree 1, execute the following.

    ```
    curveSwirl( 1.0, 30, 5, 1 );
    ```

    Because the curve has degree 1, it has linear segments rather than the smooth segments of a degree-3 curve.

5. The number of times the curve wraps around the sphere is controlled by the `$nRevolutions` parameter. To have the curve wrap a lot more, execute the following.

    ```
    curveSwirl( 1.0, 30, 10, 3 );
    ```

    The curve now wraps twice as much as before. However, the curve appears to be scaled around its center. The reason for this is that although the control vertices are located on the surface of an imaginary sphere the curve is always inside the control vertices. To get a better understanding of what is happening, turn on the curve's hull.

6. Select **Display | NURBS Components | Hulls** from the main menu.

    The hull of the curve is displayed. It is immediately clear that there are not enough control vertices to represent the sphere. Many control vertices are almost on opposite sides of the sphere.

7. To create a curve with better control vertices, execute the following.

```
curveSwirl( 1.0, 90, 10, 3 );
```

There are more control vertices, and these are better spaced around the sphere.

MEL Script: `curveSwirl.mel`

```
global proc curveSwirl(
   float $radius,
   int $nSpans,
   int $nRevolutions,
   int $degree
)
{
   int $nCVs = $degree + $nSpans;
   int $multiplicity = $degree;

   vector $cvs[];
   float $azimIncr = deg_to_rad( $nRevolutions * float(360) / ($nCVs-1) );
   float $zenIncr = deg_to_rad( float(180) / ($nCVs-1));
   float $azimuth, $zenith, $sinZenith;
   float $x, $y, $z;
   int $cvi;
   for( $i=0, $cvi=0, $azimuth=0.0, $zenith=0.0;
         $cvi < $nCVs;
         $cvi++, $azimuth+=$azimIncr, $zenith+=$zenIncr )
   {
         $sinZenith = sin( $zenith );

         $x = $radius * $sinZenith * cos($azimuth);
         $y = $radius * cos($zenith);
         $z = $radius * $sinZenith * sin($azimuth);

         $cvs[$i++] = << $x, $y, $z >>;
   }

   int $span, $m;
   float $knots[];
```

```
for( $i=0, $span=0; $span <= $nSpans; $span++ )
{
        $knots[$i++] = float($span);

        if( $span == 0 || $span == $nSpans )
        {
                for( $m=1; $m < $multiplicity; $m++ )
                        $knots[$i++] = float($span);
        }
}


string $cmd = "curve -degree " + $degree;
vector $p;
for( $i=0; $i < size($cvs); $i++ )
{
        $p = $cvs[$i];
        $cmd += " -p " + ($p.x) + " " + ($p.y) + " " + ($p.z);
}
for( $i=0; $i < size($knots); $i++ )
        $cmd += " -k " + $knots[$i];

evalEcho( $cmd );
}
```

The curveSwirl procedure has to prepare the series of control vertices and knot values that make up the curve, and then call the curve command to generate the actual curve. The $radius parameter is the radius of the imaginary sphere on which to place the control vertices. The $nSpans parameter defines the number of spans in the curve. The $nRevolutions parameter defines how many times the curve will wrap around the sphere. The final parameter, $degree, defines the degree of the curve.

```
global proc curveSwirl(
    float $radius,
    int $nSpans,
    int $nRevolutions,
    int $degree
)
```

The number of control vertices in the curve is determined from the degree and spans requested.

```
int $nCVs = $degree + $nSpans;
```

Because the curve needs to start at the first control vertex and end at the last control vertex, knot multiplicity is used to achieve this. By repeating the first and last knots as many times as the degree of the curve, the curve will start and end at the first and last control vertices. This will be clearer in material to follow, which defines the curve's knot vector.

```
int $multiplicity = $degree;
```

The $cvs array holds the control vertices of the curve.

```
vector $cvs[];
```

Positions on the imaginary sphere are calculated using spherical coordinates. These comprise two angular coordinates (azimuth and zenith). The azimuth defines the longtitude around the sphere and varies from 0 to 360 degrees. The zenith defines the vertical angle and varies from 0 to 180 degrees. The total azimuth angle the curve will travel is

$nRevolutions * 360°

This angle is divided into the number of segments that make up the hull of the curve. Recalling that the hull is simply the segments between control vertices, the total number of segments is

$nCVs − 1

The angular step of the azimuth is therefore

$nRevolutions * 360° / ($nCVs − 1)

The final anglular step, $azimIncr, has to be in radians rather than in degrees so that the 360 degrees are converted into radians using the deg_to_rad procedure. It is important to note the need for the casting of the integer constant 360 to a float.

Without this, the multiplication and division would be done using integer arithmetic, resulting in an incorrect result. Rather than casting 360 to a float, the float constant 360.0 could also have been used.

```
float $azimIncr = deg_to_rad( $nRevolutions * float(360) / ($nCVs-1) );
```

The total zenith angle the curve will cover is 180 degrees. The angular step, $zenIncr, is calculated by dividing 180 degrees into the number of segments in the curve hull.

```
float $zenIncr = deg_to_rad( float(180) / ($nCVs-1));
```

With the angular steps now determined, the control vertices are calculated.

```
int $cvi;
for( $i=0, $cvi=0, $azimuth=0.0, $zenith=0.0;
        $cvi < $nCVs;
        $cvi++, $azimuth+=$azimIncr, $zenith+=$zenIncr )
{
```

The Cartesian coordinates ($x, $y, $z) are calculated from the spherical coordinates ($azimuth, $zenith).

```
$sinZenith = sin( $zenith );
$x = $radius * $sinZenith * cos($azimuth);
$y = $radius * cos($zenith);
$z = $radius * $sinZenith * sin($azimuth);
```

The control vertex is appended to the $cvs array.

```
$cvs[$i++] = << $x, $y, $z >>;
}
```

The array of knot values, $knots, is now generated. The total number of knot values needed is

$nSpans + 2 * $degree − 1

Successive knot values must be increasing. For the curve to start at the first control vertex and end at the last vertex there must be knot multiplicity at the start and end of the knots. This means that the first and last knots must be repeated as many times as the degree of the curve. Given a curve of degree 3 with four control vertices, the number of knots needed is

```
6 = 1 + 2 * 3 - 1
```

The knot vector would be as follows.

```
0 0 0 1 1 1
```

A knot is added to the array for each span in the curve, including the last span index. The first and last knot vectors are repeated as needed.

```
int $span, $m;
float $knots[];
for( $i=0, $span=0; $span <= $nSpans; $span++ )
{
        $knots[$i++] = float($span);
```

If this is the first span or the last span index, duplicate the knot value.

```
        if( $span == 0 || $span == $nSpans )
        {
```

The knot value at the start and the end of the array is repeated for as many times as the degree of the curve. Because the knot value has been added once in the previous statement, only degree-1 repetitions still remain. This is why the loop is initialized to $m=1 rather than $m=0.

```
            for( $m=1; $m < $multiplicity; $m++ )
                $knots[$i++] = float($span);
        }
}
```

With the control vertices and knot vector now calculated, the curve command statement is generated. The statement is of the following form.

curve −degree $degree −p $cvs[0] ... −p $cvs[last] −k $knots[0] ... −k $knots[last]

```
string $cmd = "curve -degree " + $degree;
```

The control vertices are added to the command. Note that the current vector is retrieved and stored in $p. This is because it is impossible to access the vector components directly as $cvs[$i].x. Instead, $p.x is used.

```
vector $p;
for( $i=0; $i < size($cvs); $i++ )
{
        $p = $cvs[$i];
        $cmd += " -p " + ($p.x) + " " + ($p.y) + " " + ($p.z);
}
```

The knot vector values are next added to the command.

```
for( $i=0; $i < size($knots); $i++ )
        $cmd += " -k " + $knots[$i];
```

The completed curve command statement is executed. The statement is echoed to the **Script Editor**.

```
evalEcho( $cmd );
}
```

C++ API

The **CurveSwirl** plug-in demonstrates the following.

- Creating a NURBS curve based on a given radius, number of spans, revolutions, and degree

1. Open the **CurveSwirl** workspace.

2. Compile it and load the resulting curveSwirl plug-in file in Maya.

3. If the **curveSwirl.mel** file was sourced during the current session, restart Maya. Otherwise, select **File | New Scene**.

4. To create the curve, execute the following.

   ```
   curveSwirl;
   ```

   A twirled curve is created.

5. To reduce the degree of the curve, execute the following.

   ```
   curveSwirl -degree 1;
   ```

6. The number of revolutions is controlled by the `-revolutions` flag. With an increase in the number of revolutions, the number of spans also needs to be increased to have the control vertices better represent the imaginary sphere.

   ```
   curveSwirl -degree 3 -spans 60 -revolutions 10;
   ```

SOURCE CODE

Plug-in: `CurveSwirl`
File: `CurveSwirlCmd.cpp`

```
class CurveSwirlCmd : public MPxCommand
{
public:
   virtual MStatus doIt ( const MArgList& );
   virtual MStatus redoIt();
   virtual MStatus undoIt();
   virtual bool isUndoable() const { return true; }

   static void *creator() { return new CurveSwirlCmd; }
   static MSyntax newSyntax();

private:
   MDistance radius;
   int nSpans;
   int nRevolutions;
   int degree;

   MObject curveTransform;
```

```
    void genCVs( const double radius, const int nCVs,
                        const int revolutions, MPointArray &cvs );
};

const char *radiusFlag = "-r", *radiusLongFlag = "-radius";
const char *spansFlag = "-s", *spansLongFlag = "-spans";
const char *revolutionsFlag = "-rv", *revolutionsLongFlag = "-
revolutions";
const char *degreeFlag = "-d", *degreeLongFlag = "-degree";

MSyntax CurveSwirlCmd::newSyntax()
{
    MSyntax syntax;

syntax.addFlag( radiusFlag, radiusLongFlag, MSyntax::kDistance );
syntax.addFlag( spansFlag, spansLongFlag, MSyntax::kLong );
syntax.addFlag( revolutionsFlag, revolutionsLongFlag,
                    MSyntax::kLong );
syntax.addFlag( degreeFlag, degreeLongFlag, MSyntax::kLong );

    syntax.enableQuery( false );
    syntax.enableEdit( false );

    return syntax;
}

MStatus CurveSwirlCmd::doIt ( const MArgList &args )
{
    MStatus stat;

    radius.setValue( 1.0 );
    nSpans = 30;
    nRevolutions = 5;
    degree = 3;

    MArgDatabase argData( syntax(), args, &stat );
    if( !stat )
        return stat;

    if( argData.isFlagSet( radiusFlag ) )
        argData.getFlagArgument( radiusFlag, 0, radius );

    if( argData.isFlagSet( spansFlag ) )
        argData.getFlagArgument( spansFlag, 0, nSpans );
```

```
    if( argData.isFlagSet( revolutionsFlag ) )
        argData.getFlagArgument( revolutionsFlag, 0, nRevolutions );

    if( argData.isFlagSet( degreeFlag ) )
        argData.getFlagArgument( degreeFlag, 0, degree );

    return redoIt();
}
void CurveSwirlCmd::genCVs(
    const double radius,
    const int nCVs,
    const int revolutions,
    MPointArray &cvs
)
{
    cvs.clear();
    double azimIncr = revolutions * 2.0 * M_PI / (nCVs-1);
    double zenIncr = M_PI / (nCVs-1);

    MPoint p;
    double azimuth, zenith;
    double sinZenith;
    int cvi;

    azimuth = 0.0;
    zenith = 0.0;
    for( cvi=0; cvi < nCVs; cvi++, azimuth += azimIncr, zenith += zenIncr )
    {
        sinZenith = sin(zenith);

        p.x = radius * sinZenith * cos(azimuth);
        p.y = radius * cos(zenith);
        p.z = radius * sinZenith * sin(azimuth);

        cvs.append( p );
    }
}
MStatus CurveSwirlCmd::redoIt()
{
    int nCVs = degree + nSpans;
    int multiplicity = degree;
```

```
        MPointArray cvs;
        genCVs( radius.value(), nCVs, nRevolutions, cvs );

        MDoubleArray knots;
        int span, m;
        for( span=0; span <= nSpans; span++ )
        {
            knots.append( double(span) );

            if( span == 0 || span == nSpans )
            {
                for( m=1; m < multiplicity; m++ )
                    knots.append( double(span) );
            }
        }

        MStatus stat;
        MFnNurbsCurve curveFn;
        curveTransform = curveFn.create( cvs, knots, degree,
                                    MFnNurbsCurve::kOpen, false, false,
                                    MObject::kNullObj, &stat );

        return stat;
    }

MStatus CurveSwirlCmd::undoIt()
{
    MFnDagNode dagFn( curveTransform );
    MObject child;
    child = dagFn.child(0);
    MGlobal::deleteNode( child );
    MGlobal::deleteNode( curveTransform );

    return MS::kSuccess;
}

MStatus initializePlugin( MObject obj )
{
    MFnPlugin plugin( obj, "David Gould", "1.0" );
```

```
   MStatus stat;
   stat = plugin.registerCommand( "curveSwirl",
                                  CurveSwirlCmd::creator,
                                  CurveSwirlCmd::newSyntax );

   if ( !stat )
       stat.perror( "registerCommand failed");

   return stat;
}

MStatus uninitializePlugin( MObject obj )
{
   MFnPlugin plugin( obj );

   MStatus  stat;
   stat = plugin.deregisterCommand( "curveSwirl" );
   if ( !stat )
       stat.perror( "deregisterCommand failed" );

   return stat;
}
```

SOURCE CODE EXPLANATION

Plug-in: CurveSwirl
File: CurveSwirlCmd.cpp

The **CurveSwirlCmd** class contains the standard member functions for a command that is undoable/redoable.

```
class CurveSwirlCmd : public MPxCommand
{
```

The command takes four arguments. The first is the radius of the imaginary sphere the curve will twist around. The second is the number of spans in the curve. The third argument is the number of times the curve will twist around the sphere. The last argument is the degree of the curve.

```
   ...
   MDistance radius;
   int nSpans;
   int nRevolutions;
   int degree;
```

The command generates a single curve. This curve is made up of a **transform** object and a child **nurbsCurveShape** object. The `curveTransform` variable is set to the transform object generated by this command.

```
    MObject curveTransform;

    ...

};
```

The `genCVs` member function generates the control vertices that make up the curve. Refer to the previous MEL section for a complete description of how the control vertices are generated.

```
    void CurveSwirlCmd::genCVs(
        const double radius,
        const int nCVs,
        const int revolutions,
        MPointArray &cvs
    )
```

The `redoIt` member function generates the control vertices and knots. Because the command only generates one curve, it is possible that these could be generated in the `doIt` function and stored in the class. Refer to the previous MEL section for a complete description of how the knot vectors are generated.

```
    MStatus CurveSwirlCmd::redoIt()
    {
        ...
```

The curve is created by passing the control vertices, knots, degree, and form to the **MFnNurbsCurve**'s `create` function. The function's `create2D` and `rational` parameters are both set to `false`. The curve will be a nonrational curve. The curve's `transform` object is returned from the `create` function.

```
        MStatus stat;
        MFnNurbsCurve curveFn;
        curveTransform = curveFn.create( cvs, knots, degree,
                                    MFnNurbsCurve::kOpen, false, false,
                                    MObject::kNullObj, &stat );

        ...

    }
```

The `undoIt` function deletes the curve created. Because the curve wasn't generated using a simple `MDGModifier::createNode` call, but uses the `MFnNurbsCurve::create` function, the curve must be deleted manually.

```
MStatus CurveSwirlCmd::undoIt()
{
    MFnDagNode dagFn( curveTransform );
    MObject child;
```

It is important to delete the child **nurbsCurve** shape before the transform. Deleting the transform object without first deleting its child will result in Maya crashing.

```
    child = dagFn.child(0);
    MGlobal::deleteNode( child );
    MGlobal::deleteNode( curveTransform );
    ...
}
```

CURVESTAR

This section describes how to create a periodic NURBS curve in the shape of a star. Periodic curves wrap around on themselves, thereby hiding any join or seam. As a result, they appear as one continuous curve even though they have a definite start and end. Curves of different degrees will be supported. The degree of a curve affects how many duplicate control vertices are needed to hide the seam. The curve's knot vector is also quite different from the previous example. For periodic curves, the knot vector specifies knot values that take advantage of the modulus of knot values. This provides for knot values that wrap around. Figure 9.24 shows the result of applying the `curveStar` procedure with two different spike settings.

MEL

1. Ensure the `MAYA_SCRIPT_PATH` is set up correctly. (See Section 1.1.2 for further details.)

2. Execute the following.

```
source curveStar;
```

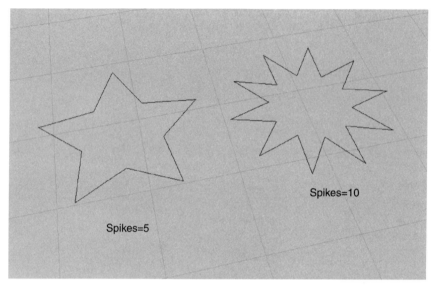

FIGURE 9.24 CurveStar result.

3. The curveStar procedure is used to create the curve.

```
curveStar( 0.5, 1.0, 5, 1, false );
```

A five-point curve is created. The curveStar procedure takes the following parameters.

```
global proc curveStar(
    float $innerRadius,     // Circle on which inner points are located
    float $outerRadius,     // Circle on which outer points are located
    int $spikes,            // Number of spikes
    int $degree,            // Degree of the curve
    int $periodic           // Whether the curve is periodic
)
```

Because the $periodic parameter is set to false, the curve is nonperiodic. Specifically, this means that the curve doesn't wrap around on itself. A nonperiodic curve will have separate and distinct control vertices. Even though the curve appears to be closed, in fact it isn't.

4. Execute the following.

```
select -r curve1.cv[0];
```

5. Select the **Move Tool**.

6. Move the selected control vertex.

   When the control vertex is moved, it is clear that the curve isn't closed. Even though the first and last control vertices were in the same position, because the curve is neither closed nor periodic, moving one of the vertices reveals the underlying form of the curve. This is now going to be compared with a periodic curve.

7. To remove the existing curve, execute the following.

```
select -r curve1;
delete;
```

8. A periodic curve will now be created.

```
curveStar( 0.5, 1.0, 5, 1, true );
```

   The curve looks the same as the previous curve. Its underlying form will become clearer as its last control vertex is moved.

9. Execute the following.

```
select -r curve1.cv[0];
```

10. Select the **Move Tool**.

11. Move the selected control vertex.

    The curve remains closed when the control vertex is moved. Because the form of the curve is set to be periodic when the first control vertex is moved, Maya will also move the last control vertex to ensure that they are coincident. It is important to note that the higher the degree of the curve, the more coincident overlapping control vertices are necessary to maintain a periodic curve.

12. Select **Edit | Undo** to restore the control vertex's original position.

13. To see the effect of using curves of different degrees, execute the following.

```
curveStar( 0.5, 1.0, 5, 3, true );
```

A more smoothly varying curve is produced. It is important to understand that the only difference between the previous curve and the current one is that the degree was changed from 1 to 3. The control vertices are the same.

14. Select **Display | NURBS Components | Hulls**.

The hull of the new curve is displayed. It is exactly aligned with the first curve. Figure 9.25 shows curves with the same control vertices but differing degrees.

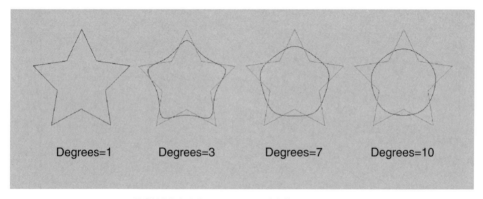

FIGURE 9.25 Curve stars of different degrees.

MEL Script: `curveStar.mel`

```
global proc curveStar(
   float $innerRadius,
   float $outerRadius,
   int $spikes,
   int $degree,
   int $periodic
)
{
   vector $cvs[];
   int $nSpikeCVs = 2 * $spikes;
```

```
float $angleIncr = deg_to_rad(180) / $spikes;
float $angle;
float $x, $y, $z, $r;
int $ci;
for( $ci=0, $angle=0.0; $ci < $nSpikeCVs; $ci++, $angle+=$angleIncr )
{
      if( $ci % 2 ) // Odd
              $r = $outerRadius;
      else
              $r = $innerRadius;

      $x = $r * cos($angle);
      $y = 0.0;
      $z = $r * sin($angle);

      $cvs[$ci] = << $x, $y, $z >>;
}

for( $ci=0; $ci < $degree; $ci++ )
      $cvs[size($cvs)] = $cvs[$ci];

float $knots[];
int $nSpans = size($cvs) - $degree;
int $nKnots = $nSpans + 2 * $degree - 1;
int $ki;
for( $i=-($degree-1), $ki=0; $ki < $nKnots; $i++, $ki++ )
      $knots[$ki] = float($i);

string $cmd = "curve -degree " + $degree +
          " -periodic " + $periodic;
vector $p;
for( $i=0; $i < size($cvs); $i++ )
{
      $p = $cvs[$i];
      $cmd += " -p " + ($p.x) + " " + ($p.y) + " " + ($p.z);
}
for( $i=0; $i < size($knots); $i++ )
      $cmd += " -k " + $knots[$i];

evalEcho( $cmd );
}
```

The curveStar procedure takes five parameters that define how the curve will be created. The $innerRadius parameter is the radius of the circle on which the inner points will be located. The $outerRadius defines the radius of the circle on which the outer points will be located. The $spikes parameter defines the number of points in the star. The $degree parameter specifies the degree of the curve. Finally, the $periodic parameter is a Boolean value that determines whether the curve is periodic or not.

```
global proc curveStar(
    float $innerRadius,
    float $outerRadius,
    int $spikes,
    int $degree,
    int $periodic
)
{
```

The star shape is created by alternately creating control vertices on the inner and outer circles.

```
vector $cvs[];
```

The number of control vertices in the star is simply twice the number of spikes. Note that the last control vertex isn't coincident with the first.

```
int $nSpikeCVs = 2 * $spikes;
```

The angular step between each point, whether it be an inner or outer point, is the same.

```
float $angleIncr = deg_to_rad(180) / $spikes;
```

The position for each control vertex is now calculated.

```
float $angle;
float $x, $y, $z, $r;
int $ci;
for( $ci=0, $angle=0.0; $ci < $nSpikeCVs; $ci++, $angle+=$angleIncr )
{
```

All odd points are on the outer circle and all even points on the inner circle. The only difference between the two circles is their radius, and thus odd points have their radius set to the outer radius and even points have their radius set to the inner radius.

```
if( $ci % 2 )
        $r = $outerRadius;
else
        $r = $innerRadius;
```

The 2D polar coordinate ($r, $angle) is converted into a 3D Cartesian coordinate ($x, 0, $z).

```
$x = $r * cos($angle);
$y = 0.0;
$z = $r * sin($angle);
```

The control vertex is added to the array.

```
$cvs[$ci] = << $x, $y, $z >>;
    }
```

For a curve to be periodic, the last degree number of control vertices must be the same. This ensures that the curve has smooth continuity at its end and that the curvature matches the start of the curve. By ensuring that the continuity and curvature at the start and end of the curve are the same, no sharp bend will occur in the curve at the junction between the start and end. The curve will appear continuous.

The continuity is achieved by simply duplicating the first degree number of control vertices and then appending them to the array. The result is that the last degree control vertices are coincident with the first degree control vertices.

```
for( $ci=0; $ci < $degree; $ci++ )
        $cvs[size($cvs)] = $cvs[$ci];
```

The knot vector for a periodic curve is different from that used for open or closed curves. Whereas the previous example used multi-knot values to ensure that the curve passes exactly from the first to last control vertices, periodic curves take advantage of the fact that knot values use the modulus to determine the control vertex index. The number of spans is calculated using the following formula

$$\textbf{spans = cvs degree}$$

```
...
int $nSpans = size($cvs) - $degree;
```

The number of knot values is the same as before. Whether a curve is open, closed, or periodic, the number of knot values still needs to be as follows.

$$\textbf{\# knots = spans + 2 * degree 1}$$

```
int $nKnots = $nSpans + 2 * $degree - 1;
```

For a periodic curve, the knot vector will resemble the following.

```
 -2 -1 0 1 2 3 4 5 6 7 8 9 10 11 12
```

This is the knot vector for a curve with 10 control vertices and a degree of 3. The first and last two knot vectors are beyond the end of the control vertex indices. Using the modulus to index the control vertex ensures that indices wrap around. The result is that spans at the start and end of the curve share control vertices from the end and start of the curve, respectively.

```
int $ki;
for( $i=-($degree-1), $ki=0; $ki < $nKnots; $i++, $ki++ )
    $knots[$ki] = float($i);
```

The curve command is now generated. The main difference with the last example is that the -periodic flag is used.

```
string $cmd = "curve -degree " + $degree +
        " -periodic " + $periodic;
vector $p;
```

```
    for( $i=0; $i < size($cvs); $i++ )
    {
        $p = $cvs[$i];
        $cmd += " -p " + ($p.x) + " " + ($p.y) + " " + ($p.z);
    }
    for( $i=0; $i < size($knots); $i++ )
        $cmd += " -k " + $knots[$i];

    evalEcho( $cmd );
}
```

C++ API

The **CurveStar** plug-in demonstrates the following.

- Creating a periodic NURBS curve based on a given inner radius, outer radius, number of spikes, degree, and form

1. Open the **CurveStar** workspace.

2. Compile it and load the resulting `curveStar` plug-in file in Maya.

3. If the **curveStar.mel** file was sourced during the current session, restart Maya. Otherwise, select **File | New Scene**.

4. To create the curve, execute the following.

   ```
   curveStar;
   ```

   A curve in the shape of a five-point star is created.

5. The number of points in the star can be increased.

   ```
   curveStar -spikes 10;
   ```

   A ten-point star is generated.

6. The inner radius can be reduced.

   ```
   curveStar -spikes 10 -innerRadius 0.25;
   ```

   The outer points don't change but the inner points are now closer to the center.

SOURCE CODE

Plug-in: CurveStar
File: CurveStarCmd.cpp

```cpp
class CurveStarCmd : public MPxCommand
{
public:
   virtual MStatus doIt ( const MArgList& );
   virtual MStatus redoIt();
   virtual MStatus undoIt();
   virtual bool isUndoable() const { return true; }

   static void *creator() { return new CurveStarCmd; }
   static MSyntax newSyntax();

private:
   MDistance outerRadius;
   MDistance innerRadius;
   int spikes;
   int degree;
   int form;

   MObject curveTransform;
};

const char *outerRadiusFlag = "-or",
   *outerRadiusLongFlag = "-outerRadius";
const char *innerRadiusFlag = "-ir",
   *innerRadiusLongFlag = "-innerRadius";
const char *spikesFlag = "-s", *spikesLongFlag = "-spikes";
const char *degreeFlag = "-d", *degreeLongFlag = "-degree";
const char *formFlag = "-f", *formLongFlag = "-form";

MSyntax CurveStarCmd::newSyntax()
{
 MSyntax syntax;

 syntax.addFlag( outerRadiusFlag, outerRadiusLongFlag,
     MSyntax::kDistance );
 syntax.addFlag( innerRadiusFlag, innerRadiusLongFlag,
     MSyntax::kDistance );
```

```
   syntax.addFlag( spikesFlag, spikesLongFlag, MSyntax::kLong );
   syntax.addFlag( degreeFlag, degreeLongFlag, MSyntax::kLong );
   syntax.addFlag( formFlag, formLongFlag, MSyntax::kLong );

      syntax.enableQuery( false );
      syntax.enableEdit( false );

      return syntax;
}

MStatus CurveStarCmd::doIt ( const MArgList &args )
{
      MStatus stat;

      outerRadius.setValue( 1.0 );
      innerRadius.setValue( 0.5 );
      spikes = 5;
      degree = 1;
      form = 2;

      MArgDatabase argData( syntax(), args, &stat );
      if( !stat )
            return stat;

      if( argData.isFlagSet( outerRadiusFlag ) )
            argData.getFlagArgument( outerRadiusFlag, 0, outerRadius );

      if( argData.isFlagSet( innerRadiusFlag ) )
            argData.getFlagArgument( innerRadiusFlag, 0, innerRadius );

      if( argData.isFlagSet( spikesFlag ) )
            argData.getFlagArgument( spikesFlag, 0, spikes );

      if( argData.isFlagSet( degreeFlag ) )
            argData.getFlagArgument( degreeFlag, 0, degree );

      if( argData.isFlagSet( formFlag ) )
            argData.getFlagArgument( formFlag, 0, form );

      return redoIt();
}

MStatus CurveStarCmd::redoIt()
{
      MPointArray cvs;
      int nSpikeCVs = 2 * spikes;
```

```
double angleIncr = M_PI / spikes;
MPoint p;
double angle;
double r;
int i;
for( i=0, angle=0.0;
        i < nSpikeCVs;
        i++, angle+=angleIncr )
{
        r = (i & 1) ? outerRadius.value() : innerRadius.value();

        p.x = r * cos(angle);
        p.y = 0.0;
        p.z = r * sin(angle);

        cvs.append( p );
}

for( i=0; i < degree; i++ )
        cvs.append( cvs[i] );

MDoubleArray knots;
int nSpans = cvs.length() - degree;
int nKnots = nSpans + 2 * degree - 1;
int ki;
for( i=-(degree-1), ki=0; ki < nKnots; i++, ki++ )
        knots.append( double(i) );

MFnNurbsCurve::Form f = (form == 0) ? MFnNurbsCurve::kOpen :
(( form == 1) ? MFnNurbsCurve::kClosed : MFnNurbsCurve::kPeriodic );

MStatus stat;
MFnNurbsCurve curveFn;
curveTransform = curveFn.create( cvs, knots, degree, f, false, false,
                                 MObject::kNullObj, &stat );

    return stat;
}

MStatus CurveStarCmd::undoIt()
{
    MFnDagNode dagFn( curveTransform );
    MObject child;
    child = dagFn.child(0);
```

```
      MGlobal::deleteNode( child );
      MGlobal::deleteNode( curveTransform );

      return MS::kSuccess;
}

MStatus initializePlugin( MObject obj )
{
      MFnPlugin plugin( obj, "David Gould", "1.0" );

      MStatus stat;
      stat = plugin.registerCommand( "curveStar",
                                        CurveStarCmd::creator,
                    CurveStarCmd::newSyntax );
      if ( !stat )
            stat.perror( "registerCommand failed");
      return stat;
}

MStatus uninitializePlugin( MObject obj )
{
      MFnPlugin plugin( obj );

      MStatus     stat;
      stat = plugin.deregisterCommand( "curveStar" );
      if ( !stat )
            stat.perror( "deregisterCommand failed" );

      return stat;
}
```

SOURCE CODE EXPLANATION

Plug-in: `CurveStar`
File: `CurveStarCmd.cpp`

The previous MEL section described the core functionality used to generate the star NURBS curves. The major difference is that this custom command supports the three different curve forms (0 = open, 1 = closed, and 2 = periodic) by using the `-form` flag.

```
      ...
      MFnNurbsCurve::Form f = (form == 0) ? MFnNurbsCurve::kOpen :
      (( form == 1) ? MFnNurbsCurve::kClosed : MFnNurbsCurve::kPeriodic );
```

The form is passed to the `create` function. Comparing the same curves but with different forms provides a clearer means of understanding the effect of different forms on the final appearance of the curve and how coincident control vertices are treated when moved.

```
MStatus stat;
MFnNurbsCurve curveFn;
curveTransform = curveFn.create( cvs, knots, degree, f, false, false,
                         MObject::kNullObj, &stat );

...
```

SURFACE CURVES

A curve can be created on a NURBS surface as easily as it can in world space. The key difference is that control vertex locations are specified in parametric coordinates (u, v) rather than the usual Cartesian coordinates (x, y, z). The parametric coordinates define locations on the NURBS surface.

1. Open the **PlaneNurbs.ma** scene.

2. To create a surface curve, execute the following (type it on a single line).

```
curveOnSurface -degree 3 -uv 0.25 0.25 -uv 0.75 0.25 -uv 0.25 0.75 -uv
0.75 0.75 nurbsPlane1;
```

A curve is created on the NURBS surface.

3. Execute the following.

```
ls -selection;
```

The result is the DAG path to the newly created surface curve.

```
// Result: nurbsPlaneShape1->curve1 //
```

As expected, the **curve1** object is in the underworld of the **nurbsPlaneShape1** object.

CURVE FITTING

The process of curve fitting involves creating a smooth curve that travels through a given sequence of points. Figure 9.26 shows a curve fitted to another.

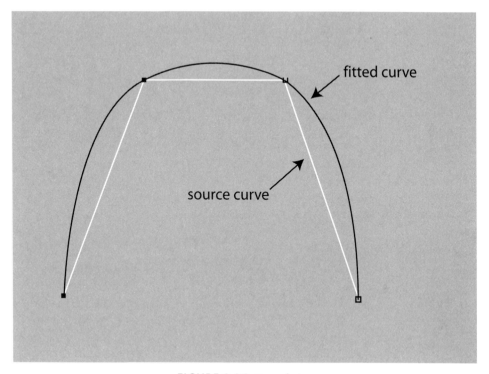

FIGURE 9.26 Curve fitting.

The fitBspline command is used to create a NURBS curve that goes through the set of control vertices of another NURBS curve.

1. Select **File | New Scene**.

2. To create a basic curve, execute the following (type it on a single line).

   ```
   curve -degree 1 -p 0.0 0.0 0.0 -p 0.25 0.0 0.75 -p 0.75 0.0 0.75 -p 1.0
   0.0 0.0;
   ```

   A curve with four straight line segments is produced.

3. A fitted curve is created from this curve by executing the following.

   ```
   fitBspline -constructionHistory true -tolerance 0.01;
   ```

A smooth curve is generated that goes through the control vertices of the selected curve. Because construction history was turned on, the resulting curve will automatically update if the source curve changes.

4. Execute the following to move one of the control vertices of the source curve.

```
select -r curve1.cv[2];
move -r 0.1 0.0 0.1;
```

The fitted curve is automatically regenerated. With construction history turned on, a **fitSpline** node is created. The source curve was fed into this node and it dynamically generated a newly fitted curve that is fed into the final curve.

9.2.4 EDITING CURVES

Once a curve is created, there are a variety of different commands to edit it. Many of the curve-editing commands share these common flags.

```
-replaceOriginal <boolean>
```

The original curve is edited in place and no new curve is created.

```
-constructionHistory <boolean>
```

A new curve is created with a construction history that has the original curve fed into the curve-editing node. This way, if the original curve changes the new curve will be automatically updated.

It is important to note that these flags are not necessarily available in all situations. In addition, the default settings for these flags are not the same for all commands. This means that some commands will, by default, create a new curve, whereas others will replace the original curve.

GENERAL

1. Open the **TwoCurves.ma** scene.

2. Select the **curve1** object.

3. Select **Display | NURBS Components | Edit Points** from the main menu.

    The four edit points in the curve are displayed.

4. To insert a new edit point, execute the following.

```
insertKnotCurve -parameter 1.5;
```

A new edit point is inserted at the given parametric position.

5. Select **Edit | Undo**.

6. To create a sharp edit point, execute the following.

```
insertKnotCurve -parameter 1.5 -add false -numberOfKnots 3;
```

A new curve is generated with an inserted edit point. Because this edit point has a knot multiplicity of 3, the curve doesn't smoothly travel through it. Instead, there is a sharp join.

7. To move the newly inserted edit point, execute the following.

```
select -r curvelinsertedKnotCurve1.ep[2];
move -r 0 0 3;
```

The edit point is moved, revealing its sharp continuity. The `hardenPointCurve` command can also be used to change smooth control vertices into sharp control vertices. This command relies on the control vertices before and after the one being sharpened having a certain multiplicity. As such, it doesn't work in all cases.

8. To reposition a point so that it lies on the smoothed curve, execute the following.

```
smoothCurve curvelinsertedKnotCurve1.cv[4];
```

The control vertex has been placed back on the smooth curve. It is important to note that the control vertex is still sharp (i.e., it has knot multiplicity), and thus moving it will once again reveal its sharpness. To remove the sharpness from a control vertex, its knot multiplicity must be removed.

9. To smooth all control vertices in the curve, execute the following.

```
rebuildCurve -rebuildType 3 -keepControlPoints true;
```

All knot multiplicity is removed from the interior curve control vertices. The knot multiplicity at the start and end control vertices isn't changed.

10. The control vertex is now moved.

```
select -r curve1insertedKnotCurve1.cv[4];
move -r 0 0 3;
```

Because the knot multiplicity was removed, the curve is now smoother when the control vertex is moved.

REBUILDING CURVES

1. Open the **TwoCurves.ma** scene.

2. Select the **curve1** object.

3. To change the degree of the curve, execute the following.

```
rebuildCurve -degree 1;
```

The curve now has a degree of 1 and is thus generated as straight line segments.

4. Select **Edit | Undo**.

5. To change the parameterization of the curve, execute the following.

```
rebuildCurve -keepRange 0;
```

Where the curve had a parametric range from 0 to 3, it now has a normalized range of 0 to 1.

6. To reduce the number of spans in the curve, execute the following.

```
rebuildCurve -spans 3;
```

The curve's spans are reduced from four to three. The surviving control vertices are moved to ensure that the resulting curve is as close to the original as possible.

REVERSING CURVES

1. Open the **TwoCurves.ma** scene.

2. Select the **curve1** object.

3. Press **F9** or right click on the object and then select **Control Vertex** from the pop-up menu.

    The second control vertex in a curve is displayed as a **U** rather than a dot. The top left control vertex is the first, and the second is the one displayed with the **U**. As such, the curve's direction is from the top left-most control vertex to the bottom right-most control vertex.

4. Press **F8** to select the curve.

5. To reverse the direction of the curve, execute the following.

    ```
    reverseCurve -replaceOriginal true;
    ```

    Because the `-replaceOriginal` flag was used, the selected curve is reversed rather than creating a new curve.

6. Select the **curve1** object.

7. Press **F9** to display the control vertices.

    The second control vertex is now near the bottom right, indicating that the direction of the curve now goes from the bottom right to the top left.

8. Press **F8** to select the curve.

9. To create a new curve that is reversed, execute the following.

    ```
    reverseCurve -replaceOriginal false;
    ```

    A new reversed curve named **curve1reversedCurve1** is created. This curve is a complete copy of the first but with its direction reversed. Because this is a distinct copy of the original curve, changes to the copy will not effect the original.

10. Select the **curve1** object.

11. To create a reversed curve that is dependent on the original, execute the following.

    ```
    reverseCurve -replaceOriginal false -constructionHistory on;
    ```

    A new reversed curve named **curve1reversedCurve2** is created. Because it has construction history turned on, it depends on the original curve.

12. Move the duplicate curve away from the original.

```
select -r curve1reversedCurve2;
move -r 0 0 4;
```

13. Move one of the control vertices in the original curve to see how it affects the duplicated curve.

```
select -r curve1.cv[2];
move -r -0.25 -0.75 0.75;
```

The reversed curve is automatically updated.

CLOSING CURVES

Given an open curve, it can be closed using the `closeCurve` command. The resulting curve is a periodic curve.

1. Open the **TwoCurves.ma** scene.

2. Select the **curve1** object.

3. To close the curve, execute the following.

```
closeCurve -constructionHistory true;
```

A closed curve named **curve1closedCurve1** is created.

DISSECTING CURVES

A curve can be cut into separate pieces using the `detachCurve` command. This command allows a curve to be split at parametric positions and at edit points. Pieces can be arbitrarily kept and or discarded.

1. Open the **TwoCurves.ma** scene.

2. Select the **curve1** object.

3. To split the curve into two pieces, execute the following.

```
detachCurve -parameter 1.5;
```

The curve is split around the center into two curves: **curve1detachedCurve1** and **curve1detachedCurve2**.

4. Select **Edit | Undo** to remove the newly created curves.

5. To split the curve at the second edit point, execute the following.

```
detachCurve curve1.ep[1];
```

6. Select **Edit | Undo** to remove the newly created curves.

7. To split the curve but only keep the first piece, execute the following.

```
detachCurve -parameter 1.5 -keep true -keep false;
```

The curve is split as before, but the second curve object, **curve1detachedCurve2**, is empty.

8. Select **Edit | Undo** to remove the newly created curves.

9. The curve can be split into three pieces by executing the following.

```
detachCurve -parameter 1.0 -parameter 2.0 -replaceOriginal on;
```

The curve is split into three curves. The three curves cover the parametric ranges [0.0, 1.0), [1.0, 2.0), and [2.0, 3.0], respectively. Because -replaceOriginal is on, the original curve is set to the first piece. The remaining two pieces are placed into the newly created curves, **curve1detachedCurve2** and **curve1detachedCurve3**.

ATTACHING CURVES

Curves can be joined to generate a single curve.

1. Open the **TwoCurves.ma** scene.

2. To join the two curves, execute the following.

```
select -r curve1 curve2;
attachCurve;
```

The two curves are joined. The first curve, **curve1**, is replaced with the resulting curve. By default, the attachCurve command simply connects the two curves. This explains the hard seam at the point where the two curves join.

3. Select **Edit | Undo** to undo the attachment.

4. To create a new curve that is blended, execute the following.

```
attachCurve -replaceOriginal false -method 1;
```

A new curve is created because the `-replaceOriginal` flag is set to `false`. The attachment method is set to 1, which means that the curves will be blended. By default, the resulting curve will be an equal mix of the two source curves.

5. To have the second curve favored more when blending, execute the following.

```
select -r curve1 curve2;
attachCurve -replaceOriginal false -method 1 -blendBias 0;
```

A new curve is created, but the blending is biased toward the second curve. This is because the `-blendBias` setting defines how the two curves are mixed. With a setting of 0, the second curve has greater preference over the first. Alternatively, with a setting of 1 the first curve is given greater preference over the second.

9.3 NURBS SURFACES

A NURBS surface is the logical extension of a NURBS curve to two parametric dimensions. Figure 9.27 shows both a NURBS curve and surface with their parametric dimensions indicated. Where a NURBS curve has only one parametric dimension (u), a NURBS surface has two, u and v. Given a parametric position u, a point in the curve can be calculated. Given both u and v parametric coordinates, a point on the surface can be calculated. A parametric point (u, v) on the surface is called a surface point.

The parametric extents of the curve and surface in Figure 9.27 are normalized; that is, they range from 0 to 1. Curves and surfaces can have other parametric extents.

9.3.1 DISPLAYING SURFACES

GENERAL

1. Open the **SphereNurbs.ma** scene.

2. Select the **sphere** object.

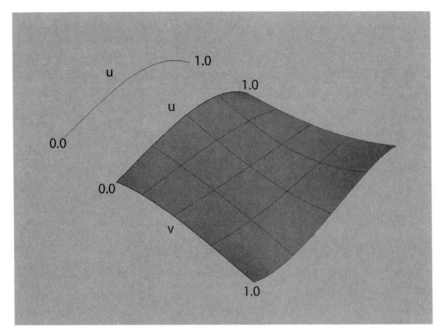

FIGURE 9.27 NURBS surface parameterization.

3. Execute the following to hide the NURBS surface.

```
toggle -geometry;
```

The object is still visible, but the NURBS surface itself is now hidden.

4. To restore the visibility of the geometry, execute the following.

```
toggle -geometry;
```

The NURBS surface is once again displayed.

5. Execute the following to display the control vertices.

```
toggle -controlVertex;
```

All control vertices are now displayed.

6. The edit points on the surface can be displayed.

```
toggle -editPoint;
```

7. The hull of the surface can be displayed.

```
toggle -hull;
```

8. The surface faces are displayed by executing the following.

```
toggle -surfaceFace;
```

9. To display the surface normals, execute the following.

```
toggle -normal;
```

The additional flags for the normal display (`-point`, `-facet`, and `-pointFacet`) are not valid for NURBS surfaces and thus can't be used.

10. The length of the normals displayed can be changed.

```
setAttr sphereShape.normalsDisplayScale 0.25;
```

The normals are now displayed at a quarter of their original size.

SURFACE DETAIL

NURBS surfaces can be quite complex. A scene that contains many complex surfaces will take longer to display and interact with. Maya provides a variety of means to simplify the display of NURBS surfaces.

1. Open the **SphereNurbs.ma** scene.

2. Select the **sphere** object.

3. The surface can be displayed as the hull by executing the following.

```
displaySmoothness -hull;
```

The hull of the surface is now displayed as a shaded object. A NURBS surface has a **simplifyMode** attribute that can be in one of two settings: full or hull.

4. When the surface is displayed in hull mode, the **simplifyU** and **simplifyV** attributes are taken into account. Execute the following to simply the display of the U divisions.

```
displaySmoothness -simplifyU 2;
```

The hull is now simplified even further. The **simplifyU** and **simplifyV** settings define the number of spans to skip in the u and v directions when the surface is displayed in hull mode. By default, these settings are set to 1.

5. To switch to the full mode, execute the following.

```
displaySmoothness -full;
```

The actual NURBS surface is displayed.

6. Press the 4 key or select **Shading | Wireframe** from the viewport menu.

The NURBS surface is displayed in wireframe.

7. When the object is displayed in wireframe, the number of divisions in the u and v directions are controlled by -divisionsU and -divisionsV flags.

```
displaySmoothness -divisionsU 2;
```

Because the default setting for divisionsU is 1, there are now double the number of u divisions. The divisionsU setting defines the number of isoparms displayed per span along the u direction. The divisionsV setting works equivalently but along the v direction.

8. To change the number of points per isoparm span used to display the surface while in wireframe, execute the following.

```
displaySmoothness -pointsWire 2;
```

The surface is now drawn with only two points per span. The default setting is 4. It can range from 1 to 128, though a high number would only be needed for extremely complex surfaces.

9. Press the **5** key or select **Shading | Smooth Shade All** from the viewport menu.

   The NURBS surface is once again displayed as a solid shaded surface.

10. To reduce the number of points to display the surface, execute the following.

```
displaySmoothness -pointsShaded 2;
```

   The surface is displayed in a more simplified way.

11. The settings used to display the surface in the viewports are quite different from those used to render the final surface. To be able to visualize the final surface that will be rendered, execute the following.

```
displaySmoothness -renderTessellation true;
```

   The surface is displayed as a tessellated surface. This shows what the final tessellated mesh of the NURBS surface will look like.

It is important to note that the displaySmoothness command can be used with the -all flag to have the display setting applied to all NURBS surfaces and curves, and not just the currently selected ones.

9.3.2 QUERYING SURFACES

GENERAL

MEL

1. Open the **SphereNurbs.ma** scene.

2. Select the **sphere** object.

3. The degrees of the u and v dimensions are retrieved as follows.

```
getAttr sphere.degreeU;
// Result: 3 //
getAttr sphere.degreeV;
// Result: 3 //
```

Although the u and v degrees of this surface match, it is possible for a surface to have different degrees in the u and v dimensions.

4. The number of spans in the surface is determined as follows.

```
getAttr sphere.spansU;
// Result: 4 //
getAttr sphere.spansV;
// Result: 8 //
```

5. To visualize how a four-sided NURBS patch can be deformed into a sphere, imagine taking a square sheet and rolling it into a cylinder. Drawing a circle around the cylinder draws a line of constant u direction (latitude), with v varying. The top and bottom edges of the cylinder are then pinched into single points, forming the top and bottom poles of the sphere. Drawing a line from top to bottom draws a line of constant v direction (longtitude), with u varying.

```
getAttr sphere.formU;
// Result: 0 //
```

The result is the form in the u direction (0 = open, 1 = closed, 2 = periodic). The form of the u direction, which is the latitude of the sphere, is therefore open.

```
getAttr sphere.formV;
// Result: 2 //
```

The form of the v direction, the longtitude of the sphere, is periodic. This is consistent with the sphere's surface being continuous in the v direction.

6. The parametric extents of the u and v parameters are now retrieved, starting with the u dimension.

```
getAttr sphere.minValueU;
// Result: 0 //
getAttr sphere.maxValueU;
// Result: 4 //
```

The surface's u parametric value varies from 0 to 4. The extent of the v dimension is retrieved similarly.

```
getAttr sphere.minValueV;
// Result: 0 //
getAttr sphere.maxValueV;
// Result: 8 //
```

The surface's v parametric value varies from 0 to 8.

7. Because the surface has rows and columns of control vertices, these are retrieved using two indices.

```
getAttr sphere.cv["*"]["*"];
// Result: 0 0 0 0 0 0 0 0 0 0 ... //
```

All control vertices are zero. The reason for this is that the NURBS surface has construction history. To retrieve the control vertices using the **cv** attribute, the NURBS surface can't have a construction history.

8. Select **Edit | Delete by Type | History** from the main menu.

The construction history of the object is removed.

9. The control vertices can now be retrieved directly.

```
getAttr sphere.cv["*"]["*"];
// Result: 0 -1 0 0 -1 0 0 -1 0 0 -1 0 0 -1 0 0 -1 0 0 -1 0 0 -1
0 0.199917 -1 -0.199917 0.282725 -1 0 0.199917 -1 0.199917 0 -1
0.282725 -0.199917 -1 0.199917 -0.282725 -1 0 -0.199917 -1 -0.199917
0 -1 -0.282725 0.61643 -0.783612 -0.61643 0.871764 -0.783612 0
0.61643 -0.783612 0.61643 0 ... //
```

It is important to note that these coordinates are in local space.

10. To retrieve just a single control vertex, use the following.

```
getAttr sphere.cv[0][0];
// Result: 0 -1 0 //
```

This retrieves the coordinates of the first control vertex (u index = 0, v index = 0).

11. To retrieve an entire row or column of control vertices, the following can be used.

```
getAttr sphere.cv["*"][0];
// Result: 0 -1 0 0.199917 -1 -0.199917 0.61643 -0.783612 -0.61643
0.867202 0 -0.867202 0.61643 0.783612 -0.61643 0.199917 1 -0.199917
0 1 0 //
```

The first row of control vertices is returned. Similarly, the third column of control vertices can be retrieved as follows.

```
getAttr sphere.cv[2]["*"];
// Result: 0.61643 -0.783612 -0.61643 0.871764 -0.783612 0 0.61643
-0.783612 0.61643 0 -0.783612 0.871764 -0.61643 -0.783612 0.61643
-0.871764 -0.783612 0 -0.61643 -0.783612 -0.61643 0 -0.783612
-0.871764 //
```

12. Open the **SphereNurbs.ma** scene.

13. Select the **sphere** object.

14. As stated before, if a NURBS surface has construction history its control vertices can't be retrieved by accessing the **cv** attribute. To determine if the object has construction history, execute the following.

```
listConnections -source true -destination false sphere.create;
// Result: makeNurbSphere1 //
```

The `listConnections` command returned the name of the **makeNurbsSphere1** node. This indicates that the **makeNurbsSphere1** node feeds into the surface's **create** attribute. As such, it has construction history.

15. When a surface has construction history or the world space coordinates of the control vertices are needed, use the following.

```
createNode surfaceInfo;
connectAttr -force sphereShape.worldSpace surfaceInfo1.inputSurface;
getAttr surfaceInfo1.controlPoints["*"];
// Result: 0 -1 0 0 -1 0 0 -1 0 0 -1 0 0 -1 0 0 -1 0 0 -1 0 0 ...//
```

A **surfaceInfo** node is created. The **worldSpace** attribute of the sphere surface shape is connected into the **surfaceInfo1** node's **inputSurface**. Finally, the

controlPoints attribute of the **surfaceInfo** node is retrieved. The **surfaceInfo** node will return the world space coordinates of the control vertices of the surface connected into its **inputSurface** attribute.

16. The knot vector of the u and v parameters can be determined as follows.

```
getAttr surfaceInfo1.knotsU;
// Result: 0 0 0 1 2 3 4 4 4 //
getAttr surfaceInfo1.knotsV;
// Result: -2 -1 0 1 2 3 4 5 6 7 8 9 10 //
```

The knot vectors are consistent with the u parameter being open and the v parameter being periodic.

17. If the NURBS surface is rational, the weights of the control vertices can be retrieved.

```
getAttr surfaceInfo1.weights;
// Warning: line 1: surfaceInfo1 (Surface Info Node): NURBS surface in
non-rational. All weights are 1. //
// Result: 1 1 1 1 1 1 1 1 1 1 1 1 1 1 1 1 1 1 1 1 1 1 1 1 1 1 1 1 1 1
1 1 1 1 1 1 1 1 1 1 1 1 1 1 1 1 1 1 1 1 1 1 1 1 1 1 1 1 1 1 1 1 1 1 1 1
1 1 1 1 1 1 1 1 1 1 //
```

Because the surface is nonrational, Maya issues a warning and returns an array of ones.

C++ API

The **SurfaceInfo1** plug-in demonstrates the following.

- Retrieving the selected NURBS surface(s)

- Accessing NURBS surface information (area, degrees, spans, forms, parametric ranges, control vertices, and knot vector)

- Printing out NURBS surface information

1. Open the **SurfaceInfo1** workspace.

2. Compile it and load the resulting surfaceInfo1 plug-in file in Maya.

3. Open the **SphereNurbs.ma** scene.

4. Select the **sphere** object.

5. Execute the following.

```
surfaceInfo1;
```

A variety of information about the curve is output.

```
// |sphere
Area: 12.541428
Degrees: 3, 3
Spans: 4, 8|
Forms: Open, Periodic
Parametric Ranges: [0, 4], [0, 8]
CVs: 7, 11
  (0, -1, 0) (0, -1, 0) (0, -1, 0) (0, -1, 0) (0, -1, 0) (0, -1, 0) (0, -1,
0) (0, -1, 0) (0, -1, 0) (0, -1, 0) (0, -1, 0) (0.199917, -1, -0.199917)
(0.282725, -1, 0) (0.199917, -1, 0.199917) ...
Knots: 9, 13
  0 0 0 1 2 3 4 4 4
  -2 -1 0 1 2 3 4 5 6 7 8 9 10
```

SOURCE CODE

Plug-in: SurfaceInfo1
File: SurfaceInfo1Cmd.cpp

```cpp
DeclareSimpleCommand( surfaceInfo1, "David Gould", "1.0" );

MStatus surfaceInfo1::doIt( const MArgList& args )
{
    MStatus stat = MS::kSuccess;

    MSelectionList selection;
    MGlobal::getActiveSelectionList( selection );

    MDagPath dagPath;
    MObject component;

    const char *formTxt[] = { "Invalid", "Open", "Closed",
                              "Periodic", "Last" };
```

```
double startU, endU, startV, endV;
unsigned int i, j, nCVsU, nCVsV, nKnotsU, nKnotsV;
MPoint pt;
MDoubleArray knots[2];

MString txt;
MItSelectionList iter( selection );
for ( ; !iter.isDone(); iter.next() )
{
      iter.getDagPath( dagPath, component );
      MFnNurbsSurface surfaceFn( dagPath, &stat );
      if( stat )
      {
            txt += dagPath.fullPathName() + "\n";

            txt += MString("Area: ") + surfaceFn.area() + "\n";
            txt += MString("Degrees: ") + surfaceFn.degreeU() + ", " +
                  surfaceFn.degreeV() + "\n";
            txt += MString("Spans: ") + surfaceFn.numSpansInU() + ", "
                  + surfaceFn.numSpansInV() + "\n";
            txt += MString("Forms: ") + formTxt[ surfaceFn.formInU() ]
                  + ", " + formTxt[ surfaceFn.formInV() ] + "\n";

            surfaceFn.getKnotDomain( startU, endU, startV, endV );
            txt += MString("Parametric Ranges: [") + startU + ", " +
                  endU + "], [" + startV + ", " + endV + "]\n";

            nCVsU = surfaceFn.numCVsInU();
            nCVsV = surfaceFn.numCVsInV();
            txt += MString("CVs: ") + nCVsU + ", " + nCVsV + "\n";

            for( i=0; i < nCVsU; i++ )
            {
                  for( j=0; j < nCVsV; j++ )
                  {
                        surfaceFn.getCV( i, j, pt, MSpace::kWorld );
                        txt += MString(" (") + pt.x + ", " + pt.y +
                              ", " + pt.z + ")";
                  }
            }
            txt += "\n";
```

```
nKnotsU = surfaceFn.numKnotsInU();
nKnotsV = surfaceFn.numKnotsInV();
txt += MString("Knots: ") + nKnotsU + ", " +
               nKnotsV + "\n";

surfaceFn.getKnotsInU( knots[0] );
surfaceFn.getKnotsInV( knots[1] );

for( i=0; i < 2; i++ )
{
        for( j=0; j < knots[i].length(); j++ )
        {
                txt += MString(" ") + knots[i][j];
        }
        txt += "\n";
    }
  }
}

MGlobal::displayInfo( txt );

return MS::kSuccess;
}
```

SOURCE CODE EXPLANATION

Plug-in: `SurfaceInfo1`
File: `SurfaceInfo1Cmd.cpp`

The command works in the same way as previous simple commands. The
MFnNurbsSurface function set is bound to the currently selected object.

```
MFnNurbsSurface surfaceFn( dagPath, &stat );
if( stat )
{
```

The full DAG path to the object is included in the output text.

```
txt += dagPath.fullPathName() + "\n";
```

The area of the surface is calculated using the `area` function.

```
txt += MString("Area: ") + surfaceFn.area() + "\n";
```

The degree of the u and v directions is retrieved.

```
txt += MString("Degrees: ") + surfaceFn.degreeU() + ", " +
            surfaceFn.degreeV() + "\n";
```

The number of spans in the u and v directions is calculated.

```
txt += MString("Spans: ") + surfaceFn.numSpansInU() + ", "
            + surfaceFn.numSpansInV() + "\n";
```

The form of the u and v parameters is determined.

```
txt += MString("Forms: ") + formTxt[ surfaceFn.formInU() ]
            + ", " + formTxt[ surfaceFn.formInV() ] + "\n";
```

The parametric range of the u and v parameters is calculated using the `getKnotDomain` function.

```
surfaceFn.getKnotDomain( startU, endU, startV, endV );
txt += MString("Parametric Ranges: [") + startU + ", " +
            endU + "], [" + startV + ", " + endV + "]\n";
```

The number of control vertices in the u and v directions is now determined. This corresponds to the number of rows and columns of control vertices.

```
nCVsU = surfaceFn.numCVsInU();
nCVsV = surfaceFn.numCVsInV();
txt += MString("CVs: ") + nCVsU + ", " + nCVsV + "\n";
```

Each control vertex is iterated over. The control vertices are processed in row order.

```
for( i=0; i < nCVsU; i++ )
{
        for( j=0; j < nCVsV; j++ )
        {
```

The world space coordinates of the control vertex are retrieved using the row (*i*) and column (*j*) indices.

```
surfaceFn.getCV( i, j, pt, MSpace::kWorld );
txt += MString(" (") + pt.x + ", " + pt.y +
           ", " + pt.z + ")";
        }
    }
    txt += "\n";
```

The knot vectors in either direction can be of different lengths, and thus the number of u knots is retrieved separately from the number of v knots.

```
nKnotsU = surfaceFn.numKnotsInU();
nKnotsV = surfaceFn.numKnotsInV();
txt += MString("Knots: ") + nKnotsU + ", " +
               nKnotsV + "\n";
```

The actual knot values are retrieved for the u and v directions. They are placed into an array of two **MDoubleArray**s.

```
surfaceFn.getKnotsInU( knots[0] );
surfaceFn.getKnotsInV( knots[1] );
```

Each knot value is iterated over, starting with the values in the u knot and finishing with the values in the v knot.

```
for( i=0; i < 2; i++ )
{
    for( j=0; j < knots[i].length(); j++ )
    {
        txt += MString(" ") + knots[i][j];
    }
    txt += "\n";
}
```

As always, the final output text is displayed in the **Script Editor**.

```
MGlobal::displayInfo( txt );

return MS::kSuccess;
}
```

SAMPLING SURFACES

Given a parametric location (u, v) on the surface, the position, normal, u tangent, and v tangent can be calculated. Figure 9.28 shows the result of sampling the surface at parametric location (u = 0.5, v = 0.5).

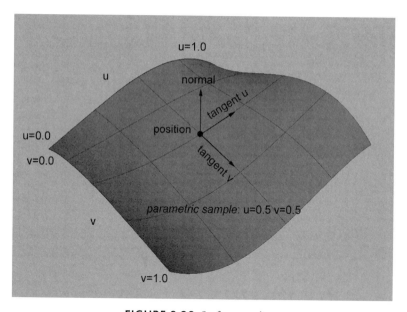

FIGURE 9.28 Surface sampling.

The tangent u and tangent v are vectors that correspond to the surface's partial derivatives dP/du and dP/dv. A particular derivative is where one of the parameters is held fixed, whereas the other is free to change. In the case of dP/du, the v parameter is fixed, whereas the u parameter is allowed to move from u to u + du. The result is a vector from the position at u, v to the position at u + du, v. The same methodology applies to the calculation of dP/dv.

The normal is the vector perpendicular to the surface. This can be calculated by performing the cross product of the two tangents.

normal = tangentU ^ tangentV
= dP/du ^ dP/dv

The normal is therefore a vector that is perpendicular to the plane formed by the u and v tangents. It has to be normalized to ensure that it is a unit vector.

Measure Tools

The Parameter tool can be used to display the u and v coordinate of a NURBS surface point.

1. Open the **PlaneNurbs.ma** scene.

2. Select **Create | Measure Tools | Parameter Tool.**

3. Click on the NURBS surface.

    A **paramDimension** node is created. It displays its (u, v) position.

4. Press the **w** key or select **Modify | Transformation Tools | Move Tool.**

5. Move the parametric dimension object across the NURBS surface.

    The u and v coordinates are updated.

MEL

1. Open the **PlaneNurbs.ma** scene.

2. Execute the following to sample the surface at several locations.

```
float $startU = `getAttr nurbsPlane1.minValueU`;
float $endU = `getAttr nurbsPlane1.maxValueU`;
float $startV = `getAttr nurbsPlane1.minValueV`;
float $endV = `getAttr nurbsPlane1.maxValueV`;
int $nSegs = 3;
float $uIncr = ($endU - $startU) / $nSegs;
float $vIncr = ($endV - $startV) / $nSegs;
float $u, $v;
int $segU, $segV;
float $pt[], $norm[], $tangU[], $tangV[];
```

```
for( $segU=0, $u=$startU; $segU < ($nSegs+1); $segU++, $u+=$uIncr )
{
 for( $segV=0, $v=$startV; $segV < ($nSegs+1); $segV++, $v+=$vIncr )
 {
 $pt = `pointOnSurface -u $u -v $v -position nurbsPlane1`;
 $norm = `pointOnSurface -u $u -v $v -normalizedNormal nurbsPlane1`;
 $tangU = `pointOnSurface -u $u -v $v -normalizedTangentU nurbsPlane1`;
 $tangV = `pointOnSurface -u $u -v $v -normalizedTangentV nurbsPlane1`;
 print ("Sample: (" + $u + ", " + $v + ")\n");
 print (" Position: (" + $pt[0] + ", " + $pt[1] + ", "+
     $pt[2] + ")" + "\n");
 print (" Normal: (" + $norm[0] + ", " + $norm[1] + ", " +
     $norm[2] + ")" + "\n");
 print (" Tangent U: (" + $tangU[0] + ", " + $tangU[1] + ", " +
     $tangU[2] + ")" + "\n");
 print (" Tangent V: (" + $tangV[0] + ", " + $tangV[1] + ", " +
     $tangV[2] + ")" + "\n");
 }
}
```

The sampled data is printed out.

```
Sample: (0, 0)
 Position: (-0.5, 0.2063039629, 0.5)
 Normal: (0.4657155149, 0.7524746629, -0.4657155149)
 Tangent U: (0.850316795, -0.5262711737, 0)
 Tangent V: (0, -0.5262711737, -0.850316795)
Sample: (0, 0.3333333333)
 Position: (-0.5060202878, 0.07980263474, 0.1629603319)
 Normal: (-0.01476708366, 0.9802314539, -0.1973023823)
 Tangent U: (0.9998862209, 0.01386910053, -0.005932391062)
 Tangent V: (-0.01433546967, -0.1975111708, -0.9801958129)
 ...
```

The parametric extents of the u and v dimensions are first retrieved.

```
float $startU = `getAttr nurbsPlane1.minValueU`;
float $endU = `getAttr nurbsPlane1.maxValueU`;
float $startV = `getAttr nurbsPlane1.minValueV`;
float $endV = `getAttr nurbsPlane1.maxValueV`;
```

The number of segments per u and v parameters is set.

```
int $nSegs = 3;
```

The step in u and v values per sample is calculated.

```
float $uIncr = ($endU - $startU) / $nSegs;
float $vIncr = ($endV - $startV) / $nSegs;
```

The surface is iterated over in row order (u parameter) first.

```
...
for( $segU=0, $u=$startU; $segU < ($nSegs+1); $segU++, $u+=$uIncr )
{
for( $segV=0, $v=$startV; $segV < ($nSegs+1); $segV++, $v+=$vIncr )
{
```

The surface is sampled at parametric location $u, $v using the pointOnSurface command. The position is sampled by using the -position flag.

```
$pt = `pointOnSurface -u $u -v $v -position nurbsPlane1`;
```

The unit normal is retrieved using the -normalizedNormal flag.

```
$norm = `pointOnSurface -u $u -v $v -normalizedNormal nurbsPlane1`;
```

The normalized u tangent is retrieved using the -normalizedTangentU flag.

```
$tangU = `pointOnSurface -u $u -v $v -normalizedTangentU nurbsPlane1`;
```

The normalized v tangent is retrieved using the -normalizedTangentV flag.

```
$tangV = `pointOnSurface -u $u -v $v -normalizedTangentV nurbsPlane1`;
```

The sampled data is then printed out.

```
print ("Sample: (" + $u + ", " + $v + ")\n");
...
```

The `pointOnSurface` command can also create a **pointOnSurface** node. Once this node is created, the surface can be sampled by requesting values directly from the node.

1. Open the **PlaneNurbs.ma** scene.

2. Execute the following to create the **pointOnSurface** node.

```
string $infoNode = `pointOnSurface -constructionHistory on nurbsPlane1`;
```

The node is created.

```
// Result: pointOnSurfaceInfo1 //
```

3. The parametric sample is specified.

```
setAttr ($infoNode + ".u") 0.5;
setAttr ($infoNode + ".v") 0.5;
```

It is also possible to set this when the `pointOnSurface` command is first called by specifying -u and -v flags.

4. The world space position on the surface can now be sampled by retrieving the **position** attribute. The node will automatically calculate the position based on the parametric sample (u, v).

```
getAttr ($infoNode + ".position");
// Result: -0.0163313 0.0624094 -0.0100707 //
```

The other attributes that can be sampled include **normal, normalizedNormal, tangentU, normalizedTangentU, tangentV,** and **normalizedTangentV.**

C++ API

The **SurfaceInfo2** plug-in builds on the **SurfaceInfo1** plug-in and demonstrates the following.

• Sampling a NURBS surface at a given parametric location (u, v)

• Accessing the sample information (position, normal, and u and v tangents)

• Printing out the sample information

1. Open the **SurfaceInfo2** workspace.

2. Compile it and load the resulting `surfaceInfo2` plug-in file in Maya.

3. Open the **PlaneNurbs.ma** scene.

4. Select the **nurbsPlane1** object.

5. Execute the following.

```
surfaceInfo2;
```

The surface is sampled at a series of locations and the sampled data is output.

```
// |nurbsPlane1
Sample: (0, 0)
 Position: (-0.5, 0.206304, 0.5)
 Normal: (0.465716, 0.752475, -0.465716)
 Tangent U: (0.850317, -0.526271, 0)
 Tangent V: (0, -0.526271, -0.850317)
Sample: (0, 0.333333)
 Position: (-0.50602, 0.0798026, 0.16296)
 Normal: (-0.0147671, 0.980231, -0.197302)
 Tangent U: (0.999886, 0.0138691, -0.00593239)
 Tangent V: (-0.0143355, -0.197511, -0.980196)
```

SOURCE CODE

Plug-in: `SurfaceInfo2`
File: `SurfaceInfo2Cmd.cpp`

```cpp
DeclareSimpleCommand( surfaceInfo2, "David Gould", "1.0" );

MStatus surfaceInfo2::doIt( const MArgList& args )
{
    MStatus stat = MS::kSuccess;

    MSelectionList selection;
    MGlobal::getActiveSelectionList( selection );

    MDagPath dagPath;
    MObject component;
```

```cpp
const int nSegs = 3;
double startU, endU, startV, endV;
unsigned int segU, segV;
double u, v, uIncr, vIncr;
MPoint pt;
MVector norm, tangU, tangV;

MString txt;
MItSelectionList iter( selection );
for ( ; !iter.isDone(); iter.next() )
{
    iter.getDagPath( dagPath, component );

    MFnNurbsSurface surfaceFn( dagPath, &stat );
    if( stat )
    {
        txt += dagPath.fullPathName() + "\n";

        surfaceFn.getKnotDomain( startU, endU, startV, endV );
        uIncr = (endU - startU) / nSegs;
        vIncr = (endV - startV) / nSegs;

        for( segU=0, u=startU; segU < (nSegs+1); segU++, u+=uIncr )
        {
            for( segV=0, v=startV; segV < (nSegs+1);
                segV++, v+=vIncr )
            {
                surfaceFn.getPointAtParam( u, v, pt,
                                        MSpace::kWorld );
                norm = surfaceFn.normal( u, v,
                                        MSpace::kWorld );
                norm.normalize();
                surfaceFn.getTangents( u, v, tangU, tangV,
                                        MSpace::kWorld );
                tangU.normalize();
                tangV.normalize();

                txt += MString("Sample: (") + u + ", " +
                                        v + ")\n";
                txt += MString(" Position: (") + pt.x + ", " +
                                    pt.y + ", " + pt.z + ")\n";
```

```
                           txt += MString(" Normal: (") + norm.x + ", " +
                                          norm.y + ", " + norm.z +
                                          ")\n";
                           txt += MString(" Tangent U: (") + tangU.x +
                                          ", " + tangU.y + ", " +
                                          tangU.z + ")\n";
                           txt += MString(" Tangent V: (") + tangV.x +
                                          ", " + tangV.y + ", " +
                                          tangV.z + ")\n";
                       }
                   }
               }
           }
       MGlobal::displayInfo( txt );
       return MS::kSuccess;
   }
```

SOURCE CODE EXPLANATION

Plug-in: `SurfaceInfo2`
File: `SurfaceInfo2Cmd.cpp`

The **MFnNurbsSurface** function set is bound to the currently selected object.

```
       ...
       MFnNurbsSurface surfaceFn( dagPath, &stat );
       if( stat )
       {
```

The full DAG path to the object is output.

```
           txt += dagPath.fullPathName() + "\n";
```

The parametric range of the u and v dimensions is calculated.

```
           surfaceFn.getKnotDomain( startU, endU, startV, endV );
```

The incremental step in the u and v parameters is determined.

```
           uIncr = (endU - startU) / nSegs;
           vIncr = (endV - startV) / nSegs;
```

The surface is iterated over in row order (u parameter).

```
for( segU=0, u=startU; segU < (nSegs+1); segU++, u+=uIncr )
{
    for( segV=0, v=startV; segV < (nSegs+1);
        segV++, v+=vIncr )
    {
```

The position on the surface is sampled at u, v using the getPointAtParam function.

```
surfaceFn.getPointAtParam( u, v, pt,
                    MSpace::kWorld );
```

The normal is retrieved using the normal function.

```
norm = surfaceFn.normal( u, v,
                    MSpace::kWorld );
norm.normalize();
```

The *u* and *v* tangent vectors are retrieved using the getTangents function.

```
surfaceFn.getTangents( u, v, tangU, tangV,
                    MSpace::kWorld );
tangU.normalize();
tangV.normalize();
```

The sampled data is then added to the output text.

```
txt += MString("Sample: (") + u + ", " +
                    v + ")\n";
...
```

The text is then output.

```
...
MGlobal::displayInfo( txt );
...
```

9.3.3 CREATING SURFACES

TUBE

This section covers how to create a tube out of NURBS surfaces. Figure 9.29 shows several examples of tubes. The tube consists of four surfaces: outer side, inner side, top cap, and bottom cap. All surfaces are periodic in the u direction and open in the v direction. By ensuring that the u direction is periodic, if a control vertex along the seam (u = 0 or u = 1) is moved no gap will be created.

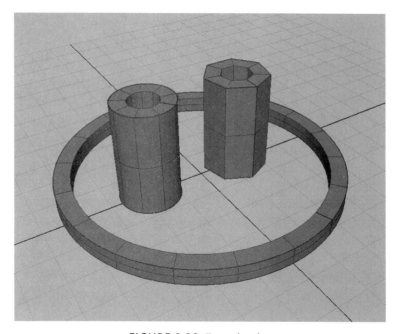

FIGURE 9.29 Example tubes.

MEL

1. Ensure that the MAYA_SCRIPT_PATH is set up correctly. (See Section 1.1.2 for further details.)

2. Execute the following.

    ```
    source tube;
    ```

3. The tube procedure is called to create the tube surfaces.

```
tube( 0.5, 1.0, 3.0, 6, 2, 3 );
```

Four NURBS surfaces are created. These are parented to the **tube** transform. The tube procedure takes the following parameters.

```
global proc tube(
    float $innerRadius,    // Radius of inner side
    float $outerRadius,    // Radius of outer side
    float $height,         // Height of the tube
    int $circumSpans,      // Number of spans around the circumference
    int $heightSpans,      // Number of spans along the height
    int $degree            // Degree of the surface
)
```

4. To create a thin wide tube, execute the following.

```
tube( 3.5, 4.0, 0.5, 15, 1, 3 );
```

SOURCE CODE

MEL Script: Tube.mel

```
proc string createPart(
    int $part,
    float $innerRadius,
    float $outerRadius,
    float $height,
    int $circumSpans,
    int $heightSpans,
    int $degree )
{
    int $uSpans, $vSpans;
    float $angleDir;
    float $radius = $outerRadius;
    float $innerRad = $innerRadius;
    float $elevation;
```

```
switch( $part )
{
     case 0: // Inner side
              $uSpans = $circumSpans;
              $vSpans = $heightSpans;
              $angleDir = 1.0;
              $radius = $innerRadius;
              break;
     case 1: // Outer side
              $uSpans = $circumSpans;
              $vSpans = $heightSpans;
              $angleDir = -1.0;
              break;
     case 2: // Top cap
              $uSpans = $circumSpans;
              $vSpans = 1;
              $angleDir = -1.0;
              $elevation = $height;
              break;
     case 3: // Bottom cap
              $uSpans = $circumSpans;
              $vSpans = 1;
              $angleDir = 1.0;
              $elevation = 0.0;
              break;
}
int $nCVsU = $degree + $uSpans;
int $nCVsV = $degree + $vSpans;
vector $cvs[];
float $x, $y, $z;
float $angleIncr = deg_to_rad( $angleDir * float(360) / $nCVsU );
float $vStart, $vIncr;
if( $part == 0 || $part == 1 )
{
     $vStart = 0.0;
     $vIncr = $height / ($nCVsV-1);
}
```

```
else
{
      $vStart = $radius;
      $vIncr = ($innerRad - $radius) / ($nCVsV-1);
}
float $angle, $v;
int $i, $j, $cvi=0;
for( $i=0, $angle=0.0; $i < $nCVsU; $i++, $angle+=$angleIncr )
{
      for( $j=0, $v=$vStart; $j < $nCVsV; $j++, $v+=$vIncr )
      {
            if( $part == 0 || $part == 1 ) // Sides
            {
                  $x = $radius * cos( $angle );
                  $z = $radius * sin( $angle );
                  $y = $v;
            }
            else // Cap
            {
                  $x = $v * cos( $angle );
                  $z = $v * sin( $angle );
                  $y = $elevation;
            }

            $cvs[$cvi++] = << $x, $y, $z >>;
      }
}

int $nDuplicates = $degree * $nCVsV;
for( $i=0; $i < $nDuplicates; $i++ )
      $cvs[$cvi++] = $cvs[$i];

float $knotsU[];
int $nCVsAlongU = $nCVsU + $degree;
int $nSpans = $nCVsAlongU - $degree;
int $nKnots = $nSpans + 2 * $degree - 1;
int $ki;
for( $ki=0, $i=-($degree-1); $ki < $nKnots; $ki++, $i++ )
      $knotsU[$ki] = $i;

int $multiplicity = $degree;
```

```
    float $knotsV[];
    int $span, $m;
    for( $span=0, $i=0; $span <= $vSpans; $span++ )
    {
        $knotsV[$i++] = float($span);
        if( $span == 0 || $span == $vSpans )
        {
            for( $m=1; $m < $multiplicity; $m++ )
                $knotsV[$i++] = float($span);
        }
    }

    string $cmd = "surface";
    $cmd += " -degreeU " + $degree + " -degreeV " + $degree;
    $cmd += " -formU \"periodic\" -formV \"open\"";
    vector $p;
    for( $i=0; $i < size($cvs); $i++ )
    {
        $p = $cvs[$i];
        $cmd += " -p " + ($p.x) + " " + ($p.y) + " " + ($p.z);
    }
    for( $i=0; $i < size($knotsU); $i++ )
        $cmd += " -ku " + $knotsU[$i];
    for( $i=0; $i < size($knotsV); $i++ )
        $cmd += " -kv " + $knotsV[$i];

    string $shapeObj = eval( $cmd );
    string $relatives[] = eval( "listRelatives -parent " + $shapeObj );
    string $transformObj = $relatives[0];

    $cmd = "sets -e -fe initialShadingGroup " + $transformObj;
    eval( $cmd );

    return $transformObj;
}

global proc tube(
    float $innerRadius,
    float $outerRadius,
    float $height,
    int $circumSpans,
```

```
        int $heightSpans,
        int $degree
    )
    {
        string $tubeTransform = eval( "createNode \"transform\" -n \"tube\"" );

        string $parts[];
        int $i;
        for( $i=0; $i < 4; $i++ )
        {
            $part = createPart( $i, $innerRadius, $outerRadius, $height,
                                $circumSpans, $heightSpans, $degree );

            eval( "parent " + $part + " " + $tubeTransform );
        }
        eval( "select -r " + $tubeTransform );
    }
```

SOURCE CODE EXPLANATION

MEL Script: `Tube.mel`

The `createPart` procedure creates the individual NURBS surfaces that make up the tube. The $part variable can be set to one of the following values: 0 = inner side, 1 = outer side, 2 = top cap, and 3 = bottom cap.

```
    proc string createPart(
        int $part,
        float $innerRadius,
        float $outerRadius,
        float $height,
        int $circumSpans,
        int $heightSpans,
        int $degree )
    {
```

The various parts share common variables. The $uSpans and $vSpans specify, respectively, the number of spans along the u and v directions of the surface.

```
        int $uSpans, $vSpans;
```

The $angleDir defines whether the angular step is positive or negative. Switching from positive to negative, or vice versa, swaps the direction of the surface. This is important for back-face culling because the surface orientation needs to be correct or the surface will be hidden.

```
float $angleDir;
```

The $radius is set to the width of the outer radius.

```
float $radius = $outerRadius;
```

The $elevation variable is only used by caps. It specifies the y height of the cap.

```
...
float $elevation;
```

Depending on which part is requested, the common variables are set differently.

```
switch( $part )
{
     case 0: // Inner side
          $uSpans = $circumSpans;
          $vSpans = $heightSpans;
          $angleDir = 1.0;
          $radius = $innerRadius;
          break;

     case 1: // Outer side
          $uSpans = $circumSpans;
          $vSpans = $heightSpans;
          $angleDir = -1.0;
          break;

     case 2: // Top cap
          $uSpans = $circumSpans;
          $vSpans = 1;
          $angleDir = -1.0;
```

```
                    $elevation = $height;
                    break;

            case 3:  // Bottom cap
                    $uSpans = $circumSpans;
                    $vSpans = 1;
                    $angleDir = 1.0;
                    $elevation = 0.0;
                    break;
    }
```

The list of control vertices is generated.

```
    ...
    vector $cvs[];
    float $x, $y, $z;
```

The `$angleIncr` variable is the angular step per control vertex. The `$angleDir` value is used to flip this direction, depending on the desired surface orientation.

```
    float $angleIncr = deg_to_rad( $angleDir * float(360) / $nCVsU );
```

For the sides, the v direction is the height. For the caps, the v direction is the radius from the outer edge to the inner edge. As such, the v parameter serves dual purposes.

```
    float $vStart, $vIncr;
```

If creating a side, the `$vStart` is set to the bottom of the height, 0.0. The `$vIncr` is the result of dividing the height into the number of control vertex segments.

```
    if( $part == 0 || $part == 1 )
    {
            $vStart = 0.0;
            $vIncr = $height / ($nCVsV-1);
    }
```

If creating a cap, the `$vStart` is set to the outer radius. The `$vIncr` is then calculated as the range between the outer radius and inner radius divided into the number of control vertex segments.

```
else
{
        $vStart = $radius;
        $vIncr = ($innerRad - $radius) / ($nCVsV-1);
}
```

The control vertices are now calculated. Starting with the u direction and then iterating in the v direction, the control vertices are added to the list.

```
float $angle, $v;
int $i, $j, $cvi=0;
for( $i=0, $angle=0.0; $i < $nCVsU; $i++, $angle+=$angleIncr )
{
        for( $j=0, $v=$vStart; $j < $nCVsV; $j++, $v+=$vIncr )
        {
```

If creating a side, the control vertex is calculated from the polar coordinate (`$radius`, `$angle`). The y coordinate is set to v value, which is the result of interpolating.

```
                if( $part == 0 || $part == 1 ) // Sides
                {
                        $x = $radius * cos( $angle );
                        $z = $radius * sin( $angle );
                        $y = $v;
                }
```

If creating a cap, the control vertex is set to the polar coordinate (`$v`, `$angle`), where `$v` is the interpolated radius from the outer radius to the inner radius. The y coordinate is the height of the cap.

```
                else // Cap
                {
                        $x = $v * cos( $angle );
                        $z = $v * sin( $angle );
                        $y = $elevation;
                }
```

The control vertex is added to the list.

```
        $cvs[$cvi++] = << $x, $y, $z >>;
    }
}
```

Because the u parameter is periodic, the first degree number of columns must be duplicated. This ensures that there is no seam and that the surface is smooth at the junction.

```
int $nDuplicates = $degree * $nCVsV;
for( $i=0; $i < $nDuplicates; $i++ )
    $cvs[$cvi++] = $cvs[$i];
```

Calculate the knot values for the u direction. Because the u direction is periodic, the knot values need to reference knots at the start and end of the surface. This ensures that the surface wraps around correctly.

```
float $knotsU[];
int $nCVsAlongU = $nCVsU + $degree;
int $nSpans = $nCVsAlongU - $degree;
int $nKnots = $nSpans + 2 * $degree - 1;
int $ki;
for( $ki=0, $i=-($degree-1); $ki < $nKnots; $ki++, $i++ )
    $knotsU[$ki] = $i;
```

The knot values for the v direction are calculated. Because the v direction is open, the surface needs to start at the first control vertex and end at the last control vertex. To ensure this, there needs to be degree knot multiplicity at the start and end of the knot vector.

```
int $multiplicity = $degree;
float $knotsV[];
int $span, $m;
for( $span=0, $i=0; $span <= $vSpans; $span++ )
```

```
        {
                $knotsV[$i++] = float($span);

                if( $span == 0 || $span == $vSpans )
                {
                        for( $m=1; $m < $multiplicity; $m++ )
                                $knotsV[$i++] = float($span);
                }
        }
}
```

The NURBS surface is created using the surface command.

```
        string $cmd = "surface";
```

The degree of the u and v directions is set to the same value.

```
        $cmd += " -degreeU " + $degree + " -degreeV " + $degree;
```

The form of the u direction is periodic, whereas the form of the v direction is open.

```
        $cmd += " -formU \"periodic\" -formV \"open\"";
```

The control vertices are added to the command arguments.

```
        vector $p;
        for( $i=0; $i < size($cvs); $i++ )
        {
                $p = $cvs[$i];
                $cmd += " -p " + ($p.x) + " " + ($p.y) + " " + ($p.z);
        }
```

The knots for the u direction are added to the command.

```
        for( $i=0; $i < size($knotsU); $i++ )
                $cmd += " -ku " + $knotsU[$i];
```

The knots for the v direction are added to the command.

```
        for( $i=0; $i < size($knotsV); $i++ )
                $cmd += " -kv " + $knotsV[$i];
```

The surface command is executed. The result is the name of the surface shape node.

```
string $shapeObj = eval( $cmd );
```

The parent transform node of the newly created shape node is retrieved.

```
string $relatives[] = eval( "listRelatives -parent " + $shapeObj );
string $transformObj = $relatives[0];
```

The node is added to the **initialShadingGroup** so that it appears correctly in Maya's viewports.

```
$cmd = "sets -e -fe initialShadingGroup " + $transformObj;
eval( $cmd );
```

The parent transform node is returned.

```
    return $transformObj;
}
```

The `tube` procedure creates the various NURBS surfaces and parents them to a "tube" transform node.

```
global proc tube(
    float $innerRadius,
    float $outerRadius,
    float $height,
    int $circumSpans,
    int $heightSpans,
    int $degree
)
{
```

The tube transform node is created. This will be the parent of all the individual NURBS surfaces.

```
string $tubeTransform = eval( "createNode \"transform\" -n \"tube\"" );
```

The four tube parts are created.

```
string $parts[];
int $i;
for( $i=0; $i < 4; $i++ )
{
        $part = createPart( $i, $innerRadius, $outerRadius, $height,
                             $circumSpans, $heightSpans, $degree );
```

The part is added as a child of the tube transform node.

```
        eval( "parent " + $part + " " + $tubeTransform );
}
```

The parent tube transform node is selected.

```
    eval( "select -r " + $tubeTransform );
}
```

C++ API

The **Tube** plug-in demonstrates the following.

- Creating NURBS surfaces in the form of a tube given an inner radius, outer radius, height, number of spans around the circumference, number of spans along the height, and degree

1. If the **tube.mel** file was sourced during the current session, restart Maya. Otherwise, select **File | New Scene**.

   When the body of a procedure is updated, its MEL script file simply needs to be resourced. However, in this case the arguments to the procedure have changed. There is no way to update the existing procedure to take new arguments because this may break code that is running in the current session. The only way to remove the previous definition of the tube procedure is to close the current session and start Maya afresh.

2. Open the **Tube** workspace.

3. Compile it and load the resulting tube plug-in file in Maya.

4. To create the tube, execute the following.

```
tube;
```

A tube composed of four NURBS surfaces (outer wall, inner wall, top cap, and bottom cap) is created.

5. Press the **z** key or select **Edit | Undo** from the main menu.

6. A tube can be created with linear segments.

```
tube -degree 1;
```

The -degree flag can be set to any positive integer. By default, the surface degree is 3.

7. Press the **z** key or select **Edit | Undo** from the main menu.

8. To create a longer tube with more vertical spans, execute the following.

```
tube -height 5 -heightSpans 3;
```

The tube now has a height of five units and three spans.

9. Press the **z** key or select **Edit | Undo** from the main menu.

10. The inner and outer radius can also be set.

```
tube -innerRadius 4 -outerRadius 4.5 -height 0.5 -circumferenceSpans 15;
```

A thin tube is created with more circumference spans than usual.

SOURCE CODE

Plug-in: Tube
File: TubeCmd.cpp

```cpp
class TubeCmd : public MPxCommand
{
public:
    virtual MStatus doIt( const MArgList& );
    virtual MStatus redoIt();
    virtual MStatus undoIt();
    virtual bool isUndoable() const { return true; }
```

```
   static void *creator() { return new TubeCmd; }
   static MSyntax newSyntax();

private:
   MDistance innerRadius, outerRadius;
   MDistance height;
   int circumSpans, heightSpans;
   int degree;

   MObjectArray objTransforms;

   enum Part { INNER_SIDE, OUTER_SIDE,
               TOP_CAP, BOTTOM_CAP,
               // ... add other parts here
               N_PARTS };
   MObject createPart( const Part part );
};

const char *innerRadiusFlag = "-ir",
           *innerRadiusLongFlag = "-innerRadius";
const char *outerRadiusFlag = "-or",
           *outerRadiusLongFlag = "-outerRadius";
const char *heightFlag = "-h",
           *heightLongFlag = "-height";
const char *circumSpansFlag = "-cs",
           *circumSpansLongFlag = "-circumferenceSpans";
const char *heightSpansFlag = "-hs",
           *heightSpansLongFlag = "-heightSpans";
const char *degreeFlag = "-d",
           *degreeLongFlag = "-degree";

MSyntax TubeCmd::newSyntax()
{
 MSyntax syntax;

   syntax.addFlag( innerRadiusFlag, innerRadiusLongFlag,
                   MSyntax::kDistance );
   syntax.addFlag( outerRadiusFlag, outerRadiusLongFlag,
                   MSyntax::kDistance );
   syntax.addFlag( heightFlag, heightLongFlag,
                   MSyntax::kDistance );
```

```
    syntax.addFlag( circumSpansFlag, circumSpansLongFlag,
                  MSyntax::kLong );
    syntax.addFlag( heightSpansFlag, heightSpansLongFlag,
                  MSyntax::kLong );
    syntax.addFlag( degreeFlag, degreeLongFlag, MSyntax::kLong );

    syntax.enableQuery( false );
    syntax.enableEdit( false );

    return syntax;
}

MObject TubeCmd::createPart( const Part part )
{
    int uSpans, vSpans;
    double angleDir;
    double radius = outerRadius.value();
    double innerRad = innerRadius.value();
    double elevation;

    switch( part )
    {
        case INNER_SIDE:
                uSpans = circumSpans;
                vSpans = heightSpans;
                angleDir = 1.0;
                radius = innerRadius.value();
                break;

        case OUTER_SIDE:
                uSpans = circumSpans;
                vSpans = heightSpans;
                angleDir = -1.0;
                break;

        case TOP_CAP:
                uSpans = circumSpans;
                vSpans = 1;
                angleDir = -1.0;
                elevation = height.value();
                break;
```

```
        case BOTTOM_CAP:
                uSpans = circumSpans;
                vSpans = 1;
                angleDir = 1.0;
                elevation = 0.0;
                break;
}

MPointArray cvs;

int nCVsU = degree + uSpans;

int nCVsV = degree + vSpans;

MPoint pt;
double angleIncr = angleDir * (M_PI * 2.0) / nCVsU;
double vStart, vIncr;
if( part == INNER_SIDE || part == OUTER_SIDE )
{
     vStart = 0.0;
     vIncr = height.value() / (nCVsV-1);
}
else
{
     vStart = radius;
     vIncr = (innerRad - radius) / (nCVsV-1);
}

double angle, v;
int i, j;
for( i=0, angle=0.0; i < nCVsU; i++, angle+=angleIncr )
{
     for( j=0, v=vStart; j < nCVsV; j++, v+=vIncr )
     {
          switch( part )
          {
               case INNER_SIDE:
               case OUTER_SIDE:
                    pt.x = radius * cos(angle);
                    pt.z = radius * sin(angle);
                    pt.y = v;
                    break;
```

```
                case TOP_CAP:
                case BOTTOM_CAP:
                        pt.x = v * cos(angle);
                        pt.z = v * sin(angle);
                        pt.y = elevation;
                        break;
            }

            cvs.append( pt );
        }
}

int nDuplicates = degree * nCVsV;
for( i=0; i < nDuplicates; i++ )
    cvs.append( cvs[i] );

MDoubleArray knotsU;
int nCVsAlongU = nCVsU + degree;
int nSpans = nCVsAlongU - degree;
int nKnots = nSpans + 2 * degree - 1;
int ki;
for( i=-(degree-1), ki=0; ki < nKnots; i++, ki++ )
    knotsU.append( double(i) );

const int multiplicity = degree;
MDoubleArray knotsV;
int span, m;
for( span=0; span <= vSpans; span++ )
{
    knotsV.append( double(span) );

    if( span == 0 || span == vSpans )
    {
        for( m=1; m < multiplicity; m++ )
            knotsV.append( double(span) );
    }
}

MStatus stat;
MFnNurbsSurface surfaceFn;
```

```
    MObject objTransform = surfaceFn.create( cvs, knotsU, knotsV,
                                              degree, degree,
                                              MFnNurbsSurface::kPeriodic,
                                              MFnNurbsSurface::kOpen,
                                              false, MObject::kNullObj,
                                              &stat );

    if( !stat )
        stat.perror( "Unable to create mesh" );

    return objTransform;
}

MStatus TubeCmd::doIt( const MArgList &args )
{
    MStatus stat;

    innerRadius.setValue( 0.5 );
    outerRadius.setValue( 1.0 );
    height.setValue( 3.0 );
    circumSpans = 6;
    heightSpans = 2;
    degree = 3;
    MArgDatabase argData( syntax(), args, &stat );
    if( !stat )
        return stat;

    if( argData.isFlagSet( innerRadiusFlag ) )
        argData.getFlagArgument( innerRadiusFlag, 0, innerRadius );

    if( argData.isFlagSet( outerRadiusFlag ) )
        argData.getFlagArgument( outerRadiusFlag, 0, outerRadius );

    if( argData.isFlagSet( heightFlag ) )
        argData.getFlagArgument( heightFlag, 0, height );

    if( argData.isFlagSet( circumSpansFlag ) )
        argData.getFlagArgument( circumSpansFlag, 0, circumSpans );

    if( argData.isFlagSet( heightSpansFlag ) )
        argData.getFlagArgument( heightSpansFlag, 0, heightSpans );

    if( argData.isFlagSet( degreeFlag ) )
        argData.getFlagArgument( degreeFlag, 0, degree );

    return redoIt();
}
```

```
MStatus TubeCmd::redoIt()
{
    MStatus stat;
    MString cmd;

    objTransforms.clear();

    MFnDagNode dagFn;
    MObject objTransform;
    unsigned int i;
    for( i=0; i < N_PARTS; i++ )
    {
            objTransform = createPart( (Part)i );
            objTransforms.append( objTransform );

            MFnDagNode dagFn( objTransform );

            cmd = "sets -e -fe initialShadingGroup ";
            cmd += dagFn.name();
            MGlobal::executeCommand( cmd );
    }

    MFnTransform transformFn;
    MObject tubeTransform;
    tubeTransform = transformFn.create();
    transformFn.setName( "tube" );

    for( i=0; i < objTransforms.length(); i++ )
            transformFn.addChild( objTransforms[i] );

    objTransforms.append( tubeTransform );
    cmd = MString( "select -r " ) + transformFn.name();
    MGlobal::executeCommand( cmd );

    return MS::kSuccess;
}

MStatus TubeCmd::undoIt()
{
    MDGModifier dgMod;
    MFnDagNode dagFn;
    MObject child;
```

```
    unsigned int i;
    for( i=0; i < objTransforms.length(); i++ )
    {
          dagFn.setObject( objTransforms[i] );
          child = dagFn.child( 0 );
          if( !child.isNull() )
                dgMod.deleteNode( child );

          dgMod.deleteNode( objTransforms[i] );
    }

    return dgMod.doIt();
}

MStatus initializePlugin( MObject obj )
{
    MFnPlugin plugin( obj, "David Gould", "1.0" );

    MStatus stat;
    stat = plugin.registerCommand( "tube",
                                   TubeCmd::creator,
                                   TubeCmd::newSyntax );
    if ( !stat )
          MGlobal::displayError( MString( "registerCommand failed: " ) +
                                 stat.errorString() );

    return stat;
}

MStatus uninitializePlugin( MObject obj )
{
    MFnPlugin plugin( obj );

    MStatus stat;
    stat = plugin.deregisterCommand( "tube" );
    if ( !stat )
          MGlobal::displayError( MString( "deregisterCommand failed: " ) +
                                 stat.errorString() );

    return stat;
}
```

SOURCE CODE EXPLANATION

Plug-in: Tube
File: TubeCmd.cpp

The tube command is a standard **MPxCommand**. It supports undoing and redoing, as well as command flag arguments.

```
class TubeCmd : public MPxCommand
...
```

The innerRadius defines the radius of the inside of the tube, whereas the outerRadius defines the radius of the outside of the tube.

```
...
MDistance innerRadius, outerRadius;
```

The height variable specifies the height of the tube.

```
MDistance height;
```

The circumSpans defines the number of spans in the circumference of the tube. The heightSpans defines the number of spans in the height of the tube. The specification of spans is simpler, for the user, than specifying the number of control vertices. The number of control vertices is determined implicitly by the degree of the final surface. The user would be required to do the mental math to calculate the number of control vertices necessary for the given degree. As such, specifying the number of spans is far easier and more intuitive for the user.

```
int circumSpans, heightSpans;
```

The degree specifies the degree of the surface. It can be any positive integer greater than zero.

```
int degree;
```

The objTransforms array holds the list of NURBS surfaces this command creates.

```
MObjectArray objTransforms;
```

The tube is composed of four separate NURBS surfaces: the inner side, outer side, top cap, and bottom cap.

```
enum Part { INNER_SIDE, OUTER_SIDE,
            TOP_CAP, BOTTOM_CAP,
            // ... add other parts here
            N_PARTS };
    ...
```

The `createPart` function creates the individual NURBS surfaces that make up the tube. Given the `part`, the function can create the cylinders forming the outer and inner sides as well as the disc forming the top and bottom caps.

```
MObject TubeCmd::createPart( const Part part )
{
```

Depending on which part is requested, the various variables are initialized. The `uSpans` and `vSpans` specify the number of spans in the u and v directions of the surface. For the sides, the `vSpans` is the number of height spans. For the caps, there is only one span in the v direction.

```
int uSpans, vSpans;
```

The `angleDir` defines whether the angle increment is positive or negative. Changing from positive to negative, or vice versa, results in the surface orientation being flipped. For the outer side, the normals need to point outward, whereas they need to point inward for the inner side. By simply changing the `angleDir`, the final surface changes orientation. This is important if the user turns back-face culling on, as the orientation of the surface becomes more obvious.

```
double angleDir;
```

The `radius` is the distance of the inner or outer side. For the caps, it is the radius of the outer side.

```
double radius = outerRadius.value();
double innerRad = innerRadius.value();
```

The `elevation` is only used by the caps. This determines at what height they are created.

```
double elevation;
```

The variables are initialized depending on what part needs to be created.

```
switch( part )
{
    case INNER_SIDE:
        uSpans = circumSpans;
        vSpans = heightSpans;
        angleDir = 1.0;
        radius = innerRadius.value();
        break;

    case OUTER_SIDE:
        uSpans = circumSpans;
        vSpans = heightSpans;
        angleDir = -1.0;
        break;

    case TOP_CAP:
        uSpans = circumSpans;
        vSpans = 1;
        angleDir = -1.0;
        elevation = height.value();
        break;

    case BOTTOM_CAP:
        uSpans = circumSpans;
        vSpans = 1;
        angleDir = 1.0;
        elevation = 0.0;
        break;
}
```

The control vertices are now created.

```
MPointArray cvs;
...
```

The angleIncr determines the angular step per control vertex along the u direction. Note that the angleDir is used to flip the direction if necessary.

```
...
double angleIncr = angleDir * (M_PI * 2.0) / nCVsU;
```

The v direction is the height for the sides and the radius for the caps. As such, it serves a dual purpose. If the part requested is a side, the vStart is initialized to the height of 0. The vIncr is initialized to the height divided by the number of control vertices in the height minus 1.

```
double vStart, vIncr;
if( part == INNER_SIDE || part == OUTER_SIDE )
{
    vStart = 0.0;
    vIncr = height.value() / (nCVsV-1);
}
```

If the part requested is a cap, the vStart is initialized to the outer radius. The vIncr is the step from the outer radius to the inner radius.

```
else
{
    vStart = radius;
    vIncr = (innerRad - radius) / (nCVsV-1);
}
```

The surface is generated by iterating in row order first (u direction), followed by column order (v direction).

```
...
for( i=0, angle=0.0; i < nCVsU; i++, angle+=angleIncr )
{
    for( j=0, v=vStart; j < nCVsV; j++, v+=vIncr )
    {
```

Given the part, the control vertex is calculated.

```
switch( part )
{
```

For sides, the x and y coordinates are derived from the polar coordinates (radius, angle). The z coordinate is the height along the v direction.

```
case INNER_SIDE:
case OUTER_SIDE:
        pt.x = radius * cos(angle);
        pt.z = radius * sin(angle);
        pt.y = v;
        break;
```

When creating a cap, the x and y coordinates are derived from the polar coordinates (v, angle). All control vertices are given the same height, as specified by the elevation variable.

```
case TOP_CAP:
case BOTTOM_CAP:
        pt.x = v * cos(angle);
        pt.z = v * sin(angle);
        pt.y = elevation;
        break;
}
```

The newly calculated control vertex is added to the list.

```
        cvs.append( pt );
    }
}
```

Because the u direction is periodic, there needs to be duplicate control vertices to ensure no seams appears. The first degree columns of control vertices are duplicated. Note that because the v direction is open no duplicate rows are needed.

```
int nDuplicates = degree * nCVsV;
for( i=0; i < nDuplicates; i++ )
    cvs.append( cvs[i] );
```

The knot vector for the u direction is generated. By derivation, it is clear that the nSpans calculation can be reduced to simply nSpans = CVsU. The complete calculation is included to help understand how it is derived.

```
MDoubleArray knotsU;
int nCVsAlongU = nCVsU + degree;
int nSpans = nCVsAlongU - degree;
int nKnots = nSpans + 2 * degree - 1;
```

The knots for the periodic u direction are calculated by ensuring that spans from before and after the seam are referenced.

```
int ki;
for( i=-(degree-1), ki=0; ki < nKnots; i++, ki++ )
        knotsU.append( double(i) );
```

The knot vector for the v direction is simpler because the surface is open in that direction. Because the surface needs to pass through the first and last control vertices in the v direction, there is knot multiplicity at the first and last spans. The first and last knots are duplicated for as many times as the degree of the surface.

```
const int multiplicity = degree;
MDoubleArray knotsV;
int span, m;
for( span=0; span <= vSpans; span++ )
{
        knotsV.append( double(span) );

        if( span == 0 || span == vSpans )
        {
                for( m=1; m < multiplicity; m++ )
                        knotsV.append( double(span) );
        }
}
```

The surface is created by calling the **MFnNurbsSurface**'s create function. The transform parent object of the NURBS surface shape is returned.

```
MStatus stat;
MFnNurbsSurface surfaceFn;
```

```
MObject objTransform = surfaceFn.create( cvs, knotsU, knotsV,
                                          degree, degree,
                                          MFnNurbsSurface::kPeriodic,
                                          MFnNurbsSurface::kOpen,
                                          false, MObject::kNullObj,
                                          &stat );
```

The transform object is returned.

```
    ...
    return objTransform;
}
```

The doIt function simply retrieves the command flags and then calls the redoIt function.

```
MStatus TubeCmd::doIt( const MArgList &args )
{
```

The command arguments are initialized to their default values.

```
    ...
    innerRadius.setValue( 0.5 );
    outerRadius.setValue( 1.0 );
    height.setValue( 3.0 );
    circumSpans = 6;
    heightSpans = 2;
    degree = 3;
    ...
```

The redoIt function takes the command arguments and generates the actual NURBS surfaces.

```
MStatus TubeCmd::redoIt()
{
```

The list of object transforms is cleared. This will contain the list of previous object transforms if the command is being redone.

```
    ...
    objTransforms.clear();
```

The four parts are generated by calling the `createPart` function.

```
MFnDagNode dagFn;
MObject objTransform;
unsigned int i;
for( i=0; i < N_PARTS; i++ )
{
        objTransform = createPart( (Part)i );
```

The transform parent object of the newly created NURBS surface is added to the list.

```
        objTransforms.append( objTransform );
```

The new object is added to the **initialShadingGroup**. Otherwise, it will display incorrectly in Maya's viewports.

```
        MFnDagNode dagFn( objTransform );
        cmd = "sets -e -fe initialShadingGroup ";
        cmd += dagFn.name();
        MGlobal::executeCommand( cmd );
}
```

A transform object is created that will serve as the parent of the four surfaces. It is named **tube**.

```
MFnTransform transformFn;
MObject tubeTransform;
tubeTransform = transformFn.create();
transformFn.setName( "tube" );
```

The four parts are added as children to the **tube** transform object.

```
for( i=0; i < objTransforms.length(); i++ )
        transformFn.addChild( objTransforms[i] );
```

The **tube** transform object is added to the list of created objects. It needs to be added so that it can be removed if the user requests an undo.

```
objTransforms.append( tubeTransform );
```

The **tube** transform object is selected.

```
cmd = MString( "select -r " ) + transformFn.name();
MGlobal::executeCommand( cmd );
...
```

The undoIt function removes the surfaces created, as well as the parent **tube** transform. Because the command only generates a few objects and operates on them, it only needs to record the objects created. The additional operations don't need to be recorded.

```
MStatus TubeCmd::undoIt()
{
    MDGModifier dgMod;
    MFnDagNode dagFn;
    MObject child;

    unsigned int i;
    for( i=0; i < objTransforms.length(); i ++ )
    {
```

As always, the child node needs to be deleted before the parent. Otherwise, Maya will crash.

```
        dagFn.setObject( objTransforms[i] );
        child = dagFn.child( 0 );
```

Because the **tube** transform is included in the objTransforms list and doesn't have a child, it needs to be tested. Only the four NURBS surfaces will have child shapes.

```
        if( !child.isNull() )
            dgMod.deleteNode( child );

        dgMod.deleteNode( objTransforms[i] );
    }

    return dgMod.doIt();
}
```

9.3.4 EDITING SURFACES

REBUILDING SURFACES

The parameterization and other characteristics of a NURBS surface can be changed using the `rebuildSurface` command.

1. Open the **PlaneNurbs.ma** scene.

2. Select the **nurbsPlane1** object.

3. To change the u degree of the surface, execute the following.

    ```
    rebuildSurface -degreeU 1;
    ```

    The *u* direction of the surface now has a degree of 1 and is thus linear. The *v* direction still maintains its degree of 3 and is thus smooth.

4. Press the **z** key or select **Edit | Undo**.

5. To change the parameterization of the surface, execute the following.

    ```
    rebuildSurface -keepRange 2;
    ```

    The parametric range of the surface has changed from u = [0,1], v = [0,1] to u = [0,4], v = [0,4]. The upper extent, 4, corresponds to the number of spans in the surface.

6. Press the **z** key or select **Edit | Undo**.

7. To reduce the number of spans along the u direction, execute the following.

    ```
    rebuildSurface -spansU 3;
    ```

    The number of u direction spans is reduced from 4 to 3. The remaining control vertices are moved to try to maintain the same shape as the original. Of course, as the spans are reduced it become more difficult to maintain the same shape.

DISSECTING SURFACES

A NURBS surface can be split into multiple NURBS surfaces at a given series of u or v isoparameters.

1. Open the **PlaneNurbs.ma** scene.

2. Select the **nurbsPlane1** object.

3. To dissect the surface along the u parameter, execute the following.

```
detachSurface -parameter 0.5;

// Result: nurbsPlane1detachedSurface1 nurbsPlane1detachedSurface2 //
```

The surface is split into two NURBS surfaces at the u = 0.5 isoparm.

4. Press the **z** key or select **Edit | Undo** to undo the dissection.

5. To dissect the surface along the v parameter, execute the following.

```
detachSurface -direction 0 -parameter 0.25 -replaceOriginal true;
```

The surface is once again split into two pieces, but this time it is along the v = 0.25 isoparm. Because the -replaceOriginal flag was set to true, the original surface is split and contains the first half (v = 0.0 to v = 0.25) of the resulting split surface. The **nurbsPlane1detachedSurfaceShape2** object contains the other half.

6. Press the **z** key or select **Edit | Undo** to undo the last operation.

7. To move the middle section of the surface, use the following.

```
detachSurface -parameter 0.33 -parameter 0.66 -keep on -keep off
-keep on;
```

The surface is split into three parts, although the middle part isn't kept.

```
// Result: nurbsPlane1detachedSurface1 nurbsPlane1detachedSurface2
nurbsPlane1detachedSurface3 //
```

The first part ranges from u = 0.0 to u = 0.33. The last part ranges from u = 0.66 to u = 1.0.

8. Press the **z** key or select **Edit | Undo** to undo the last operation.

9. To create a split but maintain a construction history with the original surface, execute the following.

```
detachSurface -parameter 0.5 -constructionHistory true;
```

The surface is split at u = 0.5 and two new surfaces are created. In addition, a **detachSurface** node, **detachSurface1**, is created.

```
// Result: nurbsPlane1detachedSurface1 nurbsPlane1detachedSurface2
detachSurface1 //
```

Because the construction history was turned on, whenever the original nurbsPlane1 surface is changed the two detached surfaces will update automatically. In addition, the attributes of the **detachSurface** node can be edited to change the split.

10. To dissect along the v direction, execute the following.

```
setAttr detachSurface1.direction 0;
```

11. To edit the parameter at which the split happens, execute the following.

```
setAttr detachSurface1.parameter[0] 0.35;
```

ATTACHING SURFACES

Two NURBS surfaces can be attached to create a single combined surface.

1. Open the **TwoPlaneNurbs.ma** scene.

2. To attach the two surfaces, execute the following.

```
select -r nurbsPlane1 nurbsPlane2;
attachSurface;
```

The attachSurface command will, by default, create a simple connection between the two surfaces. This connection is more obvious if the surface is moved.

3. To move the original surface, execute the following.

```
select -r nurbsPlane1;
move -r 0 0.5 0;
```

Seeing the two planes move in unison shows that the second plane is indeed attached to the first.

4. Press the **z** key or select **Edit | Undo** to undo the movement.

5. Press the **z** key or select **Edit | Undo** to undo the surface attachment.

6. To attach the surfaces with a blended surface, execute the following.

    ```
    attachSurface -method 1;
    ```

7. To move the original surface, execute the following.

    ```
    select -r nurbsPlane1;
    move -r 0 0.5 0;
    ```

    The attached surface is now a smoother blend between the two original surfaces.

TRIMMING SURFACES

A NURBS surface with surface curves can be trimmed.

1. Open the **PlaneNurbsTrimmed.ma** scene.

2. Select the **nurbsPlane1** object.

3. To trim the surface, execute the following.

    ```
    trim -locatorU 0.5 -locatorV 0.5;
    ```

    The portion of the surface inside the curve is kept. A **trim** node is created because construction history is on by default. To create a trimmed surface without construction history, simply include -constructionHistory false in the command arguments.

4. Press the **z** key or select **Edit | Undo**.

5. To trim the inner portion, execute the following.

    ```
    trim -locatorU 0.5 -locatorV 0.5 -selected true;
    ```

    The inner portion is now removed, leaving the outer portion of the surface.

6. To remove a trim on a trimmed surface, execute the following.

    ```
    untrim;
    ```

    The original untrimmed surface is restored. Note that this command creates an **untrim** node if the surface has construction history.

CHAPTER 10

Subdivision Surfaces

Subdivision surfaces take a polygonal mesh and successively subdivide it many times. The result is an extremely smooth surface from a hard polygonal mesh. Figure 10.1 shows an example of subdividing the polygonal mesh displayed in wireframe.

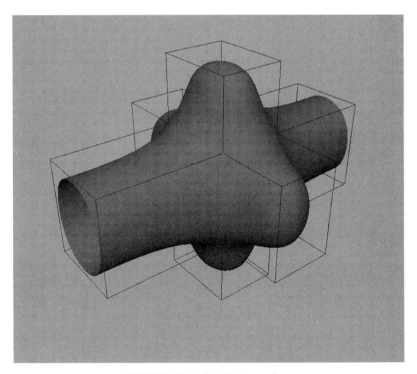

FIGURE 10.1 Subdivision surface.

Subdivision surfaces combine some of the advantages of polygon meshes and NURBS surfaces. A polygon mesh can have any arbitrary topology, whereas a NURBS surface always consists of a "sheet" of four sides. This restriction makes the modeling of complex surfaces much more difficult with NURBS. Of course, this restriction is circumvented with the use of advanced and intuitive NURBS modeling tools. The biggest challenge with creating complex models using NURBS surfaces is stitching them to create a consistently smooth surface. Even more difficult is ensuring that the NURBS surfaces remain smoothly attached to each other when arbitrary animation and deformations are applied to the surfaces.

NURBS surfaces also suffer from an inability to provide local edits easily. This means that if additional detail is required in an area, that often an entire isoparameter must be inserted. This requires the creation of a lot of control vertices, many outside the area that needs the greatest focus.

In terms of easily generating arbitrarily complex models, nothing surpasses the simplicity of a polygonal representation. Because subdivision surfaces are based on polygonal meshes, they inherit one of their weaknesses: no implicit parameterization. As such, there is no automatic parameterization for uv texture coordinates as there are for NURBS surfaces. Fortunately, Maya comes with a complete suite of uv texture assignment tools for polygonal meshes. A subdivision surface can inherit its uv texture coordinates from its base polygonal mesh.

Although Maya currently only supports subdivision surfaces, it is also possible to have subdivision curves. Whereas a subdivision surface starts with a polygon cage, a subdivision curve would start with a polyline (series of contiguous straight line segments). Like a polygon cage, this polyline would be subdivided. With a sufficient number of subdivisions, the polyline would produce a smooth curve. A subdivision curve would also have a theoretical subdivision limit curve analogous to a subdivision surface's limit surface.

10.1 CONCEPTS

10.1.1 CONTROL MESH

The control mesh is the original polygonal mesh that is first subdivided. Figure 10.2 shows a cube polygonal control mesh and its resulting subdivision surface. Maya refers to this mesh as the *base mesh*. The control mesh of a subdivision surface can be edited directly by switching to *polygon proxy mode*.

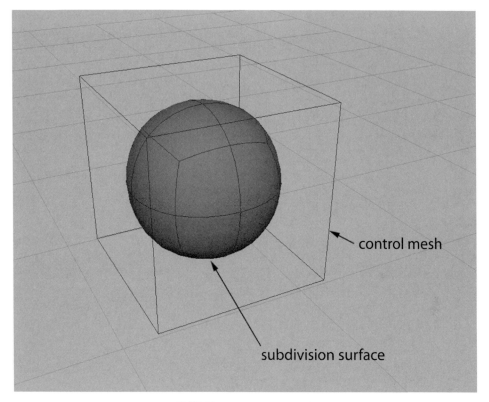

FIGURE 10.2 Control mesh.

Although Maya allows the user to edit the control mesh when in polygon proxy mode, once the switch is made back to standard mode any construction history is deleted. As such, it isn't possible to continue tweaking the construction history once switched to standard mode.

10.1.2 SUBDIVISION

Figure 10.3 shows the result of subdividing a polygonal cube several times. It is clear that the greater the number of subdivisions the smoother the final surface.

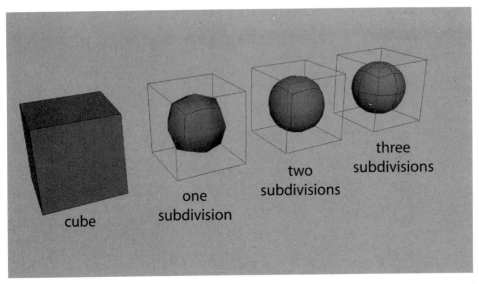

FIGURE 10.3 Subdivision surface.

Subdividing is an iterative process. The cube polygonal mesh is subdivided once, resulting in a fairly rough mesh. This mesh is then subdivided again. This process is then repeated. The result of one subdivision is then used as input into the next subdivision. For the majority of cases only a few levels of subdivision are necessary to create a smooth surface. Each subdivision is referred to as a *subdivision step*.

10.1.3 LIMIT SURFACE

Mathematically, the surface that results after an infinite number of subdivisions is referred to as the *limit surface*. Positions and tangents on the limit surface can be computed directly without having to go through the arduous task of subdividing a polygonal mesh countless numbers of times. Instead, they are calculated directly using closed form expressions. The normal on the limit surface can be calculated once the tangents are known by using the cross product.

For practical reasons a polygonal mesh will never be subdivided infinitely and thus an approximation to the limit surface can be achieved after just a few subdivisions. When a subdivision surface is converted to a NURBS surface, it provides an even closer approximation to the limit surface, without the overhead of millions of polygons.

10.1.4 CREASES

When the control mesh is subdivided, the resulting surface is smooth. It may be necessary to have some sharper points or edges in the final surface. To define where the surface should be sharper, an edge or vertex is tagged as a *crease*. The surface will then be sharper where the creased edge or vertex is located. Maya provides two levels of creasing: partial or full. Partial creasing will only sharpen the area slightly, whereas full creasing will provide a maximum amount of sharpening. Figure 10.4 shows two subdivided cubes with creases.

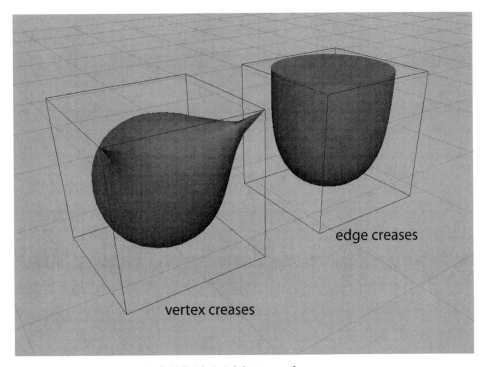

FIGURE 10.4 Subdivision surface creases.

The subdivision surface with vertex creases was created by making the two top front vertices fully creased. The second subdivision surface with edge creases was created by making all top edges fully creased. Any edge or vertex can have its crease tag removed, thereby restoring the surface to its original smoothness.

10.1.5 HIERARCHICAL SUBDIVISIONS

Maya supports multiple levels of subdivisions. At each level it is possible to transform (move, rotate, or scale) the vertices, thereby manipulating the subdivision surface at multiple levels of detail. Figure 10.5 shows a subdivided cube with three levels. Level 2 was created by selecting the foremost top left vertex and subdividing it. This explains the fact that Level 2 is confined to the region around that vertex.

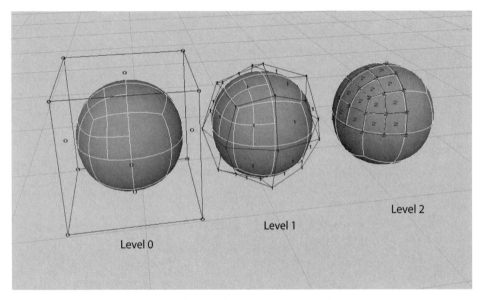

FIGURE 10.5 Subdivision surface levels.

It is important to note the distinction between the smoothness of a subdivision surface and its levels. A subdivision surface doesn't need multiple levels to be smooth. After the first subdivision, the surface will be perfectly smooth. However, it may not appear so in Maya's viewports. This is simply the surface detail that Maya is displaying in the viewports. This is analogous to the display of NURBS surfaces, where a mathematically smooth surface can be shown in low resolution as an angular sharp polygonal surface. As such, it is unnecessary to add levels to a subdivision surface to obtain a smooth result.

Support for levels is an extension to the basic subdivision surface approach. It provides for editing of the surface at multiple levels. This allows for finer detail to be added to the surface at a higher level. The great advantage of this approach is that when a component is edited at a lower level all higher-level edits will follow. This can be exploited when animating an object wherein the smaller details must follow the larger details, such as spikes on the skin.

Maya allows a maximum of 13 levels. The control mesh is counted as the first level, leaving 12 additional levels for editing and refinement. Even though 13 levels are supported, it is very unlikely that that many would be used because it would result in too many polygons. In fact, a single four-sided polygon when subdivided to the 13th level results in approximately 16,000,000 vertices.

10.1.6 ORDINARY AND EXTRAORDINARY POINTS

In a polygonal mesh, each vertex is connected to other vertices via edges. The number of vertices, connected by edges, to a vertex is called its *valence*. The classification of a point depends on the subdivision scheme. If the subdivision scheme is triangle-based, a vertex with valence 6 is called an ordinary point. Any other valence and it is called an extraordinary point. Whether a point is ordinary or extraordinary often determines the continuity (smoothness) of the resulting subdivision surface. Using the Loop subdivision scheme, an ordinary point will produce a surface of C^2 continuity, whereas an extraordinary point will produce a surface of C^1 continuity. Ordinary points are also referred to as regular points, whereas extraordinary points are also referred to as irregular points.

10.1.7 SUBDIVISION SCHEME

The subdivision scheme defines how a polygonal mesh is subdivided into a subdivision surface. The application of a subdivision scheme is composed of two phases: refinement phase and smoothing phase. The refinement phase creates new vertices and reconnects them to create new, smaller triangles. The smoothing phase typically computes new positions for the vertices. The choice of refinement method determines how the polygonal mesh is split into smaller polygons. One method may split a polygon by placing a new vertex at its center, whereas another method may split a polygon along its edges. The smoothing method determines the level of continuity of the surface, as well as whether it is approximating or interpolating.

Subdivision schemes can be further classified into those that are *stationary* or *uniform*, and whether they are *triangle based* or *polygon based*. A stationary scheme uses the same subdivision method at all levels of subdivision. A nonstationary scheme uses different subdivision methods at different levels. A uniform scheme uses the same method for every vertex or edge, as opposed to nonuniform schemes that may use different rules at different levels. A triangle-based scheme operates on triangles, whereas a polygon-based scheme operates on polygons with an arbitrary number of vertices.

Some common subdivision schemes include Loop, √3, Modified Butterfly, Doo-Sabin, and Catmull-Clark. Maya's subdivision scheme is a hierarchical implementation of the Catmull-Clark subdivision scheme. This scheme is polygon based and after the first subdivision generates only four-sided polygons (*quads*), though not all vertices have valence 4. More precisely, when the control mesh is first subdivided each face will produce as many child faces as it has edges. As such, a four-sided polygon will produce four child polygons. These child polygons will be quadrilaterials. The resulting surface tends to be more symmetrical than other schemes. Another advantage of this scheme is that if the control mesh has only ordinary points the subdivision surface can be represented as a *uniform bicubic B-spline surface*. This means that the subdivision surface can be easily converted into a NURBS surface. A uniform bicubic B-spline surface is just a specialization of a more general NURBS surface: the knot vector must be uniform, the curve is nonrational, and it uses basis functions of only degree 3 (cubic).

10.2 DISPLAYING SUBDIVISION SURFACES

A subdivision surface can have its many components (vertices, edges, faces, and so on) displayed. Because it can potentially have many levels, the components at specific levels can be displayed. At a given level it is possible to display only those vertices that have been edited, as opposed to all vertices.

1. Open the **CubeSubd.ma** scene.

2. Select the **subd** object.

    The subdivision surface is currently displayed with a rough smoothness.

3. To determine the current display smoothness, execute the following.

```
subdivDisplaySmoothness -query;
// Result: 1 //
```

    The result indicates the display smoothness is set to rough. The display smoothness can be one of the following: 0 = hull, 1 = rough, 2 = medium, or 3 = fine.

4. To display the control mesh, execute the following.

```
subdivDisplaySmoothness -smoothness 0;
```

The polygonal mesh that defines the subdivision surface is displayed. Note that one of the vertices has been moved up, creating a spike on the left side. This is due to this vertex being moved in a coarser subdivision level.

5. To display the subdivision surface with an increased smoothness, execute the following.

```
subdivDisplaySmoothness -smoothness 3;
```

The surface is now displayed much more smoothly. It is possible to set the display smoothness for all subdivision surfaces by using the -all flag.

6. To display the normals of the object, execute the following.

```
toggle -normal;
```

The normals are far too long.

7. To reduce the size of the normals displayed, execute the following.

```
setAttr subd.normalsDisplayScale 0.25;
```

The normals are reduced to a quarter of their previous size.

8. Execute the following.

```
toggle -normal;
```

The normals are no longer displayed.

9. To display the vertices, execute the following.

```
setAttr subd.dispVertices true;
```

The vertices are each displayed as a number, indicating their level.

10. To display the vertices at a finer level, execute the following.

```
setAttr subd.displayLevel 1;
```

All vertices at level 1 are displayed.

11. To display only those vertices that have been transformed from their original positions, execute the following.

```
setAttr subd.displayFilter 1;
```

Only the top left vertex is displayed. This is the only vertex at level 1 that was moved. The **displayFilter** attribute can be set to one of the following values: 0 = All or 1 = Edited.

12. Press the **z** key or select **Edit | Undo** from the main menu.

13. The faces of the mesh can be displayed by executing the following.

```
setAttr subd.dispFaces true;
```

The faces are displayed with a number in their center, specifying which level they are.

14. Press the **z** key or select **Edit | Undo** from the main menu.

15. To display the edges of the mesh, execute the following.

```
setAttr subd.dispEdges true;
```

16. Press the **z** key or select **Edit | Undo** from the main menu.

17. To display the uv texture coordinates, execute the following.

```
setAttr subd.dispVertices false;
setAttr subd.dispMaps true;
```

The display of vertices is first turned off, and then the uv texture coordinates are displayed at the vertices.

18. To display the borders of the uv texture coordinates, execute the following.

```
setAttr subd.dispUVBorder true;
```

19. Select **Window | UV Texture Editor** from the main menu.

The borders of the uv coordinates are displayed with thicker lines.

10.3 QUERYING SUBDIVISION SURFACES

A subdivision surface is the combination of a control mesh, vertex offsets if edited, and crease tags assigned to vertices and/or edges.

10.3.1 COMPONENTS

A polygonal mesh doesn't have a hierarchy of levels or edits and thus its vertices are stored as a 1D array of positions. The faces and edge lists are also 1D arrays. Referencing a component of a polygonal mesh therefore requires a single value that is the index into one of the arrays.

Because a subdivision surface can contain an arbitrary number of levels as well as edits to its vertices (transformations) and edges (crease tagging), a more flexible means of referencing components is needed. Each component in a subdivision surface is referenced based on its location in the subdivision hierarchy. This location can be defined using a path from the base mesh down through successive levels until the exact component is reached. A subdivision surface can have 13 levels of subdivision, and thus the path to a component can be long. A single 32-bit index isn't sufficient. A 64-bit integer is used instead. However, this integer doesn't simply hold an index. Instead, it is treated as a series of bits rather than a single number. For those familiar with C/C++, this is the equivalent of bit fields. The bits are grouped into logical parts. Figure 10.6 shows how a 64-bit integer is divided into groups of bits.

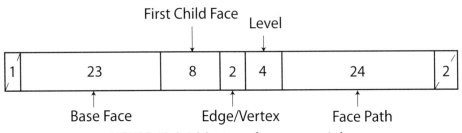

FIGURE 10.6 Subdivision surface component index.

These parts are defined as follows.

1. **Base Face**

    This identifies the face in the control mesh. It is stored using 23 bits, thereby allowing a maximum of 8,388,608 (2^{23}) faces in the control mesh.

2. **Level**

    This identifies the component's level in the hierarchy. This is stored as a 4-bit value, in that there are 14 possible levels (0 to 13).

3. **First Child Face**

    A face in the control mesh can have up to 256 edges. When this face is subdivided it will produce as many faces as it has edges, and thus there is a maximum of 256 possible child faces from a face in the control mesh. The First Child Face identifies which of the possible 256 edge faces (level 0) this face (level 1) is derived from. It is stored as an 8-bit value.

4. **Face Path**

    Given a face in the control mesh (level 0), its series of child faces (level 1) are identified by the First Child Face values. Faces in level 1 are guaranteed to divide into exactly four child faces (level 2). A child face of a level 1 face can therefore be indexed using just two bits ($2^2 = 4$). The face path is 24 bits long, and thus it can hold a series of 12 child face indices (12 * 2 bits = 24 bits). These identify all the child faces from level 2 to level 13.

5. **Edge/Vertex**

    Many of the other parts just listed are used to uniquely identify a given face. This last part provides the index of the edge or vertex of the given face. It is a 2-bit value because all child faces are guaranteed to be quadrilaterals, and thus they will have four vertices and four edges. The edge/vertex index is a face-relative index for a given vertex or edge.

To uniquely identify any face in the subdivision surface, the Base Face, First Child Face, and Face Path values are needed. Together, they define a unique path to a given face, from level 0 to the face's final level.

It is important to note that the layout of the bits as shown in Figure 10.6 shouldn't be relied on. In the future, Maya could possibly pack the values into 64 bits differently.

MEL

Unfortunately, MEL doesn't support 64-bit integers. Its integers are only 32 bits in length. To get around this problem, the 64-bit integer is split into two 32-bit integers. The two 32-bit integers are then used to index a subdivision component. The problem is that the 64-bit integer value is already difficult to decipher because it is the result of packing a lot of different bits into a single integer. In addition, the layout of the bits can't be relied on. In addition, this number is then split into two 32-bit integers. Whether the higher-order 32 bits (word) of the 64 bits is put into the first or second 32-bit integer isn't clear. In addition, MEL doesn't provide any bitwise operators (or and xor), and thus the exact value of each part of the 32-bit value is always going to be difficult to retrieve. Even if it were possible to retrieve them, it is ill advised to do this for the reasons mentioned previously. As such, it is almost impossible to intuitively interpret exactly which component the 32-bit integers refer to.

The components are accessed as if it were in a 2D array, using the two 32-bit integers. The components are retrieved using the following attribute names.

- **smp** – Subdivision mesh points

- **sme** – Subdivision mesh edges

- **smf** – Subdivision mesh faces

- **smm** – Subdivision mesh uv coordinate

1. Open the **CubeSubd.ma** scene.

2. Execute the following.

   ```
   select -r subd.smp[0][2];
   ```

   This selects the top left vertex.

3. Execute the following.

   ```
   select -r subd.smp[2][67108864];
   ```

   This selects the top left vertex at level 1. Note that the indices are quite different from those used before.

4. Execute the following.

   ```
   select -r subd.sme[257][67108864];
   ```

   This selects the front edge at level 1.

5. Execute the following.

```
select -r subd.smf[1024][0];
```

This selects the front face at level 0.

6. Execute the following.

```
select -r subd.smm[131];
```

This selects the front middle texture coordinate. Note that texture coordinates don't need two indices to access them.

C++ API

Unlike MEL, it is possible to use 64-bit integers in the C++ API. 64-bit integers are stored using the **MUint64** data type. The **MUint64** is divided into a sequence of bits to identify the various parts that reference a component.

Although it is possible to extract these values directly from the **MUint64** variable using shifts and bit masks, this isn't recommended. Fortunately, Maya provides a convenience class, **MFnSubdNames**, to access the various parts of the **MUint64** type. It includes a variety of member functions that can split an **MUint64** into its parts as well as construct a new one from a given series of parts.

10.3.2 CREASES

Each vertex and edge can be tagged as being creased. It is important to note that crease tags are inherited. If a vertex at level 0 is marked as creased, all of its child vertices at finer levels will inherit this tag and thus will also be creased. This also applies to edges.

Full and partial creases are implemented somewhat differently. This discussion covers edges, but the same approach applies to vertices. When a full crease is applied, another finer level of refinement will be created if it doesn't exist already. All finer levels, including those that might be created later, will inherit the crease tag.

When a partial crease is applied, another two finer levels of refinement around the selected edges are created if they don't exist already. The selected edges will be assigned crease tags, although none of their finer-level edges will. This means that the crease tags are not inherited by the finer-level edges. The vertices associated with the edge in the next and finer level are moved to simulate a partial crease.

When a vertex or edge at a coarser level has its creasing reset or changed, all child vertices and edges have their creasing tags removed. This effectively resets them to inherit their parent's current crease settings.

C++ API

If there is a need to retrieve all creased vertices and edges in a subdivision surface and apply that to a similar subdivision surface, the `MFnSubd::creasesGetAll` function shouldn't be used. This function will return a list of all vertices and edges that have their creases explicitly set. This means that it will not list those vertices and edges that have their creasing turned on by inheritance from their parents. As such, it is important to copy the crease information for every vertex and edge in the subdivision surface and not just those that are explicitly set.

10.3.3 UV TEXTURE COORDINATES

Texture coordinates can be optionally assigned to the subdivision surface. These texture coordinates are face-vertex texture coordinates, which means that each vertex in a given face can have its individual texture coordinates. Texture coordinates can be edited in the **Texture Editor** in the usual way.

In terms of initializing the texture coordinates at finer levels, if the control mesh has texture coordinates these will be transferred to the vertices at the next level. The new texture coordinates are calculated using the same subdivision scheme as those for calculating new vertices. The subdivision scheme is used for propagating texture coordinates through all hierarchical levels. Once the initial texture coordinates are assigned, they can be edited as usual.

10.3.4 MEL

1. Ensure that the `MAYA_SCRIPT_PATH` is set up correctly. (See Section 1.1.2 for further details.)

2. Execute the following.

```
source subdInfo1;
```

3. Open the **CubeSubdShaded.ma** scene.

4. Select the **subd** object.

5. To query the subdivision surface, execute the following.

```
subdInfo1("all");
```

All face and vertex data is output.

```
|subd
Levels: 3 Max Levels: 13
Level: 0
 Polygons: 6
 Polygon #0
 Vertices: 4
  Vertex #0
  Position: (-0.5, -0.5, 0.5)
  UV: (0, 0)
  Valence: 3
  Vertex #1
...
```

The subdInfo1 procedure takes a filter string that specifies what type of data to output.

6. To display only those vertices that have been moved, execute the following.

```
subdInfo1("editsOnly");
```

The list of edited vertices is output.

```
|subd
Levels: 3 Max Levels: 13
Level: 0
 Edited Vertices:
 subd.smp[0][0:3]
 subd.smp[256][2:3]
 subd.smp[512][2:3]
Level: 1
 Edited Vertices:
 subd.smp[2][67108864]
Level: 2
 Edited Vertices:
```

Note that the vertices are specified in compact form (subd.smp[0][0:3]) rather than the fully expected form (subd.smp[0][0], subd.smp[0][1]).

7. To display the vertices and edges that have been tagged as creased, execute the following.

```
subdInfo1("creasesOnly");
```

Those components marked as being creased are output.

```
|subd
Levels: 3 Max Levels: 13
Level: 0
 Creased Vertices:
 subd.smp[0][2]
 Creased Edges:
 subd.sme[256][1]
Level: 1
Level: 2
```

SOURCE CODE

MEL Script: `subdInfo1.mel`

```
global proc subdInfo1( string $filter )
{
   int $filterAll = true,
    $filterCreased = false,
    $filterEdits = false;
   switch( $filter)
   {
        case "all":
             break;

        case "creasesOnly":
             $filterCreased = true;
             $filterAll = $filterEdits = false;
             break;

        case "editsOnly":
             $filterEdits = true;
             $filterAll = $filterCreases = false;
             break;
```

```
        default:
            warning ("Unknown filter specified: " + $filter);
            return;
            break;
    }

string $subdShape;
string $rels[];
string $selection[] = `ls -selection -long`;
for( $sel in $selection )
{
    $subdShape = "";
    $rels = `listRelatives $sel`;
    if( size($rels) && `objectType -isType "subdiv" $rels[0]` )
        $subdShape = $rels[0];
    else
    {
        if( `objectType -isType "subdiv" $sel` )
        $subdShape = $sel;
    }

    if( $subdShape == "" )
        continue;

    print ($sel + "\n");
    int $nLevels = `subdiv -query -deepestLevel $subdShape` + 1;
    int $maxLevels = `subdiv -query -maxPossibleLevel $subdShape`;

    print ("Levels: " + $nLevels + " Max Levels: " + $maxLevels +
        "\n");

    int $level;
    for( $level=0; $level < $nLevels; $level++ )
    {
        print ("Level: " + $level + "\n");

        if( $filterEdits )
        {
            querySubdiv -action 1 -level $level
                    -relative off $subdShape;
            string $vertsCompact[] = `ls -selection`;
            print(" Edited Vertices:\n" );
```

```
            for( $vertCompact in $vertsCompact )
                    print(" " + $vertCompact + "\n");
            continue;
    }

    if( $filterCreased )
    {
            querySubdiv -action 2 -level $level
                        -relative off $subdShape;
            string $vertsCompact[] = `ls -selection`;
            if( size($vertsCompact) )
            {
                    print(" Creased Vertices:\n" );
                    for( $vertCompact in $vertsCompact )
                            print(" " + $vertCompact + "\n");
            }

            querySubdiv -action 3 -level $level
                        -relative off $subdShape;
            string $edgesCompact[] = `ls -selection`;
            if( size($edgesCompact) )
            {
                    print(" Creased Edges:\n" );
                    for( $edgeCompact in $edgesCompact )
                            print(" " + $edgeCompact + "\n");
            }

            continue;
    }

    querySubdiv -action 4 -level $level
                -relative off $subdShape;
    string $faces[] = `ls -selection -flatten`;
    print (" Polygons: " + size($faces) + "\n");

    int $f;
    for( $f=0; $f < size($faces); $f++ )
    {
        print (" Polygon #" + $f + "\n");

        string $vertsCompact[] = `subdListComponentConversion
                            -fromFace -toVertex $faces[$f]`;
        string $verts[] = `ls -flatten $vertsCompact`;
```

```
            string $uvsCompact[] = `subdListComponentConversion
                                   -fromFace -toUV $faces[$f]`;
            string $uvs[] = `ls -flatten $uvsCompact`;
            print(" Vertices: " + size($verts) + "\n");

            int $v;
            float $pos[3];
            float $uv[2];
            for( $v = 0; $v < size($verts); $v++ )
            {
                    $pos = `pointPosition -w $verts[$v]`;
                    $uv = `getAttr $uvs[$v]`;

            string $edgesCompact[] = `subdListComponentConversion
                             -fromVertex -toEdge $verts[$v]`;
                string $edges[] = `ls -flatten $edgesCompact`;

                prin/t (" Vertex #" + $v + "\n");
                print (" Position: (" + $pos[0] + ", " +
                        $pos[1] + ", " + $pos[2] + ")\n");
                print (" UV: (" + $uv[0] + ", " +
                        $uv[1] + ")\n");
                print (" Valence: " + size($edges) +
                        "\n");

            }
        }
        }
    }
    select -r $selection;
}
```

SOURCE CODE EXPLANATION

MEL Script: `subdInfo1.mel`

The subdInfo1 procedure takes a single-string parameter, $filter. This defines what type of data the procedure will output.

```
global proc subdInfo1( string $filter )
{
```

There are three data filtering options: all, only creases, and only vertex edits.

```
int $filterAll = true,
    $filterCreased = false,
    $filterEdits = false;
switch( $filter)
{
    case "all":
        break;
    case "creasesOnly":
        $filterCreased = true;
        $filterAll = $filterEdits = false;
        break;
    case "editsOnly":
        $filterEdits = true;
        $filterAll = $filterCreases = false;
        break;
```

If the filter isn't supported, issue a warning and then exit the procedure.

```
    default:
        warning ("Unknown filter specified: " + $filter);
        return;
        break;
}
```

Iterate over all selected objects.

```
    ...
    string $selection[] = `ls -selection -long`;
    for( $sel in $selection )
    {
```

Determine if the object is the parent transform of a **subdiv** shape node or the object is itself a **subdiv** shape node.

```
        $subdShape = "";
        $rels = `listRelatives $sel`;
```

```
if( size($rels) && `objectType -isType "subdiv" $rels[0]` )
        $subdShape = $rels[0];
else
{
        if( `objectType -isType "subdiv" $sel` )
        $subdShape = $sel;
}
```

No subdivision surface was selected; thus continue on to the next object.

```
if( $subdShape == "" )
        continue;
```

The finest level in the hierarchy of the subdivision surface is determined using the subdiv command with the -deepestLevel flag. The total number of levels is this plus one, in that the base mesh must be included as it is level 0.

```
...
int $nLevels = `subdiv -query -deepestLevel $subdShape` + 1;
```

The maximum number of levels is determined. This is a constant value for all subdivision surfaces.

```
int $maxLevels = `subdiv -query -maxPossibleLevel $subdShape`;
```

All levels in the hierarchy are iterated over.

```
...
int $level;
for( $level=0; $level < $nLevels; $level++ )
{
```

If only the edited vertices are requested, these are now output.

```
...
if( $filterEdits )
    {
```

The `querySubdiv` command called with the `-action` 1 flag selects all vertices that have been edited for the given level. The command returns a variety of information, depending on the setting of the `-action` flag.

```
querySubdiv -action 1 -level $level
            -relative off $subdShape;
```

Because the vertices are now selected, they are retrieved using the `ls` command. The `-flatten` flag isn't used, and thus the vertices are listed in their compact form.

```
string $vertsCompact[] = `ls -selection`;
```

The list of edited vertices is then output.

```
print(" Edited Vertices:\n" );
    ...
}
```

If the procedure was called to display only those vertices and edges tagged as creases, the next section is executed.

```
if( $filterCreased )
{
```

The `querySubdiv` command is called with the `-action` 2 flag. This selects all vertices, in the given level, that have been tagged as a crease.

```
querySubdiv -action 2 -level $level
            -relative off $subdShape;
```

The vertices are retrieved from the current selection.

```
string $vertsCompact[] = `ls -selection`;
```

The list of vertices is output.

```
if( size($vertsCompact) )
{
        print(" Creased Vertices:\n" );
        ...
}
```

To get the list of edges tagged as creases, the querySubdiv command is called with the -action 3 flag.

```
querySubdiv -action 3 -level $level
            -relative off $subdShape;
```

The list of edges is retrieved from the current selection.

```
string $edgesCompact[] = `ls -selection`;
```

The edges are then output.

```
if( size($edgesCompact) )
{
        print(" Creased Edges:\n" );
        ...
}

continue;
}
```

If the filter is set to "all", the following section is executed. The list of all faces for the given level is retrieved using the querySubdiv command with the -action 4 flag.

```
querySubdiv -action 4 -level $level
            -relative off $subdShape;
```

The list of faces is retrieved from the selection. The selection list is flattened so that the final list contains each face listed individually.

```
string $faces[] = `ls -selection -flatten`;
...
```

Each face in the level is iterated over.

```
int $f;
for( $f=0; $f < size($faces); $f++ )
{
    ...
```

All vertices in the current face are retrieved using the `subdListComponentConversion` command. It will convert the face into all vertices that make it up.

```
string $vertsCompact[] = `subdListComponentConversion
                -fromFace -toVertex $faces[$f]`;
```

Because the returned list is in expanded form, each vertex is listed individually.

```
string $verts[] = `ls -flatten $vertsCompact`;
```

The `subdListComponentConversion` command is also used to determine all uv texture coordinates for the current face.

```
string $uvsCompact[] = `subdListComponentConversion
                -fromFace -toUV $faces[$f]`;
```

The texture coordinate list is expanded. There will be one texture coordinate for each vertex in the face.

```
string $uvs[] = `ls -flatten $uvsCompact`;
...
```

Each of the vertices is iterated over.

```
...
for( $v=0; $v < size($verts); $v++ )
{
```

The world space position of the vertex is determined using the `pointPosition` command with the -w flag. If the object space position of the vertex is needed, simply use `$pos = `getAttr $verts[$v]`;`.

```
$pos = `pointPosition -w $verts[$v]`;
```

The uv coordinate is retrieved by using the `getAttr` command. It returns an array of two floats.

```
$uv = `getAttr $uvs[$v]`;
```

There is no standard MEL command to give the valency of a vertex. It can be calculated, however, by counting the number of edges sharing the vertex. The `subdListComponentConversion` command is called with the `-fromVertex` and `-toEdge` flags to retrieve all shared edges of the given vertex.

```
string $edgesCompact[] = `subdListComponentConversion
                  -fromVertex -toEdge $verts[$v]`;
```

The list of edges is expanded. The number of elements in this array is the valency of the current vertex.

```
string $edges[] = `ls -flatten $edgesCompact`;
```

The vertex data (position, uv texture coordinate, and valency) are output.

```
print (" Vertex #" + $v + "\n");
                ...
                }
            }
        }
    }
```

After all the data is output, the original selection is restored. This is because the `querySubdiv` command stores its result by changing the current selection.

```
select -r $selection;
}
```

10.3.5 C++ API

The **SubdInfo1** plug-in demonstrates the following.

- Retrieving the selected subdivision surface(s)

- Accessing the subdivision surface information (levels, maximum number of levels, polygons, assigned shader, creases, vertices, positions, normals, uv texture coordinates, and valences)

- Printing out the subdivision surface information

1. Open the **SubdInfo1** workspace.

2. Compile it and load the resulting `subdInfo1` plug-in file in Maya.

3. If the **subdInfo1.mel** file was sourced during the current session, restart Maya. Otherwise, select **File | New Scene**.

4. Open the **SubdCubeShaded.ma** scene.

5. Select the **subd** object.

6. Execute the following.

```
subdInfo1;
```

A variety of information about the subdivision surface is output.

```
// |subd
Levels: 3 Max Levels: 13
Level 0
 Polygons: 6
 Polygon #0
 Shader: initialShadingGroup
 Creased Edges:
 Vertices: 4
 Vertex #0
  Position: (-0.5, -0.5, 0.5)
  Normal: (-1.599976, -1.599976, 1.599976)
  UV: (0, 0)
  Valence: 3
 Vertex #1
  ...
```

7. To display a list of all vertex and edge creases, execute the following.

```
subdInfo1 -creasesOnly;
```

The list of vertices and edges is output to the **Script Editor**, as well as a command result.

```
// |subd
Vertex: |subd.smp[0][2] (Relevant)
Edge: |subd.sme[256][1] (Irrelevant)

// Result: |subd.smp[0][2] |subd.sme[256][1] //
```

Because the list of vertices and edges is output from the command, they can be used in other MEL statements.

8. To select all vertices and edges tagged with creases, execute the following.

```
select -r `subdInfo1 -creasesOnly`;
```

The vertex and edge, tagged with a crease, are selected.

9. The list of vertices that have been edited can be output as follows.

```
select -r subd;
subdInfo1 -editsOnly;
```

The list of edited vertices is output to the **Script Editor**, as well as a command result.

```
// |subd
Vertex: |subd.smp[2][67108864])

// Result: |subd.smp[2][67108864] //
```

10. To select all edited vertices, use the following.

```
select -r `subdInfo1 -editsOnly`;
```

SOURCE CODE

Plug-in: `SubdInfo1`
File: `SubdInfo1Cmd.cpp`

```cpp
DeclareSimpleCommand( subdInfo1, "David Gould", "1.0" );

MStatus subdInfo1::doIt( const MArgList& args )
{
    MStatus stat = MS::kSuccess;

    MSelectionList selection;
    MGlobal::getActiveSelectionList( selection );

    MDagPath dagPath;
    MObject component;

    bool filterAll = true,
            filterCreases = true,
            filterEdits = true;
    unsigned int index;
    index = args.flagIndex( "co", "creasesOnly" );
    if( index != MArgList::kInvalidArgIndex )
    {
        args.get( index+1, filterCreases );
        filterAll = filterEdits = false;
    }
    index = args.flagIndex( "eo", "editsOnly" );
    if( index != MArgList::kInvalidArgIndex )
    {
        args.get( index+1, filterCreases );
        filterAll = filterCreases = false;
    }

    unsigned int i, j, k, m, level, nLevels, nMaxLevels, nPolysLevel0;
    unsigned int index0, index1;
    MUint64Array polyIds, childPolyIds, vertIds, edgeIds;
    MUint64 polyId, vertId;
    MPoint pt;
    MVector vec, norm;
```

```
int valence;
bool isBoundary, isCreased, hasUVs, hasOffset, found;
MDoubleArray uCoords, vCoords;
MObjectArray shaders;
MUint64Array polyIdsWithShader;
MIntArray shaderIds;
MObject shader;
MUint64Array filteredComponents;
MString str;
MString relevancy;

MString txt;
MItSelectionList iter( selection );
for ( ; !iter.isDone(); iter.next() )
{
      iter.getDagPath( dagPath, component );

      MFnSubd subdFn( dagPath, &stat );
      if( !stat )
            continue;

      txt += dagPath.fullPathName() + "\n";

      nLevels = subdFn.levelMaxCurrent() + 1;
      nMaxLevels = subdFn.levelMaxAllowed();

      if( filterAll )
      {
            subdFn.getConnectedShaders( dagPath.instanceNumber(),
                  shaders, polyIdsWithShader, shaderIds );
            txt += MString("Levels: ") + nLevels +
                  " Max Levels: " + nMaxLevels + "\n";
      }

      polyIds.clear();
      nPolysLevel0 = (unsigned int) subdFn.polygonCount(0);
      for( i=0; i < nPolysLevel0; i++ )
            polyIds.append( MFnSubdNames::baseFaceIdFromIndex(i) );

      for( level=0; level < nLevels; level++ )
      {
```

```
if( filterAll )
{
      txt += MString("Level ") + level + "\n";
      txt += MString(" Polygons: ") +
            subdFn.polygonCount( level ) + "\n";
}

childPolyIds.clear();

for( i=0; i < polyIds.length(); i++ )
{
      polyId = polyIds[i];

      if( filterAll )
      {
            txt += MString(" Polygon #") + i + "\n";

            shader = MObject::kNullObj;
            for( k=0; k < polyIdsWithShader.length(); k++ )
            {
                  if( polyId == polyIdsWithShader[k] &&
                    shaderIds[k] ! = -1 )
                  {
                        shader = shaders[ shaderIds[k] ];
                        MFnDependencyNode depFn( shader );
                        txt += (" Shader: ") +
                              depFn.name() + "\n";

                        break;
                  }
            }
      }

      if( filterCreases )
      {
      if( filterAll )
            txt += " Creased Edges:";

      subdFn.polygonEdges( polyId, edgeIds );
      for( k=0; k < edgeIds.length(); k++ )
      {
```

```
            if( subdFn.edgeIsCreased( edgeIds[k] ) )
            {
                  if( subdFn.edgeCreaseRelevant(
                        edgeIds[k] ) )
                        relevancy = "Relevant";
                  else
                        relevancy = "Irrelevant";

                  if( filterAll )
                        txt += MString(" ") + k +
                              " (" + relevancy + ")";
                  else
                  {
                  found = false;
                  for( m=0;
                        m < filteredComponents.length();
                     m++ )
                  {
                        if( edgeIds[k] ==
                              filteredComponents[m] )
                        {
                              found = true;
                              break;
                        }
                  }

                  if( !found )
                  {
                  MFnSubdNames::toSelectionIndices(
                        edgeIds[k], index0, index1 );
                  str = dagPath.fullPathName() + ".sme[" +
                        index0 + "][" + index1 + "]";
                  txt += "Edge: " + str + " (" +
                        relevancy + ")\n";
                  appendToResult( MString(" ") + str );
                  filteredComponents.append( edgeIds[k] );
                  }
            }
      }
```

```
if( filterAll )
    txt += "\n";
}

if( filterAll )
{
    hasUVs = subdFn.polygonHasVertexUVs( polyId );
    if( hasUVs )
        subdFn.polygonGetVertexUVs( polyId,
            uCoords, vCoords );

    txt += MString(" Vertices: ") +
        subdFn.polygonVertexCount(polyId) +
        "\n";
}

subdFn.polygonVertices( polyId, vertIds );
for( j=0; j < vertIds.length(); j++ )
{
    vertId = vertIds[j];

    subdFn.vertexPositionGet( vertId, pt,
                    MSpace::kWorld );
    subdFn.vertexEditGet( vertId, vec,
                    MSpace::kWorld );
    hasOffset = vec != MVector::zero;
    valence = subdFn.vertexValence( vertId );
    subdFn.vertexNormal( vertId, norm );
    isBoundary = subdFn.vertexIsBoundary( vertId );
    isCreased = subdFn.vertexIsCreased( vertId );

    if( filterAll )
    {
        txt += MString(" Vertex #") + j;
        if( isBoundary )
            txt += " (Boundary)";
    }

    if( filterCreases && isCreased )
    {
    if( subdFn.vertexCreaseRelevant( vertId ) )
        relevancy = "Relevant";
```

```
        else
             relevancy = "Irrelevant";

        if( filterAll )
             txt += " (Creased - " + relevancy + ")";
        else
        {
             found = false;
             for( m=0;
                 m < filteredComponents.length();
                 m++ )
             {
                  if(vertId==filteredComponents[m])
                  {
                       found = true;
                       break;
                  }
             }

             if( !found )
             {
             MFnSubdNames::toSelectionIndices( vertId,
                       index0, index1 );
             str = dagPath.fullPathName() + ".smp[" +
                  index0 + "][" + index1 + "]";
             txt += "Vertex: " + str + " (" +
                  relevancy + ")\n";
             appendToResult( MString(" ") + str );
             filteredComponents.append( vertId );
             }
        }
    }

    if( filterAll )
         txt += "\n";

    if( filterAll )
    {
         txt += MString(" Position: (") +
              pt.x + ", " + pt.y + ", " +
              pt.z + ")";
```

```
            if( hasOffset )
                    txt += MString(" Offset: (") +
                    vec.x + ", " + vec.y + ", " +
                    vec.z + ")";
            txt += "\n";
    }
    else
    {

            if( filterEdits && hasOffset )
            {
            found = false;
            for( m=0;
                m < filteredComponents.length();
                m++ )
            {
                    if( vertId==filteredComponents[m] )
                    {
                            found = true;
                            break;
                    }
            }

            if( !found )
            {
            MFnSubdNames::toSelectionIndices( vertId,
                            index0, index1 );
            str = dagPath.fullPathName() + ".smp[" +
                    index0 + "][" + index1 + "]";
            txt += "Vertex: " + str + ")\n";
            appendToResult( MString(" ") + str );
            filteredComponents.append( vertId );
            }
    }
    }

    if( filterAll )
    {
            txt += MString(" Normal: (") +
                    norm.x + ", " + norm.y + ", " +
                    norm.z + ")\n";
```

```
                                    if( hasUVs )
                                         txt += MString(" UV: (") +
                                         uCoords[j] + ", " + vCoords[j] +
                                         ")\n";

                                    txt += MString(" Valence: ") +
                                         valence + "\n";
                               }
                          }

                          subdFn.polygonChildren( polyId, childPolyIds );
                     }

                     polyIds = childPolyIds;
               }
          }

     MGlobal::displayInfo( txt );

     return MS::kSuccess;
}
```

SOURCE CODE EXPLANATION

Plug-in: `SubdInfo1`
File: `SubdInfo1Cmd.cpp`

The **subdInfo1** command takes two command flags that define the information filtering.

```
     ...
     bool filterAll = true,
          filterCreases = true,
          filterEdits = true;
     unsigned int index;
```

The `-creaseOnly` flag will cause the command to only output vertices and edges that have been tagged as creased.

```
     index = args.flagIndex( "co", "creasesOnly" );
     if( index != MArgList::kInvalidArgIndex )
     {
          args.get( index+1, filterCreases );
          filterAll = filterEdits = false;
     }
```

The -editsOnly flag will cause the command to only output vertices that have been moved.

```
index = args.flagIndex( "eo", "editsOnly" );
if( index != MArgList::kInvalidArgIndex )
{
        args.get( index+1, filterCreases );
        filterAll = filterCreases = false;
}
```

All selected objects are iterated over.

```
...
MString txt;
MItSelectionList iter( selection );
for ( ; !iter.isDone(); iter.next() )
{
        iter.getDagPath( dagPath, component );
```

The **MFnSubd** function set is bound to the current object. If it fails, the object isn't a subdivision surface.

```
MFnSubd subdFn( dagPath, &stat );
if( !stat )
        continue;
```

The finest level in the subdivision surface is retrieved using the levelMaxCurrent function. The number of levels is this plus one, in that the base level needs to be taken into account.

```
...
nLevels = subdFn.levelMaxCurrent() + 1;
```

The levelMaxAllowed returns the maximum level any subdivision surface can have. This is a constant.

```
nMaxLevels = subdFn.levelMaxAllowed();
```

Each face, at any level, can be assigned an individual shader group. It is important to note that shaders assigned to faces at finer levels take precedence over shaders assigned at coarser levels. To get the currently assigned shader, the getConnectedShaders function is used. Given the instance number of the current object, a list of shaders, 64-bit polygon IDs, and shader indices is returned. The shaders list is a list of **MObjects** that reference individual shading groups. The **polyIdsWithShader** list contains a list of 64-bit polygon IDs for those polygons that have been assigned a shader. The **shaderIds** list is an array of indices into the shaders list. For the *i*th element in the **polyIdsWithShader** list there is a corresponding *i*th element in the **shaderIds** list. As such, the **polyIdsWithShader** list is the same size as the **shaderIds** list. Thus, the shader group assigned to the *i*th polygon is retrieved as follows.

shader[shaderIds[i]]

If the **shaderIds** element is set to -1, there is no corresponding shader.

```
if( filterAll )
{
        subdFn.getConnectedShaders( dagPath.instanceNumber(),
                shaders, polyIdsWithShader, shaderIds );
        ...
}
```

All polygon IDs from the base mesh are retrieved and stored in the polyIds array.

```
polyIds.clear();
nPolysLevel0 = (unsigned int) subdFn.polygonCount(0);
for( i=0; i < nPolysLevel0; i++ )
```

A 64-bit ID is created from the base mesh's linear polygon index.

```
polyIds.append( MFnSubdNames::baseFaceIdFromIndex(i) );
```

Each of the hierarchical levels in the subdivision surface is iterated.

```
for( level=0; level < nLevels; level++ )
{
```

The current level is output, as well as the number of polygons in the current level.

```
if( filterAll )
{
        txt += MString("Level ") + level + "\n";
        txt += MString(" Polygons: ") +
                subdFn.polygonCount( level ) + "\n";
}
```

The `childPolysIds` will eventually contain a list of all child polygons of the polygons in the current level. It is initially empty.

```
childPolyIds.clear();
```

Each polygon in the current level is iterated over.

```
for( i=0; i < polyIds.length(); i++ )
{
```

The `polyId` variable is initialized to the polygon's 64-bit ID.

```
polyId = polyIds[i];
```

This section determines if the current polygon is assigned an individual shading group.

```
if( filterAll )
{
        ...
        shader = MObject::kNullObj;
```

All polygon IDs that have been assigned as shaders are iterated over.

```
for( k=0; k < polyIdsWithShader.length(); k++ )
{
```

A shader has been assigned if the current polygon ID matches the current polygon ID in the `polyIdsWithShader` list and the shader index isn't set to −1.

```
if( polyId == polyIdsWithShader[k] &&
  shaderIds[k] != -1 )
{
```

The shader group is retrieved using the `shaderId`'s index into the `shaders` list.

```
shader = shaders[ shaderIds[k] ];
```

The shader group is an **MObject** that is used to intialize the **MFnDependencyNode** function set. The shader group's name is then output.

```
MFnDependencyNode depFn( shader );
txt += (" Shader: ") +
        depFn.name() + "\n";
break;
```

If requested, the creased edges information is now output.

```
...
if( filterCreases )
{
```

The list of edges associated with the given polygon is retrieved using the `polygonEdges` function.

```
...
subdFn.polygonEdges( polyId, edgeIds );
```

Each edge is iterated over.

```
for( k=0; k < edgeIds.length(); k++ )
{
```

If the edge is creased, it is output.

```
if( subdFn.edgeIsCreased( edgeIds[k] ) )
{
```

The `relevancy` string variable is initialized. An edge crease is relevant if it is different from its parent's.

```
if( subdFn.edgeCreaseRelevant(
    edgeIds[k] ) )
        relevancy = "Relevant";
else
        relevancy = "Irrelevant";
```

If outputting all information, the face-relative index of the edge is output as well as its relevancy.

```
if( filterAll )
    txt += MString(" ") + k +
        " (" + relevancy + ")";
```

An attempt is made to find the current edge in the list of `filteredComponents`. This list contains 64-bit IDs to all candidate components so far visited.

```
else
{
found = false;
for( m=0;
    m < filteredComponents.length();
    m++ )
{
    if( edgeIds[k] ==
        filteredComponents[m] )
    {
            found = true;
            break;
    }
}
```

If the edge isn't already in the list, two 32-bit IDs are generated from the 64-bit ID. These two 32-bit IDs are what MEL uses.

```
if( !found )
{
MFnSubdNames::toSelectionIndices(
            edgeIds[k], index0, index1 );
```

The explicit path to the component is then generated.

```
str = dagPath.fullPathName() + ".sme[" +
            index0 + "][" + index1 + "]";
```

Additional information about the edge is added to the `txt` string variable, which will ultimately output to the **Script Editor**.

```
txt += "Edge: " + str + " (" +
            relevancy + ")\n";
```

The component's path is added to the command's result.

```
appendToResult( MString(" ") + str );
```

The current edge is added to the list of already visited components.

```
filteredComponents.append( edgeIds[k] );
}
}
}
```

If the polygon has uv texture coordinates, they are stored in two separate arrays, `uCoords` and `vCoords`.

```
...
if( filterAll )
{
    hasUVs = subdFn.polygonHasVertexUVs( polyId );
```

```
if( hasUVs )
        subdFn.polygonGetVertexUVs( polyId,
                uCoords, vCoords );
```

The total number of vertices in the polygon is added to the output.

```
txt += MString(" Vertices: ") +
        subdFn.polygonVertexCount(polyId) +
        "\n";
}
```

The 64-bit IDs of all vertices in the polygon are retrieved using the `polygonVertices` function.

```
subdFn.polygonVertices( polyId, vertIds );
```

Each vertex is iterated over.

```
for( j=0; j < vertIds.length(); j++ )
{
        vertId = vertIds[j];
```

The world space position of the vertex is retrieved. Note that this is the vertex's final position after any edits are applied.

```
subdFn.vertexPositionGet( vertId, pt,
                        MSpace::kWorld );
```

The vertex's edited offset is retrieved. If the vertex hasn't been moved, this vector will be a zero vector.

```
subdFn.vertexEditGet( vertId, vec,
                        MSpace::kWorld );
hasOffset = vec != MVector::zero;
```

The valence of the vertex is next retrieved.

```
valence = subdFn.vertexValence( vertId );
```

The normal at the vertex is retrieved using the `vertexNormal` function.

```
subdFn.vertexNormal( vertId, norm );
```

If the mesh has a non-closed surface and this vertex is on the outer edge of the surface, the `vertexIsBoundary` function will return `true`.

```
isBoundary = subdFn.vertexIsBoundary( vertId );
```

Whether the vertex is tagged as creased is next determined.

```
isCreased = subdFn.vertexIsCreased( vertId );
```

If the command is outputting creasing and the vertex is creased, the next section is executed.

```
...
if( filterCreases && isCreased )
{
```

The relevancy of the vertex's crease is determined using the `vertexCreaseRelevant` function.

```
if( subdFn.vertexCreaseRelevant( vertId ) )
        relevancy = "Relevant";
else
        relevancy = "Irrelevant";
```

If outputting all information, the fact that the vertex is creased as well as its relevancy is output.

```
if( filterAll )
        txt += " (Creased - " + relevancy + ")";
else
{
```

The current vertex is searched for in the `filteredComponents` list.

```
found = false;
for( m=0;
    m < filteredComponents.length();
    m++ )
{
    if(vertId==filteredComponents[m])
    {
        found = true;
        break;
    }
}
```

If the vertex isn't found, it is output.

```
if( !found )
{
```

The 64-bit vertex ID is converted to a pair of 32-bit IDs compatible with MEL.

```
MFnSubdNames::toSelectionIndices( vertId,
                index0, index1 );
```

The complete path to the vertex component is generated.

```
str = dagPath.fullPathName() + ".smp[" +
        index0 + "][" + index1 + "]";
```

The vertex information is added to the output text.

```
txt += "Vertex: " + str + " (" +
        relevancy + ")\n";
```

The vertex's complete path is added to the command's result.

```
appendToResult( MString(" ") + str );
```

The vertex's 64-bit ID is added to the list of components already visited.

```
                    filteredComponents.append( vertId );
                }
        }
    }
```

The position and offset of the current vertex is output.

```
            ...
            if( filterAll )
            {
                    txt += MString(" Position: (") +
                            pt.x + ", " + pt.y + ", " +
                            pt.z + ")";
                    if( hasOffset )
                            txt += MString(" Offset: (") +
                            vec.x + ", " + vec.y + ", " +
                            vec.z + ")";
                    txt += "\n";
            }
            else
            {
```

If filtering all vertices that have been edited and the vertex has an offset, it is output.

```
                    if( filterEdits && hasOffset )
                    {
```

The vertex is first searched for in the list of components already visited.

```
                    found = false;
                    for( m=0;
                        m < filteredComponents.length();
                        m++ )
                    {
                            if( vertId==filteredComponents[m] )
```

```
                            {
                                found = true;
                                break;
                            }
                        }
```

Because the vertex isn't in the list it can be output.

```
                        if( !found )
                        {
```

The pair of 32-bit IDs are generated from the 64-bit vertex ID. As before, the vertex data is then output.

```
                            MFnSubdNames::toSelectionIndices( vertId,
                                        index0, index1 );

                            ...
                        }
                    }
                }
```

The normal, uv texture coordinate, and valence are added to the output string.

```
                if( filterAll )
                {
                    txt += MString(" Normal: (") +
                        norm.x + ", " + norm.y + ", " +
                        norm.z + ")\n";
                    if( hasUVs )
                        txt += MString(" UV: (") +
                        uCoords[j] + ", " + vCoords[j] +
                        ")\n";

                    txt += MString(" Valence: ") +
                        valence + "\n";

                }
            }
```

The child polygons are retrieved for the current polygon. The `polygonChildren` function will simply append the 64-bit polygon IDs of the children to the `childPolyIds` list.

```
                subdFn.polygonChildren( polyId, childPolyIds );
            }
```

Now that all polygons at the current level have been visited, the new list of polygons to visit is simply all child polygons.

```
            polyIds = childPolyIds;
        }
    }
```

The final output text is displayed in the **Script Editor**.

```
    MGlobal::displayInfo( txt );

    return MS::kSuccess;
}
```

10.4 CREATING AND CONVERTING SUBDIVISION SURFACES

A subdivision surface can be created from either a polygonal mesh or NURBS surface. It can also be converted back to a polygonal mesh or NURBS surface.

10.4.1 POLYGONAL MESH TO SUBDIVISION SURFACE

When creating a subdivision surface from a polygonal mesh, it must satisfy the following constraints.

- **Manifold Geometry**

  The polygons must be manifold; that is, an edge must have a maximum of two neighboring faces. Adjacent faces can't be flipped. Faces can't share just a single vertex rather than an entire edge.

- **Vertex Valence**

  A vertex must have a valence of at least 2.

- **Vertex Count Per Face**

  Each face must have 256 vertices or fewer.

- **Vertex Count Per Mesh**

  The total number of vertices in the polygonal mesh must be 8,388,608 (2^{23}) or less.

MEL

The simplest method of creating a subdivision surface from a polygonal mesh is to first create the polygonal mesh that will become the base mesh and then to apply the `polyToSubdiv` command.

1. Open the **CubeMesh.ma** scene.

2. Select the **cube** object.

3. To convert the cube to a subdivision surface, execute the following.

```
polyToSubdiv;
```

The **polyToSubd1** object is created with a child **subdiv** shape, **polyToSubdShape1**, as shown in Figure 10.7.

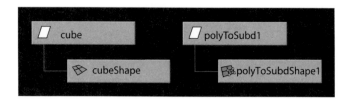

FIGURE 10.7 The polyToSubd1 object created.

The **cubeShape** node is connected to the **polyToSubdShape1** node. The **cubeShape's worldMesh[0]** attribute feeds into the **polyToSubdiv1** node's **inMesh** attribute. The **polyToSubdiv1** node produces a subdivision surface in its **outSubdiv** attribute, as shown in Figure 10.8. This is fed into the **polyToSubdShape1** shape node.

FIGURE 10.8 Subdivision surface construction history.

Because it is a subdivision surface derived from the cube, the surface is smaller than the cube and is thus inside it. As such, it isn't directly visible in the shaded viewport.

4. Press the 4 key or select **Shading | Wireframe** from the viewport's panel.

   The **polyToSubd1** object is now visible.

5. Select the **polyToSubd1** object.

6. Select **Subdiv Surfaces | Standard Mode** from the main menu.

   The cube shape is now deleted. All construction history is deleted when a subdivision surface is displayed in standard mode.

It is possible to store all hierarchical edits and crease information as blind data on another polygonal mesh. When the polygonal mesh is converted to a subdivision surface, the blind data is used to apply the hierarchical edits and crease information to the new subdivision surface.

1. Open the **CubeSubdShaded.ma** scene.

   The subdivision surface information from the **subd** object will be copied to a new polygonal mesh. Because the base mesh of the **subd** is a cube, a new cube is created to hold the blind data. If the destination polygonal mesh doesn't have the same topology or number of faces as the subdivision surface's base mesh, the blind data will be created but the validity of the results will not be guaranteed.

2. Select **Create | Polygonal Primitives | Cube**.

3. The new cube object is moved to the right by executing the following.

```
move -r 0 0 -1;
```

4. Execute the following.

```
subdToBlind -includeCreases true subdShape pCubeShape1;
```

A series of **subdBlindData** nodes is created that contains the subdivision surface edits that are necessary to transform the cube base mesh into the final subdivision surface. Because the `-includeCreases` flag is set to `true`, the crease information is also copied to the blind data.

5. To create the subdivision surface from the cube, execute the following.

```
polyToSubdiv;
```

6. Press the 4 key or select **Shading | Wireframe** from the viewport's panel.

    The subdivision surface is now visible. The surface matches the original subdivision surface. When the `polyToSubdiv` command is executed it will automatically use the **subdBlindData** nodes to apply the hierarchical edits to the cube.

There also exists a command, **subdTransferUVsToCache**, for copying the uv texture coordinate information from a subdivision surface to a **polygonToSubd** node. It is important to note that this is an internal Maya command and thus should be used with caution.

C++ API

The **SubdCube** plug-in demonstrates the following.

*   Creating a subdivision surface from scratch

There isn't an easy means through the C++ API of automatically converting a polygonal mesh to a subdivision surface. Instead, the polygonal mesh can be created using the C++ API and then converted to a subdivision surface using the `polyToSubdiv` MEL command. If a simple polygon mesh (no uv texture coordinates) is all that is needed for the base mesh, the **MFnSubd** class can be used to crease the subdivision surface directly.

1. Open the **SubdCube** workspace.

2. Compile it and load the resulting `subdCube` plug-in file in Maya.

3. Select **File | New Scene**.

4. Execute the following.

```
subdCube;
```

The cube base mesh is subdivided, resulting in a spherically shaped surface, **subdiv1**.

5. Press the **5** key or select **Shading | Smooth Shade All** from the viewport menu.

6. Press the **3** key or select **Display | Subdiv Surface Smoothness | Fine**.

   The subdivision surface is shown shaded and much smoother.

SOURCE CODE

Plug-in: SubdCube

File: SubdCubeCmd.cpp

```
class SubdCubeCmd : public MPxCommand
{
public:
    virtual MStatus  doIt ( const MArgList& );
    virtual MStatus  redoIt();
    virtual MStatus  undoIt();
    virtual bool  isUndoable() const { return true; }

    static void *creator() { return new SubdCubeCmd; }

private:
    MObject subdTransform;
};

MStatus SubdCubeCmd::doIt ( const MArgList &args )
{
    return redoIt();
}

Mstatus SubdCubeCmd::redoIt()
{
    const MPoint pts[8] =
    {
        MPoint( -0.5, -0.5, 0.5 ),
        MPoint( 0.5, -0.5, 0.5 ),
        MPoint( 0.5, 0.5, 0.5 ),
        MPoint( -0.5, 0.5, 0.5 ),
        MPoint( 0.5, -0.5, -0.5 ),
        MPoint( 0.5, 0.5, -0.5 ),
        MPoint( -0.5, 0.5, -0.5 ),
        MPoint( -0.5, -0.5, -0.5 ),
    };
```

```
const int faces[6][4] =
{
      { 0, 1, 2, 3 },
      { 1, 4, 5, 2 },
      { 4, 7, 6, 5 },
      { 7, 0, 3, 6 },
      { 2, 5, 6, 3 },
      { 0, 7, 4, 1 }
};

MStatus stat;

unsigned int i, j;
MPointArray verts;
for( i=0; i < 8; i++ )
      verts.append( pts[i] );
MIntArray polyCounts, polyConnects;
for( i=0; i < 6; i++ )
{
      polyCounts.append( 4 );
      for( j=0; j < 4; j++ )
            polyConnects.append( faces[i][j] );
}

MFnSubd subdFn;
subdTransform = subdFn.createBaseMesh( false, 8, 6, verts,
                                    polyCounts, polyConnects );

MString cmd( "sets -e -fe initialShadingGroup " );
cmd += subdFn.name();
MGlobal::executeCommand( cmd );

cmd = MString("select -r ") + subdFn.name();
MGlobal::executeCommand( cmd );

   return stat;
}

Mstatus SubdCubeCmd::undoIt()
{
   MFnDagNode dagFn( subdTransform );
   MObject child;
```

```
      child = dagFn.child(0);
      MGlobal::deleteNode( child );
      MGlobal::deleteNode( subdTransform );

      return MS::kSuccess;
   }

MStatus initializePlugin( MObject obj )
{
   MFnPlugin plugin( obj, "David Gould", "1.0" );

   MStatus stat;
   stat = plugin.registerCommand( "subdCube", SubdCubeCmd::creator );
   if ( !stat )
         stat.perror( "registerCommand failed");

   return stat;
}

MStatus uninitializePlugin( MObject obj )
{
   MFnPlugin plugin( obj );

   MStatus  stat;
   stat = plugin.deregisterCommand( "subdCube" );
   if ( !stat )
         stat.perror( "deregisterCommand failed" );

   return stat;
}
```

SOURCE CODE EXPLANATION

Plug-in: SubdCube
File: SubdCubeCmd.cpp

The subdCube command is consistent with other **MPxCommand**s that support
undoing. The main work is done in the redoIt function.

```
   Mstatus SubdCubeCmd::redoIt()
   {
```

The eight points making up the vertices of the cube are defined.

```
const MPoint pts[8] =
{
        MPoint( -0.5, -0.5, 0.5 ),
        MPoint( 0.5, -0.5, 0.5 ),
        MPoint( 0.5, 0.5, 0.5 ),
        MPoint( -0.5, 0.5, 0.5 ),
        MPoint( 0.5, -0.5, -0.5 ),
        MPoint( 0.5, 0.5, -0.5 ),
        MPoint( -0.5, 0.5, -0.5 ),
        MPoint( -0.5, -0.5, -0.5 ),
};
```

The six faces that define the cube surface have their vertex indices listed.

```
const int faces[6][4] =
{
        { 0, 1, 2, 3 },
        { 1, 4, 5, 2 },
        { 4, 7, 6, 5 },
        { 7, 0, 3, 6 },
        { 2, 5, 6, 3 },
        { 0, 7, 4, 1 }
};
```

The vertex array is created from the `pts` array.

```
...
MPointArray verts;
for( i=0; i < 8; i++ )
        verts.append( pts[i] );
```

The number of vertices and their indices are put into the `polyCounts` and `polyConnects` arrays, respectively.

```
MIntArray polyCounts, polyConnects;
for( i=0; i < 6; i++ )
{
        polyCounts.append( 4 );
        for( j=0; j < 4; j++ )
                polyConnects.append( faces[i][j] );
}
```

The subdivision surface is created by specifying the base mesh using the createBaseMesh function. The parent **transform** node of the **subdiv** shape node is returned.

```
MFnSubd subdFn;
subdTransform = subdFn.createBaseMesh( false, 8, 6, verts,
                                       polyCounts, polyConnects );
```

The new subdivision surface is assigned the initial shading group.

```
MString cmd( "sets -e -fe initialShadingGroup " );
cmd += subdFn.name();
MGlobal::executeCommand( cmd );
```

The new subdivision surface is selected.

```
cmd = MString("select -r ") + subdFn.name();
MGlobal::executeCommand( cmd );

return stat;
}
```

10.4.2 SUBDIVISION SURFACE TO POLYGONAL MESH

The subdivision surface can be easily converted to a polygonal mesh. The base mesh or an approximate polygon surface to the original subdivision surface can be created.

MEL

1. Open the **CubeSubdShaded.ma** scene.

2. Select the **subd** object.

3. A subdivision surface can be converted to a polygonal mesh that serves as the base mesh of a subdivision surface that matches the original. To create this base mesh, execute the following.

```
subdToPoly -format 3 -depth 1;
```

Note that -depth 0 wasn't used even though this is, strictly speaking, the base mesh. The mesh at depth 0 is simply the cube. Converting it to a subdivision will not give the same subdivision surface as the current one. Given the changes applied to the cube, a mesh generated from depth 1 will, when converted to a subdivision surface, match the current one. The polygonal mesh, **subdTess1**, is generated. The -format flag is set to 3 to indicate that the subdivision mesh vertices should be used.

Alternatively, the following command could be used.

```
subdToPoly -extractPointPosition true -depth 1;
```

The lag defines whether the resulting mesh vertices are on the subdivision surface or off it. Because the base mesh is needed the points need to be off the surface.

At a given level, the -extractPointPosition flag defines whether the generated mesh vertices are those on the control mesh or those on the actual subdivision surface. When the flag is set to false (the default), the vertices from the level's control mesh are subdivided to determine their corresponding location on the subdivision surface. If the flag is true, the vertices from the level's control mesh are used.

4. Move it to the left so that it is easier to see by executing the following.

```
move -r 0 0 1;
```

5. Select **Modify | Convert | Polygons to Subdiv** from the main menu.

6. Press the **3** key or select **Display | Subdiv Surface Smoothness | Fine**.

The resulting subdivision surface matches the original. A more typical use of the subdToPoly command is to create a tessellated polygonal mesh that approximates the subdivision surface.

7. Open the **CubeSubdShaded.ma** scene.

8. Select the **subd** object.

9. To tessellate the subdivision surface, execute the following.

```
subdToPoly -sampleCount 4;
move -r 0 0 1;
```

The polygonal mesh generated is a close match to the subdivision surface. The mesh has a **subdivToPoly** node, **subdivToPoly1**, as part of its construction history. This can be changed to have the mesh automatically updated.

10. Execute the following to increase the surface detail.

```
setAttr subdivToPoly1.sampleCount 6;
```

C++ API

The **SubdToMesh** plug-in can be used to demonstrate the following.

- Creating a custom command to convert a subdivision surface into a mesh

The **MFnSubd** class is the main class for tessellating a subdivision surface, resulting in a polygonal mesh. Unfortunately, the **MFnSubd** member functions, `tesselate` (this is the spelling used in the API) and `tessellateViaNurbs`, don't offer the range of options that the `subdToPoly` command does. However, they do offer enough functionality to create a variety of tessellated polygonal meshes.

1. Open the **SubdToMesh** workspace.

2. Compile it and load the resulting `subdToMesh` plug-in file in Maya.

3. Open the **CubeSubdShaded.ma** scene.

4. Select the **subd** object.

5. Execute the following.

```
subdToMesh;
move -r 0 0 1;
```

A polygonal mesh approximating the subdivision surface is created.

6. Press the **z** key or select **Edit | Undo** from the main menu.

7. Select the **subd** object.

8. To create a more detailed mesh, execute the following.

```
subdToMesh -samples 8;
move -r 0 0 1;
```

A smoother polygonal surface is created. The `-samples` flag defines the number of rows and columns of vertex samples per face to be created.

9. Press the **z** key or select **Edit | Undo** from the main menu.

10. Select the **subd** object.

11. To create a mesh with adaptive tessellation, execute the following.

```
subdToMesh -uniform false;
move -r 0 0 1;
```

Where the subdivision surface is more detailed the mesh has more polygons. By default, the `-uniform` flag is set to `true`.

12. Press the **z** key or select **Edit | Undo** from the main menu.

13. Select the **subd** object.

14. When the tessellation is uniform the depth can be set.

```
subdToMesh -depth 3;
move -r 0 0 1;
```

A finely detailed polygonal mesh is generated. It is important to specify the `-depth` and `-samples` flags carefully. Setting them to a large number will result in a lot of polygons. Given uniform tessellation, each level 1 face will tessellate into approximately the following number of triangles.

triangles = 2 * 4$^{\text{depth-1}}$ * samples^2

15. Press the **z** key or select **Edit | Undo** from the main menu.

16. Select the **subd** object.

17. In addition to uniform and adaptive tessellation, it is possible to tessellate the subdivision surface via a NURBS surface.

```
subdToMesh -viaNurbs true;
move -r 0 0 1;
```

SOURCE CODE

Plug-in: `SubdToMesh`
File: `SubdToMeshCmd.cpp`

```cpp
class SubdToMesh : public MPxCommand
{
public:
    virtual MStatus  doIt ( const MArgList& );
    virtual MStatus  redoIt();
    virtual MStatus  undoIt();
    virtual bool  isUndoable() const { return true; }

    static void *creator() { return new SubdToMesh; }
    static MSyntax newSyntax();

private:
    bool viaNurbs;
    bool uniform;
    int depth;
    int samples;

    MDagPathArray selSubds;
    MObjectArray meshes;
};

const char *viaNurbsFlag = "-vn", *viaNurbsLongFlag = "-viaNurbs";
const char *uniformFlag = "-u", *uniformLongFlag = "-uniform";
const char *depthFlag = "-d", *depthLongFlag = "-depth";
const char *samplesFlag = "-s", *samplesLongFlag = "-samples";
```

```
MSyntax SubdToMesh::newSyntax()
{
 MSyntax syntax;

 syntax.addFlag( viaNurbsFlag, viaNurbsLongFlag, MSyntax::kBoolean );
 syntax.addFlag( uniformFlag, uniformLongFlag, MSyntax::kBoolean );
 syntax.addFlag( depthFlag, depthLongFlag, MSyntax::kLong );
 syntax.addFlag( samplesFlag, samplesLongFlag, MSyntax::kLong );

    syntax.enableQuery( false );
    syntax.enableEdit( false );

    return syntax;
}

MStatus SubdToMesh::doIt ( const MArgList &args )
{
    MStatus stat;

    viaNurbs = false;
    uniform = true;
    depth = 1;
    samples = 4;

    MArgDatabase argData( syntax(), args, &stat );
    if( !stat )
        return stat;

    if( argData.isFlagSet( viaNurbsFlag ) )
        argData.getFlagArgument( viaNurbsFlag, 0, viaNurbs );

    if( argData.isFlagSet( uniformFlag ) )
        argData.getFlagArgument( uniformFlag, 0, uniform );

    if( argData.isFlagSet( depthFlag ) )
        argData.getFlagArgument( depthFlag, 0, depth );

    if( argData.isFlagSet( samplesFlag ) )
        argData.getFlagArgument( samplesFlag, 0, samples );

    MSelectionList selection;
    MGlobal::getActiveSelectionList( selection );
```

```
    MDagPath dagPath;
    MItSelectionList iter( selection, MFn::kSubdiv );
    for ( ; !iter.isDone(); iter.next() )
    {
          iter.getDagPath( dagPath );
          selSubds.append( dagPath );
    }

    if( selSubds.length() == 0 )
    {
          MGlobal::displayWarning( "Select one or more subd surfaces." );
          return MS::kFailure;
    }

    return redoIt();
}

MStatus SubdToMesh::redoIt()
{
    meshes.clear();

    MObject meshTransform, mesh;
    MDagPath dagPath;
    unsigned int i;
    for( i=0; i < selSubds.length(); i++ )
    {
          dagPath = selSubds[i];

          MFnSubd subdFn( dagPath );
          meshTransform = viaNurbs ?
                      subdFn.tessellateViaNurbs() :
                      subdFn.tesselate( uniform, depth, samples );
          if( !meshTransform.isNull() )
          {
                MFnDagNode dagFn( meshTransform );
                mesh = dagFn.child(0);

                MFnMesh meshFn( mesh );
                meshes.append( mesh );
```

```
                    MString cmd( "sets -e -fe initialShadingGroup " );
                    cmd += meshFn.name();
                    MGlobal::executeCommand( cmd );
            }
    }

    MString cmd( "select -r" );
    for( i=0; i < meshes.length(); i++ )
    {
            MFnMesh meshFn( meshes[i] );
            cmd += MString(" ") + meshFn.name();
    }
    MGlobal::executeCommand( cmd );

    return MS::kSuccess;
}

MStatus SubdToMesh::undoIt()
{
    unsigned int i;
    for( i=0; i < meshes.length(); i++ )
    {
            MFnDagNode dagFn( meshes[i] );
            MObject parentTransform = dagFn.parent(0);
            MGlobal::deleteNode( meshes[i] );
            MGlobal::deleteNode( parentTransform );
    }

    return MS::kSuccess;
}

MStatus initializePlugin( MObject obj )
{
    MFnPlugin plugin( obj, "David Gould", "1.0" );

    MStatus stat;
    stat = plugin.registerCommand( "subdToMesh"",
                                    SubdToMesh::creator,
                                    SubdToMesh::newSyntax );
```

```
   if ( !stat )
        stat.perror( "registerCommand failed");

   return stat;
}

MStatus uninitializePlugin( MObject obj )
{
   MFnPlugin plugin( obj );

   MStatus stat;
   stat = plugin.deregisterCommand( "subdToMesh" );
   if ( !stat )
        stat.perror( "deregisterCommand failed" );

   return stat;
}
```

SOURCE CODE EXPLANATION

Plug-in: SubdToMesh
File: SubdToMeshCmd.cpp

The redoIt function contains the main functionality of the plug-in.

```
   MStatus SubdToMesh::redoIt()
   {
```

The list of created meshes is initially cleared.

```
   meshes.clear();
```

Each of the selected subdivision surfaces is iterated over.

```
   ...
   for( i=0; i < selSubds.length(); i++ )
   {
        dagPath = selSubds[i];
```

The **MFnSubd** function set is applied to the current subdivision surface.

```
   MFnSubd subdFn( dagPath );
```

If the `viaNurbs` variable is set, the `tessellateViaNurbs` function is called. It doesn't take any parameters. If this variable isn't set, the `tesselate` function is called. It takes three paramaters: `uniform`, `depth`, and `samples`. When `uniform` is set to `true`, the tessellation of the surface will be uniform. Otherwise, it will be adaptive. The `depth` variable determines how deep the uniform tessellation will be. The `samples` variable specifies how many position samples to make per face. Both functions return the parent transform of the resulting polygonal mesh.

```
meshTransform = viaNurbs ?
            subdFn.tessellateViaNurbs() :
            subdFn.tesselate( uniform, depth, samples );
```

The next section of code addresses the mesh to the list of meshes and ensures that it is included in the initial shading group.

```
if( !meshTransform.isNull() )
{
    MFnDagNode dagFn( meshTransform );
    mesh = dagFn.child(0);

    MFnMesh meshFn( mesh );
    meshes.append( mesh );

    MString cmd( "sets -e -fe initialShadingGroup " );
    cmd += meshFn.name();
    MGlobal::executeCommand( cmd );
}
}
...
```

10.4.3 NURBS SURFACE TO SUBDIVISION SURFACE

A non-trimmed NURBS surface can be converted to a subdivision surface. The basic methodology for the conversion is that the NURBS surface's hull is converted to a polygonal mesh. This mesh provides the base mesh for the subdivision surface. Unfortunately, because the Catmull-Clark subdivision scheme is different from the method used to generate NURBS surfaces, the resulting surfaces are different.

MEL

1. Press **Ctrl + N** or select **File | New Scene** from the main menu.

2. Select **Create | NURBS Primitives | Sphere**.

3. To convert the NURBS sphere to a subdivision surface, execute the following.

```
nurbsToSubdiv;
```

The subdivision surface is created. The parent transform is named **nurbsToSubd1**, and the child **subdiv** shape node is named **nurbsToSubdShape1**.

4. To see the subdivision surface more clearly, execute the following.

```
move -r 0 0 2;
```

5. Press the **3** key or select **Display | Subdiv Surface Smoothness | Fine**.

Because the subdivision surface is connected to the original NURBS surface, any changes to the NURBS surface will be reflected in the subdivision surface.

6. To see what the subdivision surface's base mesh looks like, execute the following.

```
setAttr nurbsToSubdShape1.dispResolution 0;
```

C++ API

There currently isn't a means for creating a subdivision surface from a NURBS surfaces using the C++ API. Instead, the `nurbsToSubdiv` MEL command should be called from within the plug-in.

10.4.4 SUBDIVISION SURFACE TO NURBS SURFACE

A subdivision surface can be easily converted to a NURBS surface. In fact, some subdivision surfaces (typically from level 2 onward) are exactly the same as a uniform bicubic B-spline. This is a simpler version of a NURBS surface.

MEL

1. Open the **CubeSubdShaded.ma** scene.

2. Select the **subd** object.

3. To convert to a NURBS surface, execute the following.

```
subdToNurbs;
move -r 0 0 1;
```

A series of NURBS surface patches, **subdToNurbsShape1_***, are created under the **surfaceVarGroup** node, **subdToNurbsShape1**. The **surfaceVarGroup** node is used to group and display an arbitrary number of NURBS surface shapes.

The NURBS surfaces are connected to the original subdivision surface via a **subdivToNurbs** node, **subdivToNurbs1**. If the subdivision surface changes, the NURBS surfaces will be automatically updated.

C++ API

The **SubdToNURBS** plug-in can be used to demonstrate the following.

- Creating a custom command to convert a subdivision surface into one or more NURBS surfaces

1. Open the **SubdToNURBS** workspace.

2. Compile it and load the resulting `subdToNURBS` plug-in file in Maya.

3. Open the **CubeSubdShaded.ma** scene.

4. Select the **subd** object.

5. Execute the following.

```
subdToNURBS;
move -r 0 0 1;
```

A series of NURBS surfaces are generated. These surfaces are parented under the **subdivToNURBS** parent transform.

SOURCE CODE

Plug-in: SubdToNURBS
File: SubdToNURBSCmd.cpp

```
class SubdToNURBS : public MPxCommand
{
public:
   virtual MStatus   doIt ( const MArgList& );
   virtual MStatus   redoIt();
   virtual MStatus   undoIt();
   virtual bool isUndoable() const { return true; }

   static void *creator() { return new SubdToNURBS; }

private:
   MDagPathArray selSubds;
   MObjectArray nurbsTransforms;
};

MStatus SubdToNURBS::doIt ( const MArgList &args )
{
   MSelectionList selection;
   MGlobal::getActiveSelectionList( selection );

   MDagPath dagPath;
   MItSelectionList iter( selection, MFn::kSubdiv );
   for ( ; !iter.isDone(); iter.next() )
   {
        iter.getDagPath( dagPath );
        selSubds.append( dagPath );
   }

   if( selSubds.length() == 0 )
   {
        MGlobal::displayWarning( "Select one or more subd surfaces." );
        return MS::kFailure;
   }

   return redoIt();
}
```

```
MStatus SubdToNURBS::redoIt()
{
    MStatus stat;
    nurbsTransforms.clear();
    MObjectArray nurbsSurfs;
    MDagPath dagPath;
    unsigned int i;
    for( i=0; i < selSubds.length(); i++ )
    {
        dagPath = selSubds[i];
        MFnSubd subdFn( dagPath );
        subdFn.convertToNurbs( nurbsSurfs );

        MFnDagNode dagFn;
        MObject transform;
        transform = dagFn.create( "transform", "subdivToNURBS" );
        nurbsTransforms.append( transform );

        dagFn.setObject( transform );
        unsigned int j;
        for( j=0; j < nurbsSurfs.length(); j++ )
        {
            dagFn.addChild( nurbsSurfs[j] );

            MFnDependencyNode depFn( nurbsSurfs[j] );
            MGlobal::executeCommand( MString("sets -e -fe
                                    initialShadingGroup ") +
                                    depFn.name() );
        }
    }
    MString cmd( "select -r" );
    for( i=0; i < nurbsTransforms.length(); i++ )
    {
        MFnDagNode dagFn( nurbsTransforms[i] );
        cmd += MString(" ") + dagFn.name();
    }
    MGlobal::executeCommand( cmd );

    return stat;
}
```

```
MStatus SubdToNURBS::undoIt()
{
   unsigned int i;
   for( i=0; i < nurbsTransforms.length(); i++ )
   {
        MFnTransform transformFn( nurbsTransforms[i] );
        while( transformFn.childCount() )
             MGlobal::deleteNode( transformFn.child(0) );
        MGlobal::deleteNode( transformFn.object() );
   }

   return MS::kSuccess;
}

MStatus initializePlugin( MObject obj )
{
   MFnPlugin plugin( obj, "David Gould", "1.0" );

   MStatus stat;
   stat = plugin.registerCommand( "subdToNURBS",
                                         SubdToNURBS::creator );

   if ( !stat )
        stat.perror( "registerCommand failed");

   return stat;
}

MStatus uninitializePlugin( MObject obj )
{
   MFnPlugin plugin( obj );

   MStatus stat;
   stat = plugin.deregisterCommand( "subdToNURBS" );
   if ( !stat )
        stat.perror( "deregisterCommand failed" );

   return stat;
}
```

SOURCE CODE EXPLANATION

Plug-in: `SubdToNURBS`
File: `SubdToNURBSCmd.cpp`

The most important function, `redoIt`, is explained in detail in the following material.

```
MStatus SubdToNURBS::redoIt()
{
    ...
```

The list of parent transforms for the resulting NURBS surfaces is cleared.

```
    nurbsTransforms.clear();
```

The selected subdivision surfaces are iterated over.

```
    ...
    for( i=0; i < selSubds.length(); i++ )
    {
        ...
```

The `MFnSubd` function set is applied to the current subdivision surface.

```
        MFnSubd subdFn( dagPath );
```

The `convertToNurbs` function converts the subdivision surface into a series of NURBS surface shape nodes. As yet, these shape nodes have no parent.

```
        subdFn.convertToNurbs( nurbsSurfs );
```

A parent transform node, named **subdivToNURBS**, is created.

```
        MFnDagNode dagFn;
        MObject transform;
        transform = dagFn.create( "transform", "subdivToNURBS" );
```

The transform node is added to the list.

```
nurbsTransforms.append( transform );
```

The NURBS surface shape nodes are added as children to the transform node. The shape nodes are also added to the initial shading group.

```
dagFn.setObject( transform );
unsigned int j;
for( j=0; j < nurbsSurfs.length(); j++ )
{
        dagFn.addChild( nurbsSurfs[j] );

        MFnDependencyNode depFn( nurbsSurfs[j] );
        MGlobal::executeCommand( MString("sets -e -fe
                                 initialShadingGroup ") +
                                 depFn.name() );
}
}
...
```

10.5 EDITING SUBDIVISION SURFACES

In Maya, a subdivision surface consists of a base polygonal mesh with any number of hierarchical edits and crease assignments. As such, the process of editing a subdivision surface consists of editing the base mesh, adding hierarchical edits, or assigning creases to vertices or edges. Hierarchical edits include the creation of finer levels through refinement as well as moving vertices. Internally, an edge that is moved is stored as the movement to its two vertices. No edge or face movements, per se, are stored.

10.5.1 MEL

1. Select **File | New Scene** from the main menu.

2. Select **Create | Polygon Primitives | Cube** from the main menu.

3. To convert the polygonal cube to a subdivision surface, execute the following.

```
polyToSubdiv;
```

4. Press the **3** key or select **Display | Subdiv Surface Smoothness | Fine** from the main menu.

5. Press the **5** key or select **Shading | Smooth Shaded All** from the viewport menu.

6. Select **Subdiv Surfaces | Standard Mode** from the main menu.

7. Right click on the **polyToSubdShape1** object, and then click on **Edge** from the marking menu.

8. Execute the following to select the top front edge.

```
select -r polyToSubd1.sme[256][1];
```

9. The edge will now be creased by executing the following.

```
subdivCrease -sharpness true;
```

The subdivision surface now has a full crease in the area corresponding to the selected edge. Maya also allows for a partial creasing of edges. Unlike a full crease, a partial crease actually refines the subdivision surface and then moves the newly refined edges. As such, partial creases can't be toggled on or off like a full crease.

10. To restore the edge sharpness, execute the following.

```
subdivCrease -sharpness false;
```

The subdivCrease command can also be applied to selected vertices.

11. Right click on the **polyToSubdShape1** object, and then click on **Vertex** in the marking menu.

12. Right click on the **polyToSubdShape1** object, and then click on **Finer** in the marking menu.

The subdivision surface already has two levels: 0 and 1. The level 1 vertices are now displayed.

13. To select the front top vertex, execute the following.

```
select -r polyToSubd1.smp[2][67108864];
```

14. The region surrounding this selected vertex will now be refined by executing the following.

```
refineSubdivSelectionList;
createSubdivRegion;
```

Level 2 is created and its vertices are selected. The `refineSubdivSelectionList` command will create another level localized in the area selected. The `createSubdivRegion` command sets the current level and its components as the active selection.

It is important to note that once a new level is created it can't be undone. However, there is a command to remove levels that don't contain any edits.

15. Execute the following.

```
subdCleanTopology polyToSubdShape1;
```

All level 2 components are deleted because they don't contain any edits. An edit would be one of the following.

- The position of the component has changed.
- A vertex has been assigned a uv texture coordinate or that coordinate has been changed.
- Crease has been applied to the component.

If none of these conditions apply, the component can be deleted. However, there may be some vertices that satisfy these conditions but still can't be deleted. This is often due to the vertex being needed to maintain surface topology.

16. Open the **CubeSubdShaded.ma** scene.

17. Select the **subd** object.

This subdivision surface has three hierarchical levels. These hierarchical levels can be compressed into a single level.

18. Execute the following.

```
subdCollapse -level 0;
move -r 0 0 1;
```

The levels as deep as level 0 are compressed into a single level. To capture the complete shape of the subdivision surface, it is clear that all levels must be included.

19. Press **z** to undo or select **Edit | Undo** from the main menu.

    This removes the move.

20. Press **z** to undo or select **Edit | Undo** from the main menu.

    This removes the subdCollapse command.

21. Execute the following.

    ```
    subdCollapse -level 2;
    move -r 0 0 1;
    ```

    The subdivision surface at level 2 is collapsed to become the level 0 mesh. The result is the subdivision surface, **subdCollapseShape1**, with only one level (level 0) but as much detail as level 2 in the original shape.

22. Press the **3** key or select **Display | Subdiv Surface Smoothness | Fine** from the main menu.

23. Open the **CubeSubdShaded.ma** scene and select the **subd** object.

24. Execute the following.

    ```
    subdDuplicateAndConnect;
    move -r 0 0 1;
    ```

    The subdivision surface is duplicated. The actual subdivision data is fed in from a connection to the original subdivision surface. As such, any changes to the original will be reflected in the duplicate. In addition, all shaders assigned to the original are also assigned to the duplicate.

CHAPTER 11

Contexts (Tools)

This chapter deals with the creation of modeling tools. Although Maya's graphical user interface uses the term *tools*, internally they are called *contexts*. These terms can be used interchangeably. However, this book will use only *contexts* because this is consistent with Maya's development interfaces: MEL and the C++ API.

A context is a special mode Maya enters into wherein the user interacts with the scene via a mouse. While in a context, a user can pick items, make selections, drag items, and in general use the mouse to manipulate the scene. The types of mouse interactions that are possible are determined by the given context. When the **Move Tool** is activated, it is possible to both select and move items with the mouse. When the **Split Polygon Tool** is activated, the user can only select polygonal edges. A context is free to execute commands, modify the selection, perform custom drawing operations, change the cursor, and so on. The steps for creating and activating a context are as follows.

1. Select **File | New Scene** from the main menu.

2. Select **Create | Polygon Primitives | Cube** from the main menu.

3. Select **Modify | Transformation Tools | Move Tool** from the main menu.

   By selecting the **Move Tool**, a context was created and activated.

4. To determine the name of the instance of the current context, execute the following.

```
currentCtx;
// Result: moveSuperContext //
```

The currentCtx command returns the name of the currently activated context.

5. To determine the user interface title of the context, execute the following.

```
contextInfo -title moveSuperContext;
// Result: Move Tool //
```

The title is the name that will appear in Maya's user interface.

6. The context's actual type is determined by using the `contextInfo` command as follows.

```
contextInfo -class moveSuperContext;
// Result: manipMove //
```

moveSuperContext is an instance of the **manipMove** context.

7. To determine if a given context exists, execute the following.

```
contextInfo -exists moveSuperContext;
// Result: 1 //
```

8. An instance of the selection context will now be created. Execute the following.

```
string $selCtx = `selectContext`;
// Result: selectContext1 //
```

An instance of the context, **selectContext**, was created: `selectContext1`. Maya's context-creating commands are named ending in **Ctx** or **Context**. Refer to the MEL command documentation for a complete list.

9. To use a context it needs to be activated. This is accomplished using the `setToolTo` command.

```
setToolTo $selCtx;
```

The `selectContext1` instance is activated. All mouse events (clicks, drags, releases, modifier keys, and so on) will be sent to the context for processing.

Even though a context is designed to take interactive input from the user, it can still be controlled by MEL. The `ctxAbort` command will abort the current context. The `ctxCompletion` command will complete the current context. The `resetTool` command will reset the context back to its factory default settings. The `toolHasOptions` command will return `true` if the context has options.

11.1 SELECTRINGCONTEXT1 PLUG-IN

The **SelectRingContext1** plug-in demonstrates the following.

- Creating a basic context

- Selecting an edge using the mouse

- Supporting modifier keys

- Selecting edge rings

- Using the **MPxContext** and **MPxContextCommand** classes

The **selectRingContext1** context is designed to select polygonal mesh edges. The user selects an edge in a polygonal mesh and all contiguous edges opposite it are then selected. As such, this context can automatically select a ring of edges around an object. It works with polygonal meshes of any number of edges, although it works best with polygons with an even number of edges and having a uniform distribution. Figure 11.1 shows the selected edges resulting from clicking on the top middle edge.

FIGURE 11.1 Edges selected using `selectRingContext1`.

11.1.1 USAGE

1. Open the **SelectRingContext1** workspace.

2. Compile it and load the resulting `selectRingContext1` plug-in file in Maya.

3. Open the **CubeMeshDivided.ma** scene.

    The **cube** object has many quadrilateral faces.

4. To use the context, execute the following.

    ```
    string $selRingCtx = `selectRingContext1`;
    setToolTo $selRingCtx;
    ```

    The `selectRingContext1` command creates an instance of the **SelectRingContext1** context. The `setToolTo` command is then used to activate the newly created instance.

5. Click on the edge shown in Figure 11.2.

FIGURE 11.2 Edge to click.

6. The edge ring is selected. The context can be used with the *modifier keys*: Shift and Ctrl. If they are pressed when an edge is clicked on, the selection can be changed in a variety of ways. If the Shift key is held down when clicking, the selection is toggled. If the Ctrl key is held down, the edge ring is removed from the selection. If both the Shift and Ctrl key are held down, the edge ring is merged with the current selection. By using the modifier keys and the **selectRingContext1** context, a complex selection can be easily achieved.

SOURCE CODE

The creation of a context consists of creating two new classes derived from **MPxContext** and **MPxContextCommand**. The **MPxContext**-derived class is where the actual context is defined. It specifies what happens when a user clicks, drags, and releases the mouse buttons. It does all of the main work of the context, including calling commands, performing custom display, and any other operations necessary to complete the context. The **MPxContextCommand**'s main task is to create an instance of the custom **MPxContext**. The custom classes are registered with Maya in a manner similar to that of registering a command.

Plug-in: `SelectRingContext1`
File: `SelectRingContext1.cpp`

```
class SelectRingContext1 : public MPxContext
{
public:
    SelectRingContext1();

    virtual void toolOnSetup( MEvent &event );
    virtual void toolOffCleanup();

    virtual MStatus  doPress( MEvent &event );
    virtual MStatus  doRelease( MEvent &event );

private:
    MGlobal::MSelectionMode prevSelMode;
    MSelectionMask prevCompMask;
    MSelectionMask prevObjMask;

    MGlobal::ListAdjustment listAdjust;
```

```
    short pressX, pressY;
    short releaseX, releaseY;
    int clickBoxSize;

    static const MString helpTxt;
};

const MString SelectRingContext1::helpTxt( "Click on an edge" );

SelectRingContext1::SelectRingContext1()
{
    setTitleString( "Select Ring Tool" );
}

void SelectRingContext1::toolOnSetup( MEvent &event )
{
    MGlobal::executeCommand( "selectPref -query -clickBoxSize",
                             clickBoxSize );

    setHelpString( helpTxt );
    setCursor( MCursor::editCursor );

    prevSelMode = MGlobal::selectionMode();
    if( prevSelMode == MGlobal::kSelectComponentMode )
        prevCompMask = MGlobal::componentSelectionMask();
    else
        prevObjMask = MGlobal::objectSelectionMask();
}

void SelectRingContext1::toolOffCleanup()
{
    MGlobal::setSelectionMode( prevSelMode );
    if( prevSelMode == MGlobal::kSelectComponentMode )
        MGlobal::setComponentSelectionMask( prevCompMask );
    else
        MGlobal::setObjectSelectionMask( prevObjMask );
}

MStatus SelectRingContext1::doPress( MEvent &event )
{
    listAdjust = MGlobal::kReplaceList;

    if( event.isModifierShift() || event.isModifierControl() )
```

```
    {
        if( event.isModifierShift() )
        {
            if( event.isModifierControl() )
                listAdjust = MGlobal::kAddToList;
            else
                listAdjust = MGlobal::kXORWithList;
        }
        else
        {
            if( event.isModifierControl() )
                listAdjust = MGlobal::kRemoveFromList;
        }
    }

    event.getPosition( pressX, pressY );

    return MS::kSuccess;
}

MStatus SelectRingContext1::doRelease( MEvent &event )
{
    event.getPosition( releaseX, releaseY );

    if( abs(pressX - releaseX) > 1 || abs(pressY - releaseY) > 1 )
    {
        MGlobal::displayWarning( "Click on a single edge" );
        return MS::kFailure;
    }

    int halfClickBoxSize = clickBoxSize / 2;
    pressX -= halfClickBoxSize;
    pressY -= halfClickBoxSize;
    releaseX = pressX + clickBoxSize;
    releaseY = pressY + clickBoxSize;

    MSelectionList curSel;
    MGlobal::getActiveSelectionList( curSel );

    MGlobal::setSelectionMode( MGlobal::kSelectObjectMode );
    MGlobal::setComponentSelectionMask(
                MSelectionMask( MSelectionMask::kSelectObjectsMask ) );
```

```
MGlobal::selectFromScreen( pressX, pressy, releaseX, releaseY,
                           MGlobal::kReplaceList);
MGlobal::executeCommand( "hilite" );

MGlobal::setSelectionMode( MGlobal::kSelectComponentMode );
MGlobal::setComponentSelectionMask(
          MSelectionMask( MSelectionMask::kSelectMeshEdges ) );

MGlobal::selectFromScreen( pressX, pressy, releaseX, releaseY,
                           MGlobal::kReplaceList );

MSelectionList origEdgesSel;
MGlobal::getActiveSelectionList( origEdgesSel );
MSelectionList newEdgesSel;
MDagPath dagPath;
MObject component;

MItSelectionList selIter( origEdgesSel, MFn::kMeshEdgeComponent );
if( !selIter.isDone() )
{
     selIter.getDagPath( dagPath, component );

     MIntArray faces;
     MItMeshEdge edgeIter( dagPath, component );

     MIntArray edgesVisited, facesVisited;
     int edgeIndex, faceIndex;
     int prevIndex;
     unsigned int i;
     bool finished = false;
     while( !finished )
     {
         edgeIndex = edgeIter.index();
         edgesVisited.append( edgeIndex );

         MFnSingleIndexedComponent indexedCompFn;
         MObject newComponent = indexedCompFn.create(
                                    MFn::kMeshEdgeComponent );
         indexedCompFn.addElement( edgeIndex );
         newEdgesSel.add( dagPath, newComponent );
```

```
edgeIter.getConnectedFaces( faces );
faceIndex = faces[0];
if( faces.length() > 1 )
{
     for( i=0; i < facesVisited.length(); i++ )
     {
          if( faceIndex == facesVisited[i] )
          {
               faceIndex = faces[1];
               break;
          }
     }
}

facesVisited.append( faceIndex );

MItMeshPolygon polyIter( dagPath );

polyIter.setIndex( faceIndex, prevIndex );

MIntArray edges;
polyIter.getEdges( edges );

unsigned int edgeFaceIndex = 0;
for( i=0; i < edges.length(); i++ )
{
     if( edges[i] == edgeIter.index() )
     {
          edgeFaceIndex = i;
          break;
     }
}

edgeIndex = edges[ (edgeFaceIndex + (edges.length()/2) )
                     % edges.length() ];

edgeIter.setIndex( edgeIndex, prevIndex );

for( i=0; i < edgesVisited.length(); i++ )
{
     if( edgeIndex == edgesVisited[i] )
```

```
                            {
                                    finished = true;
                                    break;
                            }
                    }
            }
    }
    MGlobal::setActiveSelectionList( curSel, MGlobal::kReplaceList);
    MGlobal::selectCommand( newEdgesSel, listAdjust );
    return MS::kSuccess;
}
class SelectRingContextCmd1 : public MPxContextCommand
{
public:
    virtual MPxContext *makeObj();
    static void *creator();
};
MPxContext *SelectRingContextCmd1::makeObj()
{
    return new SelectRingContext1();
}
void *SelectRingContextCmd1::creator()
{
    return new SelectRingContextCmd1;
}
MStatus initializePlugin( MObject obj )
{
    MFnPlugin plugin( obj, "David Gould", "1.0" );
    MStatus stat;
    stat = plugin.registerContextCommand( "selectRingContext1",
                                    SelectRingContextCmd1::creator );
    if ( !stat )
        stat.perror( "registerContextCommand failed");
    return stat;
}
```

```
MStatus uninitializePlugin( MObject obj )
{
   MFnPlugin plugin( obj );

   MStatus stat;
   stat = plugin.deregisterContextCommand( "selectRingContext1" );
   if ( !stat )
        stat.perror( "deregisterContextCommand failed" );

   return stat;
}
```

SOURCE CODE EXPLANATION

The custom **SelectRingContext1** class is defined as a subclass of **MPxContext**.

```
class SelectRingContext1 : public MPxContext
{
   ...
};
```

The `helpTxt` variable holds the text that will be displayed in the help line when the mouse enters the viewport while this context is active.

```
const MString SelectRingContext1::helpTxt( "Click on an edge" );
```

The constructor sets the title text for the context.

```
SelectRingContext1::SelectRingContext1()
{
   setTitleString( "Select Ring Tool" );
}
```

When the context is activated, the `toolOnSetup` function is called. If the context is activated by clicking on a tool button, the `event` variable will contain the mouse click information. The `toolOnSetup` function's task is to prepare the context for user input.

```
void SelectRingContext1::toolOnSetup( MEvent &event )
{
```

The click box size is the width of the area over which a single click will select items. This value is stored in the `clickBoxSize` variable.

```
MGlobal::executeCommand( "selectPref -query -clickBoxSize",
                              clickBoxSize );
```

The help text that will follow the title text in the help line is set.

```
setHelpString( helpTxt );
```

The mouse cursor is set to the edit cursor. There is no need to reset the cursor when the context is deactivated because the newly activated context will set its own cursor.

```
setCursor( MCursor::editCursor );
```

The current selection mode and masks are stored because they will be changed by this context.

```
prevSelMode = MGlobal::selectionMode();
if( prevSelMode == MGlobal::kSelectComponentMode )
    prevCompMask = MGlobal::componentSelectionMask();
else
    prevObjMask = MGlobal::objectSelectionMask();
}
```

When the context is deactivated, the `toolOffCleanup` function is called.

```
void SelectRingContext1::toolOffCleanup()
{
```

The previous selection mode and masks are restored.

```
MGlobal::setSelectionMode( prevSelMode );
if( prevSelMode == MGlobal::kSelectComponentMode )
    MGlobal::setComponentSelectionMask( prevCompMask );
else
    MGlobal::setObjectSelectionMask( prevObjMask );
}
```

Whenever any mouse button is pressed, the `doPress` function is called. The `event` variable contains information about which button is pressed, as well as which modifier keys may also have been pressed.

```
MStatus SelectRingContext1::doPress( MEvent &event )
{
```

This context follows the standard selection conventions that Maya has established. When the user clicks on an item without any modifier keys, the current selection is replaced. When the user clicks with the Shift key pressed, the selection is toggled with the current selection. When the user clicks with the Ctrl key pressed, the selection is removed from the current selection. When the user clicks with both the Shift and the Ctrl key pressed, the selection is merged into the current selection. The `listAdjust` variable is updated to reflect how the current selection will be modified by this context.

```
listAdjust = MGlobal::kReplaceList;
if( event.isModifierShift() || event.isModifierControl() )
{
     if( event.isModifierShift() )
     {
          if( event.isModifierControl() )
               listAdjust = MGlobal::kAddToList;
          else
               listAdjust = MGlobal::kXORWithList;
     }
     else
     {
          if( event.isModifierControl() )
               listAdjust = MGlobal::kRemoveFromList;
     }
}
```

The position of the mouse press is recorded. The `getPosition` function returns the coordinates in the current view. The origin is located at the bottom left of the view and extends in a positive fashion both up and to the right.

```
event.getPosition( pressX, pressY );
return MS::kSuccess;
}
```

When any mouse button is released, the doRelease function is called.

```
MStatus SelectRingContext1::doRelease( MEvent &event )
{
```

The position of the mouse, when the button is released, is recorded.

```
event.getPosition( releaseX, releaseY );
```

Because the context assumes that the user will click on an edge, if the user has instead performed a marquee selection (click and drag over an area) a warning is issued and the context fails. This is not necessarily an error, per se, but this context currently only handles one-click selections.

```
if( abs(pressX - releaseX) > 1 || abs(pressY - releaseY) > 1 )
{
        MGlobal::displayWarning( "Click on a single edge" );
        return MS::kFailure;
}
```

It is very difficult to click exactly on an edge because it may be quite thin. The selection area is increased around the click point by the width of the click box size.

```
int halfClickBoxSize = clickBoxSize / 2;
pressX -= halfClickBoxSize;
pressY -= halfClickBoxSize;
releaseX = pressX + clickBoxSize;
releaseY = pressY + clickBoxSize;
```

The current selection is retrieved.

```
MSelectionList curSel;
MGlobal::getActiveSelectionList( curSel );
```

Unless the user has already highlighted an object and placed it in edge selection mode, a click on an object will not result in an edge being selected. Instead, the click must select the object, which is then highlighted. Its edges can then be selected. The selection mode is set to select entire objects.

```
MGlobal::setSelectionMode( MGlobal::kSelectObjectMode );
MGlobal::setComponentSelectionMask(
           MSelectionMask( MSelectionMask::kSelectObjectsMask ) );
```

Any object within the click box size of the mouse click is selected.

```
MGlobal::selectFromScreen( pressX, pressY, releaseX, releaseY,
                            MGlobal::kReplaceList);
```

The object is highlighted. It can now have its components selected.

```
MGlobal::executeCommand( "hilite" );
```

The selection mode is set to be polygonal mesh edge components.

```
MGlobal::setSelectionMode( MGlobal::kSelectComponentMode );
MGlobal::setComponentSelectionMask(
           MSelectionMask( MSelectionMask::kSelectMeshEdges ) );
```

The edges under the mouse click are selected.

```
MGlobal::selectFromScreen( pressX, pressY, releaseX, releaseY,
                            MGlobal::kReplaceList );
```

The currently selected edges are recorded in the origEdgesSel variable.

```
MSelectionList origEdgesSel;
MGlobal::getActiveSelectionList( origEdgesSel );
...
```

Only the first edge in the selection list is used.

```
MItSelectionList selIter( origEdgesSel, MFn::kMeshEdgeComponent );
if( !selIter.isDone() )
{
```

The dag path and component are retrieved from the current selection.

```
selIter.getDagPath( dagPath, component );
...
```

An **MItMeshEdge** iterator is bound to the selected edge.

```
MItMeshEdge edgeIter( dagPath, component );
...
```

The ring continues until all edges in the ring have been visited.

```
bool finished = false;
while( !finished )
{
```

The mesh-relative edge index is retrieved using the index function.

```
edgeIndex = edgeIter.index();
```

Include the edge in the list of those already visited.

```
edgesVisited.append( edgeIndex );
```

The edge needs to be added to a new list of selected edges. To do this, a component needs to be created that references the edge. Because edges are indexed by a single value, the **MFnSingleIndexedComponent** function set is used.

```
MFnSingleIndexedComponent indexedCompFn;
```

A component that will reference polygonal mesh edges is created.

```
MObject newComponent = indexedCompFn.create(
                        MFn::kMeshEdgeComponent );
```

The edge index is added to the component.

```
indexedCompFn.addElement( edgeIndex );
```

The object's edge, specified using the DAG path and edge component, are added to the new edge selection list.

```
newEdgesSel.add( dagPath, newComponent );
```

All faces connected to this edge are retrieved. In a nonproblematic mesh there would be a maximum of two faces per edge.

```
edgeIter.getConnectedFaces( faces );
```

Initially set the `faceIndex` to the first face sharing the edge.

```
faceIndex = faces[0];
```

If the edge has two sharing faces, it is important that the same face not be visited more than once. To ensure this, a `facesVisited` list of face indices visited is maintained. Each time a new face is visited it is put into this list.

```
if( faces.length() > 1 )
{
        for( i=0; i < facesVisited.length(); i++ )
        {
                if( faceIndex == facesVisited[i] )
                {
```

Because the first face (`faces[0]`) has already been visited, the second face, `faces[1]`, is used.

```
                        faceIndex = faces[1];
                        break;
                }
        }
}
```

The face is included in the list of faces already visited.

```
facesVisited.append( faceIndex );
```

The **MItMeshPolygon** is bound to the current face.

```
MItMeshPolygon polyIter( dagPath );
polyIter.setIndex( faceIndex, prevIndex );
```

All edge indices in the face are retrieved. The edge indices are mesh relative.

```
MIntArray edges;
polyIter.getEdges( edges );
```

The face-relative index of the current edge needs to be found. Each mesh-relative edge index in the list is compared until the current edge is found.

```
unsigned int edgeFaceIndex = 0;
for( i=0; i < edges.length(); i++ )
{
        if( edges[i] == edgeIter.index() )
        {
                edgeFaceIndex = i;
                break;
        }
}
```

With the face-relative index of the current edge now known, it is possible to select the edge directly opposite. The edge opposite is exactly half the way around the edge list. Of course, for an odd numbers of edges only an approximate opposite edge can be determined because there is no strict opposite. The edgeIndex is set to the opposite edge. This edge will be used as the initial edge in the next iteration of this main loop.

```
edgeIndex = edges[ (edgeFaceIndex + (edges.length()/2) )
                        % edges.length() ];
```

The edge iterator is set to the opposite edge.

```
edgeIter.setIndex( edgeIndex, prevIndex );
```

If the edge has already been visited, the main *while* loop can finish, in that an edge ring has now been formed.

```
            for( i=0; i < edgesVisited.length(); i++ )
            {
                    if( edgeIndex == edgesVisited[i] )
                    {
                            finished = true;
                            break;
                    }
            }
        }
    }
```

The current selection is set to the original selection.

```
    MGlobal::setActiveSelectionList( curSel, MGlobal::kReplaceList);
```

The selected edges are added to the current selection based on the listAdjust value.

```
    MGlobal::selectCommand( newEdgesSel, listAdjust );
    ...
}
```

The **SelectRingContextCmd1** class is derived from the **MPxContextCommand**. This class's main job will be to create an instance of itself as well as the custom context.

```
class SelectRingContextCmd1 : public MPxContextCommand
{
    ...
};
```

The makeObj function creates an instance of the custom context, **SelectRingContext1**.

```
MPxContext *SelectRingContextCmd1::makeObj()
{
    return new SelectRingContext1();
}
```

The creator function, like in the **MPxCommand** class, creates an instance of this class.

```
void *SelectRingContextCmd1::creator()
{
    return new SelectRingContextCmd1;
}
```

The plug-in initialization and uninitialization involve the register and deregister of the context command using the registerContextCommand and deregisterContextCommand functions, respectively.

```
MStatus initializePlugin( MObject obj )
{
    ...
    stat = plugin.registerContextCommand( "selectRingContext1",
                                    SelectRingContextCmd1::creator );
    ...
}

MStatus uninitializePlugin( MObject obj )
{
    ...
    stat = plugin.deregisterContextCommand( "selectRingContext1" );
    ...
}
```

11.2 SELECTRINGCONTEXT2 PLUG-IN

Building on the previous plug-in, **SelectRingContext1**, the **SelectRingContext2** plug-in demonstrates the following.

- More robust implementation of ring selection
- Support for loop selection
- Optional selection of vertices, edges, and faces
- Context icons
- Shelf buttons for context

- Property sheets

- Use of the **MPxToolCommand** class

The **selectRingContext2** context provides for ring and loop selections. A loop selection is where edges are followed along contiguous faces, in the direction of the original selected edge. The context can also select vertices and faces neighboring the edges. Figure 11.3 shows the result of selecting the cube with various selection types (loop and ring) and components (vertices, edges, and faces).

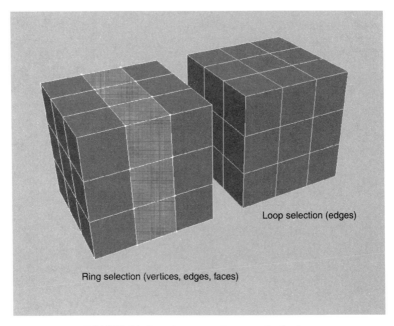

Loop selection (edges)

Ring selection (vertices, edges, faces)

FIGURE 11.3 `SelectRingContext2` selections.

11.2.1 INSTALLATION

Before the context can be used, there is some preparation needed to ensure the context's icon and property window MEL scripts are installed.

ICON

Each context can have its own icon. This icon is will be shown in the toolbox as well as any tool buttons that use the context. If a context doesn't have an icon, the button will be displayed as empty.

An icon is a bitmap with dimensions, 32 × 32, stored in the .xpm image file format. Icons can also be in the .iff or .bmp (Windows only) file formats. Figure 11.4 shows the icon for the **SelectRingContext2** context. The icon file name doesn't have to match the name of the context, but it's better if it does because this prevents confusion and is more consistent with Maya's icon naming.

FIGURE 11.4 SelectRingContext2 icon.

The program imconvert can be used to convert images to the .xpm file format. It supports a wide range of image file formats. This program is located in the *maya_install*/bin directory. The icon was created in Photoshop and saved as a .jpg file. It was converted to an .xpm by executing the following in a shell (outside Maya).

```
imconvert selectRingContext2.jpg selectRingContext2.xpm
```

1. For Maya to locate the icon file, it needs to be in one of the directories listed by the XBMLANGPATH environment variable. To get the list of directories, retrieve the environment variable as follows.

```
getenv XBMLANGPATH;
// Result: C:/ Documents and Settings/davidgould/...
```

The result is a single string with all directory names. To get a list of individual directory names, use the xbmLangPathList command.

2. Copy the selectRingContext2.xpm file from the directory containing the source code for the **SelectRingContext2** plug-in to one of the directories listed in the XBMLANGPATH environment variable.

PROPERTY SHEET

When the tool settings are requested for a given context, the **Tool Property Window** is displayed. This window contains interface elements so that the user can query and set the current context's options. Figure 11.5 shows the **Tool Property Window** for the **SelectRingContext2** context.

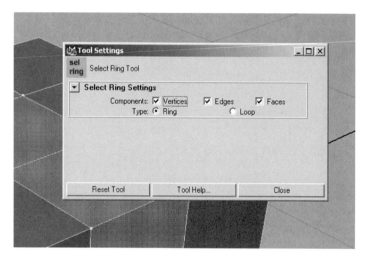

FIGURE 11.5 `SelectRingContext2` property sheet.

To install the MEL scripts responsible for managing the property sheet, continue with the following.

3. The MEL scripts need to be located in one of the directories listed in the `MAYA_SCRIPT_PATH` environment variable. To get the list of directories, retrieve the environment variable as follows.

```
getenv MAYA_SCRIPT_PATH;
// Result: C:/ Documents and Settings/davidgould/...
```

The result is a single string with all directory names.

4. Copy the following two MEL scripts from the directory containing the source code for the **SelectRingContext2** plug-in to one of the directories listed in the `MAYA_SCRIPT_PATH` environment variable.

```
selectRingContext2Properties.mel
selectRingContext2Values.mel
```

SHELF BUTTON

Maya's shelves can store two types of buttons: command buttons and tool buttons. A tool button when pressed will activate a given context instance.

5. Open the **SelectRingContext2** workspace.

6. Compile it and load the resulting `selectRingContext2` plug-in file in Maya.

7. Determine in which shelf the button should be added. In this example, the button will be added to the **Custom** shelf. Substitute `Custom` with the name of any shelf.

    ```
    setParent Custom;
    ```

8. A shelf button is created for the context by executing the following.

    ```
    shelfButton -command "if( !`contextInfo -exists selRingCtx` )
    selectRingContext2 selRingCtx;
    setToolTo selRingCtx;" -doubleClickCommand "toolPropertyWindow"
        -image1 "selectRingContext2.xpm";
    ```

    The MEL code that will execute when the button is pressed will check to see if the `selRingCtx` object exists. If it doesn't, it is created using the `selectRingContext2` command. The current tool is then set to the `selRingCtx` context. The `-doubleClickCommand` flag defines the MEL code that will be executed when the button ID is double clicked. In this case, the **Tool Property Window** will be opened. The `-image1` flag is used to specify the icon to use for the shelf button.

11.2.2 USAGE

With the various context items now installed, the context can now be run.

1. If not done already, complete all steps in the previous "Installation" section.

2. Open the **CubeMeshDivided.ma** scene.

3. Click on the **Sel Ring** shelf button.

    The **Tool Settings** window will be visible in the **Channel Box** area if the preferences are set to have the **Tool Settings** window displayed in the Maya window. If the **Tool Settings** window isn't visible, double click on the **Sel Ring** shelf button. The default context settings will select edges in a ring.

4. Click on one of the edges in the cube.

   The ring of edges is selected.

5. In the **Components** section of the **Tool Settings** window, click on the **Vertices** check box to turn it on.

6. Click on one of the edges.

   The ring of vertices and edges is selected.

7. Turn the **Vertices** and **Edges** check boxes off.

8. Turn the **Faces** check box on.

9. Click on one of the edges.

   A ring of faces is selected.

10. Turn on the **Edges** check box.

11. Turn off the **Faces** check box.

12. In the **Type** section select the **Loop** radio button.

13. Click on one of the edges.

    A loop of edges is selected.

SOURCE CODE

Plug-in: `SelectRingContext2`
File: `SelectRingContext2.cpp`

```cpp
class SelectRingToolCmd2 : public MPxToolCommand
{
public:
    SelectRingToolCmd2();

    MStatus doIt( const MArgList &args );
    MStatus redoIt();
    MStatus undoIt();
    bool isUndoable() const { return true; }
    MStatus  finalize();

    enum SelType { RING, LOOP };
```

```
      void setSelEdges( bool on ) { selEdges = on; }
      void setSelFaces( bool on ) { selFaces = on; }
      void setSelVertices( bool on ) { selVertices = on; }
      void setCurrentSelection( MSelectionList &curSel ) { prevSel=curSel; }
      void setSelectedEdgeObject( const MDagPath &dagPath )
                                           { selEdgeObject = dagPath; }
      void setSelectedEdgeComponent( const MObject &component )
                                           { selEdgeComp = component; }
      void setListAdjust( const MGlobal::ListAdjustment &la )
                                           { listAdjust = la; }
      void setSelType( SelType type ) { selType = (int)type; }

      static void *creator();
      static MSyntax newSyntax();
      static const MString commandName;

   private:
      MSelectionList prevSel;

      MDagPath selEdgeObject;
      MObject selEdgeComp;
      MGlobal::ListAdjustment listAdjust;
      bool selEdges;
      bool selFaces;
      bool selVertices;
      int selType;

      enum Location { NEXT, PREVIOUS, OPPOSITE };
      int navigateFace( const MDagPath &dagPath,
                              const int faceIndex,
                              const int edgeIndex,
                              const Location loc );
   };

const MString SelectRingToolCmd2::commandName( "selectRingToolCmd2" );

const char *edgeFlag = "-ed", *edgeLongFlag = "-edge";
const char *selEdgesFlag = "-se", *selEdgesLongFlag = "-selectEdges";
const char *selFacesFlag = "-sf", *selFacesLongFlag = "-selectFaces";
const char *selVerticesFlag = "-sv", *selVerticesLongFlag = "-
selectVertices";
```

```
const char *listAdjustFlag = "-la", *listAdjustLongFlag = "-listAdjust";
const char *selTypeFlag = "-st", *selTypeLongFlag = "-selectType";

MSyntax SelectRingToolCmd2::newSyntax()
{
 MSyntax syntax;

    syntax.addFlag( edgeFlag, edgeLongFlag, MSyntax::kString );
    syntax.addFlag( selEdgesFlag, selEdgesLongFlag, MSyntax::kBoolean );
    syntax.addFlag( selFacesFlag, selFacesLongFlag, MSyntax::kBoolean );
    syntax.addFlag( selVerticesFlag,selVerticesLongFlag,MSyntax::kBoolean);
    syntax.addFlag( listAdjustFlag,listAdjustLongFlag,MSyntax::kUnsigned );
    syntax.addFlag( selTypeFlag, selTypeLongFlag, MSyntax::kUnsigned );

    return syntax;
}

void *SelectRingToolCmd2::creator()
{
    return new SelectRingToolCmd2;
}

SelectRingToolCmd2::SelectRingToolCmd2()
{
    setCommandString( SelectRingToolCmd2::commandName );
}

MStatus SelectRingToolCmd2::doIt( const MArgList &args )
{
    MStatus stat;

    MGlobal::getActiveSelectionList( prevSel );

    selEdges = true;
    selFaces = false;
    selVertices = false;
    selEdgeObject = MDagPath();
    selEdgeComp = MObject::kNullObj;
    listAdjust = MGlobal::kReplaceList;
    selType = RING;
    MArgDatabase argData( syntax(), args, &stat );
    if( !stat )
        return stat;
```

```
    if( argData.isFlagSet( edgeFlag ) )
    {
         MString edgeSpec;
         argData.getFlagArgument( edgeFlag, 0, edgeSpec );

         MSelectionList sel;
         sel.add( edgeSpec );
         sel.getDagPath( 0, selEdgeObject, selEdgeComp );
    }

    if( argData.isFlagSet( selEdgesFlag ) )
         argData.getFlagArgument( selEdgesFlag, 0, selEdges );

    if( argData.isFlagSet( selFacesFlag ) )
         argData.getFlagArgument( selFacesFlag, 0, selFaces );

    if( argData.isFlagSet( selVerticesFlag ) )
         argData.getFlagArgument( selVerticesFlag, 0, selVertices );

    if( argData.isFlagSet( listAdjustFlag ) )
    {
         unsigned value;
         argData.getFlagArgument( listAdjustFlag, 0, value );
         listAdjust = MGlobal::ListAdjustment( value );
    }

    if( argData.isFlagSet( selTypeFlag ) )
         argData.getFlagArgument( selTypeFlag, 0, selType );

    return redoIt();
}

MStatus SelectRingToolCmd2::redoIt()
{
    MItMeshPolygon polyIter( selEdgeObject );
    MItMeshEdge edgeIter( selEdgeObject, selEdgeComp );

    MFnSingleIndexedComponent indexedCompFn;
    MObject newComponent;
    MSelectionList newSel;
    MIntArray edges;
    MIntArray faces;
```

```
unsigned int i;
const int initEdgeIndex = edgeIter.index();
int initFaceIndex;
int prevIndex, lastIndex;
int faceIndex, edgeIndex;
int newFaceIndex, newEdgeIndex;
int nInitEdgeVisits;

MIntArray remainFaces;
MIntArray remainEdges;
if( selType == RING )
{
     nInitEdgeVisits = 0;

     edgeIter.getConnectedFaces( faces );
     if( faces.length() > 1 )
     {
          remainFaces.append( faces[1] );
          remainEdges.append( initEdgeIndex );
     }
     initFaceIndex = faces[0];
     remainFaces.append( initFaceIndex );
     remainEdges.append( initEdgeIndex );

     while( remainFaces.length() )
     {
          lastIndex = remainFaces.length() - 1;
          faceIndex = remainFaces[ lastIndex ];
          edgeIndex = remainEdges[ lastIndex ];
          remainFaces.remove( lastIndex );
          remainEdges.remove( lastIndex );

          if( faceIndex == initFaceIndex &&
           edgeIndex == initEdgeIndex )
          {
               if( ++nInitEdgeVisits == 2 )
                    break;
          }
```

```
if( selEdges )
{
      newComponent = indexedCompFn.create(
                              MFn::kMeshEdgeComponent );
      indexedCompFn.addElement( edgeIndex );
      newSel.add( selEdgeObject, newComponent );
}

if( selVertices )
{
      newComponent = indexedCompFn.create(
                              MFn::kMeshVertComponent );
      edgeIter.setIndex( edgeIndex, prevIndex );
      indexedCompFn.addElement( edgeIter.index(0) );
      indexedCompFn.addElement( edgeIter.index(1) );
      newSel.add( selEdgeObject, newComponent );
}

if( faceIndex != -1 )
{
      if( selFaces )
      {
            newComponent = indexedCompFn.create(
                        MFn::kMeshPolygonComponent );
            indexedCompFn.addElement( faceIndex );
            newSel.add( selEdgeObject, newComponent );
      }
      newEdgeIndex = navigateFace( selEdgeObject,
                              faceIndex,
                              edgeIndex, OPPOSITE );

      edgeIter.setIndex( newEdgeIndex, prevIndex );
      edgeIter.getConnectedFaces( faces );

      newFaceIndex = -1;
      if( faces.length() > 1 )
            newFaceIndex = (faceIndex == faces[0]) ?
                        faces[1] : faces[0];
```

```
                                remainFaces.append( newFaceIndex );
                                remainEdges.append( newEdgeIndex );
                       }
              }
     }
     else
     {
              int reflEdgeIndex;
              int newReflEdgeIndex;
              int initReflEdgeIndex;
              MIntArray remainReflEdges;

              nInitEdgeVisits = 0;

              edgeIter.getConnectedFaces( faces );
              initFaceIndex = faces[0];
              for( i=0; i < 2; i++ )
              {
                       remainFaces.append( initFaceIndex );
                       remainEdges.append( initEdgeIndex );
                       remainReflEdges.append(
                             navigateFace( selEdgeObject, initFaceIndex,
                                         initEdgeIndex,
                                         (i == 0) ? PREVIOUS : NEXT ) );
              }
              initReflEdgeIndex = remainReflEdges[1];

              while( remainFaces.length() )
              {
                       lastIndex = remainFaces.length() - 1;
                       faceIndex = remainFaces[ lastIndex ];
                       edgeIndex = remainEdges[ lastIndex ];
                       reflEdgeIndex = remainReflEdges[ lastIndex ];
                       remainFaces.remove( lastIndex );
                       remainEdges.remove( lastIndex );
                       remainReflEdges.remove( lastIndex );

                       if( faceIndex == initFaceIndex &&
                         edgeIndex == initEdgeIndex &&
                         reflEdgeIndex == initReflEdgeIndex )
```

```
    {
        if( ++nInitEdgeVisits == 2 )
            break;
    }

    if( selEdges )
    {
        newComponent = indexedCompFn.create(
                        MFn::kMeshEdgeComponent );
        indexedCompFn.addElement( edgeIndex );
        newSel.add( selEdgeObject, newComponent );
    }

    if( selVertices )
    {
        newComponent = indexedCompFn.create(
                        MFn::kMeshVertComponent );
        edgeIter.setIndex( edgeIndex, prevIndex );
        indexedCompFn.addElement( edgeIter.index(0) );
        indexedCompFn.addElement( edgeIter.index(1) );
        newSel.add( selEdgeObject, newComponent );
    }

    if( selFaces )
    {
        newComponent = indexedCompFn.create(
                        MFn::kMeshPolygonComponent );
        indexedCompFn.addElement( faceIndex );
        newSel.add( selEdgeObject, newComponent );
    }

    edgeIter.setIndex( reflEdgeIndex, prevIndex );
    edgeIter.getConnectedFaces( faces );

    if( faces.length() > 1 )
    {
        newFaceIndex = (faceIndex == faces[0]) ?
                        faces[1] : faces[0];

        int edgePrev = navigateFace( selEdgeObject,
                        newFaceIndex, reflEdgeIndex,
                        PREVIOUS );
```

```
                        int edgeNext = navigateFace( selEdgeObject,
                                         newFaceIndex, reflEdgeIndex,
                                         NEXT );

                        edgeIter.setIndex( edgeIndex, prevIndex );
                        if( edgeIter.connectedToEdge( edgePrev ) )
                        {
                            newEdgeIndex = edgePrev;
                            newReflEdgeIndex = navigateFace( selEdgeObject,
                                             newFaceIndex, newEdgeIndex,
                                             PREVIOUS );
                        }
                        else
                        {
                            newEdgeIndex = edgeNext;
                            newReflEdgeIndex = navigateFace( selEdgeObject,
                                             newFaceIndex, newEdgeIndex,
                                             NEXT );
                        }
                        remainFaces.append( newFaceIndex );
                        remainEdges.append( newEdgeIndex );
                        remainReflEdges.append( newReflEdgeIndex );
                    }
                }
            }

        MGlobal::setActiveSelectionList( prevSel, MGlobal::kReplaceList );

        MGlobal::selectCommand( newSel, listAdjust );

        return MS::kSuccess;
}

int SelectRingToolCmd2::navigateFace(
    const MDagPath &dagPath,
    const int faceIndex,
    const int edgeIndex,
    const Location loc )
{
    int prevIndex;
```

```
    MItMeshPolygon polyIter( dagPath );
    polyIter.setIndex( faceIndex, prevIndex );

    MIntArray edges;
    polyIter.getEdges( edges );

    unsigned int i;
    for( i=0; i < edges.length(); i++ )
    {
        if( edgeIndex == edges[i] )
        {
            int offset;
            if( loc == OPPOSITE )
                offset = edges.length()/2;
            else
                offset = (loc == NEXT) ? 1 : -1;
            return edges[ (i + offset) % edges.length() ];
        }
    }

    return -1;
}

MStatus SelectRingToolCmd2::undoIt()
{
    return MGlobal::setActiveSelectionList( prevSel,
                                        MGlobal::kReplaceList);
}

MStatus SelectRingToolCmd2::finalize()
{
    MArgList command;
    command.addArg( commandString() );
    command.addArg( MString(edgeFlag) );
    MSelectionList sel;
    sel.add( selEdgeObject, selEdgeComp );
    MStringArray edges;
    sel.getSelectionStrings( edges );
    command.addArg( edges[0] );

    command.addArg( MString(selEdgesFlag) );
    command.addArg( selEdges );
```

```
      command.addArg( MString(selFacesFlag) );
      command.addArg( selFaces );

      command.addArg( MString(selVerticesFlag) );
      command.addArg( selVertices );

      command.addArg( MString(listAdjustFlag) );
      command.addArg( (int)listAdjust );

      command.addArg( MString(selTypeFlag) );
      command.addArg( selType );

      return MPxToolCommand::doFinalize( command );
}

class SelectRingContext2 : public MPxContext
{
public:
      SelectRingContext2();

      virtual void toolOnSetup( MEvent &event );
      virtual void toolOffCleanup();

      virtual MStatus doPress( MEvent &event );
      virtual MStatus doRelease( MEvent &event );

      virtual void getClassName( MString &name ) const;

      MGlobal::ListAdjustmentlistAdjust;
      bool selVertices;
      bool selEdges;
      bool selFaces;
      int selType;

   private:
      MGlobal::MSelectionMode prevSelMode;
      MSelectionMask prevCompMask;
      MSelectionMask prevObjMask;

      short pressX, pressY;
      short releaseX, releaseY;
      int clickBoxSize;

      static const MString helpTxt;
   };
```

```
const MString SelectRingContext2::helpTxt( "Click on an edge" );

SelectRingContext2::SelectRingContext2()
{
    listAdjust = MGlobal::kReplaceList;
    selVertices = false;
    selEdges = true;
    selFaces = false;
    selType = SelectRingToolCmd2::RING;

    setTitleString( "Select Ring Tool" );
    setImage( "selectRingContext2.xpm", MPxContext::kImage1 );
}

void SelectRingContext2::getClassName( MString &name ) const
{
    name = "selectRingContext2";
}

void SelectRingContext2::toolOnSetup( MEvent &event )
{
    MGlobal::executeCommand( "selectPref -query -clickBoxSize",
                             clickBoxSize );

    setHelpString( helpTxt );
    setCursor( MCursor::editCursor );

    prevSelMode = MGlobal::selectionMode();
    if( prevSelMode == MGlobal::kSelectComponentMode )
            prevCompMask = MGlobal::componentSelectionMask();
    else
            prevObjMask = MGlobal::objectSelectionMask();
}

void SelectRingContext2::toolOffCleanup()
{
    MGlobal::setSelectionMode( prevSelMode );
    if( prevSelMode == MGlobal::kSelectComponentMode )
            MGlobal::setComponentSelectionMask( prevCompMask );
    else
            MGlobal::setObjectSelectionMask( prevObjMask );
}
```

```
MStatus SelectRingContext2::doPress( MEvent &event )
{
    listAdjust = MGlobal::kReplaceList;

    if( event.isModifierShift() || event.isModifierControl() )
    {
        if( event.isModifierShift() )
        {
            if( event.isModifierControl() )
                listAdjust = MGlobal::kAddToList;
            else
                listAdjust = MGlobal::kXORWithList;
        }
        else
        {
            if( event.isModifierControl() )
                listAdjust = MGlobal::kRemoveFromList;
        }
    }

    event.getPosition( pressX, pressY );

    return MS::kSuccess;
}

MStatus SelectRingContext2::doRelease( MEvent &event )
{
    event.getPosition( releaseX, releaseY );

    if( abs(pressX - releaseX) >1 || abs(pressY - releaseY) >1 )
    {
        MGlobal::displayWarning( "Click on a single edge" );
        return MS::kFailure;
    }

    // Set the selection surface area
    int halfClickBoxSize = clickBoxSize / 2;
    pressX -= halfClickBoxSize;
    pressY -= halfClickBoxSize;
```

```
releaseX = pressX + clickBoxSize;
releaseY = pressY + clickBoxSize;

MSelectionList curSel;
MGlobal::getActiveSelectionList( curSel );

MGlobal::setSelectionMode( MGlobal::kSelectObjectMode );
MGlobal::setComponentSelectionMask(
          MSelectionMask( MSelectionMask::kSelectObjectsMask ) );

MGlobal::selectFromScreen( pressX, pressY, releaseX, releaseY,
                           MGlobal::kReplaceList);
MGlobal::executeCommand( "hilite" );

MGlobal::setSelectionMode( MGlobal::kSelectComponentMode );
MGlobal::setComponentSelectionMask(
          MSelectionMask( MSelectionMask::kSelectMeshEdges ) );

MGlobal::selectFromScreen( pressX, pressY, releaseX, releaseY,
                           MGlobal::kReplaceList );

MSelectionList origEdgesSel;
MGlobal::getActiveSelectionList( origEdgesSel );

MItSelectionList selIter( origEdgesSel, MFn::kMeshEdgeComponent );
if( !selIter.isDone() )
{
     MDagPath dagPath;
     MObject component;
     selIter.getDagPath( dagPath, component );

     SelectRingToolCmd2 &cmd = *(SelectRingToolCmd2 *)
                                                newToolCommand();
     cmd.setCurrentSelection( curSel );
     cmd.setSelectedEdgeObject( dagPath );
     cmd.setSelectedEdgeComponent( component );
     cmd.setListAdjust( listAdjust );
     cmd.setSelEdges( selEdges );
     cmd.setSelFaces( selFaces );
     cmd.setSelVertices( selVertices );
     cmd.setSelType( SelectRingToolCmd2::SelType(selType) );
```

```
        cmd.redoIt();
        cmd.finalize();
   }
   return MS::kSuccess;
}
class SelectRingContextCmd2 : public MPxContextCommand
{
public:
   SelectRingContextCmd2();
   virtual MPxContext *makeObj();
   virtual MStatus doEditFlags();
   virtual MStatus doQueryFlags();
   virtual MStatus appendSyntax();

   static void *creator();
   static const MString commandName;

protected:
   SelectRingContext2 *lastMadeCtx;
};
const MString SelectRingContextCmd2::commandName( "selectRingContext2" );

SelectRingContextCmd2::SelectRingContextCmd2()
{
   lastMadeCtx = NULL;
}

MPxContext *SelectRingContextCmd2::makeObj()
{
   lastMadeCtx = new SelectRingContext2();
   return lastMadeCtx;
}

void *SelectRingContextCmd2::creator()
{
   return new SelectRingContextCmd2;
}

MStatusSelectRingContextCmd2::doEditFlags()
{
   MArgParser pars = parser();
```

```
        if( pars.isFlagSet( selEdgesFlag ) )
            pars.getFlagArgument( selEdgesFlag, 0, lastMadeCtx->selEdges );
        if( pars.isFlagSet( selFacesFlag ) )
            pars.getFlagArgument( selFacesFlag, 0, lastMadeCtx->selFaces );
        if( pars.isFlagSet( selVerticesFlag ) )
            pars.getFlagArgument( selVerticesFlag, 0,
                                lastMadeCtx->selVertices );
        if( pars.isFlagSet( selTypeFlag ) )
            pars.getFlagArgument( selTypeFlag, 0, lastMadeCtx->selType );
        return MS::kSuccess;
    }

MStatus SelectRingContextCmd2::doQueryFlags()
{
    MArgParser pars = parser();

    if( pars.isFlagSet(selVerticesFlag) )
        setResult( lastMadeCtx->selVertices );

    if( pars.isFlagSet(selEdgesFlag) )
        setResult( lastMadeCtx->selEdges );

    if( pars.isFlagSet(selFacesFlag) )
        setResult( lastMadeCtx->selFaces );

    if( pars.isFlagSet(selTypeFlag) )
        setResult( lastMadeCtx->selType );

    return MS::kSuccess;
}

MStatus SelectRingContextCmd2::appendSyntax()
{
    MSyntax syn = syntax();

    syn.addFlag( selEdgesFlag, selEdgesLongFlag, MSyntax::kBoolean );
    syn.addFlag( selFacesFlag, selFacesLongFlag, MSyntax::kBoolean );
    syn.addFlag( selVerticesFlag, selVerticesLongFlag, MSyntax::kBoolean );
    syn.addFlag( selTypeFlag, selTypeLongFlag, MSyntax::kUnsigned );

    return MS::kSuccess;
}
```

```
MStatus initializePlugin( MObject obj )
{
   MFnPlugin plugin( obj, "David Gould", "1.0" );

   MStatus stat;
   stat = plugin.registerContextCommand(
                        SelectRingContextCmd2::commandName,
                        SelectRingContextCmd2::creator,
                        SelectRingToolCmd2::commandName,
                        SelectRingToolCmd2::creator,
                        SelectRingToolCmd2::newSyntax );
   if ( !stat )
        stat.perror( "registerContextCommand failed");
   return stat;
}

MStatus uninitializePlugin( MObject obj )
{
   MFnPlugin plugin( obj );

   MStatus stat;
   stat = plugin.deregisterContextCommand(
                        SelectRingContextCmd2::commandName,
                        SelectRingToolCmd2::commandName );
   if ( !stat )
        stat.perror( "deregisterContextCommand failed" );

   return stat;
}
```

Plug-in: `SelectRingContext2`
File: `selectRingContext2Properties.mel`

```
global proc selectRingContext2Properties()
{
   if( !`control -exists selectRing2` )
   {
        setUITemplate -pushTemplate OptionsTemplate;

        string $parent = `toolPropertyWindow -query -location`;
        setParent $parent;
```

```
        columnLayout selectRing2;
            frameLayout -collapsable true -collapse false
                -1 "Select Ring Settings" selectRing2Frame;
                columnLayout selectRing2Options;
                $parent = `setParent -query`;
                    separator -style "none";
                    checkBoxGrp -ncb 3
                        -1 "Components:"
                        -11 "Vertices"
                        -12 "Edges"
                        -13 "Faces"
                        selectRing2Components;
                radioButtonGrp -nrb 2
                    -1 "Type:"
                    -11 "Ring"
                        -12 "Loop"
                        selectRing2Type;
                setParent ..;
            setParent ..;
        setParent ..;
        setUITemplate -popTemplate;
    }
  }
```

Plug-in: `SelectRingContext2`
File: `selectRingContext2Values.mel`

```
    global proc selectRingContext2Values( string $ctxName )
    {
        string $icon = "selectRingContext2.xpm";
        string $helpTag = "Select Ring";
        toolPropertySetCommon $ctxName $icon $helpTag;

        string $parent = (`toolPropertyWindow -q -location` + "|selectRing2");
        setParent $parent;

        int $selVerts = `selectRingContext2 -q -selectVertices $ctxName`;
        int $selEdges = `selectRingContext2 -q -selectEdges $ctxName`;
        int $selFaces = `selectRingContext2 -q -selectFaces $ctxName`;
```

```
checkBoxGrp -e
    -v1 $selVerts
    -cc1 ("selectRingContext2 -e -selectVertices #1 " + $ctxName)
    -v2 $selEdges
    -cc2 ("selectRingContext2 -e -selectEdges #1 " + $ctxName)
    -v3 $selFaces
    -cc3 ("selectRingContext2 -e -selectFaces #1 " + $ctxName)
    selectRing2Components;

int $selType = `selectRingContext2 -q -selectType $ctxName`;

radioButtonGrp -e
    -on1 ("selectRingContext2 -e -selectType 0 " + $ctxName)
    -on2 ("selectRingContext2 -e -selectType 1 " + $ctxName)
    -select (!$selType ? 1 : 2)
    selectRing2Type;

    toolPropertySelect selectRing2;
}
```

SOURCE CODE EXPLANATION

Plug-in: `SelectRingContext2`
File: `SelectRingContext2.cpp`

This context makes use of the **MPxToolCommand** class. This class is derived from **MPxCommand**. An **MPxToolCommand**-derived command is designed specifically to work within a context, and as such must be capable of handling user interactivity. The command has a `cancel` function that is called when the user aborts the context. In addition, the command has a `finalize` function that is called when the context is completed. This function is responsible for creating the command and arguments so that they can be recorded and undone/redone if requested later. A context can have only one associated **MPxToolCommand**. The **SelectRingToolCmd2** class is derived from the **MPxToolCommand** class and provides the tool command functionality for the context.

```
class SelectRingToolCmd2 : public MPxToolCommand
{
    ...
};
```

The static member variable, commandName, is initialized to the command's name. This is the name Maya will use.

```
const MString SelectRingToolCmd2::commandName( "selectRingToolCmd2" );
...
```

The constructor calls the setCommandString function to set up the command name. The commandString function will then return this string.

```
SelectRingToolCmd2::SelectRingToolCmd2()
{
    setCommandString( SelectRingToolCmd2::commandName );
}
```

The doIt function initializes the parameters and then parses the command arguments.

```
MStatus SelectRingToolCmd2::doIt( const MArgList &args )
{
    ...
```

The current selection is stored. If the command is undone, this selection is simply restored.

```
    MGlobal::getActiveSelectionList( prevSel );
```

The options are initialized.

```
    selEdges = true;
    selFaces = false;
    selVertices = false;
    selEdgeObject = MDagPath();
    selEdgeComp = MObject::kNullObj;
    listAdjust = MGlobal::kReplaceList;
    selType = RING;
```

The arguments are parsed.

```
    MArgDatabase argData( syntax(), args, &stat );
    if( !stat )
        return stat;
```

The edge that will be used as the basis for the ring or loop selection is retrieved.

```
if( argData.isFlagSet( edgeFlag ) )
{
```

The edge is a string of the form <*object_name*>.e[<*edge_index*>].

```
MString edgeSpec;
argData.getFlagArgument( edgeFlag, 0, edgeSpec );
```

The edge is added to the **MSelectionList** object.

```
MSelectionList sel;
sel.add( edgeSpec );
```

The DAG path to the object and the edge component are extracted using the
getDagPath function.

```
    sel.getDagPath( 0, selEdgeObject, selEdgeComp );
}
...
}
```

As always, the redoIt function does the main work. This context has a more robust
implementation of ring selection and is thus more complex than the previous version. It also contains an implementation of ring selection.

```
MStatus SelectRingToolCmd2::redoIt()
{
```

An **MItMeshPolygon** iterator is bound to the selected mesh object.

```
MItMeshPolygon polyIter( selEdgeObject );
```

An **MItMeshEdge** iterator is bound to the mesh edge.

```
MItMeshEdge edgeIter( selEdgeObject, selEdgeComp );
...
```

The initial edge index is set to the edge originally selected.

```
const int initEdgeIndex = edgeIter.index();
...
```

The remainFaces and remainEdges arrays will provide a stack of faces and associated edges. Although Maya's array classes don't natively support stacks, the appending and removing of elements can be used to simulate the pushing and popping of elements. Using the array as a stack circumvents the need to use recursive functions to implement traversing edges in both forward and backward directions. Both stacks are guaranteed to be the same size.

An edge is uniquely identified by its face-edge combination. The face is the mesh-relative face index. The edge is the mesh-relative edge index. Face-relative edge indices are used only rarely in this plug-in.

```
MIntArray remainFaces;
MIntArray remainEdges;
```

If the selection type is set to ring, the next section is executed.

```
if( selType == RING )
{
```

The number of times the initial edge has been visited is recorded in the nInitEdgeVisits variable.

```
nInitEdgeVisits = 0;
```

The faces on both sides of the edge are retrieved using the getConnectedFaces function.

```
edgeIter.getConnectedFaces( faces );
```

If there are two neighboring faces, the second face and the initial edge are pushed onto the stacks.

```
if( faces.length() > 1 )
{
    remainFaces.append( faces[1] );
    remainEdges.append( initEdgeIndex );
}
```

The first face and initial edge are pushed onto the stacks. The stack now has the second face and first face in the stack, in that order. Why the first face is put on top of the stack will become obvious in the next section.

```
initFaceIndex = faces[0];
remainFaces.append( initFaceIndex );
remainEdges.append( initEdgeIndex );
```

While there are still elements in the stacks, the following section is executed. Because both stacks are the same size, only the length of the remainFaces array needs to be checked.

```
while( remainFaces.length() )
{
```

The current face and edge indices are pushed off the stacks.

```
lastIndex = remainFaces.length() - 1;
faceIndex = remainFaces[ lastIndex ];
edgeIndex = remainEdges[ lastIndex ];
remainFaces.remove( lastIndex );
remainEdges.remove( lastIndex );
```

If the current face and edge are the initial face and edge, the number of times this face-edge combination has been visited is recorded. If this is the second time it has been visited, the loop is complete because the edge traversal has now arrived back at the start. As such, the *while* loop is finished.

```
if( faceIndex == initFaceIndex &&
 edgeIndex == initEdgeIndex )
{
     if( ++ nInitEdgeVisits == 2 )
          break;
}
```

If the selection of edges is turned on, the edge is selected.

```
if( selEdges )
{
```

A new mesh edge component is created and the edge index added.

```
newComponent = indexedCompFn.create(
                        MFn::kMeshEdgeComponent );
indexedCompFn.addElement( edgeIndex );
```

The mesh object and its edge are added to the new selection.

```
newSel.add( selEdgeObject, newComponent );
}
```

If the selection of vertices is turned on, the vertices at the ends of the edge are selected.

```
if( selVertices )
{
```

A new mesh vertex component is created and the vertices are added.

```
newComponent = indexedCompFn.create(
                    MFn::kMeshVertComponent );
edgeIter.setIndex( edgeIndex, prevIndex );
```

The vertex indices at the ends of the edge are retrieved using the `index` function with the edge-relative index of the vertices: 0 and 1. Note that the `index` function is overloaded, so that when no parameter is passed in, it will return the mesh-relative index of the current edge.

```
indexedCompFn.addElement( edgeIter.index(0) );
indexedCompFn.addElement( edgeIter.index(1) );
```

The mesh object and its two vertices are added to the selection list.

```
newSel.add( selEdgeObject, newComponent );
}
```

Only if the current edge has more than one neighboring face will the next section be run. An edge with only one face is considered a boundary edge.

```
if( faceIndex != -1 )
{
```

If the selection of faces is turned on, the face is added to the new selection list.

```
if( selFaces )
{
        newComponent = indexedCompFn.create(
                        MFn::kMeshPolygonComponent );
        indexedCompFn.addElement( faceIndex );
        newSel.add( selEdgeObject, newComponent );
}
```

The navigateFace function is called to retrieve the edge directly opposite the current edge.

```
newEdgeIndex = navigateFace( selEdgeObject,
                             faceIndex,
                             edgeIndex, OPPOSITE );
```

The faces neighboring the new edge are retrieved.

```
edgeIter.setIndex( newEdgeIndex, prevIndex );
edgeIter.getConnectedFaces( faces );
```

The newFaceIndex is initialized to indicate a boundary edge.

```
newFaceIndex = -1;
```

If there is more than one neighboring face, the newFaceIndex is set to the face opposite the current face. The is the face across from the opposing edge.

```
if( faces.length() > 1 )
        newFaceIndex = (faceIndex == faces[0]) ?
                        faces[1] : faces[0];
```

The new face and edge indices are pushed onto the stacks.

```
                    remainFaces.append( newFaceIndex );
                    remainEdges.append( newEdgeIndex );
            }
        }
    }
```

If the selection type is set to ring, the next section is executed.

```
    else
    {
```

The reflection edge is the edge to either the right or left of the initial edge. A reflection edge is an edge that shares the same face, as well as one of the original edge vertices. These are the edges found when moving one edge forward or backward around the current face. The reflection edge is used to determine which face will be considered next.

```
        int reflEdgeIndex;
        int newReflEdgeIndex;
        int initReflEdgeIndex;
```

An edge is uniquely identified by a face index, edge index, and reflection edge index. Although the face index and edge index are sufficient to precisely identify an edge, the reflection edge index indicates the direction of the edge searching and is thus also necessary. Another stack, remainReflEdges, is created for reflection edges. As before, the stacks will be the same size.

```
        MIntArray remainReflEdges;
```

The number of times the initial edge has been visited is recorded.

```
        nInitEdgeVisits = 0;
```

The faces connected to the initial edge are retrieved.

```
        edgeIter.getConnectedFaces( faces );
```

The initial face index is the first face.

```
initFaceIndex = faces[0];
```

The same face and edge are pushed twice onto the stack. The only difference between the two is the reflection edge, which is the edge backward and forward from the initial edge. This indicates the direction in which the edges will be traversed: backward and forward.

```
for( i=0; i < 2; i++ )
{
        remainFaces.append( initFaceIndex );
        remainEdges.append( initEdgeIndex );
        remainReflEdges.append(
                navigateFace( selEdgeObject, initFaceIndex,
                                initEdgeIndex,
                                (i == 0) ? PREVIOUS : NEXT ) );
}
```

The initial reflection edge is the edge at the top of the stack.

```
initReflEdgeIndex = remainReflEdges[1];
```

While there are still elements in the stacks, the next section is executed.

```
while( remainFaces.length() )
{
```

The face, edge, and reflection edge are popped from the stacks.

```
lastIndex = remainFaces.length() - 1;
faceIndex = remainFaces[ lastIndex ];
edgeIndex = remainEdges[ lastIndex ];
reflEdgeIndex = remainReflEdges[ lastIndex ];
remainFaces.remove( lastIndex );
remainEdges.remove( lastIndex );
remainReflEdges.remove( lastIndex );
```

If the current face-edge-reflectionEdge combination is the same as the initial one, check to see if this is the second time this combination has been visited. If it has, the loop has been closed, as the traversal has now returned to the starting edge.

```
if( faceIndex == initFaceIndex &&
 edgeIndex == initEdgeIndex &&
 reflEdgeIndex == initReflEdgeIndex )
{
        if( ++ nInitEdgeVisits == 2 )
                break;
}
...
```

The faces neighboring the reflection edge are retrieved.

```
edgeIter.setIndex( reflEdgeIndex, prevIndex );
edgeIter.getConnectedFaces( faces );
```

If there is more than one neighboring face, the next section is executed.

```
if( faces.length() > 1 )
{
```

The new face index is set to the face opposite the reflection edges.

```
newFaceIndex = (faceIndex == faces[0]) ?
                        faces[1] : faces[0];
```

The edge backward from the reflection edge, along the new face, is retrieved.

```
int edgePrev = navigateFace( selEdgeObject,
                        newFaceIndex, reflEdgeIndex,
                        PREVIOUS );
```

The edge forward from the reflection edge, along the new face, is retrieved.

```
int edgeNext = navigateFace( selEdgeObject,
                        newFaceIndex, reflEdgeIndex,
                        NEXT );
```

The edge, backward or forward in the new face, that touches the current edge is determined. This edge connects directly to the current edge.

```
edgeIter.setIndex( edgeIndex, prevIndex );
if( edgeIter.connectedToEdge( edgePrev ) )
{
```

The previous edge of the new face touches the current edge.

```
newEdgeIndex = edgePrev;
```

The new reflection edge is found by moving backward one edge from the new edge. It is important to move backward because this is the same direction as the previous edge.

```
newReflEdgeIndex = navigateFace( selEdgeObject,
                newFaceIndex, newEdgeIndex,
                PREVIOUS );
}
else
{
    ...
}
```

The new face, edge, and reflection edge are pushed onto the stacks.

```
remainFaces.append( newFaceIndex );
remainEdges.append( newEdgeIndex );
remainReflEdges.append( newReflEdgeIndex );
        }
    }
}
```

The current selection is set to the selection prior to the context being activated.

```
MGlobal::setActiveSelectionList( prevSel, MGlobal::kReplaceList );
```

The new selection is integrated into the current selection, based on the list adjustment setting.

```
MGlobal::selectCommand( newSel, listAdjust );
...
}
```

The `navigateFace` function is used to move around the edges in the face, `faceIndex`, starting at the edge, `edgeIndex`. The direction of movement is given by the `loc` variable. It can be one of the following: `NEXT`, `PREVIOUS`, or `OPPOSITE`.

```
int SelectRingToolCmd2::navigateFace(
    const MDagPath &dagPath,
    const int faceIndex,
    const int edgeIndex,
    const Location loc )
{
    ...
```

The polygon iterator is set to the given face.

```
MItMeshPolygon polyIter( dagPath );
polyIter.setIndex( faceIndex, prevIndex );
```

All edges in the current face are retrieved.

```
MIntArray edges;
polyIter.getEdges( edges );
```

All edges are iterated over.

```
unsigned int i;
for( i=0; i < edges.length(); i++ )
{
```

If the current edge matches the start edge, `edgeIndex`, the next section is executed.

```
if( edgeIndex == edges[i] )
{
```

The face-relative offset index is calculated. If the location is set to OPPOSITE, the off-set is set to the index halfway around the face. If the location is set to NEXT, the offset is simply 1. Last, if the location is set to PREVIOUS, the offset is -1.

```
int offset;
if( loc == OPPOSITE )
        offset = edges.length() / 2;
else
        offset = (loc == NEXT) ? 1 : -1;
```

Given the face-relative offset, the final edge index is returned.

```
            return edges[ (i + offset) % edges.length() ];
        }
    }
```

This piece of code will never be run. It is just included to prevent any unnecessary compiler warnings.

```
    return -1;
}
```

The undoIt function restores the selection that existed before the context was activated.

```
MStatus SelectRingToolCmd2::undoIt()
{
    return MGlobal::setActiveSelectionList( prevSel,
                                    MGlobal::kReplaceList);
}
```

The finalize function generates the complete command line, including arguments, to reproduce the current action. This is a way of recording the action so that it can be redone/undone later.

```
MStatus SelectRingToolCmd2::finalize()
{
```

The command is built by starting with the command name.

```
MArgList command;
command.addArg( commandString() );
```

The edge is identified by a DAG path and edge component. This is converted to a single string by using the **MSelectionList**'s getSelectionStrings function.

```
command.addArg( MString(edgeFlag) );
MSelectionList sel;
sel.add( selEdgeObject, selEdgeComp );
MStringArray edges;
sel.getSelectionStrings( edges );
command.addArg( edges[0] );
...
```

Once all command arguments are added, the doFinalize function needs to be called.

```
    return MPxToolCommand::doFinalize( command );
}
```

The **SelectRingContext2** context class is now defined.

```
class SelectRingContext2 : public MPxContext
{
    ...
};
```

The static variable, helpTxt, is set to the text that will be displayed in the help line when the context is active.

```
const MString SelectRingContext2::helpTxt( "Click on an edge" );
```

The constructor initializes the member variables. These variables are duplicates of the member variables available in the **SelectRingToolCmd2** class.

```
SelectRingContext2::SelectRingContext2()
{
    listAdjust = MGlobal::kReplaceList;
```

```
selVertices = false;
selEdges = true;
selFaces = false;
selType = SelectRingToolCmd2::RING;
```

The title text is set.

```
setTitleString( "Select Ring Tool" );
```

The setImage function is used to specify the icon file to use with the context. A context can have up to three images associated with it. Maya will use the image whose size is best suited to that needed to be displayed.

```
setImage( "selectRingContext2.xpm", MPxContext::kImage1 );
}
```

The getClassName function is implemented in this version of the context. The previous context, **SelectRingContext1**, didn't implement this function. This function is used to get the context name when looking for the Property Sheet MEL scripts. These MEL scripts must be named <*class_name*>Properties.mel and <*class_name*>Values.mel, respectively.

```
void SelectRingContext2::getClassName( MString &name ) const
{
    name = "selectRingContext2";
}
```

The doRelease function is very similar to that in the previous version, with one important difference. The tool command is used to do the work rather than having it done internally to this function.

```
MStatus SelectRingContext2::doRelease( MEvent &event )
{
    ...
```

Given the first selected edge, the DAG path and edge of the mesh are retrieved.

```
MItSelectionList selIter (origEdgesSel, MFn::kMeshEdgeComponent);
if( !selIter.isDone() )
```

```
{
        MDagPath dagPath;
        MObject component;
        selIter.getDagPath( dagPath, component );
```

An instance of the **MPxToolCommand**-derived command associated with this context is created using the newToolCommand function. This function knows which tool command to create, in that it was registered during the plug-in initialization.

```
        SelectRingToolCmd2 &cmd =
                        *(SelectRingToolCmd2 *) newToolCommand();
```

The various accessor member functions (set*) are used to set the command's parameters.

```
        cmd.setCurrentSelection( curSel );
        cmd.setSelectedEdgeObject( dagPath );
        cmd.setSelectedEdgeComponent( component );
        cmd.setListAdjust( listAdjust );
        cmd.setSelEdges( selEdges );
        cmd.setSelFaces( selFaces );
        cmd.setSelVertices( selVertices );
        cmd.setSelType( SelectRingToolCmd2::SelType(selType) );
```

The redoIt function is called directly. Note that the doIt function isn't called. The doIt function expects a list of command arguments. Instead, the command parameters are set explicitly, and thus the redoIt function can be called directly. Note that there is nothing preventing the creation of a **MArgsList** and passing it to the doIt function instead.

```
        cmd.redoIt();
```

The finalize function must be called after the command is executed. This creates the command line that will reproduce the same action. This command line is saved by Maya for later redoing or undoing.

```
        cmd.finalize();
    }
    return MS::kSuccess;
}
```

The **SelectRingContextCmd2** context command class is now defined. It contains a protected member, lastMadeCtx, which is a pointer to the last context object created by this command. The class also implements command querying and editing. This is necessary for the Property Sheet of the context. The Property Sheet MEL scripts need to query and edit the current parameters of the context. They do it through this command.

```
class SelectRingContextCmd2 : public MPxContextCommand
{
   ...
protected:
   SelectRingContext2 *lastMadeCtx;
};
```

The static string, commandName, is initialized to the context command name.

```
const MString SelectRingContextCmd2::commandName( "selectRingContext2" );
```

The makeObj records the last context object created before returning it.

```
MPxContext *SelectRingContextCmd2::makeObj()
{
   lastMadeCtx = new SelectRingContext2();
   return lastMadeCtx;
}
```

The doEditFlags function retrieves the command arguments and changes the appropriate context parameters.

```
MStatus SelectRingContextCmd2::doEditFlags()
{
```

The command arguments parser is retrieved using the parser function.

```
   MArgParser pars = parser();
```

If a given flag is set, the member variable of the context is updated.

```
    if( pars.isFlagSet( selEdgesFlag ) )
            pars.getFlagArgument( selEdgesFlag, 0, lastMadeCtx->selEdges );
    ...
}
```

The `doQueryFlags` function extracts the command arguments and then returns the value(s) of the requested context parameters.

```
MStatus SelectRingContextCmd2::doQueryFlags()
{
    ...
```

Given a flag, the appropriate parameter is returned by calling the `setResult` function.

```
    if( pars.isFlagSet(selVerticesFlag) )
            setResult( lastMadeCtx->selVertices );
    ...
}
```

The `appendSyntax` function must be implemented to add any flags to the given syntax object.

```
MStatus SelectRingContextCmd2::appendSyntax()
{
```

The command's syntax object is retrieved using the `syntax` function.

```
    MSyntax syn = syntax();
```

All query and edit flags this context command supports are added using the `addFlag` function.

```
    syn.addFlag( selEdgesFlag, selEdgesLongFlag, MSyntax::kBoolean );
    syn.addFlag( selFacesFlag, selFacesLongFlag, MSyntax::kBoolean );
    syn.addFlag( selVerticesFlag, selVerticesLongFlag, MSyntax::kBoolean );
    syn.addFlag( selTypeFlag, selTypeLongFlag, MSyntax::kUnsigned );
    ...
}
```

The `initializePlugin` function registers the context command.

```
MStatus initializePlugin( MObject obj )
{
    ...
```

The `registerContextCommand` is called to register the context command
SelectRingContextCmd2, the tool command **SelectionRingContextCmd2**, and the
syntax-creating function, `newSyntax`.

```
stat = plugin.registerContextCommand(
                      SelectRingContextCmd2::commandName,
                      SelectRingContextCmd2::creator,
                      SelectRingToolCmd2::commandName,
                      SelectRingToolCmd2::creator,
                      SelectRingToolCmd2::newSyntax );

    ...
}
```

The `uninitializePlugin` function unregisters the context command and tool command.

```
MStatus uninitializePlugin( MObject obj )
{
    ...
    stat = plugin.deregisterContextCommand(
                      SelectRingContextCmd2::commandName,
                      SelectRingToolCmd2::commandName );

    ...
}
```

Plug-in: `SelectRingContext2`
File: `selectRingContext2Properties.mel`

The `selectRingContext2Properties.mel` script contains a global procedure by the
same name. This procedure is called by Maya to set up the user inteface in the **Tool
Property Window** for the context.

```
global proc selectRingContext2Properties()
{
```

If the `selectRing2` control already exists, this procedure has already been called and therefore the interface already exists.

```
if( !`control -exists selectRing2` )
{
```

The current template for the interface is set to the `OptionsTemplate`.

```
setUITemplate -pushTemplate OptionsTemplate;
```

The parent control of the **Tool Property Window** is retrieved. This is set to the parent for all further controls.

```
string $parent = `toolPropertyWindow -query -location`;
setParent $parent;
```

A `columnLayout` control provides the main layout control for the interface. Multiple frames or other controls can now be added.

```
columnLayout selectRing2;
```

A frame is created that will hold all controls. A `columnLayout` control is added to the frame.

```
frameLayout -collapsable true -collapse false
    -l "Select Ring Settings" selectRing2Frame;
    columnLayout selectRing2Options;
    $parent = `setParent -query`;

    separator -style "none";
```

A `checkBoxGrp` control is used to group all component selection types.

```
checkBoxGrp -ncb 3
    -l "Components:"
    -l1 "Vertices"
    -l2 "Edges"
    -l3 "Faces"
    selectRing2Components;
```

A `radioButtonGrp` control is added to group all selection types.

```
radioButtonGrp -nrb 2
        -l "Type:"
        -l1 "Ring"
        -l2 "Loop"
                selectRing2Type;
        setParent ..;
    setParent ..;
setParent ..;
```

The previous user interface template is now made the current one.

```
        setUITemplate -popTemplate;
    }
}
```

Plug-in: `SelectRingContext2`
File: `selectRingContext2Values.mel`

The `selectRingContext2Values` procedure is called to initialize the interface controls, created previously by the `selectRingContext2Properties` procedure.

```
global proc selectRingContext2Values( string $ctxName )
{
```

The icon and help text of the current context are set using the `toolPropertySetCommon` procedure.

```
        string $icon = "selectRingContext2.xpm";
        string $helpTag = "Select Ring";
        toolPropertySetCommon $ctxName $icon $helpTag;
```

The `selectRing2` control is retrieved and set to be the current parent.

```
        string $parent = (`toolPropertyWindow -q -location` + "|selectRing2");
        setParent $parent;
```

The component selection types are retrieved by calling the `selectRingContext2` context command with the `-q` (query) flag.

```
int $selVerts = `selectRingContext2 -q -selectVertices $ctxName`;
int $selEdges = `selectRingContext2 -q -selectEdges $ctxName`;
int $selFaces = `selectRingContext2 -q -selectFaces $ctxName`;
```

The check boxes' values are updated to the latest values. In addition, the `-cc#` (`changeCommand`) flags are set to MEL code that will automatically update the associated context parameter.

```
checkBoxGrp -e
    -v1 $selVerts
    -cc1 ("selectRingContext2 -e -selectVertices #1 " + $ctxName)
    -v2 $selEdges
    -cc2 ("selectRingContext2 -e -selectEdges #1 " + $ctxName)
    -v3 $selFaces
    -cc3 ("selectRingContext2 -e -selectFaces #1 " + $ctxName)
    selectRing2Components;
```

The current selection type is queried.

```
int $selType = `selectRingContext2 -q -selectType $ctxName`;
```

The radio buttons are updated with the latest values. When one of the buttons is turned on, the associated MEL code will be executed.

```
radioButtonGrp -e
 -on1 ("selectRingContext2 -e -selectType 0 " + $ctxName)
 -on2 ("selectRingContext2 -e -selectType 1 " + $ctxName)
 -select (!$selType ? 1 : 2)
 selectRing2Type;
```

The selected tool property is set to the context's control.

```
toolPropertySelect selectRing2;
}
```

11.3 SELECTVOLUMECONTEXT1 PLUG-IN

The **SelectVolumeContext1** plug-in demonstrates the following.

- Supporting mouse dragging

- Using a custom locator for drawing 3D guides

- Reacting to the Delete, Backspace, and Enter keys

- Supporting Maya's numerical input field

The **selectVolumeContext1** context is designed to allow the user to draw a series of 3D volumes (spheres and tubes) across the ground plane. All mesh vertices within these 3D volumes will be selected. Figure 11.6 shows a flat mesh plane. Several 3D guide volumes have been created using the **selectVolumeContext1** context.

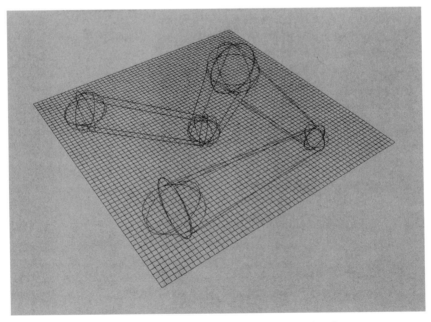

FIGURE 11.6 selectVolumeContext1 3D guide volumes.

When the Enter key is pressed, all mesh vertices in the volumes are selected, resulting in the selection shown in Figure 11.7.

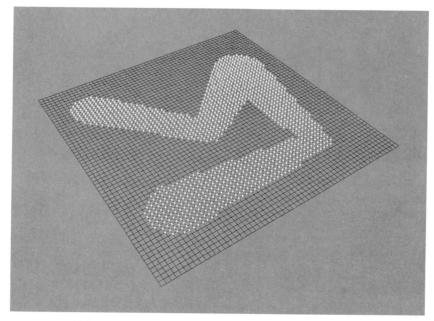

FIGURE 11.7 selectVolumeContext1's resulting selection.

11.3.1 INSTALLATION

1. Copy the selectVolumeContext1.xpm icon file from the directory containing the source code for the **SelectVolumeContext1** plug-in to one of the directories listed in the XBMLANGPATH environment variable.

2. Copy the following two MEL scripts from the directory containing the source code for the **SelectVolumeContext1** plug-in to one of the directories listed in the MAYA_SCRIPT_PATH environment variable.

    selectVolumeContext1Properties.mel
    selectVolumeContext1Values.mel

3. Open the **SelectVolumeContext1** workspace.

4. Compile it and load the resulting selectVolumeContext1 plug-in file in Maya.

11.3.2 **USAGE**

5. Complete the steps in the previous "1.3.1 Installation" section, if not done already.

6. Open the **PlaneMeshDetailed.ma** scene.

7. To create and activate the context, execute the following.

```
setToolTo `selectVolumeContext1`;
```

The cursor changes and the **Sel Vol** icon is shown in the toolbox.

8. Left click and drag in the center of the mesh plane.

    A 3D guide sphere is drawn.

9. Press the Enter key.

    All vertices inside the sphere are selected.

10. Hold down the Shift key.

    This indicates that the selection should be toggled.

11. Left click and drag at the left of the mesh plane.

    A 3D guide sphere is drawn.

12. Release the Shift key.

13. Left click and drag at the right of the mesh plane. Ensure that the tube crosses the previously selected vertices.

    Another 3D guide sphere is drawn, along with a connecting tube. Additional volumes can be created by continuing to click and drag.

14. Press the Enter key.

    The volumes are converted into a selection. Note that the vertices that were already selected are now unselected.

15. Hold down the Ctrl key.

    This will remove vertices from the selection.

16. Left click and drag on the left of the mesh plane.

17. Release the Ctrl key.

18. Left click and drag on the right of the mesh plane.

19. Press the Backspace key.

   The last 3D guide sphere is deleted. The Delete key can also be used for this purpose.

20. Left click and drag on the right of the mesh plane.

21. Ensure that the **Status Line** is displayed by selecting **Display | UI Elements | Status Line**.

22. The **Numeric Input Field** is located on the right, as shown in Figure 11.8.

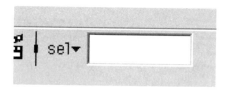

FIGURE 11.8 Numeric Input Field.

23. Click on the **sel** drop-down button.

24. Select **Numeric Input: Absolute** from the drop-down list.

   The **Numeric Input: Relative** option could also be used, in that the context doesn't make a distinction between relative and absolute.

25. Type the following into the **Numeric Input Field**.

   0.5 0 0.5 0.1

   This specifies a new sphere: x y z radius. To use the default value for any value, simply use the period character (.). Thus, the text

   2 5 3 .

   would create a sphere at (2.0, 5.0, 3.0) with a default radius of 0.25.

26. Press the Enter key.

    A sphere is created on the bottom left corner of the mesh plane. It has a radius of 0.1 unit and is located at (0.5, 0.0, 0.5).

27. Press the Enter key.

    The vertices in the volumes are removed from the selection.

SOURCE CODE

Plug-in: `SelectVolumeContext1`
File: `SelectVolumeLocator1.h`

This file declares the **SelectVolumeLocator1** class, which is used to perform custom OpenGL drawing of guide volumes.

```
class SelectVolumeLocator1 : public MPxLocatorNode
{
public:
   SelectVolumeLocator1();

 virtual void draw( M3dView &view,
                              const MDagPath &path,
                              M3dView::DisplayStyle style,
                              M3dView::DisplayStatus status );

   virtual bool isBounded() const;
   virtual MBoundingBox boundingBox() const;

   static void *creator();
   static MStatus initialize();

   static const MTypeId typeId;
   static const MString typeName;

     void addSphere( const MPoint &s );
     void setLastSphereRadius( const double rad );
     void deleteLastSphere();
     void refresh();

  private:
    MPointArray spheres;
```

```
      MPointArray circlePts;
      void generateCircle( const unsigned int nCirclePts );
      void drawSphere( const MPoint &s ) const;
      void drawTube( const MPoint &start,
                                 const MPoint &end ) const;

      static const int N_CIRCLEPTS;

      static MObject tickle;
   };
```

Plug-in: `SelectVolumeContext1`
File: `SelectVolumeLocator1.cpp`

```
   MObject SelectVolumeLocator1::tickle;

   const MTypeId SelectVolumeLocator1::typeId( 0x00339 );
   const MString SelectVolumeLocator1::typeName( "selectVolumeLocator1" );
   const int SelectVolumeLocator1::N_CIRCLEPTS = 20;

   SelectVolumeLocator1::SelectVolumeLocator1()
   {
      generateCircle( N_CIRCLEPTS );
   }

   void SelectVolumeLocator1::draw( M3dView &view,
                                    const MDagPath & path,
                                    M3dView::DisplayStyle style,
                                    M3dView::DisplayStatus status )
   {
      view.beginGL();
      glPushAttrib( GL_CURRENT_BIT );

      if( spheres.length() )
      {
          unsigned int i;
          for( i=0; i < spheres.length(); i++ )
              drawSphere( spheres[i] );
          for( i=0; i < spheres.length()-1; i++ )
              drawTube( spheres[i], spheres[i+1] );
      }
```

```
   glPopAttrib();
   view.endGL();
}
void SelectVolumeLocator1::addSphere( const MPoint &s )
{
   spheres.append( s );
}
void SelectVolumeLocator1::deleteLastSphere()
{
   if( spheres.length() )
         spheres.remove( spheres.length()-1 );
}
void SelectVolumeLocator1::setLastSphereRadius( const double rad )
{
   if( spheres.length() )
         spheres[ spheres.length()-1 ].w = rad;
}
const double M_2PI = M_PI * 2.0;
void SelectVolumeLocator1::generateCircle( const unsigned int nCirclePts )
{
   circlePts.setSizeIncrement( nCirclePts );

   MPoint pt;
   const double angleIncr = M_2PI / (nCirclePts - 1);
   double angle = 0.0;
   unsigned int i=0;
   for( ; i < nCirclePts; i++, angle+=angleIncr )
   {
         pt.x = cos( angle );
         pt.y = sin( angle );
         circlePts.append( pt );
   }
}
void SelectVolumeLocator1::drawSphere( const MPoint &s ) const
{
   unsigned int i;

   glBegin(GL_LINE_STRIP);
```

```
        for( i=0; i < circlePts.length(); i++ )
             glVertex3d( s.x + s.w * circlePts[i].x,
                            s.y,
                            s.z + s.w * circlePts[i].y );
        glEnd();

        glBegin(GL_LINE_STRIP);
        for( i=0; i < circlePts.length(); i++ )
             glVertex3d( s.x + s.w * circlePts[i].x,
                            s.y + s.w * circlePts[i].y,
                            s.z );
        glEnd();

        glBegin(GL_LINE_STRIP);
        for( i=0; i < circlePts.length(); i++ )
             glVertex3d( s.x,
                            s.y + s.w * circlePts[i].x,
                            s.z + s.w * circlePts[i].y );
        glEnd();
}

void SelectVolumeLocator1::drawTube( const MPoint &start,
                                     const MPoint &end ) const
{
   MPoint p0 = start;
   MPoint p1 = end;
   p0.w = p1.w = 1.0;

   MVector uAxis, vAxis, wAxis;
   uAxis = p1 - p0;
   uAxis.normalize();
   wAxis = MVector( 0.0, 1.0, 0.0 );
   vAxis = wAxis ^ uAxis;
   wAxis = uAxis ^ vAxis;

   unsigned int i;
   MPoint pt;

   MPointArray startPts, endPts;
   startPts.setSizeIncrement( circlePts.length() );
   endPts.setSizeIncrement( circlePts.length() );
```

```
for( i=0; i < circlePts.length(); i++ )
{
     pt = p0 + start.w * circlePts[i].x * vAxis +
          start.w * circlePts[i].y * wAxis;
     startPts.append( pt );

     pt = p1 + end.w * circlePts[i].x * vAxis +
          end.w * circlePts[i].y * wAxis;
     endPts.append( pt );
}

glBegin(GL_LINE_STRIP);
for( i=0; i < startPts.length(); i++ )
{
     pt = startPts[i];
     glVertex3d( pt.x, pt.y, pt.z );
}
glEnd();

glBegin(GL_LINE_STRIP);
for( i=0; i < endPts.length(); i++ )
{
     pt = endPts[i];
     glVertex3d( pt.x, pt.y, pt.z );
}
glEnd();

const int incr = startPts.length() / 4;

glBegin(GL_LINES);
for( i=0; i < endPts.length(); i+=incr )
{
     pt = startPts[i];
     glVertex3d( pt.x, pt.y, pt.z );
     pt = endPts[i];
     glVertex3d( pt.x, pt.y, pt.z );
}
glEnd();
}
```

```
bool SelectVolumeLocator1::isBounded() const
{
    return true;
}

MBoundingBox SelectVolumeLocator1::boundingBox() const
{
    MBoundingBox bbox;
    MPoint pt;
    double rad;
    unsigned int i;
    for( i=0; i < spheres.length(); i++ )
    {
        pt = spheres[i];
        rad = pt.w;
        pt.w = 1.0;

        bbox.expand( pt - MPoint( rad, rad, rad ) );
        bbox.expand( pt + MPoint( rad, rad, rad ) );
    }
    return bbox;
}

void *SelectVolumeLocator1::creator()
{
    return new SelectVolumeLocator1();
}
void SelectVolumeLocator1::refresh()
{
    MStatus stat;
    MObject thisNode = thisMObject();
    MFnDagNode dagFn( thisNode );

    MPlug tkPlug = dagFn.findPlug( tickle, &stat );
    int tkValue;
    tkPlug.getValue( tkValue );
    tkPlug.setValue( tkValue + 1 );
}
```

```
MStatus SelectVolumeLocator1::initialize()
{
   MFnNumericAttribute numFn;
   tickle = numFn.create( "tk", "tickle", MFnNumericData::kInt );
   numFn.setDefault( 0 );
   numFn.setHidden( true );
   addAttribute( tickle );

   return MS::kSuccess;
}
```

Plug-in: `SelectVolumeContext1`
File: `SelectVolumeContext1.h`

This file declares the classes for the context tool command **SelectVolumeToolCmd1**, the context **SelectVolumeContext1**, and the context command **SelectVolume ContextCmd1**.

```
class SelectVolumeToolCmd1 : public MPxToolCommand
{
public:
   SelectVolumeToolCmd1();

   MStatus doIt( const MArgList &args );
   MStatus redoIt();
   MStatus undoIt();
   bool isUndoable() const { return true; }
   MStatus finalize();

   void setPrevSel( const MSelectionList &sel ) { prevSel = sel; }
   void setListAdjust( const MGlobal::ListAdjustment &la )
                                             { listAdjust = la; }

   void addSphere( const MPoint &s );

   static void *creator();
   static MSyntax newSyntax();
   static const MString commandName;

 private:
   MSelectionList prevSel;
```

```
    MGlobal::ListAdjustment listAdjust;
    MPointArray spheres;

    bool inVolume( const MPoint &p ) const;
};

class SelectVolumeContext1 : public MPxContext
{
public:
    SelectVolumeContext1();

    virtual void toolOnSetup( MEvent &event );
    virtual void toolOffCleanup();

    virtual MStatus doPress( MEvent &event );
    virtual MStatus doDrag( MEvent &event );

    virtual void deleteAction();
    virtual void completeAction();
    virtual void abortAction();

    virtual bool processNumericalInput( const MDoubleArray &values,
                                        const MIntArray &flags,
                                        bool isAbsolute );
    virtual bool feedbackNumericalInput() const;
    virtual MSyntax::MArgType argTypeNumericalInput(unsigned index) const;

    virtual void getClassName( MString &name ) const;

private:
    short pressX, pressY;
    short releaseX, releaseY;
    bool addNewSphere;
    MSelectionList prevSel;
    MObject volumeLocatorObj;
    MGlobal::ListAdjustment listAdjust;
    MPointArray spheres;

    void updateViewport();
    void addSphere( const MPoint &s, bool updateLocator = true );
    void reset();
```

```
    MPoint intersectGround( const MPoint &rayOrigin,
                                        const MVector &rayDir );

    static const MString helpTxt;
};

class SelectVolumeContextCmd1 : public MPxContextCommand
{
public:
    virtual MPxContext *makeObj();

    static void *creator();
    static const MString commandName;
};
```

Plug-in: `SelectVolumeContext1`
File: `SelectVolumeContext1.cpp`

```
const MString SelectVolumeToolCmd1::commandName( "selectVolumeToolCmd1" );

const char *sphereFlag = "-sp", *sphereLongFlag = "-sphere";
const char *listAdjustFlag = "-la", *listAdjustLongFlag = "-listAdjust";

MSyntax SelectVolumeToolCmd1::newSyntax()
{
 MSyntax syntax;

    syntax.addFlag( sphereFlag, sphereLongFlag,
                    MSyntax::kDistance, MSyntax::kDistance,
                    MSyntax::kDistance, MSyntax::kDistance );
    syntax.makeFlagMultiUse( sphereFlag );

    syntax.addFlag( listAdjustFlag, listAdjustLongFlag,
                    MSyntax::kUnsigned );

    return syntax;
}

void *SelectVolumeToolCmd1::creator()
{
    return new SelectVolumeToolCmd1;
}
```

```
SelectVolumeToolCmd1::SelectVolumeToolCmd1()
{
    setCommandString( SelectVolumeToolCmd1::commandName );
}

MStatus SelectVolumeToolCmd1::doIt( const MArgList &args )
{
    listAdjust = MGlobal::kReplaceList;

    MStatus stat;
    MArgDatabase argData( syntax(), args, &stat );
    if( !stat )
        return stat;

    const unsigned int nUses = argData.numberOfFlagUses( sphereFlag );
    MArgList sphereFlagArgs;
    MDistance dist;
    MPoint s;
    unsigned int i, j;
    for( i=0; i < nUses; i++ )
    {
        argData.getFlagArgumentList( sphereFlag, i, sphereFlagArgs );
        s = MPoint::origin;
        for( j=0; j < sphereFlagArgs.length(); j++ )
        {
            sphereFlagArgs.get( j, dist );
            s[j] = dist.value();
        }
        addSphere( s );
    }

    if( argData.isFlagSet( listAdjustFlag ) )
    {
        unsigned value;
        argData.getFlagArgument( listAdjustFlag, 0, value );
        listAdjust = MGlobal::ListAdjustment( value );
    }

    return redoIt();
}
```

```
MStatus SelectVolumeToolCmd1::redoIt()
{
    MSelectionList newSel;

    MStatus stat;
    MPoint pt;
    MDagPath dagPath;
    MItDag dagIter( MItDag::kDepthFirst, MFn::kMesh );
    for( ; !dagIter.isDone(); dagIter.next() )
    {
        dagIter.getPath( dagPath );

        MItMeshVertex vertIter( dagPath, MObject::kNullObj, &stat );
        if( !stat )
            continue;

        bool isVisible = true;
        MDagPath searchPath( dagPath );
        do
        {
            MFnDagNode dagFn( searchPath );

            MPlug visPlug = dagFn.findPlug( "visibility" );
            MPlug intPlug = dagFn.findPlug( "intermediateObject" );
            bool vis, interm;
            visPlug.getValue( vis );
            intPlug.getValue( interm );

            if( !vis || interm )
            {
                isVisible = false;
                break;
            }

        } while( searchPath.pop() );

        if( !isVisible )
            continue;

        MFnSingleIndexedComponent indexedCompFn;
        MObject newComponent;
        newComponent = indexedCompFn.create( MFn::kMeshVertComponent );
```

```
                for( ; !vertIter.isDone(); vertIter.next() )
                {
                    pt = vertIter.position( MSpace::kWorld );
                    if( inVolume( pt ) )
                        indexedCompFn.addElement( vertIter.index() );
                }
                if( !indexedCompFn.isEmpty() )
                    newSel.add( dagPath, newComponent );
        }
    MGlobal::setActiveSelectionList( prevSel, MGlobal::kReplaceList );
    MGlobal::selectCommand( newSel, listAdjust );

    return MS::kSuccess;
}
MStatus SelectVolumeToolCmd1::undoIt()
{
    return MGlobal::setActiveSelectionList( prevSel,
                                            MGlobal::kReplaceList);
}

MStatus SelectVolumeToolCmd1::finalize()
{
    MArgList command;
    command.addArg( commandString() );
    command.addArg( MString(listAdjustFlag) );
    command.addArg( (int)listAdjust );

    MPoint s;
    unsigned int i;
    for( i=0; i < spheres.length(); i++ )
    {
        s = spheres[i];
        command.addArg( MString(sphereFlag) );
        command.addArg( s.x );
        command.addArg( s.y );
        command.addArg( s.z );
        command.addArg( s.w );
    }

    return MPxToolCommand::doFinalize( command );
}
```

```
void SelectVolumeToolCmd1::addSphere( const MPoint &s )
{
   spheres.append(s);
}

bool SelectVolumeToolCmd1::inVolume( const MPoint &p ) const
{
   double dist;
   MPoint pt;
   unsigned int i;
   for( i=0; i < spheres.length(); i++ )
   {
        pt = spheres[i];
        pt.w = 1.0;
        dist = pt.distanceTo( p );
        if( dist <= spheres[i].w )
              return true;
   }

   double len;
   double projDist;
   double t, rad;
   double startRad, endRad;
   MPoint start, end;
   MPoint projPt;
   MVector vecToPt, vecCentre;
   MVector vecProjPtToPt;
   for( i=0; i < spheres.length()-1; i++ )
   {
        start = spheres[i];
        end = spheres[i+1];
        startRad = start.w;
        endRad = end.w;
        start.w = 1.0;
        end.w = 1.0;

        vecToPt = p - start;
        vecCentre = end - start;

        len = vecCentre.length();
```

```
        vecCentre.normalize();
        projDist = vecToPt * vecCentre;
        if( projDist >= 0.0 && projDist <= len )
        {
                projPt = start + projDist * vecCentre;
                vecProjPtToPt = p - projPt;
                t = projDist / len;
                rad = (1 - t) * startRad + t * endRad;
                if( vecProjPtToPt.length() <= rad )
                        return true;
        }
    }

    return false;
}

const MString SelectVolumeContext1::helpTxt(
            "Click and drag to create spheres. Press Enter to finish." );

SelectVolumeContext1::SelectVolumeContext1()
{
    setTitleString( "Select Volume Tool" );
    setImage( "selectVolumeContext1.xpm", MPxContext::kImage1 );
}

void SelectVolumeContext1::getClassName( MString &name ) const
{
    name = "selectVolumeContext1";
}

void SelectVolumeContext1::toolOnSetup( MEvent &event )
{
    reset();

    setHelpString( helpTxt );
    setCursor( MCursor::editCursor );
}

void SelectVolumeContext1::toolOffCleanup()
{
    reset();
}
```

```
MStatus SelectVolumeContext1::doPress( MEvent &event )
{
    if( event.mouseButton() != MEvent::kLeftMouse )
        return MS::kFailure;

    event.getPosition( pressX, pressY );

    addNewSphere = true;

    return MS::kSuccess;
}
MStatus SelectVolumeContext1::doDrag( MEvent &event )
{
    short dragX, dragY;
    event.getPosition( dragX, dragY );

    if( abs( pressX - dragX ) <= 2 && abs( pressY - dragY ) <= 2 )
        return MS::kFailure;

    MPoint pressW, dragW;
    MVector pressWV, dragWV;

    M3dView view = M3dView::active3dView();
    view.viewToWorld( pressX, pressY, pressW, pressWV );
    view.viewToWorld( dragX, dragY, dragW, dragWV );

    MPoint sphereCentre = intersectGround( pressW, pressWV );
    MPoint sphereExtent = intersectGround( dragW, dragWV );

    double dist = sphereCentre.distanceTo( sphereExtent );

    if( addNewSphere )
    {
        if( spheres.length() == 0 )
        {
            listAdjust = MGlobal::kReplaceList;

            if( event.isModifierShift() || event.isModifierControl() )
            {
                if( event.isModifierShift() )
                {
                    if( event.isModifierControl() )
                        listAdjust = MGlobal::kAddToList;
```

```
                                    else
                                            listAdjust = MGlobal::kXORWithList;
                            }
                            else
                            {
                                    if( event.isModifierControl() )
                                            listAdjust = MGlobal::kRemoveFromList;
                            }
                    }

                    MGlobal::getActiveSelectionList( prevSel );
            }

            MPoint sphere = sphereCentre;
            sphere.w = 0.0;
            addSphere( sphere );
            addNewSphere = false;
    }

    MFnDependencyNode depFn( volumeLocatorObj );
    SelectVolumeLocator1 *loc = (SelectVolumeLocator1 *) depFn.userNode();

    if( spheres.length() )
            spheres[ spheres.length()-1 ].w = dist;
    loc-> setLastSphereRadius( dist );

    updateViewport();

    return MS::kSuccess;
}

void SelectVolumeContext1::deleteAction()
{
    if( spheres.length() )
            spheres.remove( spheres.length()-1 );

    if( !volumeLocatorObj.isNull() )
    {
            MFnDependencyNode depFn( volumeLocatorObj );
            SelectVolumeLocator1 *loc = (SelectVolumeLocator1 *)
                                    depFn.userNode();
```

```
            loc-> deleteLastSphere();

            updateViewport();
    }
}

void SelectVolumeContext1::completeAction()
{
    SelectVolumeToolCmd1 &cmd = *(SelectVolumeToolCmd1 *)
                                            newToolCommand();

    cmd.setPrevSel( prevSel );
    cmd.setListAdjust( listAdjust );
    unsigned int i;
    for( i=0; i < spheres.length(); i++ )
        cmd.addSphere( spheres[i] );

    cmd.redoIt();
    cmd.finalize();
    reset();
}

void SelectVolumeContext1::abortAction()
{
    reset();
}

bool SelectVolumeContext1::processNumericalInput(
    const MDoubleArray &values,
    const MIntArray &flags,
    bool isAbsolute )
{
    unsigned int nValues = values.length() > 4 ? 4 : values.length();

    MPoint newSphere( 0.0, 0.0, 0.0, 0.25 );
    unsigned int i;
    for( i=0; i < nValues; i++ )
    {
        if( !ignoreEntry( flags, i ) )
            newSphere[i] = values[i];
    }
```

```
    addSphere( newSphere );
    updateViewport();
    feedbackNumericalInput();

    return true;
}
bool SelectVolumeContext1::feedbackNumericalInput() const
{
    MString className;
    getClassName( className );

    MFeedbackLine::setTitle( className );
    MFeedbackLine::setFormat( "^6.3f ^6.3f ^6.3f ^6.3f" );

    MPoint sphere;
    if( spheres.length() )
        sphere = spheres[ spheres.length()-1 ];

    unsigned int i;
    for( i=0; i < 4; i++ )
        MFeedbackLine::setValue( i, sphere[i] );

    return true;
}

MSyntax::MArgType SelectVolumeContext1::argTypeNumericalInput(
    unsigned index ) const
{
    return MSyntax::kDistance;
}

void SelectVolumeContext1::reset()
{
    listAdjust = MGlobal::kReplaceList;
    prevSel.clear();
    spheres.clear();
    if( !volumeLocatorObj.isNull() )
    {
        MGlobal::removeFromModel( volumeLocatorObj );
        volumeLocatorObj = MObject::kNullObj;
    }
}
```

```
void SelectVolumeContext1::addSphere( const MPoint &s, bool
                                      updateLocator )
{
    spheres.append( s );

    if( updateLocator )
    {
        if( volumeLocatorObj.isNull() )
        {
            MFnDagNode dagFn;
            MObject transformObj = dagFn.create(
                                     SelectVolumeLocator1::typeId );
            volumeLocatorObj = dagFn.child( 0 );
        }

        MFnDependencyNode depFn( volumeLocatorObj );
        SelectVolumeLocator1 *loc = (SelectVolumeLocator1 *)
                                    depFn.userNode();
        loc->addSphere( s );
    }
}

void SelectVolumeContext1::updateViewport()
{
    if( !volumeLocatorObj.isNull() )
    {
        MFnDependencyNode depFn( volumeLocatorObj );
        SelectVolumeLocator1 *loc = (SelectVolumeLocator1 *)
                                    depFn.userNode();
        loc->refresh();
    }

    M3dView view = M3dView::active3dView();
    view.refresh();
}

MPoint SelectVolumeContext1::intersectGround( const MPoint &rayOrigin,
                                              const MVector &rayDir )
{
    MPoint hitPt;
    MVector groundNorm( 0.0, 1.0, 0.0 );
```

```
        double denom = groundNorm * rayDir;
        if( fabs( denom ) < 1.0e-8 )
        {
                double d = 0.0;
                double t = (d - (groundNorm * rayOrigin)) / denom;
                hitPt = rayOrigin + t * rayDir;
        }

        return hitPt;
}

const MString SelectVolumeContextCmd1::commandName(
                                        "selectVolumeContext1" );
MPxContext *SelectVolumeContextCmd1::makeObj()
{
    return new SelectVolumeContext1();
}

void *SelectVolumeContextCmd1::creator()
{
    return new SelectVolumeContextCmd1;
}
```

Plug-in: `SelectVolumeContext1`
File: `Plugin.cpp`

```
    MStatus initializePlugin( MObject obj )
    {
        MFnPlugin plugin( obj, "David Gould", "1.0" );

        MStatus stat;

        stat = plugin.registerNode( SelectVolumeLocator1::typeName,
                            SelectVolumeLocator1::typeId,
                            &SelectVolumeLocator1::creator,
                                &SelectVolumeLocator1::initialize,
                                MPxNode::kLocatorNode );
        if ( !stat )
        {
                stat.perror( "registerNode failed");
                return stat;
        }
```

```
    stat = plugin.registerContextCommand(
                        SelectVolumeContextCmd1::commandName,
                        SelectVolumeContextCmd1::creator,
                        SelectVolumeToolCmd1::commandName,
                        SelectVolumeToolCmd1::creator,
                        SelectVolumeToolCmd1::newSyntax );

    if ( !stat )
        stat.perror( "registerContextCommand failed");

    return stat;
}

MStatus uninitializePlugin( MObject obj )
{
    MFnPlugin plugin( obj );

    MStatus stat;

    stat = plugin.deregisterNode( SelectVolumeLocator1::typeId );
    if( !stat )
    {
        stat.perror( "deregisterNode failed" );
        return stat;
    }

    stat = plugin.deregisterContextCommand(
                            SelectVolumeContextCmd1::commandName,
                            SelectVolumeToolCmd1::commandName );
    if ( !stat )
        stat.perror( "deregisterContextCommand failed" );

    return stat;
}
```

Plug-in: `SelectVolumeContext1`
File: `selectVolumeContext1Properties.mel`

```
global proc selectVolumeContext1Properties()
{
    if( !`control -exists selectVolume1` )
    {
        setUITemplate -pushTemplate OptionsTemplate;
```

```
        string $parent = `toolPropertyWindow -query -location`;
        setParent $parent;

        columnLayout selectVolume1;
            frameLayout -collapsable true -collapse false
                -l "Select Volume Settings" selectVolume1Frame;
                columnLayout selectVolume1Options;
                $parent = `setParent -query`;

                    separator -style "none";

                    text -align "center"
                        -label "No options";

                setParent ..;
            setParent ..;
        setParent ..;

        setUITemplate -popTemplate;
    }
}
```

Plug-in: `SelectVolumeContext1`
File: `selectVolumeContext1Values.mel`

```
    global proc selectVolumeContext1Values( string $ctxName )
    {
        string $icon = "selectVolumeContext1.xpm";
        string $helpTag = "Select Volume";
        toolPropertySetCommon $ctxName $icon $helpTag;

        string $parent = (`toolPropertyWindow -q -location` +
                        "|selectVolume1");
        setParent $parent;

        toolPropertySelect selectVolume1;
    }
```

SOURCE CODE EXPLANATION

The **selectVolumeContext1** context creates a series of 3D guide spheres. The interconnected 3D tubes are derived from the spheres. To represent a sphere, a class with four floating-point numbers is required. Rather than define a new class, the **MPoint** class is used. It has four members: x, y, z, and w. The w value is normally used for representing homogeneous coordinates. In this case, it is used to hold the radius of the sphere. Lists of spheres can be created by using the **MPointArray** class.

Plug-in: `SelectVolumeContext1`
File: `SelectVolumeLocator1.cpp`

The context needs to be able to draw a series of 3D guide volumes. Unfortunately, the **MPxContext** class only has member functions for when the mouse is clicked, held, dragged, and released. Only during these actions can custom OpenGL drawing be performed in the context. When the user isn't holding down the mouse, there is no way to provide custom OpenGL drawing. In order that the 3D guide volumes be displayed at all times, a custom locator, **SelectVolumeLocator1**, is defined. It is a utility locator designed specifically for the context. It is only used when the context is active and the user is clicking. It is automatically deleted when the context is deactivated.

A locator is tagged for redrawing whenever one of its attributes changes. This locator doesn't have any attributes, but one is included for the purpose of initiating a redraw. The **tickle** attribute is defined for this purpose.

```
MObject SelectVolumeLocator1::tickle;
...
```

The constructor generates a circle of points. This pregenerated circle is used later by the various drawing functions.

```
SelectVolumeLocator1::SelectVolumeLocator1()
{
    generateCircle( N_CIRCLEPTS );
}
```

The `draw` function calls the `drawSphere` and `drawTube` functions for each sphere and interconnected spheres, respectively.

```
void SelectVolumeLocator1::draw( M3dView &view,
                                 const MDagPath & path,
                                 M3dView::DisplayStyle style,
                                 M3dView::DisplayStatus status )
```

```
{
    view.beginGL();
    glPushAttrib( GL_CURRENT_BIT );

    if( spheres.length() )
    {
        unsigned int i;
        for( i=0; i < spheres.length(); i++ )
            drawSphere( spheres[i] );
```

It is important not to do the operation spheres.length()-1 if the array is empty. The length function returns an unsigned integer, which has a valid range of values $[0, 2^{32-1}]$. As such, the result of the calculation $0 - 1$ is -1, which is outside its range. A *underflow* occurs and the final value is -1 modulus 2^{32}, which is 2^{32-1} (over 4 billion), the largest unsigned integer possible. The consequence of using this result is a very long loop. This is why this section of code is only run after the if(spheres.length()) statement is successful.

```
        for( i=0; i < spheres.length()-1; i++ )
            drawTube( spheres[i], spheres[i+1] );
    }

    glPopAttrib();
    view.endGL();
}
...
```

The generateCircle function generates a series of points around the circumference of a unit circle.

```
void SelectVolumeLocator1::generateCircle( const unsigned int nCirclePts )
{
    circlePts.setSizeIncrement( nCirclePts );

    MPoint pt;
    const double angleIncr = M_2PI / (nCirclePts - 1);
    double angle = 0.0;
    unsigned int i=0;
```

```
for( ; i < nCirclePts; i++, angle+=angleIncr )
{
        pt.x = cos( angle );
        pt.y = sin( angle );
        circlePts.append( pt );
}
}
```

The drawSphere function draws three circles, each one on a different plane: y = 0, z = 0, and x = 0.

```
void SelectVolumeLocator1::drawSphere( const MPoint &s ) const
{
    unsigned int i;

    glBegin(GL_LINE_STRIP);
    for( i=0; i < circlePts.length(); i++ )
```

The final coordinate is calculated by expanding the unit circle by the radius of the sphere (s.w) and moving it to the position of the sphere (s.x, s.y, s.z).

```
        glVertex3d( s.x + s.w * circlePts[i].x,
                    s.y,
                    s.z + s.w * circlePts[i].y );
    glEnd();

    glBegin(GL_LINE_STRIP);
    for( i=0; i < circlePts.length(); i++ )
        glVertex3d( s.x + s.w * circlePts[i].x,
                    s.y + s.w * circlePts[i].y,
                    s.z );
    glEnd();

    glBegin(GL_LINE_STRIP);
    for( i=0; i < circlePts.length(); i++ )
        glVertex3d( s.x,
                    s.y + s.w * circlePts[i].x,
                    s.z + s.w * circlePts[i].y );
    glEnd();
}
```

The `drawTube` function draws an open-ended tube between the two spheres.

```
void SelectVolumeLocator1::drawTube( const MPoint &start,
                                     const MPoint &end ) const
{
    MPoint p0 = start;
    MPoint p1 = end;
```

The homogeneous coordinate, w, is reset because it currently holds the spheres' radii.

```
    p0.w = p1.w = 1.0;
    ...
```

Three orthogonal axes are defined: u, v, and w. The u axis points from the first sphere to the second.

```
    uAxis = p1 - p0;
    uAxis.normalize();
```

The w axis points directly upward.

```
    wAxis = MVector( 0.0, 1.0, 0.0 );
```

The v axis is perpendicular to the u and w axes.

```
    vAxis = wAxis ^ uAxis;
```

Because the w axis isn't guaranteed to be orthogonal to the u axis, it needs to be recalculated so that it is perpendicular to both the u and v axes.

```
    wAxis = uAxis ^ vAxis;
    ...
```

The `startPts` and `endPts` are two arrays for holding 3D circles of points at the start and end spheres.

```
    MPointArray startPts, endPts;
    startPts.setSizeIncrement( circlePts.length() );
```

```
endPts.setSizeIncrement( circlePts.length() );
for( i=0; i < circlePts.length(); i++ )
{
```

The 3D circle is placed in the plane defined by the center of the sphere and having axes u, v, and w. The points are placed on the u = 0 plane.

```
        pt = p0 + start.w * circlePts[i].x * vAxis +
              start.w * circlePts[i].y * wAxis;
        startPts.append( pt );
        ...
}
```

The two circles are drawn.

```
    glBegin(GL_LINE_STRIP);
    ...
```

The tube surface is indicated by lines running from the first circle to the second. Only every fourth line is drawn.

```
    const int incr = startPts.length()/4;

    glBegin(GL_LINES);
    for( i=0; i < endPts.length(); i+=incr )
    {
        pt = startPts[i];
        glVertex3d( pt.x, pt.y, pt.z );
        pt = endPts[i];
        glVertex3d( pt.x, pt.y, pt.z );
    }
    glEnd();
}
```

The `boundingBox` function is necessary for the zoom selected and general zooming of the locator to work correctly.

```
MBoundingBox SelectVolumeLocator1::boundingBox() const
{
    MBoundingBox bbox;
    MPoint pt;
```

```
double rad;
unsigned int i;
for( i=0; i < spheres.length(); i++ )
{
        pt = spheres[i];
        rad = pt.w;
```

The homogeneous coordinate is reset, so that it isn't taken into account.

```
pt.w = 1.0;
```

The bounding box is expanded by a box that would completely contain the sphere.

```
        bbox.expand( pt - MPoint( rad, rad, rad ) );
        bbox.expand( pt + MPoint( rad, rad, rad ) );
}

    return bbox;
}
```

The `refresh` function doesn't actually do any redrawing. By changing one of the locator's attributes the shape will be tagged as needing a redraw. The next time Maya refreshes the viewport it will therefore redraw the locator.

```
void SelectVolumeLocator1::refresh()
{
    MStatus stat;
    MObject thisNode = thisMObject();
    MFnDagNode dagFn( thisNode );

    MPlug tkPlug = dagFn.findPlug( tickle, &stat );
    int tkValue;
    tkPlug.getValue( tkValue );
```

The **tickle** attribute is simply incremented to give it a different value. It isn't a problem if the result of the increment *overflows*, in that the value isn't used anywhere.

```
    tkPlug.setValue( tkValue + 1 );
}
```

Plug-in: `SelectVolumeContext1`
File: `SelectVolumeContext1.cpp`

The `newSyntax` function defines the two flags, `-sphere` and `-listAdjust`, for the tool command.

```
MSyntax SelectVolumeToolCmd1::newSyntax()
{
    ...
```

The `-sphere` flag takes four distance values. It can also be specified multiple times in the command arguments.

```
syntax.addFlag( sphereFlag, sphereLongFlag,
                MSyntax::kDistance, MSyntax::kDistance,
                MSyntax::kDistance, MSyntax::kDistance );
syntax.makeFlagMultiUse( sphereFlag );
    ...
}
```

The `redoIt` function changes the selection based on the guide volumes.

```
MStatus SelectVolumeToolCmd1::redoIt()
{
    MSelectionList newSel;

    MStatus stat;
    MPoint pt;
    MDagPath dagPath;
```

It is important to specify a filter for the DAG node traversal. The **MItMeshVertex** function set accepts the parent transform of a mesh shape as well as the mesh shape itself. When the DAG network is being traversed, the **MItMeshVertex** will find the parent transform and get the mesh data from the child shape. It will do the same with the mesh shape. This means that the mesh data is, in effect, traversed twice. To prevent this, the **MItDag** iterator is initialized to filter only mesh shape nodes.

```
MItDag dagIter( MItDag::kDepthFirst, MFn::kMesh );
for( ; !dagIter.isDone(); dagIter.next() )
{
        dagIter.getPath( dagPath );
```

```
MItMeshVertex vertIter( dagPath, MObject::kNullObj, &stat );
if( !stat )
        continue;
```

Only if the node is visible will it be considered. An object's visibility is inherited, and thus all parent nodes must be tested to determine if they have their visibility turned off. If an object is tagged as an *intermediate object*, the parent nodes will not be considered.

```
bool isVisible = true;
MDagPath searchPath( dagPath );
do
{
        MFnDagNode dagFn( searchPath );

        MPlug visPlug = dagFn.findPlug( "visibility" );
        MPlug intPlug = dagFn.findPlug( "intermediateObject" );
        bool vis, interm;
        visPlug.getValue( vis );
        intPlug.getValue( interm );

        if( !vis || interm )
        {
                isVisible = false;
                break;
        }

} while( searchPath.pop() );

if( !isVisible )
        continue;
```

Create a new mesh vertex component.

```
MFnSingleIndexedComponent indexedCompFn;
MObject newComponent;
newComponent = indexedCompFn.create( MFn::kMeshVertComponent );
```

Each vertex in the mesh is iterated over.

```
for( ; !vertIter.isDone(); vertIter.next() )
{
```

The world space position of the vertex is retrieved.

```
pt = vertIter.position( MSpace::kWorld );
```

The `inVolume` function is called to test if the point is inside any of the guide volumes. If it is, the vertex's index is added to the component.

```
if( inVolume( pt ) )
        indexedCompFn.addElement( vertIter.index() );
    }
```

The vertices found inside the guide volumes are added to the new selection list.

```
if( !indexedCompFn.isEmpty() )
        newSel.add( dagPath, newComponent );
    }
```

The previous selection is restored.

```
MGlobal::setActiveSelectionList( prevSel, MGlobal::kReplaceList );
```

The new selection is merged with the existing selection based on the `listAdjust` setting.

```
MGlobal::selectCommand( newSel, listAdjust );
    ...
}
```

The tool command is undone by restoring the previous selection.

```
MStatus SelectVolumeToolCmd1::undoIt()
{
    return MGlobal::setActiveSelectionList( prevSel,
                                    MGlobal::kReplaceList);
}
```

The `finalize` function generates a command argument list for the current command settings.

```
MStatus SelectVolumeToolCmd1::finalize()
{
    MArgList command;
    command.addArg( commandString() );
```

The `listAdjust` argument is added.

```
    command.addArg( MString(listAdjustFlag) );
    command.addArg( (int)listAdjust );
```

Each of the spheres is included as an argument to the command.

```
    MPoint s;
    unsigned int i;
    for( i=0; i < spheres.length(); i++ )
    {
        s = spheres[i];
        command.addArg( MString(sphereFlag) );
        command.addArg( s.x );
        command.addArg( s.y );
        command.addArg( s.z );
        command.addArg( s.w );
    }
```

The `doFinalize` function must be called after all arguments have been included.

```
    return MPxToolCommand::doFinalize( command );
}
```

The `inVolume` function returns `true` if the given point is inside any of the guide volumes.

```
bool SelectVolumeToolCmd1::inVolume( const MPoint &p ) const
{
```

The point is tested with each of the spheres.

```
...
for( i=0; i < spheres.length(); i ++ )
{
        pt = spheres[i];
        pt.w = 1.0;
        dist = pt.distanceTo( p );
```

If the distance from the point to the sphere's center is less than or equal to the sphere radius, the point is inside the sphere.

```
        if( dist <= spheres[i].w )
                return true;
}
```

The point is tested with each of the tubes connecting the spheres.

```
...
for( i=0; i < spheres.length()-1; i++ )
{
```

The start and end spheres of a tube are initialized.

```
        start = spheres[i];
        end = spheres[i+1];
        startRad = start.w;
        endRad = end.w;
```

The homogeneous coordinate is reset.

```
        start.w = 1.0;
        end.w = 1.0;
```

The vector from the start sphere's center to the point is calculated.

```
        vecToPt = p - start;
```

The vector from the start to the end spheres' centers is calculated. Its length is recorded and then it is normalized.

```
vecCentre = end - start;
len = vecCentre.length();
vecCentre.normalize();
```

The distance from the start sphere and the point projected onto the vecCentre vector is determined by calculating the dot product of the vecToPt vector and the vecCentre vector. The result is the length of the projected vector. This is a *signed* length and thus is negative if the vector projects to a point behind the start sphere and positive if it projects to a point in front of the start sphere. Thus, only if the length is positive and under the distance to the second sphere is the point within the perpendicular area between the two spheres.

```
projDist = vecToPt * vecCentre;
if( projDist >= 0.0 && projDist <= len )
{
```

The test point is projected onto the vecCentre vector.

```
projPt = start + projDist * vecCentre;
```

The vector from the test point to the projected point is calculated.

```
vecProjPtToPt = p - projPt;
```

The parametric distance of the projected point along the line between the two spheres is calculated.

```
t = projDist / len;
```

The radius of the tube at the projected point is calculated by linearly interpolating the radius at the two spheres.

```
rad = (1 - t) * startRad + t * endRad;
```

If the test point is at a distance less than or equal to the calculated tube radius, the point is inside the tube.

```
            if( vecProjPtToPt.length()<= rad )
                return true;
        }
    }
```

The test point isn't inside any of the volumes.

```
    return false;
}
```

The functions for the **SelectVolumeContext1** context will now be covered. The `toolOnSetup` function resets the internal values and then sets the help string and current mouse cursor.

```
void SelectVolumeContext1::toolOnSetup( MEvent &event )
{
    reset();

    setHelpString( helpTxt );
    setCursor( MCursor::editCursor );
}
```

The cleaning up of the context involves resetting the internal values.

```
void SelectVolumeContext1::toolOffCleanup()
{
    reset();
}
```

The `doPress` function handles all mouse click events.

```
MStatus SelectVolumeContext1::doPress( MEvent &event )
{
```

Only left-mouse button clicks are considered. The middle-mouse button is ignored. The right-mouse button is controlled exclusively by Maya and can't be overridden in a custom context.

```
if( event.mouseButton() != MEvent::kLeftMouse )
    return MS::kFailure;
```

The current mouse position, in viewport coordinates, is recorded.

```
event.getPosition( pressX, pressY );
```

The addNewSphere flag is used to determine if a new sphere should be created. The doDrag function will handle this.

```
addNewSphere = true;
...
}
```

When the user clicks, the doPress function is called. Before any dragging occurs, the doHold function is called. This context doesn't handle the doHold event, in that it isn't needed. When the user then drags the mouse, the doDrag function is called.

```
MStatus SelectVolumeContext1::doDrag( MEvent &event )
{
```

The current mouse position in the viewport is retrieved.

```
short dragX, dragY;
event.getPosition( dragX, dragY );
```

If the mouse has moved less than 3 pixels in any direction from the initial click position, the drag is ignored.

```
if( abs( pressX - dragX ) <= 2 && abs( pressY - dragY ) <= 2 )
    return MS::kFailure;

...
```

The current view is retrieved.

```
M3dView view = M3dView::active3dView();
```

The world space position and direction of the initial position and current position are calculated by using the `viewToWorld` function.

```
view.viewToWorld( pressX, pressY, pressW, pressWV );
view.viewToWorld( dragX, dragY, dragW, dragWV );
```

The `intersectGround` function is called to calculate where the given world space rays (origin and direction) hit the ground plane.

```
MPoint sphereCentre = intersectGround( pressW, pressWV );
MPoint sphereExtent = intersectGround( dragW, dragWV );
```

The distance, in world space coordinates, from the initial mouse position to the current mouse position is calculated.

```
double dist = sphereCentre.distanceTo( sphereExtent );
```

If the `addNewSphere` flag is set, the user has just clicked and now dragged a sufficent distance from the initial mouse position. A sphere can now be created.

```
if( addNewSphere )
{
```

If this is the first sphere in the list, it is important to note that there could have been other spheres, but they have been deleted by pressing the Backspace key. When the first sphere is created, the modifier key state is recorded. This will have a bearing on the final list-merging behavior.

```
if( spheres.length() == 0 )
{
    listAdjust = MGlobal::kReplaceList;

    if( event.isModifierShift() || event.isModifierControl() )
```

```
        {
            if( event.isModifierShift() )
            {
                if( event.isModifierControl() )
                    listAdjust = MGlobal::kAddToList;
                else
                    listAdjust = MGlobal::kXORWithList;
            }
            else
            {
                if( event.isModifierControl() )
                    listAdjust = MGlobal::kRemoveFromList;
            }
        }
```

The current selection is recorded.

```
            MGlobal::getActiveSelectionList( prevSel );
        }
```

The sphere is created at the location, in world space coordinates, of the first click.

```
        MPoint sphere = sphereCentre;
```

The sphere width is initialized to be zero. It will be updated in the next section.

```
        sphere.w = 0.0;
```

The sphere is added to the list. The addSphere function will automatically create the custom locator.

```
        addSphere( sphere );
```

The sphere creation flag is reset. Further dragging will not produce a new sphere. This would require a new left-mouse click.

```
        addNewSphere = false;
    }
```

The instance of the **SelectVolumeLocator** class is retrieved using the userNode function. Care must be taken when using this method because the returned pointer is not guaranteed to be non-null.

```
MFnDependencyNode depFn( volumeLocatorObj );
SelectVolumeLocator1 *loc = (SelectVolumeLocator1 *) depFn.userNode();
```

The radius of the last sphere is updated both in the context and the locator.

```
if( spheres.length() )
        spheres[ spheres.length()-1 ].w = dist;
loc->setLastSphereRadius( dist );
```

The viewport is updated.

```
updateViewport();
    ...
}
```

When the user presses the Delete or Backspace key, the deleteAction function is called.

```
void SelectVolumeContext1::deleteAction()
{
```

The last sphere is removed from the context.

```
if( spheres.length() )
        spheres.remove( spheres.length()-1 );
```

If the custom locator exists, its last sphere is deleted, and then the viewport is updated. The number of spheres in the context and the locator must be the same. In a commercial plug-in, this should be tested for during development.

```
if( !volumeLocatorObj.isNull() )
{
        MFnDependencyNode depFn( volumeLocatorObj );
        SelectVolumeLocator1 *loc = (SelectVolumeLocator1 *)
                            depFn.userNode();
```

```
        loc->deleteLastSphere();

        updateViewport();
    }
}
```

When the user presses the Enter key, the `completeAction` function is called.

```
void SelectVolumeContext1::completeAction()
{
```

A new instance of the **SelectVolumeToolCmd1** command is created by using the `newToolCommand` function.

```
SelectVolumeToolCmd1 &cmd = *(SelectVolumeToolCmd1 *)
                                    newToolCommand();
```

The command's previous selection is now set. Because the locator still exists, it will have changed the current selection. This is why the current selection can't be used instead of the selection that existed when the first mouse click and drag happened.

```
cmd.setPrevSel( prevSel );
```

The list adjustment setting is updated.

```
cmd.setListAdjust( listAdjust );
```

The spheres are added to the command.

```
unsigned int i;
for( i=0; i < spheres.length(); i++ )
    cmd.addSphere( spheres[i] );
```

With all parameters now set, the command can be executed.

```
cmd.redoIt();
```

The command and its arguments are recorded.

```
cmd.finalize();
```

The context's settings are reset.

```
    reset();
}
```

When the context is quit without finishing, the `abortAction` function is called. This can happen as a result of the `ctxAbort` MEL command being executed.

```
void SelectVolumeContext1::abortAction()
{
```

The context's settings are reset.

```
    reset();
}
```

When a user enters text in the **Numeric Input Field**, the context's `processNumericalInput` function is called.

```
bool SelectVolumeContext1::processNumericalInput(
    const MDoubleArray &values,
    const MIntArray &flags,
    bool isAbsolute )
{
```

The maximum number of values is four because that is the maximum number of components in the sphere.

```
unsigned int nValues = values.length() > 4 ? 4 : values.length();
```

A default sphere is initialized. If the text input doesn't contain explicit values, the default ones will be used instead.

```
MPoint newSphere( 0.0, 0.0, 0.0, 0.25 );
```

Each of the values is iterated over.

```
unsigned int i;
for( i=0; i < nValues; i++ )
{
```

If the value isn't to be ignored, it is set. A value is ignored if the text is set to a period character (.).

```
    if( !ignoreEntry( flags, i ) )
        newSphere[i] = values[i];
}
```

A new sphere is created and the viewport is updated.

```
addSphere( newSphere );
updateViewport();
```

The feedbackNumericalInput function is called to update the numerical field with the final setting.

```
feedbackNumericalInput();
...
}
```

The feedbackNumericalInput function is called when the numerical field needs to be updated to the actual context settings.

```
bool SelectVolumeContext1::feedbackNumericalInput() const
{
```

The feedback title is set to the context's name.

```
MFeedbackLine::setTitle( className );
```

The text formatting of the feedback data is set.

```
MFeedbackLine::setFormat( "^6.3f ^6.3f ^6.3f ^6.3f" );
```

The last sphere is retrieved.

```
MPoint sphere;
if( spheres.length() )
      sphere = spheres[ spheres.length()-1 ];
```

The components of the last sphere are included in the feedback line.

```
unsigned int i;
for( i=0; i < 4; i++ )
      MFeedbackLine::setValue( i, sphere[i] );
   ...
}
```

This function is used to specify the data type of each element in the feedback field. Because the position and radius of a sphere can be specified as distance, the **MSyntax::kDistance** value is returned.

```
MSyntax::MArgType SelectVolumeContext1::argTypeNumericalInput(
   unsigned index ) const
{
   return MSyntax::kDistance;
}
```

The reset function restores the context to its initial state. This includes removing the custom locator node, if it has been created.

```
void SelectVolumeContext1::reset()
{
   listAdjust = MGlobal::kReplaceList;
   prevSel.clear();
   spheres.clear();
   if( !volumeLocatorObj.isNull() )
   {
      MGlobal::removeFromModel( volumeLocatorObj );
      volumeLocatorObj = MObject::kNullObj;
   }
}
```

The context's `addSphere` function adds the given sphere to both the context and the custom locator.

```
void SelectVolumeContext1::addSphere( const MPoint &s, bool
                                      updateLocator)
{
```

The sphere is added to the list of spheres.

```
spheres.append( s );
```

If the `updateLocator` setting is `true`, the custom locator is updated to include the new sphere. It is rare when the locator wouldn't also be updated (the number of spheres in both the context and the locator should be the same), and thus the default setting of `updateLocator` is `true`.

```
if( updateLocator )
{
```

If the custom locator doesn't exist, it is created.

```
if( volumeLocatorObj.isNull() )
{
    MFnDagNode dagFn;
    MObject transformObj = dagFn.create(
                               SelectVolumeLocator1::typeId );
    volumeLocatorObj = dagFn.child( 0 );
}
```

The sphere is added to the locator.

```
MFnDependencyNode depFn( volumeLocatorObj );
SelectVolumeLocator1 *loc = (SelectVolumeLocator1 *)
                           depFn.userNode();
loc->addSphere( s );
    }
}
```

The updateViewport function will update the active viewport.

```
void SelectVolumeContext1::updateViewport()
{
    if( !volumeLocatorObj.isNull() )
    {
        ...
```

The locator's refresh function is called to tag the locator as needing to be redrawn.

```
        loc->refresh();
    }
    ...
```

The view's refresh function is called. Only the current view is updated and the redrawing isn't forced. This means that only those objects that have changed will be redrawn. Calling M3dView::refresh(true, true) can be very intensive and therefore should be avoided.

```
    view.refresh();
}
```

The intersectGround function calculates the point of intersection between the given ray (rayOrigin and rayDir) and the ground plane (y = 0).

```
MPoint SelectVolumeContext1::intersectGround( const MPoint &rayOrigin,
                                              const MVector &rayDir )
{
    ...
```

The normal to the ground plane is specifed.

```
    MVector groundNorm( 0.0, 1.0, 0.0 );
```

The denominator of the intersection calculation is computed using the dot product of the ground plane's normal and the ray direction.

```
    double denom = groundNorm * rayDir;
```

If the denominator is zero, the ray is parallel to the ground plane. There can't be any possible intersection. Because floating-point precision isn't exact, the denominator is compared with a small tolerance very close to zero.

```
if( fabs( denom ) < 1.0e-8 )
{
```

The value, d, is the result of computing the dot product of the ground plane normal and a point on the ground plane. Because the point (0,0,0) is on the ground plane, calculating the dot product with any vector will always result in 0.

```
double d = 0.0;
```

Calculate the parametric intersection, t, of the ray and the ground plane.

```
double t = (d - (groundNorm * rayOrigin)) / denom;
```

The intersection point is calculated by using the parametric intersection value. Note that the sign of the parametric intersection isn't tested. It is completely valid that the ground plane be behind the ray.

```
hitPt = rayOrigin + t * rayDir;
}
```

The intersection point is returned. If there is no intersection, the point returned is the origin (0,0,0).

```
return hitPt;
}
```

Further Learning

To continue your learning of Maya programming, there is a wide variety of online and offline resources available.

A.1 ONLINE RESOURCES

The Internet contains a enormous variety of computer graphics programming resources. Although it is possible to locate information about a given topic using your favorite web search engine, there are some sites that have specific Maya programming information.

A.1.1 COMPANION WEB SITE

The official companion site for this book is located at:

www.davidgould.com

A list, though not exhaustive, of the information available at the site includes:

- MEL scripts and C++ source code for all examples in the book
- Additional example MEL scripts
- Additional example C++ API source code
- Errata for this book
- Continually updated glossary
- Updated list of other relevant web sites and online resources

A.1.2 ADDITIONAL WEB SITES

Of particular note are the following web sites, which provide specific Maya programming information and forums.

ALIAS

www.alias.com

This is the complete reference site for the Maya product. It contains the latest product development news, example scripts, and plug-ins. Of particular interest to Maya developers is the Support Knowledgebase. It contains a great deal of information for almost all Maya programming tasks. The frequently asked questions (FAQ) sections can be very helpful for specific programming topics.

If you intend to create commerical plug-ins, be sure to look at the Alias Conductors program. This is an Alias program that provides greater development and marketing support to developers who are going to commercialize their products. There is even support for developers who want to distribute their plug-ins as shareware or freeware.

HIGHEND3D

www.highend3d.com

Best known for its in-depth coverage of the major animation and modeling packages, the Highend3D site is also a great repository of MEL scripts and plug-ins. It also hosts the Maya Developers forum, where you can ask questions of other developers.

BRYAN EWERT

www.ewertb.com/maya

This site contains a large number of MEL and C++ API tutorials and examples. The MEL basics are covered, as well as some of the more advanced topics. The "How To" sections are interesting for developers needing a fix to a particular problem.

MATHWORLD

http://mathworld.wolfram.com

This site contains a comprehensive encyclopedia of mathematical concepts. Quite a few of the concepts are explained with interactive demonstrations.

A.2 MAYA APPLICATION

The Maya product ships with an extensive collection of Maya programming documentation and examples. In addition, don't forget that you can often learn how Maya performs a given set of tasks by turning on **Echo All Commands** in the **Script Editor**. This can be a great starting guide if you want to do something similar.

A.2.1 DOCUMENTATION

In particular, the MEL and C++ API reference material will be a constant source of important programming information. All documentation can be accessed from within Maya by pressing **F1** or by selecting **Help** from the main menu. The main documentation page will be shown. From here, the MEL tutorials and reference documentation can be accessed. The Developer guide includes information on creating plug-ins and using the C++ API.

   The help documetation's search functionality is quite extensive. All online documentation can be searched, including the MEL and C++ API reference documentation.

   If you happen to be using the older version 5.*x* of Maya, it is highly recommended that the **Maya 5.0 Tech Docs Update** be downloaded and installed. The documentation has a far better layout and is more accessible than the standard documentation. It is available at the Alias web site.

A.2.2 EXAMPLES

The standard Maya product comes with a large number of example MEL scripts and C++ plug-ins.

MEL EXAMPLES

Because Maya's interface is written entirely in MEL, the scripts it uses are provided with the application. There is no better insight into learning how to write professional MEL scripts than by looking at the scripts written by the Maya software engineers. You will find a host of scripts in the following directory, as well its subdirectories.

```
<maya_install>\scripts
```

I strongly recommend perusing them to see how well-designed scripts are written. Note, however, that all scripts provided are the copyright of Alias and cannot be used for derived works. Instead, study them and learn from their example but don't be tempted to copy and use them as is.

In addition, be careful that when you are reviewing the scripts that you don't accidently change them. Because they are used by Maya, any changes may cause the system to become unstable and potentially crash. For this reason, it is best to make a copy of the scripts beforehand.

C++ API EXAMPLES

The C++ API example directories include source code for plug-ins, stand-alone applications, and motion-capture servers. The examples are located at:

```
<maya_install>\devkit
```

Further Reading

Computer graphics encompasses a wide variety of disciplines. However, the foundation of all computer graphics is, undoubtedly, mathematics. In particular, discrete mathematics, linear algebra, and calculus provide the major foundation for almost all computer graphics theory and practice. In addition to mathematics, a solid undertstanding of programming practices will help you in developing efficient and robust programs.

With both a good understanding of mathematics and programming, you will have a solid base from which to learn the particular techniques and methods used in computer graphics. Even though the field is continually evolving, there are many computer graphics principles that once learned will hold you in good stead for all future work. The following is a non-exhaustive list of books that provide a good grounding in their respective areas.

B.1 MATHEMATICS

Selby, Peter, and Steve Slavin. *Practical Algebra*. New York: John Wiley & Sons, 1991.

Thompson, Silvanus P., and Martin Gardner. *Calculus Made Easy*. New York: St. Martin's Press, 1998.

Van Verth, James M., and Lars M. Bishop. *Essential Mathematics for Games & Interactive Applications*. San Francisco: Morgan Kaufmann Publishers, 2004.

Mortenson, Michael E.. *Mathematics for Computer Graphics Applications*. New York: Industrial Press, 1999.

Lengyel, Eric. *Mathematics for 3D Game Programming & Computer Graphics*. Hingham, Mass.: Charles River Media, 2001.

B.2 PROGRAMMING

B.2.1 GENERAL

Deitel, Harvey M., and Paul J. Deitel. *C How to Program* (3d ed.). Upper Saddle River, N.J.: Prentice-Hall, 2000.

Knuth, Donald E. *The Art of Computer Programming*, 3 vols. Boston: Addison-Wesley, 1998.

Cormen, Thomas H., Charles E. Leiserson, Ronald L. Rivest, and Clifford Stein. *Introduction to Algorithms* (2d ed.). Cambridge, Mass.: MIT Press, 2001.

B.2.2 C++ LANGUAGE

Liberty, Jesse. *Sams Teach Yourself C++ in 21 Days Complete Compiler Edition* 4th ed.). Indianapolis: Sams Technical Publishing, 2001.

Deitel, Harvey M., and Paul J. Deitel. *C++ How to Program* (3d ed.). Upper Saddle River, N.J.: Prentice-Hall, 2000.

Stroustrup, Bjarne. *The C++ Programming Language* (special 3d ed.). Boston: Addison-Wesley, 2000.

Meyers, Scott. *Effective C++: 50 Specific Ways to Improve Your Programs and Design* (2d ed.). Boston: Addison-Wesley, 1997.

Bulka, Dov, and David Mayhew. *Efficient C++: Performance Programming Techniques.* Boston: Addison-Wesley, 1999.

B.3 COMPUTER GRAPHICS

B.3.1 GENERAL

Foley, James D., Andries van Dam, Steven K. Feiner, and John F. Hughes. *Computer Graphics: Principles and Practice in C* (2d ed.). Boston: Addison-Wesley, 1995.

Watt, Alan H. *3D Computer Graphics* (3d ed.). Boston: Addison-Wesley, 1999.

Glassner, Andrew S. *Graphics Gems I*. San Francisco: Morgan Kaufmann Publishers, 1990. Also see *Graphics Gems II, II, IV, V*.

Schneider, Philip, and David H. Eberly. *Geometric Tools for Computer Graphics*. San Francisco: Morgan Kaufmann Publishers, 2002.

B.3.2 MODELING

Rogers, David F. *An Introduction to NURBS, with Historial Perspective*. San Francisco: Morgan Kaufmann Publishers, 2001.

Warren, Joe, and Henrik Weimer. *Subdivision Methods for Geometric Design: A Constructive Approach*. San Francisco: Morgan Kaufmann Publishers, 2001.

B.3.3 ANIMATION

Parent, Rick. *Computer Animation: Algorithms and Techniques*. San Francisco: Morgan Kaufmann Publishers, 2002.

B.3.4 IMAGE SYNTHESIS

Watt, Alan, and Mark Watt. *Advanced Animation and Rendering Techniques*. New York: ACM Press, 1992.

Akenine-Moller, Tomas, and Eric Haines. *Real-time Rendering* (2d ed.). Natuck, Mass.: A K Peters, 2002.

Glassner, Andrew S. *Principles of Digital Image Synthesis*. San Francisco: Morgan Kaufmann Publishers, 1995.

Ebert, David S. F. Kenton Musgrave, Darwyn Peachey, Ken Perlin, and Steven Worley. *Texturing and Modeling*. San Diego: Academic Press, 1998.

Shirley, Peter. *Realistic Ray Tracing*. Natick, Mass.: A K Peters, 2000.

Blinn, James. *Jim Blinn's Corner: A Trip Down the Graphics Pipeline*. San Francisco: Morgan Kaufmann Publishers, 1996.

Glossary

affine transformation A transformation that involves a linear transformation followed by a translation.

animation controller Many 3D packages have specific functionality for animating objects. In 3dsmax, they are referred to as controllers. In Softimage, they are fcurves. In Maya, the standard animation controls are the **animCurve** nodes. They allow you to create and edit a curve that then controls a parameter over the range of the animation.

ANSI This an abbreviation for the American National Standards Institute. The institute is involved in defining standards for many computer languages, including C and C++.

API Abbreviation for Application Programming Interface. A system will provide a programmer with an API. This API defines the complete methods by which a programmer can access and control the given system.

argument An argument to a command or procedure is simply a value given to the command or procedure as input to perform its operation.

array An array is a list of items.

ASCII Abbreviation for American Standard Code for Information Interchange. This is a system for encoding characters using 7 bits.

assignment Assignment consists of storing a value into a variable. The assignment operator ($=$) is used to store values; for example, $a = 2$.

attribute This is a particular property of a node. For instance, the **makeNurbsSphere** node has a **radius** attribute. By changing this attribute, the sphere will change in size.

axis An axis is a direction. A 3D object will have three axes: x, y, and z.

axis of rotation The axis about which a point or vector is rotated.

back-face culling For display purposes, all those faces that point away from the camera will not be visible and therefore don't have to be drawn. Back-face culling discards all such faces before display. As such, only front-facing faces are drawn.

base mesh See *control mesh*.

basis vector A vector that is linearly independent of other vectors. A series of basis vectors and a single origin are used to define a coordinate frame.

black box When the exact operations of a given system are not known outside the system, it is referred to as a black box. This means that its inner workings can't be seen.

Boolean Booleans are used to denote the result of a logical operation. A Boolean can be either `true` or `false`.

breakdown key This is a key that depends on keys before and after it. A breakdown key will automatically maintain its relative position to the other keys when they are moved.

C^0 continuity As it applies to curves, C^0 continuity across the junction between two piecewise curves indicates that the two curves touch each other. For example, the end of the first curve touches the start of the second curve. It is for this reason that C^0 continuity is also referred to as *positional continuity*.

C^1 continuity As it applies to curves, C^1 continuity across the junction between two piecewise curves indicates that the first-order derivatives $f'(x)$ are equal. This can be thought of as the velocity across the junction being the same. As such, C^1 continuity is also referred to as *tangential continuity*. C^1 continuity implies that C^0 continuity also exists.

C^{-1} continuity There is no continuity at all.

C^2 continuity As it applies to curves, C^2 continuity across the junction between two piecewise curves indicates that the second-order derivatives $f''(x)$ are equal. This can be thought of as the acceleration across the junction being the same. C^2 continuity is also referred to as *curvature continuity*. C^2 continuity implies that C^1 and C^0 continuity also exist.

C++ This is an object-oriented programming language based on the C language.

Cartesian coordinates A coordinate system that defines positions based on their projection onto a series of orthogonal axes.

case sensitive When an operation is case sensitive it makes a distinction between two names that don't have the same case. For instance, the terms *bill* and *Bill* will be considered different in a case-sensitive system.

child This is something that has a parent.

class In C++, a class is the basic construct for defining a self-contained object. Classes have their own member functions and data.

class hierarchy Using standard object-oriented design methods, most complex systems are broken into a hierarchy. At the root (top) is a class with very basic functionality. Other classes are derived (child) from this class to add more specific functionality. As this process continues, you end up with a tree hierarchy of classes.

closed polyline A series of line segments where the last segment joins to the first, creating a continous loop with no gaps.

command A command is used to perform a particular operation. The sphere command, for example, is used to create and edit spheres. Commands are used throughout Maya to perform almost all of its various operations.

command modes A single command can operate in the following variety of modes: creation, edit, and query. When a command is executed in a given mode, it will perform a restricted set of operations. When in query mode, it will retrieve values. When in creation mode, it will create things.

comment This is some descriptive text a programmer includes in source code so that other people can read and understand what they were doing. It is a means of documenting the functionality of a program. A *multiline comment* is a comment that spans more than one line of text.

compile-and-link Compiled languages such as C and C++ need to have the source code compiled and linked into machine code in order to run. This is in contrast to scripting languages, such as MEL, that interpret instructions and execute them immediately.

component This is the individual value of a vector, point, and so on. A point has three components: x, y, and z.

compound attribute This is an attribute that consists of combining other attributes. The attributes are compounded into another, more complex, attribute.

compute function This is the function in a node that does the calculation of a node's output attributes. The compute function takes the input attributes and then calculates the final values for the output attributes.

concatenation With regard to the concatenation of transformations, this is the process of multiplying a series of matrices together resulting in a single matrix that incorporates all transformations.

connection When the value of one attribute feeds into another a connection is established between the two. It is possible to freely make and break connections.

construction history The process of an object's construction is recorded as a series of interconnected nodes. This allows any step in the object's construction to be later revisited and altered.

context (a) When the compute function of a node is called, the context defines when, in time, the node is being recalculated. (b) See *tool*.

continuity This is a measure of how smoothly one piecewise curve flows into another. There are geometric (G^0, G^1, . . ., G^n) and parametric continuities (C^0, C^1, C^2, . . ., C^n).

contravariant Vectors that are transformed by the usual transformation matrix are contravariant.

control mesh The initial polygonal mesh that is first subdivided to produce a subdivision surface.

coordinate frame A combination of an origin and n basis vectors define a coordinate frame. The origin (0,0,0) and three basis vectors (1,0,0), (0,1,0), and (0,0,1) form the 3D Cartesian frame.

covariant Vectors that are transformed using the inverse transpose matrix are covariant.

creation expression An expression that is run when a particle's age is 0; that is, when it just born.

cross product The cross product of two vectors is another vector that is perpendicular to the two. It is often used to determine the direction of a vector that is normal to a surface.

cubic polynomial Polynomial equation with its highest exponent of three:

```
x(u) = a*u3 + b*u2 + c*u1 + d*u0
     = a*u3 + b*u2 + c*u + d
```

curvature This is a measure of how much a curve curves at a given point. It is the reciprocal of the radius of a circle (1/radius) that would fit snugly at the given point. The circle's first- and second-order derivatives match those of the curve at the given point.

curveAnim node These are curve animation nodes. These nodes hold an animation curve that you can edit and modify to animate a particular parameter. These nodes can do standard keyframing and driven-key animation.

DAG Abbreviation for *directed acyclic graph*. This is a technical term for a hierarchy where none of the children can themselves be their own parents. If you walked from the first node in the hierarchy to the very last you would never see the same node twice.

DAG path This is the complete path to a given node. The path lists the node and all of its ancestor nodes.

data flow model A conceptual model where data flows through a series of nodes from the first node to the last. Data is modified by each subsequent node.

deformer A deformer takes one or more points and moves them to a new location.

degree (a) Unit of measurement for angles. There are 360 degrees in a circle. (b) The degree of a curve defines the number of control vertices per span plus one.

dependency node A general dependency graph node. All Maya nodes are dependency nodes.

dependent attribute This is an output attribute. When an attribute depends on other attributes for its final value, it is considered a dependent attribute. The `MPxNode::attributeEffects` function is used to set this dependent relationship between attributes.

DG Abbreviation for *dependency graph*. The DG consists of all Maya nodes and their connections.

dirty bit This is a flag an attribute contains to indicate whether it needs to be updated.

dirty bit propagation This is the process where a dirty bit message is passed through the DG from one node to another. The message eventually passes from the first attribute to all other attributes this one affects.

displacement The translation of one position to another, often represented using a vector.

dot product The dot product is simply the result of multiplying all components of two vectors together and adding the results: `dot product(a,b) = a.x * b.x + a.y * b.y + a.z * b.z`. The dot product is often used to calculate the cosine of the angle between two vectors.

double In C++, this is a data type for storing numbers with decimal digits. It often, although not always, has a higher precision than the float data type.

dynamic attribute This is an attribute that is added to a particular node. This attribute isn't shared by all nodes of the same type, but is unique to a given node.

dynamic link library This is a library of programming functionality that is loaded into memory only when needed.

ELF Abbreviation of *extended layer framework*. This is the framework used in MEL to define interfaces. Interfaces are designed by creating layouts to which controls are then attached. The framework supports arbitrary nesting of layouts and controls.

entry point This is the function that is called when a dynamic link library is loaded into memory.

exit point This is the function that is called when a dynamic link library is unloaded from memory.

expression In the context of Maya, an expression is a series of MEL commands that control one or more node attributes. This allows you to programmatically control attributes.

face See *polygon.*

face-relative index See *face-relative vertex ID.*

face-relative vertex ID An index into the list of vertices that make up a face. A face with five vertices will have a list of five vertex indices. The *i*th index in the list is the face-relative index. The actual value of the *i*th indexed element will be a mesh-relative vertex index.

face vertex A means of referencing a specific vertex within a face. This reference is made up of a combination of the face's index and the face-relative index of the vertex. The face-relative index is the vertex's order in the list of vertices that make up the face. This face-relative vertex index is independent of the mesh vertex index.

face-vertex uv coordinate A uv coordinate assigned to a specific vertex within a face.

flag A flag is used to indicate if something is on or off. It is used as a means of signaling.

float This the data type for storing numbers with decimal digits. The size of a float in MEL is not necessarily the same as in C++.

floating-point A floating-point number is how computers store numbers with decimal digits. The term refers to the fact that the decimal point can change.

forward kinematics/FK This is where an animator must explicitly define the orientations of all joints.

function In the C/C++ programming languages, a function defines how to perform a particular operation. A function can, for instance, add two numbers or rotate an object, or just about any operation. Functions are *called* to execute them.

function set Under Maya's scheme of separating the data from the functions that operate on them, a function set is a C++ class that provides the programmer with access to the data. A function set can be used to create, edit, and query the data without having to know its specific details.

G^0 continuity As it applies to curves, G^0 continuity across the junction between two piecewise curves indicates that the two curves are touching. This is the equivalent of C^0 continuity.

G^1 continuity As it applies to curves, G^1 continuity is similar to C^1 continuity. Given two connected curves, there will be C^1 continuity across the joint if the end tangent vector of the first curve is exactly the same as the first tangent vector of the second curve. This implies that the first-order derivatives $f'(x)$ are the same. G^1 continuity is the same as C^1 continuity except that the tangent vectors only need to be pointing in the same direction, although they don't have to have the same length.

gimbal lock The loss of one or more degrees of freedom due to a colinear alignment of dependent axes. Gimbal lock is a possibility when using Euler angles.

global This defines the scope of a variable or procedure. If variables or procedures are made global, they can be accessed from anywhere.

gouraud shading A simplified shading method where the shading color is only calculated at the vertices of an object. The interior surface of the object is shaded not by calculating it directly but by interpolating the shading color from the vertices.

group In Maya, a group is simply a transform node that becomes the parent of all child nodes in the group.

GUI Abbreviation for *graphical user interface*. This is the system of windows, dialog boxes, and other user interface elements you interact with when using Maya.

hierarchy Any system where there is a parent-child relationship.

identity matrix A transformation matrix that doesn't have any effect when applied to a point. Technically, the matrix is composed of all 0s with just the diagonal having 1s.

identity transformation See *identity matrix*.

IK solver Maya allows you to write your own inverse kinematic systems. An IK solver determines the orientations of intermediate joints.

initialization This is the value assigned to a variable when it is first defined.

input attribute This is an attribute that provides input to a node. The input attribute's value is often used by the compute function to calculate the value of one or more output attributes.

instance An instance of an object is the same as an exact duplicate of the object. An instance is really an object that shares the exact same properties as the original. It will always stay the same as the original no matter what changes are made to the original.

int This data type is used to store whole numbers; integers.

interface The specific communication methods through which you communicate with a system. The graphical user interface provides a set of graphical elements you can use to effectively communicate your intentions to the underlying system.

intermediate object A hidden shape node that provides the input into the construction history of an object. Because an object can only have one shape node, the hidden shape node is used to feed the start of the construction history but isn't displayed.

interpreted language This is a computer language where the source code is interpreted and run immediately. This is different from a compiled language, where the source code must first be compiled, then linked, before being run. Interpreted languages tend to be slower than compiled languages, although they are often better for rapid prototyping.

inverse kinematics/IK This is where an animator can control a series of joints by simply placing the last one. All intermediate joints are calculated by the computer.

isoparm See *isoparametric curve*.

isoparametric curve Curve across a NURBS surface when either the u or v coordinate is set to a fixed value and the other coordinate is allowed to vary. This traces out a curve across the NURBS surface along the fixed coordinate.

joint A joint is like a bone. Joints can be connected to create appendages. Joints are often what the animator moves to control a character.

keyframe animation This is where you define the animation for a parameter by specifying its exact value at a given set of times. The computer can then work out by interpolating what the value should be between the keys.

keystroke This is when a key on the keyboard is pressed.

knot Parametric position assigned to the end of each span. This is the point where two spans join.

knot vector Sequence of knot values for a curve.

library In the context of C++, a library is a repository of functionality that can be used in other programs. A library for handling files will allow you to create, open, and edit files. By using a library in your program, you don't have to develop the technology yourself.

limit surface The mathematically precise surface of a subdivision surface. If a polygonal mesh were subdivided an infinite number of times, the resulting surface would be the limit surface.

linear polynomial Polynomial equation with its highest exponent of 1:

```
x(u) = a*u¹ + b*u⁰
     = a*u + b
```

This is the commonly used equation for a straight line:

```
y(x) = a*x + b

where "a" is the slope and "b" is the y axis intercept
```

local This defines how a procedure or variable can be accessed. By making them local they can only be accessed within the script file or current block.

local space This is the coordinate space in which an object is first defined. In this space no transformations have been applied to the object.

locator A locator is a 3D shape that is displayed in Maya. The main difference is that it will not show up in the final render.

loop This is where you repeat an operation several times.

magnitude Length of a vector.

manipulator This is a visual control the user manipulates in 3D to change an attribute.

matrix A matrix is a series of rows and columns of numbers. Matrices are used in computer graphics to transform points.

matrix transpose An operation where the row and column positions of all matrix elements are interchanged: $M[i,j] = M[j,i]$.

MEL Abbreviation of Maya Embedded Language. This is Maya's interpreted scripting language. It is very close to the C language in syntax, but is easier to learn and allows you to quickly write programs to access and control Maya.

mesh A mesh is a series of polygons grouped to form a surface.

mesh-relative index See *vertex ID*.

mesh-relative vertex ID See *vertex ID*.

modifier keys The Shift and Ctrl keys.

Name space A name space is where a set of names resides. Because they are all in the same set, their names must be different from each other. If you have names that are the same, a *name space conflict* results.

node A node is the fundamental building block of Maya's Dependency Graph. Nodes contain attributes a user can change. They also contain a compute function that automatically calculates certain attributes.

noise This is a pseudo-random number. For consistent inputs it generates consistent, though random, numbers.

non-undoable command An MEL command that doesn't alter Maya's state. Such a command will often query the scene without changing it.

normal A normal is a vector perpendicular to a surface.

normalize To scale a vector so that its length is 1.

NURBS Abbreviation for *nonuniform rational B-spline*. This is a mathematical representation for smooth curves and surfaces.

object space See *local space*.

operator An operator is a shorthand method of defining an operation between one or more values. The addition operator is written using the plus sign (+). Other operators include multiply (*) and division (/).

order The number of control vertices that influences a span of a NURBS.

output attribute This is an attribute that holds the result of a computation. One or more input attributes are fed into the node's compute function that then create an output value that is stored in an output attribute.

overflow When an operation of a data type outside its maximum range is performed, an overflow results. For instance, a 32-bit unsigned integer will store the resulting out-of-range value.

```
value = out_of_range_value % 2^32
```

Essentially, the value wraps around at 2^{32-1}.

parent A parent is something that has one or more children. Because a parent can also have a parent, its children will have indirect parents. These are parents (grandparent, great-grandparents, and so on) about their direct parents.

parent attribute In a compound or array attribute, this is the topmost attribute. It is the parent of all child attributes under it.

particles A particle defines a point in space. Particles are often animated and controlled by applying forces and other physics to them.

patch An area of a NURBS surface that is enclosed by four isoparametric curves (two u curves and two v curves).

phong shading A shading method where all points interior to a surface are calculated rather than interpolated. In particular, the normals are interpolated from the normals at the vertices. This is in contrast to *Gouraud shading*. Phong shading isn't to be confused with phong reflectance.

pipeline In the context of a production studio, the pipeline includes all of the various steps that go into making a film. Starting with modeling, then progressing to animation, lighting, and finally rendering, the pipeline often consists of separate specialized departments.

pitch Direction of rotation that tips the object forward or backward.

pivot point A position about which scales and rotations are performed.

platform A platform is a particular computer configuration. It includes the operating system and other specific components (CPU and so on). Example platforms include Irix, Linux, and Windows.

plug A plug identifies a particular node's attribute. It is used to access a specific node's attribute values.

Plug-in A plug-in is a program written by someone that is integrated into another application. The program *plugs into* the application. Plug-ins often provide additional functionality that isn't available in the application.

point A point defines a position with Cartesian coordinates. A 2D point has two coordinates (x and y), whereas a 3D point has three coordiantes (x, y, and z).

polygon A flat surface area with its boundary defined by line segments through three or more vertices.

polygon proxy A polygonal mesh that represents the control mesh to a subdivision surface. See also *control mesh*.

polygon proxy mode Operating in this mode allows the subdivision surface's control mesh to be edited. See also *control mesh* and *standard mode*.

polyline A series of line segments that passes through vertices.

polymorphism With regard to an object-oriented programming language, such as C++, polymorphism refers to an object's ability to behave differently depending on its type. This provides a powerful means of making extensions to objects.

polynomial A mathematical equation with one or more terms. For example,

$$y = a^2 + bx + c$$

is a quadratic (highest exponent is 2) polynomial equation.

post-infinity This is any frame after the last key in an animation curve.

precedence In a programming language, the precedence of an operator determines in what order it will be evaluated. An operator with a higher precedence will be evaluated before another with a lower precedence. For instance, multiplication has a higher precedence than addition.

pre-infinity This is any frame before the first key in an animation curve.

procedure A procedure is a means of defining a particular operation in MEL. A procedure is used to perform some operation and often return a result. This is conceptually the same as the C language's function.

pseudocode Pseudocode is a shorthand way of describing a computer program. Rather than use the specific syntax of a computer language, more general wording is used. Using pseudocode, it is easier for a nonprogrammer to understand the general workings of the program.

push-pull model A conceptual model where data is both pushed and pulled through a series of nodes. This model differs from the data flow model in that it is more efficient because only nodes that need updating are updated. Maya's dependency graph works on this principle.

Pvertices One or more vertices.

quad Abbreviation for *quadrilateral.*

quadratic polynomial Polynomial equation with its highest exponent of 2, as in the following.

$$x(u) = a*u^2 + b*u^1 + c*u^0$$
$$= a*u^2 + b*u + c$$

quadrilateral A polygon with four sides.

quartic polynomial Polynomial equation with its highest exponent of 4, as in the following.

$$x(u) = a*u^4 + b*u^3 + c*u^2 + d*u^1 + e*u^0$$
$$= a*u^4 + b*u^3 + c*u^2 + d*u + e$$

quaternion A means of specifying an orientation using a 4D vector.

random number A number that is determined entirely by chance.

redo When an command is undone, it can be reexecuted by choosing to redo it.

render To take the scene information, models, lights, camera, and so on and make a final image.

roll Direction of rotation that spins an object about its front-facing axis.

root This is the fictitious node that is the parent of all other nodes in the scene. There is the concept of a root node so that the entire scene can be thought of as a tree, starting at the root.

rotate/rotation Rotating an object is the same as spinning it around. This changes its orientation. The point about which it will rotate is called the rotation pivot. A wheel will have its rotation pivot in its center.

runtime expression An expression that is run when a particle is older than zero.

scalar A single value.

scale Scaling an object means resizing it. A uniform scale is where the object is resized evenly. By doing a nonuniform scale an object can be made wider, higher, or deeper, without keeping its original proportions.

scene The scene consists of all Maya data. It includes all models and their animation, effects, settings, and so on.

scope The scope of a variable defines whether or not it can be accessed. If a variable has a global scope, it can be accessed everywhere. If it has a local scope, it can only be accessed in the block it is defined and all inner blocks.

script A text file that contains MEL statements.

scripting language A scripting language differentiates itself from other typical languages in that they are usually simpler to learn and use as well as not needing to be compiled. The language is interpreted at runtime so that you can execute instructions immediately.

seam NURBS geometry with closed or periodic forms have seams. This is where Maya ensures that control vertices that should be coincident remain coincident after a control vertex is moved.

set A set is simply a list of items. When an object is put into a set, it is made a part of the list.

set-driven keys Set-driven keys are used to define a relationship between one parameter and another. Unlike keyframes that assume you are using time, a set-driven key can use any parameter (driver) to drive another parameter. The relationship is defined by editing a curve.

shader A shader defines the final surface properties of an object. For example, a shader can define the color, reflectivity, and transluscency of a surface.

shape This is the general term for all 3D data that can be displayed in Maya. Shapes include curves, surfaces, and points.

shape node A node that holds a shape, such as a polygonal mesh, curve, NURBS surface, or particle.

shell A mesh is a group of polygons. These can be connected or disconnected. Any group of polygons that share connectivity via one or more vertices or edges is considered a shell. As such, a mesh can contain multiple shells.

sibling A sibling is a child that shares the same parent.

signed A value that can be either negative (−) or positive (+).

skeleton A hierarchy of joints that defines the inner structure of a character.

skinning This is the process where a model is wrapped around a skeleton. When the skeleton moves, the model will move correspondingly. The model effectively forms a skin over the skeleton joints.

sourcing This is the process where a MEL script is loaded into Maya and then executed.

space A space is a particular frame of reference for an object. Specifically, it defines the transformations applied to an object to put it into the frame of reference.

spring A spring provides a means of describing and calculating the elasticity, mass, damping, and so on between two points.

standard mode Operating in this mode allows for the editing and refinement of subdivision surface components.

string This is series of characters; text.

structured programming This is a design approach where complex systems are broken down into smaller, more manageable pieces.

subd, subdiv Abbreviation of *subdivision surface*.

subdivision surface A smooth surface resulting from subdividing a polygonal mesh multiple times.

tangent In the context of an animation curve key, the tangents define how values are interpolated between successive keys. By changing a key's tangents, you can make the animation faster or slower between keys.

time node The time node is used to store time. It has a single attribute, **outTime**, that holds the time. Whereas the **time1** node holds the current time, it is possible to create additional time nodes.

tool A tool defines a set of specific steps that must be completed in order to perform an operation. They often require the user to select with the mouse before the operation can be completed on the given selection.

transform node A DAG node used to specify the position, orientation, and size of a shape.

transformation See *transformation matrix*.

transformation hierarchy A single transformation will position, orient, and size a given object. By putting the transformations into a hierarchy, you can have a series of transformations applied to an object. An object that has parent transformations will also be affected by those transformations.

transformation matrix A transformation matrix is a shorthand way of describing the positioning, rotating, and sizing of an object. When a transformation matrix is applied to an object, it will often be in a different place, orientation, and size afterward. The *inverse* of a transformation matrix will restore the object to its original place, orientation, and size.

translate/translation Translating an object is the same as moving it.

translator In Maya, a translator is a piece of software that can translate data from one format into a format that Maya can understand. A translator may, for example, take a Softimage file and convert it to a Maya file. Translators are also referred to as importers/exporters because they can take information into and out of Maya.

tree This is the metaphor used to describe hierarchies.

truncate Truncating is when something is removed to make it compatible with something smaller. A decimal number can often be truncated to an integer by removing the decimal digits.

tweak (a) This refers to the general process of editing something. When you tweak an object you are simply changing it. Before a scene is final, it will often undergo a lot of tweaking. (b) The movement of a vertex or position. The relative difference between the new position and the original position is stored as a vector known as a tweak.

tweak node A tweak node is used by Maya to store all individual moves to some geometry's points.

underflow When a computation results in a value that is less than the minimum value a data type can store, an underflow occurs. For instance, given an unsigned 32-bit integer, the result of the calculation $0 - 1$ will result in an underflow. The final stored value will be 2^{32-1} because the result will always be modulo 2^{32}.

underworld This is a parametric space for defining the positions of objects. The parameteric space is often the surface of a NURBS surface.

undo To remove the effect of a command, it can be undone. Undoing a command restores Maya to its state before the command was executed.

uniform bicubic B-spline A basis spline that uses degree-3 polynomials for its basis functions. Its knot vector also has uniform spacing between knots.

unit vector A vector with a length of 1.

uv coordinate A 2D position with coordinates (u and v) that is often associated with texturing. The positon defines a location in a 2D image or plane. Assigning an object a texture coordinate provides a means of mapping a 2D image onto an arbitrary surface.

uv ID A vertex's or face-relative vertex's index into the uv coordinates array.

valence The number of neighboring vertices, connected directly via edges, to a given vertex.

vector A vector defines a direction. They can also have a magnitude that defines their length. A vector that has a length of 1 is called a unit vector.

vertex See *position*.

vertex ID An index into a mesh's vertex array.

vertex uv coordinate A texture coordinate assigned to a given vertex.

world space This the space where all objects in the scene are displayed. The world space is the result of applying all of an object's parent transformations.

Index